A Cry For Help

Why the Self-Help Books Can't Make You Happy

*Please Help Change the World
So They Can*

John B. Duffield

Life's all about choices, but when all is said and done, there are only two. Two different ways of seeing the world to choose from. Choose the wrong one and you'll go to school, get good jobs, retire, and die, never knowing who you are, or why you're here. Choose the right one and you'll heal yourself and our world. Both ways of seeing things are here for you. The choice is yours.

Copyright © 2009 by John B. Duffield

All rights reserved, including the right to reproduce this work in any form whatsoever, without permission in writing from the publisher, except for brief passages in connection with a review.

Cover Design: The Celtic Tree of Life depicted here is a generic version of an ancient symbol representing the deep unification of all things great and small. Branches and roots become each other in this profound sign of wholeness.

In Memoriam: *I would like to dedicate this book to my dear friend John Gerolami, who died of cancer before his time. I wish you could have continued this Great Journey with me old buddy. See you later botcha.*

ISBN: 978-0-578-02823-1

CONTENTS

Is This Book For You?..p5

Introduction: Why The Self-Help Books Don't Help…………...p6

Chapter One: You Don't Know Your Own Dreams………..p15

Chapter Two: What You're Called to Do……………………p23

Chapter Three: The Plan You Came With…………………..p35

Chapter Four: Don't Believe You Lost Your Calling? ……..p53

Chapter Five: Still Not Sure You've Lost Your Way? ……..p65

Chapter Six: Does This Look Like You? …………………...p74

Chapter Seven: I Hope You Aren't This Lost……………....p84

Chapter Eight: My Journey of Discovery Begins…………..p93

Chapter Nine: Something Big is Revealed to Me ………….p100

Chapter Ten: But I Still Don't Get It For 20 More Years…..p105

Chapter Eleven: Finally I See (The Key to Our Lives)….…..p110

Chapter Eleven Point Five: (Stop and Think Right Here)....p118

Chapter Twelve: 8 Ways You Won't Find Your Dreams….p119

Big Chapter Thirteen: Still Just Want Money?......................p132

Chapter Fourteen: Want To Know Why You're Here?........p156

Chapter Fifteen: Six Rule of Life Exercises…………………p163

Chapter Sixteen: Mission Exercises………………………….p190

Chapter Seventeen: The Rule of Life Restores Vision……..p201

Chapter Eighteen: Seeds of Vision…………………………p226

Chapter Nineteen: Seven Roadblocks……………………...p233

Chapter Twenty: How to Know Vision's Returning……….p248

Chapter Twenty-One: Why Vision Stops Growing………..p269

Chapter Twenty-Two: A Journal Tool...…………………...p281

Chapter Twenty-Three: My Example Journal...…………...p286

Chapter Twenty-Four: An Example Winter Journal...……..p289

    (What it's Like to be Lost)

Chapter Twenty-Five: A Spring Journal…………………...p332

    (What Waking Up Feels Like)

Chapter Twenty-Six: The Summer of Life: A Journal……..p377

    (Discovering Yourself Will Be Like This)

Chapter Twenty-Seven: A Journal of Autumn Life………..p409

    (Your Life Mission and Mine)

Chapter Twenty-Eight: A Cry For Help..………………....p437

Chapter Twenty-Nine: Not The Final Chapter… I Hope….p446

Reading List.…………………………………………….p448

Is This Book For You?

Joseph Campbell on How to Live Life .--- The Power of Myth

"....How do you do it? My answer is, "Follow your bliss". There is something inside you that knows when you are in the center, that knows when you are on the beam or off the beam. And if you have got off the beam to earn money, you have lost your life. And if you stay in the center and don't get any money, you still have your bliss".

Hello there dear reader. Joseph Campbell wrote that famous line a long time ago, but it's as true today as it was then. It could be the best piece of advice in the Universe too, because the only way to find what you're looking for in Life is to follow your Bliss. If you're anything like I was though, you won't honestly be able to say your world is filled with the kind of love and happiness Bliss is made of. You'll probably be collecting cars and carpets and cash, and wondering what's missing, like I was. There's a good chance you think that blissful happy life professor Campbell speaks of is nothing but a fairy tale as well. But it's not. Truth be told, it's actually possible to let torrents of Bliss into your universe again, flooding your life with meaning and purpose and giving you a real shot at finding your soul mate. If that sounds a lot better than what you're doing now, this book is for you. It will teach you how to find your Bliss and follow it forever.

John B. Duffield

Introduction
Why The Self-Help Books Don't Help

"Before your dreams can come true, you have to have those dreams.". - Joyce Brothers, U.S. psychologist

What Should You Be Doing With Your Life?

If you're anywhere between zero and a hundred years of age, you've probably wondered what you should be doing with your life. If you're closer to a hundred, you might have noticed hardly anyone seems to solve that famous puzzle before they die. But have you ever wondered why that is? It's certainly not because nobody's trying to figure it out. Having no real purpose causes so much grief, we've launched a kind of Manhattan Project to help find ourselves. It's called the "self-help" industry, and literally thousands of gurus write hundreds of books every year proposing solutions to this unhappy mystery of meaning missing in our lives. Despite their best efforts, it isn't helping. It didn't help me find what I was looking for and it rarely helps anyone. No doubt about it, the problem of discovering what we want to be when we grow up is so big and old and difficult, it qualifies as a true enigma. I certainly cannot claim to have figured it out, but I do know what the solution is.

If that sounds suspiciously like nonsense to you, it isn't. It's revelation. Before you run away, let me explain. Revelation is a kind of seeing or sudden understanding that comes to you when you're ready for it, like a Divine gift. It has nothing to do with brain power or ability. People with huge intellectual abilities certainly are gifted with revelation on occasion of course, but so too are the rest of us. I know that for sure, because yours truly is an average guy every which way you look at it and revelation happened to me.

In essence then, what you're about to read is a result of three separate revelations gifted upon me over a period of twenty years. Sudden surprising insights arriving without notice, that let me see why the self-help books don't help. But please do not misunderstand what this book is about. It's about *your* life. It's painstakingly crafted to give you the single kernel of knowledge that will let you discover who you are and why you're here. It chronicles my Journey to revelation, so you see where I'm coming from, but goes on to show you precisely how to use this newfound knowledge to get what you want out of life.

These pages also reveal how this single spark of know-how transformed one aimless, wallflower of a man stuck at the top of the corporate ladder, hiding his sorrows behind booze…to an outgoing, vibrant human being driven to carry out a calling. In case you're not sure who that might be….you're looking at him. I'm not shy about revealing my lost and found self here either, so you can identify with me and follow my examples. Here's something I want you to know right now too. If you follow the Rule of Life offered later in this book, something very special will be revealed to *you* as well. You'll see what you're here on earth to do. Impossible as that might sound to you right now, it's true. Sounds hopeful at least? Good. Let's carry on.

You Don't Know Your Own Heart?

Let's take a quick look at those million self-help books out there. I can tell you something interesting about all of them. Every single one can help you achieve your heart's desires, but even if you read the whole lot you probably won't be helped. The reason for this is so simple it's almost ridiculous. You don't know what your own heart desires. As a matter of fact, you might never know.

Just in case you somehow impossibly missed the point here, there's no way you can achieve your heart's desires if you have no idea what they are. And there's almost no chance you do. I'll bet the idea you don't know your own dreams sounds so bizarre you can't believe a word of it. Right? Exactly, and I'm with you on that one. I certainly wouldn't have bought the idea twenty-five years ago. Even so, I can ask you one simple little question that will reveal whether you know what your heart really desires or not. Ready? Do you get up every day absolutely *driven* to fulfill some mission? No? I rest my case. You have no idea what your own dreams are. If you did, they'd be pushing you like a hurricane to make them come true….right now. You'd feel a high-voltage current of passion for those dreams flowing through you as we speak too, because real dreams are the stuff legends are made of. Believe me, if you'd been gifted with a real dream, you'd notice that huge force within you, pushing you towards your destiny.

But don't get me wrong here. I'm not saying you don't have all kinds of "wants, wishes, and desires" you picked up from T.V. or heard parents and friends say will make you important. But guess what? They're not coming from your heart. You probably desire every big expensive thing under the sun too, because you've been taught to from the day you crawled into your stroller, but those aren't *real* dreams. Real dreams light up your life and speak to you from the soul. True dreams can't be mistaken for anything else, any more than your image in a mirror can be mistaken for someone you once met. So? Can you feel the giant hand of fate at your back, urging you forward like a locomotive? Do you feel this Divine Force behind you with absolute certainty? A Life Force telling you why you're here? No and no again and again, like a little red chicken or big black hen? You haven't got a clue what your very own heart desires, whether you believe it right now or not.

Who Can Help Find Your Dreams?

No question about it. You don't know where your Bliss is, or how to find it, and you don't even realize it. Have I got your attention? Not yet? Alright, so maybe you're just like I used to be. Maybe you still believe some guru or mentor can tell you what that heart of yours desires. You're in good company too, because lots of people think like that. By far most of them believe an inspiring man or woman who's been to the promised land themselves can take the rest of us there. All the gurus have to do is draw up a good map. Yes? More bad news I'm afraid. No one but you can tell you what to do with your life. I'm sure you've heard that one before, but, sadly, it's as true now as it ever was. It's simply not possible to find your own dreams anywhere out there in the world, no matter how many experts you've got helping you. Even so, all is not yet lost, because the self-help experts can still help. They can help you make adopted dreams come true.

"If one advances confidently in the direction of his dreams, and endeavors to live the life which he has imagined, he will meet with success unexpected in common hours". - Henry David Thoreau

Millions Can Help You Adopt Dreams

What the heck are adopted dreams? They're ways of making a living that will make you rich and important. You'll find lots in any good book of careers or in mom's big list of things son or daughter should aspire to. Just pick one off the shelf like I did. If money's what you want, try movie star, sports pro, or Big-Act rocker. If showing your smarts to the world is your thing, how about professor or scientist. Lawyer, physician or engineer might put you nicely up in the social pecking order too. But here's the thing. If you can't say with total certainty that you're drop-dead passionate about the way of making a living you picked out of a book, it isn't *your* dream.

It's a dream you've been taught to want since the cradle. A dream of being better than the next man or woman. Dreams and desires for sure, but not coming from your soul. So go ahead and go that way if you want, but don't be surprised if you can't put everything you've got into your adopted dream…...like I couldn't. Don't be surprised if those dreams ring hollow when you make them come true either… like mine did. Am I depressing you now? Sorry. But take heart, there's hope. There *is* a way to get your own dreams back. Dreams that however big or small will knock the socks right off of you with their beauty and joy. I'll show you how, and here's a little teaser for you, to keep you reading. It doesn't matter whether your real dream is to climb Everest or rule the world or just become a good carpenter. Every single true dream comes with the same share of Bliss. If you learn how to find and follow the Golden Braid of Destiny, (don't worry, I'll explain this amazing Path of your life later), you'll get all the happy success every soul ever got or will get.

And here's something else. Remember all those self-help books I mentioned? The ones that can help make dreams picked from books true? They're just as good at helping make *real* dreams come to life. Can you imagine what that means? Once you get your very own passionate aim in life back, you'll have hundreds …. no …. thousands…. of different tools to assist you in going where you *really* want to go. Every single self-help book has tons of useful tips and pointers in it that can help you go *your* way faster and better. You'll go from famine to feast when it comes to help making your dream life. But don't forget. To know where you *really* want to take your life, you have to get your dreams back first. "I'm in!" you say? "As long as it makes me rich quick".

Dreams That Fill Your Life With Byproducts

Oh boy, here we go. All you want is money? Are you trying to tell me you want your life filled with byproducts?

You want to be like a hot-dog, filled with bits of wasted cow parts? O.K., so I'm exaggerating a bit, but there's a lot of truth to it. More than you might want to know. If you're not sure what I'm getting at here, let me fill you in. It took me nearly fifty years to really figure this one out, but I've got it down pat now. You might even have heard it before, so listen up. Money's just a *byproduct* of making dreams come true. If you make your *own* dreams come true, you'll get your share of material wealth. An abundance of it....like the gurus say. But believe it or not, money's not what you were put here to get. You're here to get something else. Something you might even have heard about before, even if you've never actually seen the real thing up close and personal yourself. So what were you put on earth to have by making your very own dreams come true?

If you guessed it's that famously elusive thing called "happiness", you're correct. Otherwise called "authentic success". That brings us to a really sad fact of life. Every single man or woman gets their fair share of true happiness by following *their* dreams. Unfortunately, in the world today, hardly anyone knows what their very own dreams are. In short, authentic success is rare as horses on mars. Which brings us back full circle, so let's review. Can't honestly say you know why you're here? You've lost your own dreams and there won't be much happiness in the direction you're headed. Better pluck up your courage and face it. You're destined to be a hot-dog all your life unless you take down the wall.

An Extraordinary Wall Between You and Your Dreams

Every psychologist, sociologist, and people-person out there knows there's a great big wall that stops men and women from finding happy success in life. A wall of fear. Fear of failure, making mistakes and being judged.

Inhibiting fear that stops folks from trying and succeeding and realizing their potentials in every land. Does that ring a little bell? If you've ever been afraid to speak in public or ask the girls to dance it will, because it's that fear we're talking about here. But this wall of fear isn't your everyday, ordinary wall. As a matter of fact, it's truly extraordinary, because we know pretty much every fact, figure and thing about it, except two. Which two? We don't know why it's there. Or how to get past it. Why is that so extraordinary? Let's put it in perspective. In today's computer world we put up walls to keep out spammers and identity thieves. They're called "firewalls", but as soon as hackers gain enough knowledge about these walls, they find a way to break through. In fact, no wall will keep hackers out if they learn enough about it. Same holds with guys in prison. It doesn't matter what kinds of brick and barbed wire walls of security are put up, someone will eventually figure out how to get past them and escape. To get past ordinary walls then, all you need is knowledge, but the wall of fear that stands between you and your destiny is a completely different animal altogether. Despite having entire libraries of knowledge about it, nobody has a clue why it's there or how to break through it. How do I know that?

A Wall Few People Ever Get Past

It's pretty easy to see we have no idea how to breach this terrible wall of fear that plagues our lives. All you have to do is open one eye and look around. You'll soon see there are more lives stalled by it today than ten decades ago. In fact, at the dawn of the twenty-first century, this wall-of-fear is stopping millions from being happy. Still don't get it? Why do you think there are people on every corner thanking God for Fridays and waiting to retire, never knowing who they are? The wall of fear is keeping them from knowing why they're here. How come men and women of every persuasion flock to the self-help gurus looking for happy success….but don't get it?

Same wall of fear. The gurus can help alright, but only if you and I have a dream to work with first. A dream that's being kept from us by that wall of fear. Why is it that hardly anyone ever knows what they want to be when they grow up? It's because that wall is stopping pretty much all of us from "knowing thyself". The truth of it is, there are so many people with no idea what to do with their lives today, we think it's normal. Sure enough, it's normal alright. About as normal as a four headed opera-singing camel with three faces of St. Nicolas and one that looks like you. You heard me. Maybe the world has been like this for a very long time, but it isn't *supposed* to be this way. In reality, every single soul is supposed to know who they are and what to do with their lives…..from beginning to end. Each of us arrives with a bona fide Life-Mission to carry out. A real, true plan to do something unbelievably important. And here's something scary to think about. Most of us even stick to our appointed path in life for a few years. Then we give it up. Yes….we abandon our Life-Missions.

The Purpose You Came With is Beyond That Wall

Each of us comes with a simple purpose in life that's rather obvious if you think about it. Your purpose and mine is to be ourselves. We're all supposed to grow Human in our own unique way until we blossom. We'd all do exactly that too, and get our fair share of true success, if the wall of fear didn't stop us. Some folks get into their teens before giving up on their Life's purpose. Others get lost earlier. I was completely aimless by the age of ten for instance, but my departed brother Brian lost his way before he was eight. So where does this wall come from and why is it all but impossible to get past? It comes from our deepest, most basic beliefs about how the world works. Beliefs that just happen to be absolutely mistaken, but are extremely difficult to give up because they're so ancient and all but sacred.

Unfortunately, these misguided beliefs also make the truth we must see to get our dreams back look like nonsense. This latter amazing and sad feature of the wall of fear is probably the worst. Imagine a wall beyond which is everything you ever dreamed of. A wall that convinces you there's nothing good on the other side. It's something like that. But you *can* get past this wall to find your purpose again. It took me decades to do it because I had to stumble around lost in the dark for many years just to figure out what was wrong. Luckily, you don't have to, because everything you need for the job is right here.

"The world we see that seems so insane is the result of a belief system that is not working. To perceive the world differently, we must be willing to change our belief system, let the past slip away, expand our sense of now, and dissolve the fear in our minds". - William James

Chapter One
Joke of the Century!
(You Don't Know What Your Own Dreams Are)

Gaston to the Maitre de in Monty Python's "The Meaning of Life"………. *"You know, one day, my-- my mother, she put me on her knee and she said to me, 'Gaston, my son, the world is a beautiful place. You must go into it and… love everyone, try to make everyone happy, and bring peace and contentment everywhere you go,' and so, I became a waiter. Well, it's-- it's not much of a philosophy, I know,… but, well,… F**! you. I can live my own life in my own way if I want to. F**! off."*

The Meaning of Life is a Joke Today

The meaning of our lives is one big joke today. You wouldn't think something of such sobering importance would be….or *should* be…but it is. If you're not sure about that, just go tell a few friends you're really serious about trying to find yourself….but watch out for the snickers. No…not the chocolate bar kind. The raised eyebrows, gagging from laughing, rolling in the aisles kind of snickers that will make you blush. You won't have to worry about all the name-calling though, because they'll be doing *that* behind your back. No question about it. Mr. Python had it right. The meaning of our lives is a comedy act today. But why is that anyway? Here's why. Everyone wants that famous meaningful life, but it's been so hard to find for so long, we have to make a joke of it. If we didn't, we'd be torturing ourselves looking for something we desperately need….but can't find. See what I mean? No? Think of it like this then. Imagine the meaning of your life is a Treasure approximately the size of ten elephants. Lucky for you too… it's in the house next door. But unfortunately, the door's locked up tighter than a rusty bolt. You're sure not getting in that way.

But, but, but …. THERE IT IS! You can see it through a window and it's got *your* name on it! The thing is, you can't get in through there either because the window is two inches of impenetrable plate glass. You want that treasure more than anything of course, but you're not having it. Now what? Here's where the joke comes in.

We Laugh Out Loud to Stop From Crying

So there you are, staring at Treasure you need to come alive, but you can't get at it. How can you stop from going insane? Convince yourself you don't even want it. Make a joke of it even. The more convinced you are treasure is ridiculous, the easier it'll be to forget. Forget what? How bad you really want it. Idiotic as it sounds, it works. It's been working for men and women in the real world for a long time. We've made the meaning of our lives a big joke for many generations because we desperately want this treasured possession…. but can't find it. All you have to do is mention the subject today and you'll get laughed at, called stupid… or worse. But I have some news for all of us. That stupid meaning of our lives is no joke. Every single one of us was put here to have it, and here's something you might want to think about.

Your life was once filled with this passionate meaning, before you let it go away. Yes, you heard right. You left behind the most important thing in the world, but not because you wanted to. You were taught to throw it down those tubes, letting your reason for being swim home to the sea. Thankfully though…..you can get it back, if you want it. Not interested? Sounds like me ten years ago. I would've passed on this book myself way back when. Like everyone else, I thought the meaning of Life was one big slap-stick comedy act. Sadly….I couldn't have been more wrong.

We're Lost Without Our Callings

Now I know this. There's something more important than air and water to your life, called "meaning and purpose". A reason for living. If you don't have one, you'll go to school, get good jobs, retire and die, never knowing who you are. While marrying the wrong person to have ten kids who will very probably do the same. A real dynasty of lost people. But guess what a living person with no purpose is? Not sure? O.K., I'll tell you. A Zombie. A lost man or woman carrying out the motions, but never putting heart and soul into anything. How does that sound to you? Not the life you'd hoped for? Probably not, but without a real aim in life, it can get a lot worse. There's a good chance you might wander around all your life, drinking and drugging to hide from the pain of being lost for example. Or live a dramatically boring life of quiet desperation, doing almost nothing, because you can't get at those potentials you know you've got. A life with no point might even make you go postal. O.K., so how do you get this famous meaning of your life? You take up the Mission or "calling" you came with and followed for years before giving up. A Mission you've never actually forgotten, and still have dim recollections of as we speak. Complete nonsense you say? Here's a little test. Try it.

"True happiness...is not attained through self-gratification, but through fidelity to a worthy purpose".- Helen Keller

Everyone Has Memories of Their Purpose in Life

I'm here to tell you there's a point to your life. You came into this world with a real, genuine calling, like you hear folks on T.V. talking about. Right here, right now, you can get a tiny inkling of this truth of your life too. I'd be surprised if you hadn't already performed this little test on yourself before. All set? Try swallowing the idea your life's absolutely meaningless.

Imagine anything you do is just one big accident of chemistry that will eventually be washed away by the rain. Stretch your mind to see yourself from birth to death as having absolutely no meaning, value, point or purpose. If you're like me, and pretty much everybody I've ever met, it just won't compute. Even if you have no idea at all right now what you're here for, the idea you're here for *nothing* just won't sit right. If there's any idea that's all but incomprehensible, it's the idea our lives are worth absolutely nothing. I sure hope your brain has a hard time making sense of it. Mine always did, even when I had no clue what to do with my life. But why is it you and I can't believe there's no reason we're here, even if we have no idea what it is?

The answer is pretty darn simple. It's because there *is* a reason we're here, and our souls can't ever forget it. Way down deep where our hearts live, we know for sure there's a place in the sun for each of us. The fundamental, inescapable, and awe-inspiring truth is, you were put here to do something with your life. Not just anything either, something that makes sense for you and only you. Something that's going to make you feel real bad if you don't do it. It's to fulfill the life-mission you came with. I know, I know. You've been taught callings, Life-Missions, and destiny are all complete nonsense. I was too, but if you look very closely you'll discover memories of your very own calling. Memories of the Mission you started life with. Stunning recollections of your destiny.

Why Don't We Recognize Our Callings?

I can hear you calling me bad names from here, because you can't remember a single scrap of *any* Life-Mission…..much less your own. You can't accept the idea you came with a calling either. Am I right? I thought so, but you're wrong on both counts. You really do have lots of memories of a time when you were relentlessly pursuing your Life's dream.

Your soul knows it full well, but your mind probably won't get it, because it's been taught wrong-headed ideas about callings. Whether you believe it or not, you don't really know what a calling is. That's why you don't recognize memories of your Life-Mission. You don't know what you're looking for. As matter of fact, you probably wouldn't know one if you fell over it. I didn't. I stumbled over memories of my destiny decade after decade without seeing them for what they were. So don't feel bad if you peer back into the mists of time and can't see your true aim in life. You'll need a brief introductory course in callings first. It's coming up next. It's the story of my life.

An Introductory Course in Callings

I grew up in a decent, caring family, with parents who tried hard to give their kids a good shot at life. How about you? I hope so, because it means you didn't get your life-mission scared out of you for a few years anyhow. Like me. I hung in there until I was about ten before I dove for the ditch and got well and truly lost. On the other hand, my departed brother Brian was a lot smarter than me. Too smart for his own good maybe, because he learned the lessons of fear faster. Brian got off track by the age of seven. Even so, Brian and I stuck to our callings long enough to lay down lots of memories. Memories of real direction and self-esteem and a sense of purpose. Amazing, wonderful memories of going the proper way. If you came from ordinary parents that didn't inflict violence upon their children, you'll have lots. If you'd like to start seeing yours, just watch me get lost first and point to mine. It'll help you spot your own life-mission memories.

One Man Loses His Way

In my teens, after a few false starts, I did what was expected.

From one of those big famous career books, I picked a college course off the shelf and knuckled under. To become an engineer. But there was a little bitta trouble under the covers. Like what? I didn't have a single engineering bone in my body anywhere. No sir, not one. Not even half of one. So why on earth did I go that way? To "get a good job" of course. I wasn't no dummy. Was I? Well....maybe, but I had another reason to go that route. I've told many people this awe-inspiring story over the years, but nobody ever believes me. They think I'm joking. But I'm not, and it's no joke either. Here it comes. I liked the spiffy gold leather jackets engineering students wore. I just had to have one. Ridiculous? Yes it is. It's idiotic, crazy, totally senseless and a waste of time. Unfortunately, it's also absolutely true. My career was based on nothing but a weird fashion choice.

As you might expect of a guy with the wrong bones though, I was swimming uphill against a current from day one. A blind man without arms would have been better at arranging flowers....if you get my drift. Even so, some years later I got out mostly alive. Five church-sanctioned miracles let me pass, and I came out as a cross between a lost soul and an engineer. Which is.... I think ...what's called a Donkey. But not to worry. Soon I got one of those "good jobs" everyone talks about, and things looked fine for a few brief weeks, as I basked in the light of my own smartness. Then big doubts crept in.

How I Discovered Some Famous Doubts

O.K., so there I am, freshly minted graduate with Canadian-style iron engineering ring in my first "good job" when some famous doubts rolled in. Like a freight train. Just one or two at first. I thought I'd worked my tail off to get to the promised land. Not so. I soon started asking myself a few painful three-word questions. Like ..."is this it?". Why? The work was absolutely, completely, utterly, and....um...totally meaningless to me.

It wasn't really meaningless of course, I just had the wrong darn bones for it. Those with proper bones were in heaven, but to me it was more like hell. That's when memories of my calling started to show up. Old dim memories of having a real mission on earth that got in my face and whacked me on the snout. They kicked me in the butt, trying to tell me my life wasn't always meaningless. But…. of course…..I didn't get it. I hate to say it…but it took me several more decades to get it. So what did these memories feel like? Like this.

I Missed My Own Mission Memories

So there I was, lost in the dark, looking for meaning in all the wrong places. Then came the flashbacks. Old feelings flooded into my head and I slipped into a trance, wishing I was a kid again. Have you ever done that? I'll bet you have. Me? I'd remember playing kick the can over the wire with Bill and Bob and Norm, or playing with my treasured Trixie dog like we were brothers. Other fun things came to mind as well, like exploring. By the age of ten, good old buddy Ken and I would ride our bikes to six mile creek and explore every nook and cranny. We discovered trout and bears and foxes. And bees nests! Not to mention how to swim bare-bum down rocky falls. But those weren't my only exploring memories. When the fish weren't biting we'd explore with microscopes and chemistry sets. Ken discovered microscopic elephants in pond water, and I created home-made bombs that blew us both up several times. No question about it. We were amateur scientists exploring brand new worlds, and I wished I was back there. Back when I'd learn for the heck of it and be stunned by the wonder of the night sky. How about you? Have you ever caught yourself wishing for happy days? Yes? Ever wonder why?

We Call Them "Happy Days"

Why do you think we all wish for youthful happy days now and then? Most people say it's because those are the days when we don't have big worries. You know, mouths to feed, bills to pay, and jobs we don't want to get up for. Worrisome things like that. But they're wrong. Those wishes are messages trying to tell us we left our callings behind. Unfortunately, if you don't really know what a calling is….like me for the first forty years of my life….you won't see why those happy words are such big clues. Happy words like playing, exploring, wondering, and learning, that all point directly to the meaning of your life. If you have a clear idea what you were put on earth to do, those words are a dead giveaway. If not, they'll be intriguing, suggestive, tantalizing and maybe even hopeful. But they won't hit the bulls-eye. So? Can you see why folks keep on dreaming for Happy Days yet? Do those happy words paint a picture so clear it's painful? Is it so obvious it's hardly worth mentioning? No? Let's look into callings a little bit more. First we'll dig up some conventional wisdom. What most people think about Life-Missions or callings.

"My advice is to live your life….allow that wonderful inner intelligence to speak through you….Don't climb the ladder of success, only to find it is leaning against the wrong wall."--- Bernie Siegel, M.D., Love, Medicine, and Miracles

Chapter Two
What You're Called to Do
(With Your Life)

"Use what talents you possess; The woods would be very silent if no birds sang there except those that sang best." (William Blake)

What Those in the Know Say About Callings

It's fair to say that most highly educated men and women today don't really believe callings even exist. By and large, that includes knowledgeable professional or professorial people who teach at our schools and head up our institutions. These folks in-the-know certainly believe some people have work that turns them on and fits them like a tailored shirt. They accept the idea that jobs can be meaningful and people can be fulfilled by doing them. Lots of professors or businessmen enjoy what they're doing and find it satisfying themselves. But there's something right at the very core of bona fide Life Missions most educated people reject with ferocity. Ferocity means they'll laugh you right out of the building if you bring up the single word that describes the heart of every calling. That one word is destiny. By far most knowledgeable people today can't imagine the possibility that you and I and everyone else came here with a single purpose set out for us before we were born. Destiny is senseless to most folks with diplomas because it conflicts with what we call "free will". How on earth can we be free to choose, if our lives were already pre-planned somehow?

When all is said and done then, most highly educated men and women today stop short of believing in real, absolute, callings because they can't believe in destiny. There are millions and millions of people in that state of mind, and they can't all be wrong. Can they? Sadly, they can.

But I'm getting a bit ahead of myself here, so let's slow down for a moment. Maybe most educated people don't cotton to callings, but that doesn't include everyone. If you diligently look around, you might be lucky enough to find a real person with a true calling or Life Mission. It might be worth your while to listen closely to what *they* say. They could be professors. They could be CEOs. They could be butchers, bakers, or candlestick makers. Wouldn't you think real people with real Life Missions would have something meaningful to say about it? Go ahead, look one right in the eye and he or she will promise you destiny is real. Just last week I heard a lady on T.V. talk like this in fact.

What People Nearing Death Say

Last Wednesday night I turned on the television to find myself watching an inspirational documentary about people with life-changing experiences. One story was about a saleswoman who traveled the world selling big-ticket computer systems. For those of you not familiar with sales careers, very large money can be made in the selling profession, and this lady was doing exactly that. She was way up into six figures and had a very generous expense account that put her into five star hotels and first class plane seats. Maybe she wasn't a millionaire, but she was far into the well-off leagues. Then one day on the way to an airport she had a car crash that broke pretty much every bone in her body and left her in a coma for months. By some miracle she eventually woke up and healed completely. But something had changed dramatically and she tells the story this way. On the very day she awakened from her coma, she realized something. Her big sales career had been a kind of lie. Forever in her heart-of-hearts, this lady had wanted to start an animal shelter and take care of neglected creatures. But of course, there's little money or power in this line of work, and even less travel and public glory. So she listened to the call of cash instead of her heart, until her life was almost taken from her. Then she saw something stunning and said so.

This woman saw clearly that she was always *meant* to care for animals. She realized that anything else would be counter to her very *being*. From that day onward she did exactly that as well. And here's what she said about it on that television show. "Now I'm following my destiny" she said, "it's what I'm here for". Her total conviction and absolute belief in destiny was so powerful, it should have made even the most hard-bitten skeptics stop and think. But it almost always takes a near-death experience to change the minds of those in the know. Hearing about near-death experiences won't do it. If you're like most folks though, you probably don't know anyone who's had a life-altering experience. So who can you turn to for the scoop on Divine purpose? There's all kinds of street-smart men and women around you who probably have something to say about it. In my former life, that's where the bulk of my education came from. Schooling that kept me in the dark about the true nature of callings for decades.

What Street Smart People Say

I don't know about you, but I'm sure not knowledgeable, professorial, or a world-class businessman like people in-the-know mentioned above. Never burdened by too much knowledge, I was always open to ideas about callings from the street. So what do street-smart people say a calling is? A fabulous job that suits someone to a tee. That sounded eminently sensible to me in my lost years, and I swallowed it hook, line and sinker. Back then, if someone asked me to explain the idea, here's what I'd say. Apparently each of us is born like an uniquely shaped peg, and somewhere out there is a similarly shaped job. Find the right fit and you've found your calling. Seems to make sense too, because a perfect fit would make the work fun and easy and people with callings are always talking about having fun. So there I was thirty years ago, wandering around expecting to find a hole to fit in.

I wasn't having any luck at the time, and often wondered where it was. What if *my* hole was in China, or some other distant place I'm not likely to visit? My calling would be sitting there waiting in a place I'm never going to. I'd be completely out of luck. There's millions of different shaped holes out there too....so how on earth am I ever going to find the right one? Maybe the right hole is six hundred jobs down the line and I can only try out the first ten in my lifetime? Lots of panicky thoughts like that crossed my mind when I was young. Lots of ways me and my calling could cross paths in the dark somewhere without meeting. Maybe you've wondered some of these things yourself? If you haven't, you've probably already given up on finding out why you're here on earth. At any rate, in my lost years, I thought those were the everyday practical problems everyone must solve to find their calling. Sure it's tough, like trying to find a needle in a haystack. But the proper shaped hole is out there somewhere, and we've just got to knuckle under and find it. It's just a fact of life. Or so I thought at the time.

In reality though, callings are nothing like that at all. The *real* problem behind callings is supremely different. It's this. You're not looking for some job, occupation or career to fit in out there at all. You're called to come out of a very special place of potential at your "center". You can't go to this place, but you can free yourself from imprisonment there. Setting yourself free is called "knowing thyself" and knowing thyself is what callings are all about. So how do we get started on a Journey to "Know Thyself"? We can begin with any decent dictionary. A good dictionary will tell us why callings are called callings and point us at the heart of it all.

Why Callings Are Called Callings

Dictionaries say people with real Life-Missions follow an "inner voice", that "calls" to them from within. A voice that tells them which way to go with their lives.

Something whispering way down deep. If you've ever wondered why callings are called callings, now you know. It's those tiny voices. Sounds ridiculous? Not really. Go take a survey and you'll find people with callings aren't crazy at all. Inventors, leaders, and go-getters yes. Artists, poets and scientists for sure. But spaced-out, nearly insane loop-headed waakkos? Not at all. So what do the dictionaries mean? They mean "ideas". They're telling us people with callings get ideas about their mission on earth. Once they get them, they know what to do with their lives. There you go. Nothing crazy about ideas is there? No there isn't, but in case you didn't notice, dictionaries don't tell us how to get these special calling-ideas or why some folks get them and others don't. Doggone it, now what? Now let's get down to brass tacks and give you the goods on callings

Callings Are About Growing

Remember all those happy words up there, like playing, exploring, wondering, and learning? They all describe growing. Growing Human I mean. That's exactly what a calling is. It's growing ourselves into who we can be. And becoming all we can become….by growing…..is what makes us happy. That's what most folks are doing with their lives at first too. Following a calling to grow themselves into a unique happy Human being, by playing, exploring, wondering and learning. Unfortunately, a terrible fear stops most of us from growing real early on. It stops those ideas the dictionaries talk about from coming into our lives, taking our callings from us so quietly we don't even realize it's happened. For a while anyhow. But eventually almost everyone begins to discover something is missing from their lives. Most people can't quite put their finger on what it is, but they sure know some kind of meaning has disappeared. Their hearts tell them there was once more to life than they have now.

Their souls know they left something important behind, back in youth when they were still growing.

Happy Days Are Days Growing Human

Can you guess what all that missing meaning makes you and I do? You got it, we wish for happy days. We wish we were kids again, but not because those were easy days without responsibilities and worries. Not even remotely. We wish for youth because that's when we were still becoming all we can become. We wish the fear hadn't taken our callings from us. And so, let's stop and contemplate for a moment. Guess what happens if you don't learn how to take down that wall of fear…. to get your calling back? Not sure? Look up. Way up. Up where the Zombies are. Find it? No? Well, let me tell you again. You'll go to school, get good jobs, retire, and die, never knowing who you are. So? Would you like to spend your life in a daze because you don't know what to do with it? Do you want to be an immature Human Being at the age of eighty? I didn't think so, but that means you have to learn how to start growing again. But watch out because there's still something critically important you need to know about callings. Believe me…you better get this part right, because growing's not enough.

Growing Is Not Enough

You can't just grow any which way. You've got to grow in the appropriate direction. The direction you're called to grow in. Just growing any way at all is a really bad thing. Bad, bad, bad. Don't think so? Think again. I have an example of growing without proper direction that'll make you shiver. Cancer. Cancer's all about growing too, but cancer cells grow wildly. They don't stop when they're supposed to, or stick to their proper place in the body because they've stopped following the plan they came with, and gave up their calling. And you?

If you want this kind of pointless growth in your life you can just go ahead and pick a few life goals off the shelf and go get them. Choose a path that'll get you heaps of money and the grandest job on the block for example. Create a career that takes you to the top of some mountain where all the important people are. But here's the bad news about this kind of choice. If this isn't the way you're called to grow, you and those big cancer tumors are like twins. Twins? Exactly. You're both products of senseless, purposeless growth. Scary sounding? Yes indeed it is.

We Have to Grow *Our Way*

Now we're at the bottom line. Sort of. Now you know exactly what a calling really is. It's growing *your* Way. I've got to grow "my way" and you've got to grow yours, from the beginning of our lives to the end. By now you've probably realized that there's a bit of a problem here. You have to know what *your* way is first. And how do you figure that out? That's a question bazillions of people would probably kill to answer. You too? Good. But you don't have to kill for it, because I'll give you the answer. All you have to do is remove that wall of fear and *your way* will come to you. Ideas about who you are and what to do with your life will flow to you, like the dictionaries said. Just like water would if you opened a tap. In fact, that's the only possible way to "go with the flow" everyone talks about. If you don't open the tap….no flow. There's only one single thing keeping you from knowing what your Life-Mission is. That fear I mentioned. Take it away and your inner voice will tell you which way to grow again. When that happens, you'll be able to follow the plan you came with and fulfill your very own dreams. But here's the best part. That is precisely what will bring you as much happiness as any soul ever gets. There you go. Dump that single fear and the most astonishing happy, heavenly life you could imagine comes to you like magic. All you have to do is get out of the way. End of story.

Don't get it? I know. We have a bit more work to do before you do. To start off we'll just go take a look at the Plan you arrived here with.

You Came With a Plan to Grow *Your Way*

Lets not forget this. Your calling is to grow yourself and all your own unique potentials from the beginning of your life until the end. Just like any flower grows from seed until it blossoms. Sounds great doesn't it......but flowers seem to have it a lot easier than we do. Flower seeds have little DNA plans at their center that tells them what they need to know to grow *their* way. That special little plan tells the seed how to take nutrients from the soil and build a plant that will go on to flower. A flower's plan for growing is there right at the beginning of its life then, and never goes away. It doesn't have to worry about who it is, or which way to take its life, because that Plan keeps on giving it direction. The Plan for today's flowers' lives goes back millions of years as well, because their DNA can be traced back to the very beginning of all life on earth.

But you and I are different. Aren't we? Yes and no. The "no" part goes like this. We too come with a DNA plan that starts us off growing in the womb, and we continue growing human as very young babies. Everybody knows we follow this Plan from conception for the first nine months of our lives. It's obvious we keep on following it for some time after birth too. Why? Because nobody knows how to build a baby Human Being, so we have to stick to that Plan. In the beginning of our lives then, you and I are following some kind of direction. We're relentlessly heading in the direction of becoming Human, according to a Plan. Now comes the "yes" part. The part that makes us different from flowers. Once old enough, we give up following this "inner direction" and consciously start making our own choices about which way to go.

That's where most of us get lost, because we have no idea which way to go. The reason we get lost is very simple too. We stop following that Plan we came with.

Your Plan is Still There For You

In today's world we believe the DNA plan we come with is just there to build our bodies. Once it's grown all our body parts, including our brains, a "conscious Mind" emerges, giving us ideas to direct our lives with. With a Mind of our own, we're free to choose our own Path and find what we're looking for in life. Ideas coming from our brains let us do that. Perhaps we need that DNA Plan to show us how to grow human in the beginning, but once we're conscious, choice-making people, we have our own ideas about which way to grow. Right?

Certainly that's conventional wisdom. But the truth is, that magical double-helix we call DNA also contains the Golden Braid of Destiny. Buried within it is the inner direction you and I must heed if we're to discover what to do with our lives. And contrary to what you might think at the moment, it is possible to find that Golden Plan you came with and begin growing Human once more. Believe it or not, your Plan is still there for you. All you have to do is learn how to release it into your life once more. No idea what I mean? Let's flesh it out a bit more.

Your Plan is Something Like This

Imagine a thread in an ocean, rising straight as an arrow towards the sky. Eventually it reaches the surface of the sea and continues into the air above. In reality, it's supposed to keep on pointing straight up towards a distant destination, but it isn't. Something has gone wrong and now the thread is blowing about in the wind. And here's a funny thing.

People watching this thread don't even realize something has gone wrong. How come? They think the thread in the air is a completely different thing from the thread in the ocean. They don't even realize they're two different parts of one thread. So it never even occurs to them that the once-directed thread has somehow become aimless. To these people, the airborne part of the thread waving aimlessly in the wind began its life like that. In fact, there are millions of similar threads aimlessly flapping about in the air, so it looks like directionless threads are normal. Nobody recognizes that each of these threads has lost the direction it came with. Your problem finding the Way in life and mine is much like that. The direction present in our earliest years growing Human, before we were born and thereafter, is supposed to continue in our conscious lives. It's supposed to show up as the right ideas that will tell us which way to go. Ideas we need to have first, before we can make the right choices. The same ideas those dictionaries say should be calling us. So why don't we even realize we've lost the direction we came with?

You Don't Recognize the Plan For Your Life?

Why is it we don't recognize we've stopped growing Human and lost the direction we once had? Well, the short answer is, we're looking at the world the wrong way to see it. I'll tell you how and why and what to do about it later. Just bear with me for now. Certainly anyone can see the thread of direction our body follows in growing Human for the first years of our life. But once we're old enough to be conscious decision-making people, with a Mind of our own, nobody expects that thread of direction to run through our ideas. As far as we're concerned today, Mind and Body are just too different to have the same thread of direction running through them. So radically different in fact, it's a gigantic, mysterious puzzle as to how they fit together.

As it turns out, it's that puzzle we'll have to solve so you can see the Golden Braid of Destiny in your life. We'll do that together later. But I want to tell you something about it right now anyway. Every single person who discovers who they are and what to do with their lives, sees that thread of inner direction going from one end of their life to the other. I know that for sure because I can see it in my life right now as I write these words. I also know it's very, very difficult to convince folks in-the-know that the purpose of our lives goes back to the very beginnings of the Cosmos, and flows through all life on earth. Because they're stuck in a worldview that won't let them see it. Later you'll see what I mean. But for now let's begin a Journey to teach you to grow *your* way like any seed, to receive your share of Bliss.

Jobs Are O.K. Too

Oh yeh. Jobs are O.K. too. In fact, if you learn how to overcome fears of being yourself, you'll find a way to make a living... being yourself. No. I'm not kidding. When you're unafraid to go about life *your* way, a special magic flows. You get the courage you need to explore and try and fail and succeed. You'll find your way by trial and error into a job that keeps you growing.... your way.... all your life, until you fully blossom. You'll get the *Joy* of Being yourself too. What kind of Joy is that? Supercharged contentment. Works like this. You won't feel bad or sad if you don't make much money or have the smallest, simplest job ever, because you already *have* what most folks with big jobs and money never get. Something they'd trade places with you in an instant for.... if they could. Which is? Knowing who you are. That will make you *super* contented... with your life. But don't misunderstand me here. Contented doesn't mean you reluctantly accept your lot in life...but you'd rather give it up.....for money. Contented means you know something for sure. Like what?

You're at the absolute peak of Human success, because being yourself is the best thing you can possibly get in life. It's the pinnacle of things Human Beings hold near and dear. If that's not supercharged contentment, I don't know what is.

Now Let's Watch You on Your Mission

Now I want you to see something important. I want you to see you once were driven to fulfill a mission and had absolute direction, because you probably don't believe it. So please read the next part careful as a cat with a fifty pound mouse. I want you to see *you* following a very special plan from conception, growing straight as an arrow in the right direction….for you. Soon as egg met sperm you were headed there like an atomic arrow, absolutely *DRIVEN*…. on a real live Life-Mission to become fully Human. If you hadn't been scared off your path, you'd still be getting up every day, driven to succeed in your very own way. Letting your inner voice guide you. Still with me? Great. We're off.

"Efforts and courage are not enough without purpose and direction". - John F. Kennedy

Chapter Three
The Plan You Came With
(And How I Gave Up Mine)

"All you need is the plan, the road map, and the courage to press on to your destination". - Earl Nightingale (1921 - 1989)

We're All Called to Grow Human

If you're a parent, midwife, babysitter, or scholarly professor studying Human development, you will have seen Human Beings growing from scratch before. It happens billions of times all over the world and has been going on for a very long time. So long and often in fact, most folks don't think anything of it anymore. But they should. Here's two reasons why. First off, how a conscious Human Being emerges from one big biological soup of atoms, proteins, chemicals and lots of water is profoundly mysterious. Nobody has the foggiest idea how that happens. If you run into someone who says they do, be sure to have your salt-shaker handy....because they're mistaken. Sounds like a reason to be in awe of conception and birth and growing babies? Yes it does, but there's another reason we should all be wonder-struck by the growth of each and every one of us from seed. That reason is "uniqueness".

Uniqueness is direction plain and simple. Each Human Being has a clear direction or purpose in life which is to grow into a one-of-a-kind person. We all come with a plan to do that, and we're supposed to stick to it all our lives. We would too, if the wall of fear I mentioned didn't stop us. And here's what I want you to think about as you read the next few paragraphs. You're looking at your calling. You and I and everyone else is called to grow Human from conception 'til death. All that familiar Human growth you see below is how people set off following a Plan for their life. A plan you can get going on again to find real Happiness.

Yes, I know, you just plain won't recognize all this baby growing stuff as the Life-Mission you came with, because you're still looking at the world the wrong way. But that's O.K. I'll teach you how to see things clearly later so you can re-discover your very own calling. For now just see how we all follow our Life's direction at first, to become Human.

In the Beginning You Grew *Your* Way

"Each man has his own vocation; his talent is his call. There is one direction in which all space is open to him." Ralph Waldo Emerson

Maybe you don't like the words "plan", "purpose", and "direction", because it seems to imply someone or something is directing your life. That's alright, because you don't have to ask where the plan comes from or if it was put there by some greater power. Those are very interesting questions of course, but I'm not asking you to answer them right now. All I'm trying to do is get you to see something obvious. This. No one can possibly deny the fact that each of us is headed in a very clear direction right from conception. As soon as egg meets sperm, we begin growing Human. Beginning with an impossible symphony of assembling cells, we grow in one direction and one direction alone. Cells are organized into organs and organs into a staggeringly complex Human body, including the most complex thing in the known universe. The Human brain.

Is there a single absolute direction in all this amazing growth? You'd have to be brain dead to miss it. Every single cell of it is being directed to become a very particular and unique thing. And after nine months of following this Plan, it's born. A baby Human Being.

The path from conception to birth of all creatures great and small, and especially Human Beings is probably the most stunning example of absolute and unerring direction we know of. But that superb and mind-boggling direction doesn't stop at birth. If anything, growth this way gets even more spectacular.

You Stuck to the Plan After Birth Too

From conception to birth you and I headed like a guided missile in the direction of growing ever more Human. But after birth we grew the same way even faster. Organs matured, vision became clear, teeth showed up, and every single part of us continued growing Human. Then what? Our relentless, purposeful growth got even more spectacular. Following the plan, we learned to walk and talk and read and write. Any one of these is an earth-shaking accomplishment, but altogether they define us as Being Human. Something we've been aiming to do since conception. Can it possibly get any more impressive? Yes it can. In a few years we're doing handsprings, reciting poems from memory and riding bicycles. Soon were driving cars, flying airplanes and even piloting rockets to the moon. Some of us anyhow. If you look closely you'll see this kind of planned growth is so astonishing, it should be impossible. But it isn't. It's just you or I growing *our* way. Following the plan we came with.

And here's something even more mind-blowing to think about. If you learn how to stick to this plan, you'll continue growing in your own unique way all your life, until you become all you can become. And how do you do that? Learn how to hear your inner voice again, so it can tell you which way to grow. That little DNA-plan was just assembling the proper parts, so you could carry on growing in the same direction after you were born. The direction that would culminate in a fully grown mature and unique Human Being.

But if you're like most folks, there's a big bad fear in the world that's soon going to stop you cold, leaving you with no choice but to grow the wrong way. Like a cancer.

Too Many People Grow the Wrong Way

I hope this doesn't make you sad, but it's true. Ninety five percent of boys and girls stop growing their way by the time they're ten. You heard me right, but don't get me wrong. That doesn't mean they stopped growing. They just gave up listening to their inner voices, and let other folks tell them what to do with their lives. Sure thing. Off they go in one big rush, growing some way Nature never meant them to. Like what? Well….musicians-at-heart become accountants, and accounting guys try to play the piano. Poetic souls take to banking careers too…..much like pussycats take to water. You name it and folks who shouldn't be doing it are. They look a lot like Mr. Tee when growing the wrong way as well. Mr. Tee? Yeh. Mr. big directionless Tumor. Bad joke eh? No kidding. Specially bad for folks who lose their way. Here's a couple of real life examples for you.

Erin Grows the Wrong Way

How do you grow the wrong way? Simple. Don't listen to your inner voice to tell you what to do with your life. Listen to someone else instead. Books, parents, teachers or bosses will be happy to tell you what to do. Like this youngster I know headed the wrong way as we speak who's always wanted ….desperately…. to be a helicopter pilot. It's fair to say he loves helicopters more than horses love hay. Just mention the word helicopter, and his face lights up like….well… a Christmas tree on fire maybe. But my friends his parents have thrown a wet blanket on that one by hitting him with good old "get a good job Routine # 7". Maybe you've heard this gem yourself. It goes like this.

"Ain't many jobs in *that* field sonny-Jim…..so don't even *try* goin' there". I'm sure this popular mantra was repeated every day plus Sunday, but I think they had to hit him with Routine # 28 before he finally gave up on helicopters. I'll bet you've heard *it* too. "Go *that* way Mr. and you're gonna hafta move to the wilderness to get a job!". Sure enough, that did it. Erin isn't thinking helicopters any more. Now he's been dropping in and out of one course after another because the love of his life went elsewhere. Poor guy doesn't know it yet, but he's stopped listening to his heart and it's going to come back to bite him some day big-time. Does that sound at all familiar? Too familiar perhaps? Like maybe I'm talking about you? Or every single one of your best friends?

An Old Friend Grows the Wrong Way

Here's another way you can grow in the wrong direction. By listening to bosses. I have a dear old friend who is a lot smarter than I am and has more talents. I'm sure about that because I've known him all my life. Matter of fact, back in highschool he was my hero. I was in awe of his energy and big fearless ideas because nothing was going to stop this guy from being King of the world. Well…Prince of Canada anyhow. "Gee" said me who was dragging his feet every which way in those years, "this guy's a real leader". And he was, until he stopped listening to his inner voice. Then what? He began thinking other folks could tell him what to do with his life. Mentors maybe, or those down home folk we call "bosses". Trouble is, that's nothing but bad ideas in a tin cup. Thirty years later I have some tough news for all of us. Unless you can hear your inner voice, the best boss in the world won't help you find your way. My old buddy's been proving it for quite a while.

Taking Direction From Bosses Doesn't Work

How's that? Well, he's been taking direction from bosses now for close to forty years. Not from his soul. From bosses. Don't misunderstand me here though. He's been doing a first class job all the way. He's been growing personally for decades as well, by taking seminars, and reading tons of books. No question about it, he's been growing steadily year after year. The wrong way. How do I know it's the wrong way? He still doesn't know what to do with his life. If you back him into a corner with a big stick he'll admit it. Sounds a bit sad? Yes it is, but I know someone a heck of a lot worse than that. Me. I stopped growing completely by the age of ten and stayed there for a long time. Would you like to see what a real lost soul like that looks like? O.K., let's go look at yours truly way back when. Then we'll fast forward to where I got on the Personal Growth Bandwagon, growing any which way but my own. I have to admit…my head hurts just remembering.

I Stopped Growing Completely

Most sane people realize that schoolwork is a kind of growing, and that to grow you need to work at it. Do homework or study for instance. Real complicated stuff like that. So what about me? I gave up growing by my tenth birthday. Forget about growing *my* way, I was stalled completely. I'd show up in class, listen half-way to Mr. or Mrs. the teacher, and go home for dinner, and at least ten hours of T.V.. Believe it or not, it never occurred to me that studying might help. By some strange twist of fate, I got by doing nothing for a while too, until high-school showed up. Then, somewhat predictably, I hit the skids. Did I get it when my marks turned tail and went straight down the drain? No I didn't.

Was I just plain stupid, like seven way silly Serge, who'd bite himself and others for fun? It must have looked like it to everyone around me, but smartness tests revealed I had almost one third a brain, so something sad was wrong somewhere. Unfortunately, no one seemed to know what it was. Certainly not that guy in the mirror I stared at every day. Lots of folks tried in vain to figure me out though. I spent many months listening to guidance counselors. "Yer like a car with a great engine" said Mr. helpful advisor …… "but you're not gettin' power to the wheels". I found that really interesting, and it even raised a teensy little red flag somewhere in the back of my head. But it didn't help.

Mom Couldn't Help Me Find My Way

Even Mom couldn't help, who threatened to take me to a psychiatrist. Lucky for me she didn't or I might have got wired up backwards or something. So what the heck was wrong with me? Now I know it's as simple as steps on a very slippery porch. In plain talk, I'd stopped growing. One single big bad fear stopped me. I didn't know that at the time of course, and neither did anyone else. But sad to say…I'd been frightened out of growing my way by the age of ten and I stayed that way for decades. I was like a poor little seed stuck in barren ground, stalled by a fright I couldn't even imagine. We'll get to those terrible fears later, but now I'll bare my soft underbelly again, by telling you how I stopped growing other ways. Looking back even I find it hard to believe, but the truth is, I'd been scared off every kind of growing you could think of. It really is too bad it took me so long to start growing up again. But that old "better late than never" saying really hits home to me now. Unfortunately, I stayed a pre-teen until starting growing again…in my forties.

Another Way I Gave Up Growing

Looking back now, all these first little stories about a lost guy are gruesomely clear and stunningly sad to me. Even back then I knew something was terribly wrong, but didn't have a clue what it was. I knew I could really do something with my life for instance, but I had no idea what that might be. You'll see this little riff of heart-song show up later in the book as well....putting it into stark perspective for you. But for now let's carry on with me completely stalled in life. As a teen I loved swimming a whole heck of a lot. I was born with several webbed feet and two pink fins behind each ear, so it was natural I'd try swimming contests. But guess what? That's right. With no idea what growing meant, I never trained. I didn't realize that to grow as a swimmer, you have to work at it to build up your stamina. You know. Do lengths....swim and swim and swim....to grow and grow and grow. Things even the brain-dead would do. Not me. I'd just dive in, with predictable results.

Would you like a real live example? No problem at all. I've got a nice one for you. Back in the fifties, we had an annual summer cottage lake swim I entered at least once. One of those two or three miles across the lake and back things popular in summer lake country. Fine, but have you ever tried swimming a few miles without training? No? It's a real treat. I'll describe what it feels like for you....just in case you'd like to try it out for yourself. About half a mile out you're done in. Absolutely and completely exhausted with arms like wet noodles and feet pointing just about straight down. You're riding pretty darn low in the water as well. So low you're lucky there's anything above water to scoop air with. But...completely ignorant of the sins you're committing... you keep at it. By the time you're a mile and a half out, drowning is becoming a real and scary option too, because boats following the swimmers would never get to you in time. You'd go straight to the bottom.

I'm Not Growing at All

So there you are approaching a near-death experience when it gets worse. Much worse. When you reach the end of your life…..get to the other side I mean….. you have to turn around and swim back. Is somebody kidding? It would certainly be easier just to flap your arms and fly back. Or shoot yourself. But not to worry. You think this self-inflicted punishment is normal because the other kids are doing it. Aren't they? No they're not, they trained for it, which is something you can't comprehend. So off you go, trying hard to swim with the fishes. Through a tunnel of light you travel to consult the angels…..and finally…. by the Grace of something powerful…. out comes Mr. dead body onto the beach. Barely a pulse left. Lest you think this is just a silly made-up story about ridiculous and dangerous things…it is not. Every single word of it is true and I tried as best I could to pass the pain of it on to you. I actually did this crazy thing myself. I jumped in as a totally untrained swimmer and somehow clawed my way several miles.

And why the heck would anyone do anything so dumb? Easy. I had no ideas about growing anything by that time because they'd all been scared out of me. Yes I had a few small swimming bones, but I spent no time growing them. I had my own share of other little talents too of course, like every soul does. But sadly, by ten years of age, I'd given up growing every single one. I was too darn scared to be myself. A pretty sobering story eh? No kidding. But it's just a symptom of losing a calling. It's a sign I'd stopped growing *my* way to release my potentials. Sure enough, I stopped following the plan meant for me. But eventually I joined all the other folks out there, going for goals that aren't really theirs. Following some wonderful plan I picked off a shelf. Want some advice? Don't.

I'm So Lost I Don't Know It

Let's see here. How about a little quiz with a surprising answer? Who do you think would bust their butt to go get something they don't really want at heart? I'm talking about working their lives away as hard as possible, to get something they really don't care a rat's bum about. Think hard now. Don't know who'd be crazy enough to waste their whole life for....pretty much nothing? Millions of people, that's who. Men and women from horizon to horizon who pick dreams off the shelf. Dreams of being important people, like CEO's or rich lawyers or twinkly stars. Lots of folks get those goals too, and kick the bucket never knowing who they are. As a matter of fact, if you stand up right now and swing a baseball bat, you should hit a whole bunch of them. Statistically speaking....if you like that kind of stuff...I'd be willing to say at least 90% of everyone falls into this category. No. I didn't go do a scientific experiment to get this answer. I just looked around me for the last fifty-odd years and saw them. Still refusing to believe this amazing state of affairs? Not quite sure what's it like to follow other people's goals? Let's watch yours truly do it. As a bona fide member of that illustrious crowd for a very long time, I am supremely qualified to tell you. Here we go.

Remember my engineer's bones I don't have? Well, my first shot at adopted dreams was in engineering jobs when I left school. Blind as a bat to who I was and still in that "get a good job" frame of mind, I thought I should become an engineering guru. Little did I know, I was more like an engineering Emu. So off I went and engineered a whole lot of things. Mostly things that didn't work at all when I was done. Pumps, heaters and oil refineries for example. Did those stark failures stop me? No they didn't. I was not aware that I had no skills, talents, abilities or interest in engineering.

And so I went on to bungle up quite a few big complicated machines that were working fine before I got to them. Pumps, heaters and oil refineries for instance. Precisely like whales with gossamer wings, I was flying high. Wasn't I? No I wasn't because monkeys can type better than I can engineer. This little monkey didn't much like what he was doing either.

I Climb a Ladder to Nowhere

Eventually the sheer drudgery and pure stupidity of pretending to be an engineer overcame me and I decided to give it up. Probably within days of someone suing me for single-handedly destroying their multi-million dollar project. So what did I do? I headed for that big magical mountain called "management" of course. If you can't manage to engineer anything, maybe you can manage engineers. I said to myself. Or just go tell people what to do. Or something ignorant like that. And so off I went to make myself a different career, and it went like this. <u>*WARNING*</u>. *Don't try this at home*. I should probably add that some of you may read this in total disbelief as well. For that I'm sorry, but it is the absolute and complete truth. Here's the story. Without planning, thinking, or any real direction at all, I blindly stumbled up the ladder. To the very top. Like a drunken sailor to where the guy or gal in the corner office sits. The one called chief, boss, and…. um…other things.

Yes you read right. I went from dysfunctional engineer to general manager in no time at all. Even best friends thought something had to be wrong somewhere. Why? They still thought you had to be smart and talented and capable of planning a big career like a military campaign to climb to the top. None of which described me at all. It's all true in fantasy land of course, but in the real world things are heaps different. But I'm getting a bit off track here.

I want to tell you what it feels like to achieve big goals picked off the shelf. Remember? O.K., so try this on. It rings hauntingly hollow like half a Halloween pumpkin. It also feels like you won something really big alright….something you have no use for and would happily throw away. If you didn't need it to pay the bills. So there I was, sitting at the top of the totem pole when I heard the personal growth parade going by. Deep down I knew I needed a dream to follow. And for goodness sakes what do you know. There are all kinds of "How To Achieve Your Wildest Dreams" books out there in personal growth territory. Unfortunately, I didn't know I'd left my own dreams behind. And the thirteen books I read from cover to cover didn't tell me how to find them either. But they did offer lots of wild dreams I could go for. Other people's dreams of course. Would you like to see me really go for broke now? Here you go. But first here's a little bit of useful advice where concerns picking wild dreams from books. You'd be better off sticking your tongue in a live light socket.

Trying To Achieve Somebody Else's Dreams

Now I have my substantial nose in the self-help world, turning to gurus to help me find my way. And there I sat, book in hand, writing out my Financial Dream Plan, Family Dream Plan, Health Dream Plan, and a half dozen others. You know….. cars, boats, dogs, houses and families. And cars. In that order. Did I mention cars? Sorry. I forgot money. I already had a bit of money of course, but the books talked about big money. Who wants paltry six figure money when you can have seven? Not me. "Attract everything known to man and wanted by women into your life" the books said. And so out came my pen and I planned. Starting with timetables I figured things down to the month. There were spreadsheets and decision trees and critical paths and neat little bars of uncertainty that seemed sensible at the time.

For those of you unfamiliar with those little bars by the way, they're like grease paint. You smear them over your paperwork to hide the fact you don't have a clue what you're doing. Then there were goals. Between us guys, I didn't really have any of course…but I was good at making them up. Any casual bystander inspecting my plans would have been truly impressed. Heck…..even me the executive guy was impressed! Only mature Human Beings would have seen right through it all…but there weren't many of those in my vicinity at the time.

So false goals I had in spades. Alright, but what about those famous obstacles all go-getters-gotta overcome? Challenges and roadblocks and pitfalls it's good to notice before you run into them. No problem. I made them up too. Now that I think of it, in hindsight it was a lot like writing a novel. Everything made sense and it told a decent story. A big, bold fiction tale certainly, but a good story nonetheless. When it was all finished I tackled those invented aims, adopted wishes, bogus wants and fictitious desires head on. So what happened?

My Heart Isn't in It

It didn't take me long to notice something about all those wonderful plans. A little niggling bit of a thing actually. Like what? I didn't have an ounce of real passion for any of it. None of it turned me on, swept me off my feet or even vaguely held my attention. Save perhaps dreams of seven…nay…eight figures. Not buying it? Just try carrying out some big fancy plan you don't believe in. Sure you *can* do it… if you're just plain stubborn like me, but your soul's going to know your heart isn't in it. Believe me, it is simply impossible to fake that Bliss we opened the book with….to yourself anyhow. You may be able to fool lots of other people, but not that authentic person hiding somewhere in its shell.

Having been around now for close to a hundred years, I can also tell you there are a whole lot of people out there still pretending to build huge careers that mean everything to them. But don't. These folks won't dare admit it to you though….and not even to themselves. Why? They'd have to admit they were completely lost…..at forty, sixty or eighty years old. So I suggest you stop for a minute and listen to what I'm trying to tell you. Without dreams, I had no choice but to achieve other people's goals. And Yessiree for sure, I did. I got families, cars, big houses with acres and dogs. Well, actually, I never had a dog. But I did have some nice cats. Money too. And here's what I can tell you about it now, but you might want to sit down first. Probably you've read this gem of wisdom before, but I'm here to shout it in your face up close and personal.

All that stuff you can pick out of a book isn't even worth half a soiled damn if it's not your dream. It's a pitifully staggering waste of life actually, if you want me to say it like it is. So how about it? Would you like to pick crap off the shelf and wallow around in it until you die? Or would you rather have a real dream of your own to put heart and soul into forever? The dream sounds better? Good, so let's go get yours back. But now I have to tell you this. The very first step is a big hard one that can be just a wee bit daunting. A classic tough row to hoe in the Garden of Life you might say. If you're not willing to climb your way over this first obstacle on the way to everything you ever dreamed of….that's O.K. Just don't expect to get anything you ever dreamed of.

Now It's Time to Look at Yourself

Take a deep breath, because step one on the path to your dreams is tough. You've probably had some first step blues yourself like this before.

Putting stuff off because getting going is painful for example. Like starting jogging, losing weight, or turning over a new leaf. Yes? Okay, so step number one is tough like that, except worse, because it's real personal. Spooky personal actually, because it is going to ask you to put at least a little part of your soul right out on the table for everyone to see. Unfortunately, if you're like most people in most places, you could well be a world-class expert at not doing exactly that. So take a minute to compose yourself if you have to. All set? The first thing you have to do is admit you're lost. You have to start with yourself, graduate to friends, parents and spouses and...finally....tell it to the world. Still there? Thank goodness. The mere thought of such a thing would have scared me away toot sweet back in my wandering years. However spooky-scary it is though, there's no way around it. It's simply not possible to find your way if you don't admit you're lost first. The truth is, you've been infected with a disease that's taken your reason for being from you. And so, in case you didn't notice, you're sitting right now in a big nervous jar of pickles. If you can't admit you're ill, you won't take the cure. Who takes medicine for something they don't have? Sad folks on drugs maybe, but not you....I hope. So pluck up your courage right now and admit you're lost. Or stay lost.

Don't Think You're Lost?

You don't even have to tell me, because I already know what you're thinking. There is just no possible way you're lost, because you have a nice big job and ten kids. You've got a house and cottage and five 401(k)'s too. Nobody you know says you're lost either. Right? Sure, but here's something to think about. You have no idea why you're here....but you're not lost. You haven't got a real life-mission to put heart and soul into. But you're not lost. There's no supercharged passion for what you're doing flowing through your life....but that doesn't mean you're lost. Does it?

Well, why don't we try the quack test on you. First go find a mirror to look in. See that fellow or lady waddling and quacking like a lost duck? Can you guess what that means? Mr. and Mrs. duck is lost. No? Gee. I better say it like it is. So what is it? It's denial. Sorry, but you've become an expert at denying you're lost. A bit skeptical are you? Not to worry, it's not a hanging offence, but you really don't have a choice. If you want to find your life-mission again, you have to realize you're lost....and ADMIT IT. How the heck am I going to get you to do that against your wishes? How can I get you to stick your neck out when every fiber of your body doesn't want to? I'll give you a whole bunch of symptoms of being lost to look for in your life. Take a very hard long look at all of them....and know this. If you've got symptoms, you've got the disease.

No way around it, if you find more than a couple, you've lost your reason for being here. Scared to admit you've lost anything that big and important? I know, I would have turned tail and ran the other way myself a few decades ago. So to help you overcome your fright, I'll do it first. I'll admit how unbelievably lost I really was for a very long time, just to make you feel better. Then it's your turn to check out the signs of losing a calling below. Don't forget to remember though. If you don't admit you're lost…at least to yourself…there's maybe one chance in two billion you'll ever find your way. Probably less. But I promised you could see my bare lost bottom first so let's go.

I'll Admit How Lost I Was First

Before I regale you with embarrassing stories of how aimless I was for decades, I'd like to tell you this. If you're lost right now like I was, you can stare at the evidence for it in your life and see absolutely zero signs of the disaster. I did.

It's a truly bizarre thing really, much like looking in a mirror and not seeing yourself there. But true. Just so you know then, the next little story about refusing to grow is one of them and you might just find snippets of this sign in your own life. Here it is, a true-life story. Remember a few pages back where I refused to study to grow? Well, I made history that way, by writing a history exam. Don't get it? Think about it. How can you write history exams without studying? Keep in mind, back in those days, history was nothing but facts and figures. The whole idea was to memorize stuff and cough it back up again. Me? Never memorized a darn thing. Didn't pay attention during my lessons either, so by the time exams came along I didn't have a single drop of history between my ears. Was I worried about my complete ignorance as I sat down to write the test? Not at all. I had a great time writing this particular exam. How can that be?

Now It's Your Turn

Some fifty years later I still remember the fun I had …making it all up. Yes, that's right, I made up history. Like this. Say the question was…. "describe England in the 1800's". Now what? I wrote a novella. A dozen nice bogus tales about geography, politics, and the industrial revolution, all tarted up to sound pretty much like real history. But it was all utter fabricated fiction. Not just small fiction either. We're talking thirty pages of surreal history here that closely resembled swine swill. Kids destined to get decent grades handed in five pages of true facts and figures. Real concrete, truthful history. I can still remember that stunned look on the teacher's face, like she was watching a turtle taking to the air. "More paper please ma'am!" I kept asking again and again. That poor unsuspecting young lady must have expected a Nobel prize winning book….not industrial strength poop on a bun. But here's something for you. I passed. Just barely, but I got a passing mark.

How on earth is that possible? All I can say about it today is she must have subscribed to the "Big Bulls Can't Be Wrong" theory of the world. You know….tell a big enough lie and you're a hero? Wadda donkey eh? I'm blushing just from telling the story. But there you go, I went first and admitted I was rudderless. Now you. Look closely at what comes next, because each and every one is a sign of losing a calling. See one or two or twenty two in your life? You're lost. You had better admit it too, or you might never find your way. Like that ant you put on a plane to China last week who still can't find his way home either.

"Not until we are lost do we begin to understand ourselves". - Henry David Thoreau

Chapter Four
Don't Believe You've Lost Your Calling?
(Check Yourself For These Doubts)

Our doubts are traitors and make us lose the good we oft might win by fearing to attempt. - William Shakespeare

When Do Doubts About Direction Start?

I call the very first sign of losing a calling "growth of doubts about direction", because no one has doubts about which way to grow in the beginning. At conception for example, or birth. But somewhere along the line, seeds of doubt get planted in our lives, and they most often keep on growing. Eventually these doubts leave us with no idea why we're here. Remember those little vignettes I offered you about following a Plan from the moment egg met sperm? The first few little descriptions about doubtless direction coming up parallel those stories for obvious reasons. You won't be able to test yourself for doubts in those. But in a few moments you'll get to where you'll probably see doubts about direction showing up in your own life. If you begin to identify with this soul-destroying aimlessness, you've found the hallmark of losing a calling. But don't despair. When you get your calling back, you'll have absolutely zero doubts about which way to go. Not one. You'll have certain knowledge of who you are and what to do with your life. I can tell you with total confidence, because it happened to me. I can tell you this as well. It is an absolutely fabulous feeling to have true direction.

We're Certain Which Way to Go at Conception

You won't be able to check out the beginnings of your life for doubts. I don't think you'll remember many days between conception and birth. So just think about it.

Think you doubted which way to go when egg met sperm? Hardly. It was relentless, purposeful, growth all the way. No wandering, aimless hunting, and above all, no doubting. You didn't waste a minute mistakenly trying to become a flower or elephant. With absolute confidence you grew "your way", following Nature's plan for you from the start. O.K., so you started off with no doubts about direction. Then you were born. If you got a decent caring family, you kept growing your way, with zero doubts about which way to go.

All Babies Grow With Certainty Too

Right after you were born you had no doubts about which way to grow either, but my guess is you don't have too many baby memories to confirm it. I didn't. But you could go look at your own baby or babies of friends if you don't have any yourself. I can pretty much guarantee you won't see any doubts about direction there either. Chances are that little creature is still following Nature's plan with certainty, still listening to his or her inner voice. Growing like a weed to become a unique person. Like you likely were in your baby days. Same for the toddling years when you were learning to walk, talk, read and write, without hesitation.

Unsure and fuzzy about which way to grow in those years? Not at all. You were still making a bee-line for all you can be. You won't find any doubts about direction in those early years. But by ten or eleven, seeds of doubt were probably planted. That's when your inner voice probably began to get quiet, making you give up Nature's plan and doubt which way to go. Now we're getting to where you really can begin to test yourself for doubts about direction. Now you can use your memory, so peel back the layers and peek back.

Before Our Teens, Doubts Show Up

Ready to find seeds of doubt? Think back to when you were ten or so. A small feisty bull shot terrier like me maybe. By now you should be able to see doubts about direction in your life. Not sure what to look for? Here's a test. Pretend you're little and ask yourself "what do I want to be when I grow up?". Now stand back and watch. Do you look like a deer caught in the headlights with that wide-eyed stunned look? Did you answer ….. "duh…..I dunno"?. There you go. You just tested positive for doubts about direction. Seeds of doubt have grown so big already, you have no idea what to do with your life anymore. You're lost, even if you don't think so. While you're chewing on that, I'll tell you how well I did on this snappy little test. I was exactly ten years old when the bomb was dropped. I remember that because it was on my birthday. April to be exact and I'm at supper with mom, dad, and brother Brian, ready to wade into a three pound piece of birthday cake. I was just about to stuff the sucker down my throat whole when the atomic missile was launched. "So John", says dad, "what do you want to be when you grow up?".

Pause. No sounds. Brian's staring. Mom and dad watching. Me? I'm confused. Something about that question really hit home. Something told me I was supposed to know the answer, but I didn't. That made me nervous. I felt like I'd forgotten something I was supposed to know. Have you ever forgotten something you studied for an exam? I felt like that. But halleluiah brother!.... in a few seconds I was saved. I remembered an answer I'd heard other kids give. "Doctor, lawyer or engineer" I said, and everyone was happy. Except me, because I still had nagging doubts. How about you? Did you fail this little test miserably when you were a kid? You're in trouble already. You've stopped listening to your inner voice. No? Maybe you need to get a bit older before it hits you. So check out your teen years.

Doubts About Direction Keep Growing

When you're a teeny-bopper you can say you want to be anything. Astronaut, Pope, Princess or Penguin are all good. But soon someone is going to ask you to put your money where your mouth is. Soon you'll have to pick a career, so you can take the right school courses. You might even get a Big Book of Careers to choose from. The one with every good job in it. If you didn't have doubts about direction before, this might just do it. If you're like me, you'll see at least fifty careers that look nifty, along with "doctor, lawyer, and engineer" of course. Trouble is, how do you decide? Nothing leaps out and grabs you. But you have to make a choice, so you do. If you're lucky, you won't start worrying now. About what? Well, think about it. You have no idea whatsoever which way to take your life….but you're taking it somewhere anyway. Does that not sound a bit dangerous to you? Like driving down the freeway blindfolded perhaps? No? Well, I have to admit, it didn't bother me either, but it sure should have. Like you probably, I figured I had all kinds of time to figure out all that life-goal stuff. I was told I needed more knowledge to sort it out too, so I just put my nose to the grindstone and forgot.

Forgot what? The simple fact I had no idea where I was headed. Like everyone around me, I thought it was O.K. to let doubts about my direction in life fester a while longer. And I was right too. They can fester right to the end of life if you let them. So test yourself right now. Ever stare blankly at that big book of career options, with no idea which way to go? But you picked one out anyhow? Did it make the hair on your neck stand up because deep down you know you have big doubts about where you're headed? No? Well, O.K.. You still have some time before those doubts blow up in your face, like an exploding rotten egg. Seeds of doubt are like that. Like cancer actually. They can grow undetected until it's too late.

By Twenty We Should Be Building Our Dream Life

Doubts about direction often grow big enough to hurt bad by our mid-twenties. So look at that twenty-something carcass of yours right now. You're supposed to be building your dream life......but are you? Do you have a perfectly clear vision of what you want to do until you die? Are you driven to carry out this mission come hell or high water? Don't feed me bull twaddle either. Or yourself. If you're on a mission you'll be absolutely sure. If not, you'll have doubts. You won't honestly be able to say you know why you're here. Trouble is, these doubts can give you trouble, because without your own dream, you can't build your dream life. "Duh....gee....I guess so" you say? You guessed it. Sure you can wander aimlessly from one good job to the next like me. Yes you can pick someone else's goals and go get them. Like I did. But that's not building a dream life. That only leads to depression and anger, not the things dreams are made of. I know darn well because I've been there. For me it was like this.

By Twenty I Was Hiding From Doubts

By my mid twenties I had another one of those good jobs. Sure it was the wrong kind for me, but it was a good one anyhow. Paid great. Doing what? Well, my business card said "engineering consultant". Yes...you heard right....a guy without engineering bones advising people how to engineer. Looking back I'd say I was a bit like a doctor who doesn't know which end of the body the brains are in. A neurosurgeon perhaps, if you get the picture. Certainly I knew I was on the wrong track, but I couldn't find the right one, so my doubts started to turn bad on me. First I got depressed, then I turned to that big famous helpmate called booze and more booze.... for comfort. Just in case you don't know by the way, no such thing as comfort is found in alcohol. Instead you become deaf, dumb, blind and comatose.

A close second to comfort? Hardly. But me and all my equally lost buddies didn't know that, so we partied 'til the cows died. All night sometimes, pretending it was macho and thinking it was normal. But normal isn't staggering in at four A.M. and trying to get to work by eight. Is it normal to waste half your income on toilet fuel? Yes it is, if you're brain dead or wannabe. But the truth of it all is this. I was hiding. Scared and hiding from big doubts about what I was doing with my life. I wasn't just depressed and juiced either, I was angry. I was angry at people who had dreams to follow. Yes I heard about folks who couldn't wait to get up in the morning, but I sure as hell wasn't one of them. Those lucky S.O.B.'s had something I wanted. They knew who they were and what to do with their lives, but I didn't. They were getting their own brand of success that made them happy. I wasn't, and it made me want to strike out at the world. Thankfully I didn't go over the edge and take up grand theft, or go postal, like some poor souls do when they lose their reason for being here. Had the cards fallen slightly differently, I absolutely could have. Believe me, if you take a man's dream from him he can get angry enough to do anything. That's why so many guys and gals are so violent today. Their hearts know their dreams have been ripped from them.

How I Got on the Wagon

So how did yours truly the medicated space-cadet make out? Well, somewhere along the line my heart, lungs, liver and pancreas suggested all-out partying might just kill me. Soon. So I got on the wagon. No, not the booze wagon. The denial bandwagon. Not exactly sure what that is? It's pretending you're not absolutely lost, by picking a dream off the shelf and trying to make it come true. The big house, money, and cars thing. Between me and you though, I was so lost, I didn't even realize it was someone else's dream. It worked fairly well for me, like it does millions of others.

As long as I boozed as much as I could in the comfort of my own home too. Just on the weekends of course, like you're supposed to. Aren't you? No you're not, but quite a few million guys and gals do. Normal men and women who get up, go to work and come home every day. Everyday people who quietly blow their brains out with booze in the confines of their own homes way too often. Waiting, like me, for crisis. Crisis happens when nothing helps you deny you're lost any more. Not money made, or booze drank or big houses built. Real crisis is when you can't deny the obvious to yourself. Then you're faced with the fact you don't know who you are or what you're doing with your life. Sometimes that's called a "mid-life crisis". You can have it at fifteen, fifty or thirty plus fifty years of age.

That Famous Mid-Life Crisis

That real and true mid-life crisis we've all heard about isn't just being forced to admit you're lost. Being pushed past denial can be sad, scary, disconcerting and depressing. But "crisis" means something yet more terrifying. You get crisis when you begin to realize you could be lost forever. When it dawns on you that you might never have the true Joys life has to offer....because you could die before finding your way....crisis happens. It's a truly panicky feeling knowing you have no idea which way to turn to find what you're looking for in life. If you've ever actually gotten lost in the woods for instance, you might have felt a similar panicky feeling. I did once and later in life I recognized this terror, when I knew I had lost my way and didn't know how to find it. I still remember that forest misadventure very well in fact. I was out camping as a kid with my buddies and strayed off the beaten path into the woods a ways. I was only a hundred yards from the trail, but somehow I'd gotten turned around and lost track of which way I'd come.

For a minute or so I hunted around for the way to head back, and wasn't worried. But slowly I realized every direction I looked in yielded a dense sea of trees that all looked the same. I also knew I'd wandered into a gigantic patch of forest that stretched literally hundreds of miles north, west, and east. There was only one way back to the trail and I had no idea which it was. It's when you realize you have zero idea which way to go and nothing you are doing is helping…that panic sets in. A very big kind of terror sweeps up from your gut and overcomes you. Anyone who really has been lost in the woods will identify with this nauseating feeling I'm describing here. Lucky for me though, I eventually heard my friends calling and found my way out again. But it's the same sort of feeling you get with a bona fide mid-life crisis. You have no idea where to go to find the Path you must be on to get your share of Life. It is a sickeningly scary feeling. Then what? Some give up living and just exist, going through the motions, waiting for retirement and death. Others head back to the bottle and drown themselves there. A few go postal. Lots of good alternatives, all ending in disaster.

Your Doubts Can Lead to Disaster

Let me see here. If you're anything like I used to be and just about everyone I ever met, you'll have doubts about direction written all over you. You'll easily identify with all my little stories about these doubts. But big deal. Everyone does….don't they? Sure. Millions and millions. Every single man jack of them lost as sailors in the Sahara. Each pooh-poohing destiny, life Missions and callings with the best of 'em. All having taken a wrong turn somewhere, heading down a very well traveled road, where nobody's dreams are. A road with millions of folks on it who think it's normal to be lost like a dollar down deep in the ocean. And you? Are you beginning to suspect you might just be on this path yourself? No?

That's O.K., but don't stop reading yet, because there are many different signs of losing a calling you need to inspect yourself for coming up. You still have a good shot at getting past denial so you can stop, turn around, go back, and take that wall of fear down. So you can begin working towards your destiny once more. I know you can do it, because that's exactly what I did. Everything you'll need for your trip is in this book too. Still with me? O.K., so WAKE UP. Look real close at the next signs of losing a calling. Those doubts about direction you've just read about are only the biggest. If you find lots of other signs in your life you qualify for taking the cure I'm offering later. You don't have to take the cure of course. You can go to your grave never knowing who you are if you want. Just don't come back to haunt me after you're gone.

A Ray of Hope

"While there's life, there's hope". - Marcus Tullius Cicero

Now that I've depressed you down to your bones, how about a cheery little story before the tough work of admitting you're lost? About a ray of hope I had thirty years ago, when still lost as lambs on ice myself. Hope I might find myself somewhere. Listen closely and you'll find yourself there too. Back in the early seventies, I worked in a little gas production plant way the heck out in Northern Alberta, somewhere by the North West Territories border. At a place called "Rainbow Lake". Go ahead, try find it. It's half a pinprick some 400 miles north of Edmonton. Rainbow Lake means "nothing by nowhere" in Cree I think. Anyway, everyone commuted to Rainbow by plane and lived there 24 hours a day in a trailer camp. Like rats in a tin box you might say. After three weeks, you better get out or go nuts. I'd fly back to Calgary to half recover.

Can you picture the place? Fifty or sixty young guys working during the day and boozing all night. A real community of like-minded folks. Not. And what exactly is yours truly doing there? No one knows. Mom thought I had a sweet job, but between us guys, I was just aimlessly wasting my life. I wandered into it like a brain-dead donkey on rusty roller skates. My soul knew it too, and began to give me trouble. Soon I had a hard time sleeping…. without a nice big bottle of brain blasting booze that is. Anyhow, one sleepless night I had a panic attack that came when my soul softly whispered something to me. "I think maybe you are so lost you will never, ever, in a million years, find your way"…. it said with great confidence. To say the least, that struck big terror in my heart and bathed me in a scary, nervous, panicky feeling. So there I am in my little trailer room, surrounded by darkness, scared spitless, being battered by waves of nameless fears. Up they rise….trying to drown me, then back they fall to the great ocean of fear I lived in. Finally….after one huge wave… the ocean fell back so far it disappeared. Just for a moment the fear was nowhere to be seen. Then something strange happened.

My Strange Experience

What happened to me that day was so striking it stuck with me forever after. I didn't really know what to make of it at the time, but I knew it was something special. I'm now going to muster up my best attempt to describe it to you. Like I said above, I'd been lying there in a kind of nervous, panicky state, rather like you might have the night before some huge important exam. It was a combination of worry, fear, and trepidation when all of a sudden this ocean of angst fell away. It felt as if I had somehow gone deep "inside" myself to a place where there was no pain and suffering from worries. It was like the real and true "me myself" lived in a safe haven at the core of all this fear. I felt a stunning sense of peace I'd never known before.

A warm, protected, comforting feeling swept over me as I just relaxed more than I had thought it was possible to do. Then something hit me like a ton of bricks. I realized I had found that inner place gurus talk about. I also knew instantly and without any doubt that what I was searching for was there. Who I was and can be was there for sure. I'd tried to go to that inner place many times before....looking for myself...but failed miserably. So many times in fact, I had almost concluded that there was nobody to be found. But in that little trailer room that night I was privy to the Truth. The Truth was, the soul-whom-I-am is always there for me. That was the astonishing insight that gave me true undying hope. Sadly, that experience didn't last long. Soon the ocean of fear swept back in. And I didn't have a clue how to get back to that "inner place" of peace and real joy. But I knew with certainty that it was there to be found. I knew I would never give up trying to find myself, because I'd always be there.

A good thing too, because it took me twenty more years to understand why I and who-knows-how-many others can't find ourselves. It's because we can't go to that inner place. It's completely out of bounds. But it *can* come to us....if we learn how to make that happen. On that fateful day in Rainbow Lake, my fears went away and it came to me. That's what this book is all about. It will show you how to let that inner place...and your heart's desires....come back to you. That person you know you can be is there for you as well, waiting to come out. So go ahead. Take it. Take what? This ray of hope. It's yours. From me to you. But don't forget to pass it on to someone else after you get your own life-mission back. That's the deal. Promise? Thank you. Now we can go look at signs of losing a calling. Admitting you're lost won't be so bad now you got your hope back.

"Hope is the thing with feathers --/ That perches in the soul --/ And sings the tunes without the words --/ And never stops --at all --." Emily Dickinson

OUR WORLD

You live in the same world I do. In this world, history keeps telling us what's right today is wrong tomorrow. So keep an open mind. You might think it's impossible you've lost the calling you once had, but soon it'll be tomorrow. History tells us you could be wrong tomorrow.

Chapter Five
Still Not Sure You've Lost Your Way?
(Look For These Signs)

"Alice came to a fork in the road. 'Which road do I take?' she asked. 'Where do you want to go?', responded the Cheshire cat. 'I don't know.' Alice answered. 'Then,' said the cat, 'it doesn't matter".
- Lewis Carroll…Alice in Wonderland

Do You Live in a Cave?

Do you live in a cave at the top of a mountain? No? O.K., all the signs below should be familiar to you. They're on T.V., in the movies, and around the office water cooler. I used to think they were normal everyday things. Things that don't mean a darn thing. Just the way it is. But they're not. They're terrible signs that something's taking people's dreams away, from one continent to another. You won't find every sign in your life, but I can guarantee you'll find some. Finding a man or woman free of them today is about as easy as finding a dry fish in the ocean. Here's a tip for you as well. Pay attention to your feelings as you read, because when you hit one connected to your heart-strings, you'll know you've lost your way. Sure you can try denying it, but your soul won't let you. Maybe you'll read five or six signs before one grabs you where it hurts. But take heart…..I put these signs here to help you get you past denial, so you'll let me teach you how to see the world differently and get your very own life-mission back. Ready or not, here they are. Real stories about real lost people. Me and others.

Are You Mystified?

Fifteen years ago, my wife and I visited a marriage counselor to help us iron out our irreconcilable differences.

Like all sage counselors, he poked and prodded and pulled us out from under our rocks. When I crawled out, two big signs were strapped to my chest, and both told the world I'd lost my calling. The first one I call "mystification", because that's what my counselor called it. "You're mystified Mr." he said….as I stared back blankly. Mystified? About what? I thought he was nuts, but he knew mystification when he saw it. And what did he see? He saw I was mystified by the meaninglessness of my life. It was obvious as a dog on a dinner plate….if you knew what to look for. It didn't take him long to figure it out either, by prying feelings out of me. In those days that was quite a feat, because a crowbar was needed to get any out. But this man was relentless and forceful enough to squeeze out a few.

Here's one. I felt like a racehorse who stopped running five steps out of the gate. In everyday words, that means I knew I could really do something with my life….if I could just figure out what it was. But I couldn't, so I was stuck. I knew there was something wrong too… but I couldn't figure out what it was. See what I mean? I was mystified by the meaninglessness of my life. Ever feel like that yourself? You absolutely know you have potential to do bigger and better things….but you just can't seem to release it? Yes? There you go, that's one of the biggest and most famous signs of losing a calling.

Pretending is a Big Sign

Sign-on-my-chest number two was a foot high and bright red. It said… "JUST PRETENDING". Mr. counselor saw I was pretending to be something I wasn't, making me sweat like a pressed pig and pretend even harder. O.K., so what was I pretending? To be smart. I wanted people to think I was a very smart fellow. Why the heck would I want folks to think that?

Well....smart guys and gals are important people ....aren't they? So they say, and that's what I wanted to be. 'Portant people. The trouble was, I wasn't what you'd call smart, so I had to fake it. Looking back today I must admit, I was pretty good at it. As a matter of fact, you might even say I was a world-class expert at gobbledygook. What's gobbledygook? Most folks call it Bull Shuffle. Here's how it works. Using 100% of my one-third brain, I'd wow passersby with phony smarts like big words, bigger sentences, or complicated nonsense. Examples? Why not. I love embarrassing myself, so let's listen to me back in those days.

I Pretended Like This

Here's something only a real Bull Ship artist would say. "I have a penchant for the ambulatory art of culturing canid cardiopulmonary efficiency". Spastic centipedes on parade!.....what the heck's that? Thank you for asking. I'll translate. I like walking the dog. Duh.... ....O.K....so why didn't I say so? Because I was pretending to be smart of course. And what exactly did that do for me? Well, it fooled me into thinking I was smart, but pretty much everyone else saw right through it. They saw a weirdo guy tripping over his own tongue trying to impress any brain-dead people who might be watching. And you? Mumble Jumbo ain't your style? No problem. There's lots of ways you can pretend to be something you're not. You can spend money you can't afford on a fancy car for example. Pretending to be rich. You can build a big career you have no passion for. Pretending to be something mom and dad want you to be. You can abuse people that work for you, pretending to be powerful. You have lots of choices, but here's something to think about. If all this talk about pretending makes you a wee bit nervous.....like maybe I'm talking about you...... you've lost your calling. Sorry to be the one to tell you.

Every Lost Soul is Hiding

"Everybody wants to be somebody; nobody wants to grow."
- Johann Von Goethe

Here's an iron-clad rule that everyone who loses their calling follows. Everyone without a calling is hiding. No question about it, you can take it to the bank. It's easy to see why too, if you think about what a calling is. A calling is just being yourself. It's coming out of your shell, to grow your very own way. People with callings are busy showing the world who they are, because they're proud to be themselves. Alright, but guess what happens if you are terrified of being yourself? Not much. You refuse to come out of that seed-shell of yours. In other words, you're hiding. There are all kinds of different ways to hide as well. Here's a few I'm sure you know about. Shy about raising your hand in class? You're hiding. Scared to ask the girls to dance? Hiding again. Afraid to take reasonable risks in life? Hmmmm ...…more hiding. Any time you don't feel free to be yourself you're hiding. Unfortunately, folks hiding themselves from the world have lost the Life-Mission they came with. I can say that with great confidence as well, because people with real Missions are doing exactly the opposite. They're coming out of shells and closets like crazy to be themselves.

There's more ways to hide than rats on a high-floating ship too, but I won't bore you with more. Well, just one maybe, because I have a real-life story about this one. A story about how fear of failure keeps people in hiding. I'm going to call on my old pal John to tell us this fear of failure story. John's in heaven now. He died of cancer a few years ago, but I have a direct line to him. He says "go ahead botcha, tell 'em MY story". I never learned what "botcha" meant in Italian by the way, or how to spell it. But it meant buddy to me and always will. Anyway, here's John's story.

John's Story

John came to Canada from Italy when he was about thirteen. Unfortunately perhaps, John was put in grade three or four because he didn't speak English. A big strapping teenager towering over little kiddies he was, but it didn't slow him down. It couldn't, because John was one of the smartest people I ever met. Smart enough that he skyrocketed right to the top of his class in high-school in a couple of years. Four years later he was in college with me. You'd think a man with that kind of brain power wouldn't fear failing. Wrong. John feared failing almost as much as I did. He'd worry himself sick over exams for example, even though he aced every darn one. But fear of failing's got nothing to do with marks. It's thinking your soul's worth less than someone else's, even if you're best in class. So John felt like a failure, even when he got 100%. One day in school John showed me exactly what that means. We'd just done a test and Mr. professor called the class's attention. Anyone a mark or two shy of passing could bring their exam up and he'd try and squeak them by. O.K., but next thing I know, John is lining up. Wait a sec here. He'd already scored 98%? Yes, that's right….ninety-eight percent. What the ding dong heck's he doing?

He Thinks He's Failed?

He wants two more points to get a perfect score?! Exactly. Sure enough, the professor thought he was crazy and sent him packing. Me? I felt like breaking his legs, because I'd just aced the thing myself….with my normal barely scraping by marks. But here comes back John, completely dejected. He looks and feels like the poor guys who actually failed.

Holy dazed dingbats! Me I mean. I could hardly believe it at the time, but now I know better. Now I know even the biggest successes can judge themselves failures. Sounds insane? Yes it does, but it's true, so John wasn't alone... and I wasn't far behind him. And what about you? Have you ever been paralyzed by fears of failing? Did you ever freeze up completely on an exam after making sure you knew everything the night before? Were several species of undiscovered butterfly found in your stomach at the mere thought of being tested for something? Have you ever been afraid to be yourself? Just a tad? It's a sign you've left your calling behind. But don't worry, you can go get it again.

"Commit yourself to a dream. . . . Nobody who tries to do something great but fails is a total failure. Why? Because he can always rest assured that he succeeded in life's most important battle -- he defeated his fear of trying". - Robert Schuller

Too Many Formulas For Success

Have you ever tried one self-help book after another, looking for your own brand of success? Riches maybe? Or peace of mind and a sense of freedom…..but you got nowhere fast? I have news for you. What you're looking for isn't on the shelf. Sure those books can help you get what you want out of life, but you have to know what you want out of life first. The books are nothing but tools. Not sure what I mean? Well, just remember what a calling is. It's growing yourself into all you can be. It's making yourself and your dream life. O.K., so now imagine making something. Say a doghouse. The first thing you'll need is tools, so which ones will you pick from the shelf? How about some teensy little dental tools and a few things blacksmiths use to shoe horses? Hardly. You'll want doghouse making tools. Makes sense? Of course, but what if you didn't have a clue what you were making? It could be a doghouse, or a computer chip, or even a milk-bottle.

You just don't know. Alright so what kind of tools are you going to pick now? You have no idea. A million to pick from won't help either because….surprise, surprise….. you don't have a clue what you're making. Same holds true of your life. If you've left your calling behind, you won't know *who* you're making, so there's no way you can pick a self-help book or guru to help. Sure you can gamble. You can flip a few coins or try out your Ouija board. They'll help you get nowhere even faster. "Gee….I never thought of it that way" you say? Me neither for at least forty years.

I Tried Them all Myself

I have to admit, I'm one of those people who actually bounced from shelf to shelf for decades looking for a helpful self-help book. I still have them all on my bookshelves today. New Age, Old Age, you name it and I half-heartedly tried it with no real success. Like what? At one point I actually believed success came to those who dressed for it. So of course I bought books that told me what to wear. And? I looked good, but it didn't bring me the authentic success I was desperate for. I tried copying successful people as well, like some books say will do the trick. To people who don't know what they're looking at, it probably made me look successful. But that kind of superficial success doesn't go deeper than the skin, and without a successful heart I was still lost.

Eventually, out of pure desperation, I tried that popular affirmation thing. Not understanding what true affirmations are about, all I could do was repeat wishes out loud. Like "I'm rich I'm rich I'm rich I'm rich" for instance. Folks within earshot might have thought I was successful, but I was still lost. Sadly, I stayed lost until I discovered how to fix the broken switch and discovered who I really am. Then I got the surprise of my life. Suddenly all those books that didn't work before did.

I mean.....all of them had neat tips and pointers I could use to grow myself *my way* better and faster. But don't forget. Before I knew who I was making, not one of them did a darn thing for me. Still there? O.K., so now you know why you can try one formula for success after another without success. It's because you've lost your calling and don't have a clue what dream life to create. In fact, you wouldn't know your own brand of success if you fell over it. Sorry. Mean but true.

Busy Bees

Everyone knows successful folks are always busy. Those lucky guys and gals are always busy making the most of every moment. But here's a surprise for you. People who lose their callings are often even busier. Why? Aimless people also want to look successful, so they frantically pretend to have direction and purpose, by keeping busy. It all looks great from a distance too, but deep down all those zooming guys and gals know something we don't. It's nothing but denial. They're just busy denying they're lost. So check your life over right now. Are you busy, busy, BUSY? Yes, yes, YES? Good for you, but ask yourself this. Can you honestly say you know why you're here? No? Guess what? You've lost your calling, and it doesn't matter how busy you are. You're just hiding behind a sad kind of busyness.

"I write of melancholy, by being busy to avoid melancholy". -- *Robert Burton, 'The Anatomy of Melancholy'*

A Busy Bee Story

Back when I lived in the big city of Toronto, I actually knew a real busy Bee myself. Gerald K. Gerald was a bona fide stock broker focused on the whole truth and nothing but the truth twenty five hours a day.

Bucks, dollars, cash, and coin that is. O.K., so let's picture Gerry for a moment. He has a cell phone plugged into one ear and a Personal Electronic Organizing Assistant physically attached to him all the time. I mean *all* the time. I once saw him talking on the phone and checking out his schedule while peeing in the men's room for example. Oh yes. Gerry had a pager of course. No real busy person is ever without a pager. He had a stupid little calculating watch that would ding dong every few minutes to remind him of something as well. That silly thing drove me nuts. No question about it, Gerry had machines telling him what to do ten times an hour. Matter of fact, his schedule was so packed I'm not sure if he slept. Have you ever met someone like this? A world-class, state-of-the-art, pushing-the-envelope busy bee? That was Gerry. To the uninformed, Gerry must have looked like he was driven to achieve some aim in life his soul couldn't do without. Making the most of every moment, and then some.

But no. That wasn't it at all. Gerry was a pretend-bee. Here's how I knew that for sure. There was no light. Lost you there did I? Let me explain. One day I asked Gerry what he was getting out of all this spastic, busy being. "Money" said he, staring at me with eyes dull as ditch water. Eyes with no light in them. It was those eyes that told me he was just busy buzzing. Playing make-believe. Why do the eyes say it all? Simple. Folks who aren't lost will light up like volcanoes if you ask them what they're doing with their lives. You'll get hit with a payload of passion. They'll breathe fire all over the place and shower you with sparks of Joy. Not Gerald. All he could do was mechanically tell you how much money he made last week. A busy Bee if there ever was one.

Chapter Six
Does This Look Like You?
(Your Dreams Are Gone)

Wake Up and See The Daisies

Have you ever heard that "wake up and smell the roses" story? Pretty much everyone has, but here's one about daisies I'm sure you've never heard before, because I just made it up. Imagine a one way road at the end of which is a big treasure. How can you know treasure's down there if the road is one way? That's a very interesting question. No one has ever come back to confirm it, but you're certain treasure is down there anyway. Needless to say, this is a very curious road indeed. It's a beautiful road as well because billions of bright daisies grow on either side, and you'd notice them, if you weren't running as fast as you can to get treasure. Now let's fast forward fifty years. Here comes the end of the road and, lo and behold there's a huge door with a sign on it ahead. With huge excitement you read the sign. It says… "BIG TREASURE ON THE OTHER SIDE". Leaping to yank it open, you're stunned into silence when you see the treasure for yourself. It's a single daisy. As the poet William Blake would say, you just discovered heaven in a wild flower. But you discovered something else as well. You missed heaven every day of your life along that long and winding road. Don't think this applies to you? If you've lost your calling it does, because you're missing the heavenly life you were put here to get.

Do You Feel Incomplete?

Belinda's Song

Once upon a time long ago, Adam and Eve shared One soul. Failing to understand this simple truth however, they behaved badly towards each other and the world, and the God of Wrath tore their single soul apart. Forever after, each Adam and every Eve has desperately sought to unite their souls with he or she who holds the other half.

Here's a sign of losing a calling I'll bet you'll never guess. It's that sad feeling of being "incomplete" most of us have sometime or the other, like someone's missing from our lives. A soul-mate we can't find maybe. Have you ever felt like that? Yes? Well, here's the surprise. It's not someone else you're missing, it's you. The real and profound truth is, you and your soul-mate are really different parts of each other, like two different petals on one flower. That means something very simple but sad. If you don't know who *you* are, you won't recognize your soul mate, even if you fell over him or her tomorrow morning at seven A.M. You have to "know thyself" to be able to pick your soul mate out of a crowd.
And in case you forgot, that's exactly the pickle you'll be in if you've lost your calling. You won't know who you are and will have zero chance of finding your soul mate. Just in case I've frightened you half-way to Venus with this thought, here's another idea that can calm you back down again. But be prepared, because it is a truly magical and awe-inspiring concept.

Right now, as you read this, wherever you are, your soul mate is waiting for you. Where? Somewhere along the Golden Braid of Destiny. What on earth does that mean? Learn how to grow yourself *your* way, and you'll begin to manifest your destiny. You'll slowly but surely grow.... to where your soul mate is.

I call that "climbing the Golden Braid of Destiny" and it's rather like Rapunzel's suitor climbing her golden hair to claim his mate. Don't believe it? Don't pass judgment until you've given the Rule of Life a try. For now though, you can read about an old friend of mine who didn't have this Joyous Rule to work with. A fellow who married his soul mate. Or so he thought.

Tony and His Soul Mate

By the eighties I'd drifted into another swell job, this time in Toronto Canada. Doing what? You got me, but my business cards still said "engineering consultant". The same guy with no engineering bones? Scary maybe….but true. Anyhow, I was still single in those days, and hung around with all the other out-to-lunch guys. Tony was one of them. Tony and I got along fabulously, because we were both completely lost. Birds of a feather flocking together you might say. So what do two stunted sailors do in their spare time? Mostly we got drunk. It's an occupational hazard for folks who lose their callings, so I got to know Tony pretty well through the beer glasses. He was a movie-star handsome guy who'd attract babes from five hundred yards. I am not kidding either. They would come out of the woodwork from nowhere at Tony. Going fishing maybe? Holy moley Miranda, where did all the ladies come from? Skydiving perhaps? Gee….I never knew so many gals jumped out of planes. Anyway, when Tony wasn't fighting off women, he was mouthing his famous one-liners. "I feel incomplete" he'd say….five times before lunch. "I just have to find my soul mate" Tony would say ten times a day. It's fair to say Tony was obsessed with the fact something was missing from his life.

They Don't Know Who They Are

But Tony had a bit of a problem to contend with. He had no clue who he was, which was making it impossible for true love to show up. Anyone could tell Tony didn't know who he was too, because he was always wondering out loud what to do with his life. Then Caroline arrived. Caroline was a cross between Marilyn Monroe and her twin sister. A bona fide brunette bombshell ranking twelve out of ten on the gorgeous scale. And guess what? Sure enough. Like some kind of heat seeking missile, she made a bee-line for Tony, running over the rest of us with hob-nailed boots to get there. And Tony? "She's my soul mate" he said fifty times in the first hour. But I had my doubts. Lost as I was, I knew something was wrong because Mr. in-over-his-head-and-heels kept asking me… "do you think I should marry her?". "You don't know?" I said… stunned by the confession. "Hmmmmm" I thought to myself, "if you gotta ask, you gotta problem!". No question, Tony was so darn lost he would have married a serial killing, baby stomping, arsonist….if it came in a pretty enough package. Caroline was none of that of course, but she was about to cause Tony some grief anyway.

How? Ten weeks in, Tony proposed to Miss Femme Fatale, and sure enough, she accepted. Where's the grief you ask? Don't worry, it's coming, because Tony kept asking…."do you think I'm doing the right thing?". I should have said, "you got the wrong soul mate mate", but I didn't. I know I was a weenie, but I couldn't bring myself to trash Tony. I didn't have to though. A few months after the Big Day…they split up. Grief city you could say. And the moral of the story? If you don't know who you are before taking the plunge, you will receive your share of grief. Guaranteed.

Waiting to be Found

"How much of human life is lost in waiting". - Ralph Waldo Emerson

Here's a sign of losing a calling I have personally seen dozens of times. I call it "waiting to be found".... because that's what it is. It's waiting for someone to come along and take charge of your life because you have no idea what to do with it yourself. It's hoping someone will show you what to do with that potential you know you have, but just don't know how to release. What does that look like in real life? Like a guy who graduated from college with me. I've changed his name to protect the innocent. Bill started his career as an Ontario scholar with marks out of highschool in the stratosphere. If anything, Bill's grades got better in engineering school. He was so much higher above me on the academic totem pole, I could barely see him up there. Professors, Deans, and students alike patted Bill on the back for his brains all throughout his college days. Then Bill graduated at the top of his class and was instantly offered a dozen jobs by recruiters on campus looking for the best of the best. Needless to say, Bill chose the highest paying one and settled in for his big rush to success.

But for all Bill's smarts, there was something he didn't comprehend about real life in the real world. Bill believed getting a 100% score on every project he was given would automatically create the kind of career dreams are made of. He thought people would recognize his potential and promote him. Sadly for way too many people, this is as untrue today as it ever was. For one thing, most bosses can't see potential at all, and wouldn't know what to do with it if they did. They want "track record" not potential. When a job opening comes up, it's usually filled with someone who's done the same job before. Can you guess what that means? People with potential can sit in the same job forever. Like Bill.

My Old Colleague Bill

Believe it or not, Bill is still more or less in the same job thirty odd years later. Now he's a "senior" engineer, with more junior people reporting to him. He makes a pretty good professional living as well, but Bill is very disappointed with his career. Down where his heart lives he knows he probably could have run America if he'd kept growing himself *his* way. But he didn't, he just kept waiting for someone to push him up the ladder. Waiting for someone to show him which way to go. Trouble is, that never works. In the real world you have to know which way to go yourself. If you do, you'll use your very own talents to try and fail and take risks. You'll make your way by trial and error to where destiny is. If you don't, you won't. And you? Waiting to be found? Hoping someone's going to show you how to tap into your potential? How much time did you say you have? Just one lifetime? Sorry, that isn't enough.

Nothing is Possible

"If I were to wish for anything, I should not wish for wealth and power, but for the passionate sense of the potential, for the eye which, ever young and ardent, sees the possible. Pleasure disappoints, possibility never. And what wine is so sparkling, what so fragrant, what so intoxicating, as possibility!" - Søren Kierkegaard - Either/Or, "Diapsalmata"

When I was a kid, my parents often repeated ancient words of wisdom to my brother and I. Wisdoms learned from *their* parents. One such phrase was...."*who do you think you are?*". This advice was offered when we would aspire to things that made us look "too big for our britches". Writing books, starting businesses, leading countries or other day-dreams for example. Brian and I listened closely and learned the lessons.

Soon we didn't need parents, teachers or other folks to help us disbelieve in possibilities. Eventually we were able to say to ourselves….*"who am I* to do amazing things?". By the time we'd left school, we could look around us in the world and see all kinds of neat things people were doing with their lives. And sure enough, we'd say to ourselves…..*"who am I* to have such adventures and create such dreams and believe in miracles?" By the time we reached our thirties, we knew for sure that anything is possible….for everyone but us. "*Who am I* to have true love and real authentic success and skyrocket dreams?" we would say again and again. We weren't alone either, because millions of folks take this wisdom to heart and stand on the sidelines of life, watching truly successful people from afar. Repeating endlessly…"*who am I* to be like them?. Does this sound vaguely like you I'm describing here? Don't worry. It means you've lost your calling….but you can get it and your life back.

Where Do You Belong?

"The greatest thing in the world is to know how to belong to oneself". -- Montaigne, 'Essays', ``To the Reader"

When I was young, I felt like I didn't belong anywhere. Not in school. Not in workplaces. Not even in my own family. My old best buddy John G. felt like that too, and had an interesting way of describing what it was like. He said he felt like he was "on top of the world", but he didn't mean he was having a great time at all. He meant he felt like he was not a part of the world….like he was suspended above it perhaps, not really participating. John and I felt like this because we'd both lost our way. We'd lost the Life-Mission or calling we came here with. So why does losing our reason for being make us feel like that? It's simple really, but you'll have to read more of the story coming up to fully appreciate what I mean.

For now though, think about this. You and I feel like we belong when we believe we're really a part of something. If you play sports for example and really participate in the game you'll probably feel like you belong on the team….because you're *part* of it. If your family shares things from the heart and has all kinds of fun together, you'll be part of a close-knit group and feel like you *belong* there. Alright, but now imagine your most basic beliefs make you think you and the world are very separate things. As you'll see later, it will make you lose your calling and you won't know what to do with your life. But those mistaken beliefs will also make you feel like you don't belong, because it won't look like you're a part of anything. When all is said and done then, if you don't feel like you belong, it's because you're looking at the world the wrong way. A way that's taking your reason for being from you and making you feel lonely. So check yourself over now. Do you feel like there just isn't a place for you in the world…but you'd sure like to find one? Would you like to have the most potent feelings of belonging possible? The Rule of Life can get those things for you.

Hoping for Luck

"Luck never made a man wise". -- *Seneca, 'Letters to Lucilius'*

Here's a sign of losing a calling you'll find at every corner store on Lottery day. Folks hoping for luck to show them what to do with their life. All they need is dollars…don't they? No they don't. If those winners didn't know what to do with their lives before the Big Win, they're not going to know after either. I know, I know. You'd rather be a rich aimless soul than a poor one. Me too, but you're missing the point. I'm not offering you an iron-clad bank account the size of Mississippi. Just a real shot at happiness. You choose. But first ask yourself this. Are you expecting to get happy by winning lotteries?

Yes? Here's your chance of success. Same chance a blind jeweler would have trying to take a tiny watch apart with mittens on and both hands tied behind his back. You'll need impossible luck to succeed. But here's something to think about. You can make your own luck. You heard me. I said....make it. How? I'm going to give you a rule to follow to make luck with. Yes I mean exactly what I said. Same Rule of Life I mentioned above. Successful people have been making luck with this Rule forever. Stay tuned, it's coming up.

A Lucky Little Story

One Saturday morning not long ago, I stopped in at the corner store to get some breakfast muffins, when a baby faced fellow and his infant looking wife pull in beside me. They were driving an amazing orange car with blue spots. No, I'm not kidding. It was a Ford so absolutely swarmed by rust the blue was in a small minority. It was so full of holes you could've strained spaghetti with it. It made me think those folks weren't real rich. But something else told me they probably weren't flush with cash as well. There were two little kiddies in the back, each wearing clothes so dingy you could barely see the moth holes. Rich kids? I don't think so. Anyhow, the exotic car man and I head into the store and soon we're standing there side-by-each. Me for my two muffins. Him for two hundred and fifty dollars worth of lottery tickets. In case you missed that, I said TWO HUNDRED AND FIFTY BUCKS! Dwinkle sputter donk went my poor little brain. I'd never seen *anybody* fork out that much cash for lottery tickets before. I've never seen anything like it since either. I had to take my left hand and push my lower jaw back up from where it fell. Then it dawned on me. These folks were *really* hoping for luck. Matter of fact, they thought upping the ante would make big luck. Enough luck to grab at least half the fourteen million dollar jackpot to get all the happy stuff you could see in his eyes he wanted.

You could tell by looking he was unhappy having less things than others. I couldn't help but feel sad watching this guy come and go with his stash of lottery tickets. It was like watching some poor soul trying to climb out of quicksand by struggling harder. He was sinking before my eyes, but there was nothing I could do. He didn't know how to make real luck. The kind that makes you rich, even if you haven't got two cents to rub together. Maybe some day he'll read about the Rule of Life and see how. Like you. I hope.

Chapter Seven
I Hope You Aren't This Lost
(Bad Signs You Have No Dreams)

Lost Forever

One of my aunts died lost many years ago. I have to admit, I didn't know her at all, but I have no doubt she died lost, because she spent half her life trying to one-up everyone. There's no better sign of being lost, and her death scared me. It told me something about life I didn't want to know. If you get lost you can stay there until the day you die, never knowing who you are.

Striking Out

When you get your calling back, you'll discover a truth that is truly beyond amazing. In fact, words simply cannot do justice to how stunning this truth is, but it can be described. As your fears of being judged go away, you'll realize with shocking clarity that your life is as important as any life anywhere, any time. You'll also recognize that it has always been so, even when you couldn't see it. Whether you can believe it right now or not, you'll know with perfect confidence that your own personal worth is equal to that of the most talented, accomplished, revered man or woman. In reality you're the equal of anyone, anywhere, over all time.

Just to make sure you understand what I'm getting at here, let's pick a few real-life practical examples of "important people" to apply the idea to. How about the President of America, Mother Teresa, Albert Einstein and Moses. No doubt these people are worshiped for their deeds and accomplishments and positions held. If I gave you ten minutes, you could probably make up a list a thousand long of equally "important folks". Alright, so what I'm saying is this.

You actually, really, and truly rank up there with any of them. Your very own life absolutely must be equally important. As you'll see later, there's no way around it. It can't be otherwise, because a fundamental Law of Nature guarantees it, much like gravity guarantees things must fall to the surface of the earth. When all is said and done, the world is put together in such a way that nobody can possibly be worth more or less than anybody else. So how come hardly anybody can see this fact of Nature? We've all been taught fundamentally mistaken ideas about how the world works. Ideas that are embedded in our souls like barbed spears and held sacred. Ideas that have convinced human beings for a long time that their lives can be and are worthless.

That's where the striking out often begins. When everything around you suggests your life is worth very little, it's flying in the face of what your soul knows down deep. It's a bit like being imprisoned for a crime you didn't commit, and it makes most people very angry. Angry enough to start striking out at the world. Don't believe it? You're surrounded by folks doing exactly that every day of the week. Just look around and you'll see crimes committed by people angry at the world because they've lost their reason for being. No doubt about it. When souls get trapped inside by fear....they're desperate to be set Free. Desperate enough to turn mean and ugly. Lying, cheating and stealing, they strike out at everything around them. Some get violent enough to turn to murder.

Sounds far-fetched? Don't kid yourself. Hold any soul down too long and he or she will bite. I think I might have been close myself, after a few decades of going without a real Life Mission. Lucky for me I didn't go bananas, but I could have. Mostly I had big bad jealous thoughts about all those successful folks out there, who had what I wanted....but didn't know how to get. Sound familiar? Yes?

So look at yourself right now. See a wee bit of jealous, angry person there? One that's not striking out yet, but might some day? Don't worry, you've just lost your calling, that's all. But you can get it back.... before you really do strike out. Now for some entertainment. I'm going to tell you a real life striking-out story from the late 1950's. Woody's story.

Woody Strikes Out

Everyone's got a bully story. But Woody was special. Woody was a few years older than me, when he drifted into our neighborhood. His dad was nowhere to be found and his mom worked, so Woody was pretty much on his own. The first time I ran into Woody, he up and kicked me in the butt.... for nothing. Just a swift boot to the aspidistras for hello. A Woody-style introduction I guess you'd say. Surprised? You bettcha. Next time I saw him he was at our school, on the front steps... scaring the pants off kids dumb enough to get close. How? By biting the heads off live grasshoppers. No......I am not making it up. I was dumb enough to go see for myself.

One day I was even dumber. Woody came over to where my friends and I were playing marbles. There I was, down on my knees knocking 'em around with the other guys, when Woody treated us to another sick trick. He chewed a few warts on his fingers until they bled like little stuck pigs. Then he bloodied up his face like a crazed vampire while grinning insanely. Guess who jumped up and squealed..... "that's gross!". You got it. Yours truly. That really made Woody's day too, because my buddies disappeared over the horizon as he beat the poop right out of me. Like my dad used to say... he had nothing better to do with his life. Now I know why. He lost his calling. By the age of twelve, this poor soul had already started striking out at the world. Sadly, he kept at it until he got to the "Big House".

Kingston Penitentiary. Fifty years later, I still get the heebee jeebees thinking about Woody.

Knowing it All

"To know yet to think that one does not know is best; Not to know yet to think that one knows will lead to difficulty" Lao-Tzu (6th century B.C.). Tao-te-ching

Have you ever met a know-it-all? Someone who won't let you get a word in edgewise, because there's no need for you to say anything? They already know better every which way. It's hard to live very long on planet earth without running into one of these folks eventually. So what's with these people anyhow? Do they really know it all? Oddly enough, some almost do. There are amazingly knowledgeable people amongst the know-it-alls. But there are also completely ignorant folks who "know everything". That's because knowing-it-all has nothing at all to do with knowledge. It has to do with low self-esteem. Know-it-alls are simply sad men and women who try to one-up everyone around them with facts or figures, to make themselves feel important because they've lost their callings and can't see the truth. The Truth is, if they simply learned how to be themselves they'd have as much importance as they could handle. Being a know-it-all makes it really tough to learn the Art of Being Human too, for obvious reasons. In short, it's because you can't tell a know-it-all anything. Here's a little story to illustrate the kind of pickle know-it-alls are in. Imagine a know-everything man imprisoned in a room where all the doors are locked. The windows have bars too and the skylights are closed. Sort of like Alcatraz perhaps, except for one little thing.

A Know-it-all Story

Here's the little thing. In the middle of one wall is an unlocked door perfectly disguised as a painting of a door. Can you guess what that means? The know-it-all's in trouble. He's not getting out, even with an unlocked door sitting there. Why? Think about it. Is he going to try opening a painting of a door? No he isn't. He knows paintings can't be opened. He's a know-it-all…..remember? O.K., but maybe we can help him. Let's go tell him there's a door there. Now he's out in a flash, isn't he? Nope. You can't tell a know-it-all anything either. Like a blind fly caught in a box with no roof, walls, or floor, this fellow is in big trouble. He's got Freedom in front of his eyes, but he's not going there.

And what exactly does that have to do with you? Let's review. You know for sure you didn't come into this world with a Mission. You're completely certain you're not lost. The idea your life is as important as Einstein or Moses is ridiculous. Right? Hmmmmm. See a know-it-all pattern there? No? Let me put it to you this way then. Would you like to be driven until you die to make your own dreams come true? Would you like to know that Bliss Professor Campbell speaks so glowingly of? "Yes please" you say? Alright, so maybe ….. …..just maybe….there might be something in this book you don't know. Something you need to know to get your calling back. "Can't be" you say? Fine by me, but don't say I didn't warn you.

An Ocean of Naysaying

Naysaying is the most common sign of losing a calling there is. It's the billions of ways we try to put other people down to make ourselves feel important because we've lost the true self-esteem we came with.

It's the endless ways we try to elevate ourselves for the same purpose. There are so many ways we do this, we don't even notice them anymore. Making more money, having more things, achieving bigger goals are all geared to propping up our low self-worth. Movies, televisions, and billboards all reinforce the idea we have to be bigger or better one way or the other to have value. But it's all naysaying. Every bit of it is a blatant or disguised way of trying to get personal value by pretending to be better than the next guy or gal. And here's a scary idea for you. It is all absolutely and completely unnecessary. In today's world, everyone believes bigger money, jobs, or smarts give us value and importance. But everyone is wrong. Not about biggest and best. They really are great things. But they have nothing to do with the importance of our lives. I am now going to tell you a little story that contains the essence of why. You won't really get it yet, but it should give you something to think about.

A Rabbit in Wonderland

Imagine you have a pet rabbit. Big ears, furry as heck, and cute as a button. Can you picture him flopping all over your couch? O.K. Now ask yourself this. Is the life of his foot more important than the life of his tail? Stop and think about it now. That sounds like one of those nonsense questions doesn't it? I mean there's only one life there, so the life of his tail can't be more important than the life of his foot. It makes no sense. Anyone who thinks the life of the bunny's foot is more important than the life of his tail is sadly mistaken at best. Right? No kidding. Alright, but the same holds for all the people and creatures you see around you. In reality, there is only one life in the Universe that all things great and small share. There simply aren't many different living things, each with its own separate life. Now I want you to think about it for a moment. You don't have to believe it yet.

Just think about it. Imagine it really was true. Imagine that you and I and everyone else are all part of one life. Now ask this. Is your life less important than mine? Is the life of some big-wig somewhere more important than yours? Those are nonsense questions too, because there's only One Life we all share. It is total horse pucks to think your life is worth less than any other life. Yes? Yes. So would you be naysaying if the world was like this? Would you try to get more money to pretend to be worth more than other people? No you wouldn't. O.K., enough said about this for the moment. Later I will explain to you how and why the world really is like this. Even better, I will give you a bunch of tools to help you train your brain to see it clearly. Why? Seeing it will give you your calling back. Yes it will, and I will show you exactly why later. For now here's a little story for you. It illustrates how hard it is to give up naysaying.

I'm Guilty of Naysaying

You and I have been taught to naysay all our lives, from the cradle, though school, and into adulthood, so it's tough to shake. Take me for example. I began to see what my Life-Mission was about ten years ago now, and my naysaying has diminished ever since. But now and then I catch myself doing it…out of habit. Here's what I mean. Yesterday was a really nice long weekend, so my wife and I went out to do some shopping for shingles and have lunch. Our roof finally needed replacing so off to the shingle store we went to check out colors. But shingles weren't at the top of my mind. "Why don't we swing by the fancy car dealer and see what they've got" I said. "Sure, sure" said my wife, used to the dumb car thing after a few decades. Did we need to? No. We already had fancy cars. So what on earth was I thinking? I guess way down in my brain I was still thinking bigger fancier car means more important person. Otherwise called naysaying.

But here's the good news. At least I know it when I see it these days. Even when it's in myself. Don't get me wrong though, there's nothing wrong with having stuff. Cars, boats, clothes....even money. But everything's wrong with thinking all this stuff makes you more important than other folks, because it'll keep you from carrying out your life-mission.

A Shocking Truth

Now we're done with signs of losing a calling. There's lots more I could have mentioned, but you've had enough already. Haven't you? Thought so, but I made naysaying the last sign along with that bunny story, to introduce you to an idea. An idea you won't swallow easily or quickly, but with time, effort, and the Rule of Life to help you, you can. I did. O.K, so try this on for size. Naysaying is calling people names to make yourself feel more important of course, but it's actually a really bizarre thing to do. Why? Because the person you're calling names is.....you. Here's where you should stop for a minute and collect yourself. I don't mean he or she is just a bit like you. I'm not saying other people out there are similar to yourself. I mean your brother, a stranger, or a friend is you. A different part of who you are, like you and they were different flowers on one plant. That guy you looked down on yesterday because he's fat and you aren't? He's every bit as much you as you are. Truth is, you were mean-mouthing yourself. And that gal you made fun of last week because she can't afford the latest cool jeans? You were making fun of yourself. Same with all those people on the wrong side of the tracks you called scum of the earth last week. They are you.

A Promise of Hope

"Hell is not other people; it is yourself." (Ludwig Wittgenstein)

Don't believe it? I don't blame you because we've been taught to see the world in a way that makes it tough to believe. To see this truth clearly, you'll have to retrain your brain. Later I'll give you a training plan that will do precisely that, and bring your very own dreams back. But be advised. Unless you're gifted with the kind of revelation that comes with near-death or other experiences, you won't see the world differently immediately. Hardly anyone changes their beliefs just like that. A few rare birds do, but ordinary folks like you and I have to train ourselves for it, like training to run a marathon. Every day you do a little bit more until you can go the distance. No way around it. You won't see the world differently just by reading this book. You'll have to do the work I give you. Unless you're one of those amazing, rare people who train for marathons by reading books about marathons of course.

Are You Ready to Find Yourself?

If you're brave enough to admit you're lost, you're ready to rediscover who you are and find your share of authentic success. Just follow me as I stumble my way into the Truth that set me Free and show you how to find what you're looking for. On the other hand, if you just can't identify with a single sign of losing a calling, you can read everything else just for fun. Coming up is nothing but little real-life stories designed to take you where you want to go. Some are funny, and some aren't. But they're all absolutely true.

Chapter Eight
My Journey of Discovery Begins
(How I Discovered My Dreams Disappeared)

"Our first journey is to find that special place for us." Earl Nightingale (1921 - 1989)

My Journey Begins

The Journey that would eventually take me through the wall of fear began when I was about seven or eight. Unfortunately, it took me 35 more years to actually get to the other side, but you can shave decades off that by reading this book. So let's head back to my pre-teen years to begin this great voyage together. But be warned. If you happened upon me in those days, you wouldn't see much of a candidate for any kind of big Journey. Why not? I was just your everyday, ordinary, average guy with a perfectly normal set of brains. Nothing too big, nothing too small. Enough to get by, but nothing to shout about either. Except maybe for one thing. Where curiosity was concerned, I had more than my fair share. As a matter of fact, it's fair to say I was the most curious kid for miles and miles. Maybe you couldn't say I was smart….but I was curious as a cat in a barrel of minced mice. In a very curious way. Like how? My somewhat undersized brain was designed for odd, peculiar, nonsense puzzles.

Most kids my age were asking questions like "how come the sky is blue?", or "why does water run downhill?", or "what time is supper?". Regular questions with clear comprehensible answers you can hang your hat on or find a seat at the dinner table with. Not me. I'd spend my daylight saving time wondering strange things nobody else seemed to bother with. Like what was going on where I wasn't for instance. In case you don't recognize it, that's the ancient… "what sound does a cannon make when there's nobody there to hear it?" question.

"Sounds like a cannon Mister" said Mom, but I wasn't convinced. I'd worry myself silly over other strange puzzles as well. Like…"where does tomorrow come from?" If you haven't tried that one yourself, I can tell you it's a tuffy. I didn't just ask myself these crazy questions either. Teachers were assaulted with bizarre queries too. "How do I know I'm not you?" for example. Sure enough, I got back answers. "Sit down and shut up" is one I can still recall, all these years later.

I'm Called a Fool

Alright, so picture little yours truly for a moment, filled with curiosity about the world and asking strange questions. My soul told me I was toying with great mysteries, but everybody else had different ideas. My heart said there were wonders to behold at the roots of my puzzles, but nobody seemed to agree. In fact, I was called weird, stupid, and other bad names for my efforts. Teachers, parents, and friends alike thought I was a nutcase. And so, to avoid bringing grief upon myself, I stopped asking crazy questions out loud. Even so, my heart-of-hearts was smitten with absurd puzzles, and I let them bounce around in my head anytime they wanted. Nary a word was whispered in public of course, because I wanted to fit in as best I could. But trying to keep my passion for those odd puzzles to myself still didn't keep me out of trouble.

"All of us have wonders hidden in our breasts, only needing circumstances to evoke them".
- Charles Dickens

I Have Big Wonder

Soon after vowing to keep the enigmatic puzzles to myself, I learned something interesting about souls.

They really do not want to be trapped inside. Mine sure didn't, and it found a way to sneak a shadow of itself out. How? Those absurd riddles rattling around in my head morphed themselves into absurd jokes that would suddenly burst into the light of day when I least expected it. What's an absurd joke? Well, it's a joke that's funny because it's not. An odd reflection on the world that makes so little sense it has to be funny. To me anyhow. These crazy jokes that look suspiciously like riddles themselves began flowing out before I was ten and continue to this very day. Just ask any poor soul forced to work alongside me over the last thirty years. Example? No problem. I can invent idiotic stuff at the drop of a hat. "What meows like a cat, has no tail, and looks a teensy bit like you?". Answer? "You and your cat!". Haw, haw, haw, haw eh? No? Well excuse me while I roll around on the floor laughing insanely like usual. What's funny you ask? Good question. Sometimes I'm not even sure myself…which is kind of funny if you think about it. Isn't it? It isn't? That's alright, because most of the time I'm the only one laughing. O.K., I'm done laughing now, so let's get back on track. I want to tell you where my hyper curiosity and pitifully dumb jokes took me.

They took me to a place called "Big Wonder". Big Wonder begins with a curiosity that makes you dig into the world until something happens. Little mysteries get bigger. Big puzzles become awe-inspiring. Everything in the world begins to have a magical, mysterious beauty to it. But Big Wonder is still to come. Big Wonder happens when something stunning begins to dawn on you.

"All the wonders you seek are within yourself". - Thomas Browne (1605 - 1682)

What is Hidden in the World?

Slowly but surely you begin to realize something astonishing is hidden in the world somewhere. At first it's just an inkling, but as the awe-inspiring mysteries fuse together, you know for sure it's there. That's when you start wondering BIG. You wonder what it is, and how to find it. Big Wonder drives you to seek it out. As my twelfth birthday came and went, I had Big Wonder about the world. I didn't know then that people in every Age have Big Wonder. Scientists, Historians, Religious leaders. Explorers of every kind. All trying to discover what's hidden before our eyes in the world, but hidden so deeply, no one has managed to dig it up. In those years I knew none of this, so I just kept on digging, even while I was completely lost.

I Seek What's Hidden

So how does a fellow with less than a full deck dig, while daydreaming in school or getting decent jobs? It begins with reading. At first I read anything I could get my hands on. Poetry, physics, music, art, medicine, mathematics. You name it, I read it, whether I wanted to or not, because I didn't know what I was looking for, or where it might be. It could be anywhere of course, so I looked anywhere. Animal books? Sure. Books on Buddha? You bet. Big ugly volumes on logic? Even more interesting. If you dropped your shorts I'd read the label! But, believe it or not, it gets worse, because I didn't follow reading rules either. I wasn't reading to become an encyclopedia, or pass tests for example. I was searching for something, so I'd scan through book after book as fast as I could, looking for who-knows-what. Like what? I didn't know of course, but I was sure I'd know it when I saw it. I was like the girl whose mom says "you'll know Mr. Right when he comes along".

Same sort of thing. She doesn't know what she's looking for either, but she knows she'll know it when she sees it. O.K., so there I was, reading and digging and digging and reading for a long time. Half bookworm, half nuts. Then one day I knew I needed to begin digging fresh dirt. Something inside told me.

A Voice Speaks Up

I still remember that day, because a little voice from deep inside spoke up. I didn't actually hear any words of course, but a huge conviction overcame me in a way I've never forgotten. Suddenly I knew with total certainty I had to do my own thinking. Now it was time to explore on my own. But that presented a little problem. Doing my own thinking and exploring on my own meant nothing more or less than being myself. Each of us comes with a brain designed to work in its own unique way of course, and not just to learn how other people think. For you and I to make our way in the world, we must eventually let our brains "do their thing". That's exactly what my soul said to me on that fateful day. It said…"if you really want to explore the world, you must do it *your* way". Unfortunately, that was exactly what I was most fearful of doing. My heart was saying I had to be myself…but every time my soul ventured out…someone laughed at me or called me names for it.

Now what? Well, I was way to scared to be myself right out in public, so all I could do was be myself to myself. I had to stay in the closet for years before I would speak my half-witted mind out in the open, like a scarecrow fluttering around in the breeze. As a matter of fact, my earliest exploring was in a real closet. The kind you hang clothes in.

"Deep into that darkness peering, long I stood there, wondering, fearing, doubting, dreaming dreams no mortal ever dared to dream before". - Edgar Allan Poe (1809 - 1849)

In a Clothes Closet

Remember what else I was doing besides digging? Aimlessly wandering. After my first engineering job, I was so badly lost I had no idea who I was or what I should be doing with my life, so I dropped out for a year. Lots of people did in the late sixties and early seventies. Me? I headed to England where I could work without papers, because Mom was an English war bride who married my Canadian dad. In those days, kids with British moms could go work in England without any fuss, muss, or red tape. So I did. During the day I waited tables, tied trout flies and helped farmers bale hay. Not to mention my personal favorite....washing dishes! I actually made enough to survive on mushy British peas and soggy sausages. Have you ever had a few English sausages on a big gooey cow-splat of muddy peas? No? You're missing out. I'd feast on them daily, until they and I looked suspiciously alike. O.K., so I pigged out on pork a lot, but what else did I do on the other side of the pond? I was still exploring queer looking riddles on my own. After work I'd retire to a dinky little room in my room, and slam the door shut. The closet.

A Dirt Poor Explorer

My tiny English flat was always freezing, and the only source of heat I had was a coin-operated electric heater. I'd never seen such a thing in North America, but England had them in spades in those days. What a bummer. It might have been good for guys with spare coins, but I was poorer than dirt down the drain at the time. There was no way I could afford to keep that voracious thing fed. So to keep warm, I took the stupid little thing in the closet with stupid little me. Plus one rickety chair to hold my scrawny butt above the floor. And a lamp....hung upside down from the clothes pole so I could see.

Then I shut the door. No…..I'm not fibbing. It was the only way I could stay warm. With the door shut, it warmed up fast and stayed that way for hours. So there I sat, scribbling notes in a Journal, digging into ancient, mysterious puzzles about the world. Eventually I dug down to something strange.

Something Strange Beneath My Feet

Can you picture me, an amateur explorer, trying to figure out how the world works….in a closet? There I was, digging into puzzles big and small, scooping turf in a teensy room. Every once and a while I'd put another coin in the heater as my toes cooled down. After some considerable time digging I hit something hard. Metaphorically speaking, there was a resounding big ………. CLINK as I encountered something very big and solid in my explorations. Beating my little brain mercilessly, I tried to get around it, but it was not yielding to my efforts. Straining and struggling, I tried getting over or under or past it any which way I could. It was like I'd hit a basement floor made of iron. The floor seemed to stretch off forever in all directions as well, because I couldn't find a way past it. Then it dawned on me. I'd seen this puzzling obstacle before. All kinds of different people exploring different aspects of the world had run into it. So many in fact, this curious barrier at depth in the world had been given a name. It's called "dualism". What's Dualism? That's a very good question. Let's go see.

"Curiosity is lying in wait for every secret." Ralph Waldo Emerson

Chapter Nine
Something Big is Revealed to Me
(Mistaken Beliefs That Steal Our Dreams)

"How wonderful that we have met with a paradox. Now we have some hope of making progress."
Niels Bohr (1885 - 1962) Danish physicist

Dualism is a Jekyl and Hyde Puzzle

Dualism is a real Jekyl and Hyde kind of puzzle. If you remember those two totally opposite characters, Dr. Jekyl was a savage, murderous, evil man who killed other folks for fun. On the other hand, Mr. Hyde was a mild-mannered guy…. who wouldn't step… on his brother the fly. The thing is, they were one and the same person. Absolutely different characters fused into one man who behaved in totally incompatible ways. That might sound a bit odd, but Jekyl and Hyde aren't like a ball that's half black and half white. They're like a ball that's completely black and completely white…. at the same time. Did that make your brain slip a gear or two? If so, you've grappled with the essential puzzle at the heart of Jekyl and Hyde….and Dualism. There is no dividing line between Doctor Jekyl and Mister Hyde, even though they are absolutely divided. Maybe that's impossible nonsense to you, but scientists have dug into the world and found this kind of craziness there in many places, so it's real. That's what I'd found in my closet and was trying to figure out.

Our Knowledge of the World is Like a Poem

"The opposite of a fact is falsehood, but the opposite of one profound truth may very well be another profound truth". – Neils Bohr

To come to grips with Dualism, I want you to imagine all our knowledge of the world is like a gigantic Poem that has this strange Dual Jekyl and Hyde character to it, only more so. Here's what I mean. Dr. Jekyl and Mr. Hyde are two completely different things at the same time, namely "good and bad". On the other hand, any or all of our knowledge is billions upon billions of completely different things at the same time. It's One Poem and Many parts….at the same time. It's Dualism writ large. But what does this Poem mean? If you've ever been asked to say what a poem means in school, you'll have faced this kind of puzzle yourself. Take that old *"roses are red and violets are blue"* poem for instance. Teacher might say it means "nature is beautiful", but some kid in the back might argue it means "nature is ugly" because he got stuck by a rose thorn yesterday. So who is right? Good question. Sometimes ten people will give ten meanings to the same poem, and nobody is really sure which is right. The Dualism poem of our knowledge is like that too. Nobody is sure what it means either.

What Does the Dualism Poem Mean?

So there I am in my closet. I've discovered our knowledge of the Universe is like a Poem and I'm wondering what it means. At the time I thought it might mean some interesting scientific or philosophical thing, and began struggling to cipher it out. I had no idea the right meaning of this great poem would let me discover the meaning of my life. Even worse, I didn't even suspect the wrong meaning of Dualism was making the world sick. It would be twenty more years before that was revealed to me, but I'm getting ahead of myself here. Right now we'll go back to England and watch me struggle with Dualism. Something important was revealed to me about this great Poem at the time, but not enough to help me find my way.

The Meaning of Dualism is Hidden

My closet was in Barnstaple North Devon, England to be exact. If I remember rightly it was Saturday mid-summer nineteen seventy six. I'd been racking my brain non-stop for something like five or six hours over the meaning of Dualism, with zero success. My mind was still doing flip-flops over things that are absolutely different and absolutely the same. Then something a little odd happened. It had never happened to me before and has never happened to me since. I think my brain blew a fuse. One second I was mulling over the Dualism puzzle, and the next I was just sitting there in a kind of fog. I can't say I was thinking about anything. Looking back it was a bit like the exhaustion runners encounter when every scrap of energy has been used and they're forced to quit. Marathoners call this the "wall" and I'd hit something like it. It was a little bit frightening actually, because it wasn't just like I'd stopped thinking. It was more like I *couldn't* think, even when I tried. Forced into a dazed state, I had to get up and out of that closet right away.

At the time my digs were a few miles from some old Montreal friends living in the nearby village of Lynton, so I decided to bus over and see them. Even today I recall that odd dream-like state my brain was in as I stumbled out to the bus stop and made my way to see Dave and Polly. When I got there, they weren't home. Still dozy from my blown fuse, I thought a climb to the top of Lynton's famous giant hill might do me some good. No longer can I remember what that hill's called, but I made my way to the top and stood looking out over gorgeous ocean views with my battered brain stuck in neutral.

Revelation Reveals the Meaning of Dualism

"The revelation of Thought takes men out of servitude into freedom". - Ralph Waldo Emerson

Standing on the top of that hill, I had a very curious kind of waking dream. It was one of those "out of body" experiences you read about, and it took my breath away. Suddenly I seemed to be outside my body, looking at the sum total of our knowledge of the world. I was staring at the curious way it was One Poem and Many pieces at the same time when I had what people call "revelation". The experience of revelation is something like this. Imagine you're struggling to understand what's in a box by shaking it and feeling its weight. You have a vague, foggy idea what's inside, but can't figure out how to get it open. Then… unexpectedly….the box springs open all on its own to reveal its contents. You don't have a clue how or why it opened up, and still don't know how to make it do that. But now its contents are revealed to you with absolute clarity. You have had a revelation. In my case what was revealed was the meaning of Dualism.

A Poem of Life

My revelation went something like this. I was staring at all our knowledge of the world when suddenly I saw it had two meanings. One meaning brings life into the world, but the other inhibits life everywhere. That makes our knowledge a "Poem of Life" because it can give or take life, depending on the meaning it's given. Unfortunately, we gave this Poem the wrong meaning Ages ago and it's been taking life from us ever since. Here's how we did that. Seeing the way our knowledge is always "One and Many at the same time", we tore it into two separate ideas called "sameness" and "difference".

Then we wove those ideas into a selfish view of the world called "Reason". Reason makes us think the world is filled with many different, separate things. "Selfish" means we mistakenly believe everything is a separate "thing unto itself", but in reality, there aren't many different, individual, separated things in the world at all. The Truth is, everything is a different part of one whole. In a nutshell then, my revelation was that we've chosen to see the world in a way that separates each of us from everything. So what you ask? That is a very good question indeed, because I asked myself that right there on Lynton hill, but didn't have a good answer. It would take me decades to see why you and I desperately need to see that we and the world are parts of one whole.

I Saw the Truth, but Missed It

Several days after my revelation on Lynton hill, something happened that took me back to Canada. Out of the blue came a call from my old fishing buddy Ken. If you recall, Ken and I swam bare-bum together in six-mile creek hundreds of years ago. Ken was getting married in our old home-town of Fort William, and was calling to ask me to be best man. One of three times I would do the honor for great friends. So off across the Atlantic I went, to begin my long aimless climb up the corporate ladder for decades. Eventually I'd have two more revelations that would show me how our misguided way of seeing the world had taken my dreams from me. And millions of other unsuspecting people.

"Who in the world am I? Ah, that's the great puzzle." - Charles Lutwidge Dodgson (Lewis Carroll)

Chapter Ten
But I Still Don't Get It
(For Twenty More Years)

"Cease trying to work everything out with your minds. It will get you nowhere. Live by intuition and inspiration and let your whole life be Revelation". - Eileen Caddy

Mr. Lost Soul Returns

After returning from England, I joined the great crowd of lost souls "getting good jobs" and accumulating as many big and little things as possible. My salary got steadily bigger in figures and my cars slowly turned European. From a distance you'd think I was a real success story. But if you and I got up close and personal in those days, you'd discover I was just as lost as I ever was. I still had no idea what to do with my life two decades after leaving behind the British Isles. During all those years I'd never actually met an authentically successful person with a real Life Mission either. In fact, with everyone around me completely lost, I'd almost started to believe it's normal to have no idea why we're here. I'd just about bought into the idea we're here to "get good jobs", wait for retirement, and die lost. But that little ray of hope from Rainbow Lake kept me from giving up on finding my reason for being. I will admit that my hopes were pretty faint twenty years later. Thankfully, my second revelation happened before they disappeared completely.

And So Does Revelation

Revelation number two arrived when I was living in a place called Kingsville Ontario, just east of Detroit Michigan.

By this time I was a bona fide head honcho running a Windsor based company painting metal parts for car makers twenty four hours a day. Complete with expense account, company car, and a big figure income that gave Mom bragging rights. You know....... "he's gotta really good job". But good job or not, I still didn't have a purpose in life to call my own. I'd been achieving other people's goals for decades. So there I was, big man on campus, with no idea what to do with my life. Not having grown *my way* for decades, I still couldn't answer the "who am I?" question. Then one morning out jogging, another revelation showed up on a little bridge over a creek. It happened on June 19th, 1996. I remember exactly when, because it was the thirtieth anniversary of a motorcycle accident I had on the very same day in 1966. So there I was cooling down on the bridge after a nice long run, thinking back over my life. Amazed at how much has changed over the years, except one little thing.

Me. Way down deep, where my soul is, I'm just the same. I'm in my ancient forties by this time, but still feel like a kid inside. Same old young guy. Sound familiar? It should. Everyone stays the same as they change....to the end of it all. So I started to wonder. "How come my soul escapes change?" I asked myself. "Isn't everything supposed to change constantly?". "Maybe my soul's not part of the world at all"... I wondered out loud... knowing full well it was. Then I saw something.

The Poem of Life Again

Sitting on that bridge, I suddenly saw the Poem of Life again. Same Poem I did hand-to-hand combat with twenty years earlier, but this time I saw it differently. Real personal you might say. The same way everyone sees it as they get older. I saw I was the same person at heart, even though I'd wrinkled up like raisins and grayed around the edges like pewter.

I was exactly the same, but completely different. BOOM! Poem of Life. Same Poem everyone eventually notices. If you haven't noticed yet, you will. It doesn't matter whether you're a mathematical professor or master mouse catcher either. You'll eventually see that everything around you will change except your soul. It stays the same. There you go. That's the dualism Poem of Life. Before we get to my second revelation though let's review the two meanings you can give that Poem. The wrong meaning is that everything in the world, including you and I, are completely different, separate things. The right meaning sounds a lot like the wrong one, but it's not. The correct meaning is that you and I and everything in the Universe are different parts of one whole. Why is one meaning better than the other? I had no idea myself back in my England days. At the time I thought these meanings were only something philosophers were interested in arguing over. I didn't realize then that the proper meaning of this great Poem is the most important thing ever to each human being on the planet. And the wrong meaning is so wrong it is truly terrifying.

More Is Revealed

That June day on the bridge is burned into my head many years later. As we speak, I can see the place like it was in front of me now. I'm sitting there dangling my feet over the water, staring down a foggy creek. Weeping willows frame a reflected sunrise and spider webs glitter with red-gold light. I'm in one of those afterburner highs you get when cooling down from a hard run. Every last bit of workday stress has disappeared and my frame of mind is warm and fuzzy as I meditate on the Poem of Life. Then suddenly I'm confused. For a moment the scene before me changes in an impossibly odd way. I'll describe it to you, but it won't come across too well in words. It's like describing the Grand Canyon with words.

They'll give you some idea what the canyon's like, but to really know what it's all about, you have to see it yourself. Anyway, here goes.

The Right Meaning of Life

One minute I'm looking at trees and grass and water and the next I'm looking into a crazy mirror. An Alice in Wonderland kind of mirror with yours truly staring back. Staring at the world around me, I was looking at myself, except for one little itty bitty problem. I was looking at trees and grass and water....but they were me. Everything I could see everywhere was me. This's the part that's hard to describe to folks who haven't seen it. Those trees and clouds and spider webs didn't look like me, but I knew they were. I could see they were different *parts* of me, just like my own arms and legs are. Certainly the water and stones and sky were amazingly different parts, but parts of me just the same. Then and there I saw that everything around me was just a different part of who I am. I saw it clearly, like I'd taken a pair of foggy glasses off.

Then....after maybe 30 seconds, the peculiar "mirror" disappeared and I couldn't see the world like that anymore. But I remembered how stunningly clear it was. I remembered what I'd seen as well. To say the least, it was totally shocking. It didn't even seem to make sense after the fact. But I could not deny what I'd just seen. It left me shaken too. I'd liken it to the shock you'd get if you saw one of those aliens we've all read about. You see it....but you can hardly believe what your own two eyes are telling you. It was rather like that. But in my case, I hadn't seen an alien spaceship or group of leprechauns. I'd seen the right meaning of our lives. The trouble was, I still didn't fully understand what I was seeing. I would have to have one more revelation for the full truth of it to dawn on me. That happened about a year later.

"A human being is part of a whole, called by us the 'Universe,' a part limited in time and space. He experiences himself, his thoughts and feelings, as something separated from the rest--a kind of optical delusion of his consciousness. This delusion is a kind of prison for us, restricting us to our personal desires and to affection for a few persons nearest us. Our task must be to free ourselves from this prison by widening our circles of compassion to embrace all living creatures and the whole of nature in its beauty." (Albert Einstein)

Chapter Eleven
Finally I See
(The Key to Our Lives)

"There is one evident, indubitable manifestation of the Divinity, and that is the laws of right which are made known to the world through Revelation" - Leo Tolstoy, Anna Karenina

A Big Revelation

Back on that bridge I saw the whole Truth of the world for a few minutes, but I still didn't know what to make of it. The Poem of Life still just looked like something professors want to argue about, but so what? Most of us aren't professors, and hardly anyone gives a turkey's bottom about poems. I didn't have a clue how it would help my own aimless life either, until one early morning a year later on Point Pelee. Pelee is a little peninsula pointing to America across Lake Erie from Canada. It's a provincial park actually, and draws crowds every year to see bird migrations that flock over it like a plague of locusts. My home town of Kingsville wasn't far from the point, so one Saturday I decided to drive over and jog down before anyone got up. It's a real treat of a place to jog in before it opens, so I parked at the highway before daybreak and set off. Eventually I hit the lake just as a huge sunburst sun dangled itself above the horizon. And what a showy sunrise that day. Copper-gray-green clouds washed across the entire sky, like liquid fireworks in an ocean of air. Blue-white waves lapped at my feet as terns and gulls swept through the bright morning. Embraced by the light and surrounded by water… there I stood at the southernmost tip of Canada, drying off from a spirited run. I was meditating as usual when it happened. Another waking dream. A revelation of revelations.

I See the Tree of Life

Standing there in a kind of trance, I saw my left and right hands held up before me like puppets. Strange as it sounds, these animated figures were behaving like little people. In fact, my right hand was calling the left one names. Why? Mr. right was a whiz at writing, but lefty just couldn't do it. Like Human Beings everywhere, one hand with greater skills and abilities was calling the other a loser. So there I stood for a moment, watching this odd scene with one of my hands berating the other for having less writing skills. It was a bit like one of those Punch and Judy shows old-time entertainers used to put on. On and on went my own right hand, calling my left one every name in the book. But then....suddenly.....I heard a little voice speak up from somewhere deep within me. It was sternly addressing both my hands like an angry school teacher or parent. "STOP IT!" said this voice to the hands before me. "Are you two blind! Can't you see it's impossible one of you can be worth less than the other!! Both of you are different parts of one whole. You *ARE* each other. Only crazy people would call themselves names.".

Then my inner voice went silent and I woke up. In an instant I saw what I'd been digging and searching for all those years. Remember I'd been looking for something? Something I knew I'd know when I saw it, like girls know Mr. Right when they see him. There it was right in front of me and I had zero doubt it was what I'd been looking for. It was the Tree of Life.

There's Only One Life

Standing there on the tip of Point Pelee, I suddenly realized that the entire Universe is like a great Tree made up of each star and galaxy and grain of sand and man and woman. Completely contrary to what we believe today though, there simply aren't many different, separate, individual lives in the Universe at all.

What we call "Life" emerges from the sum of everything. Each and every thing on earth and planet and star and galaxy merges seamlessly together so this One Life can emerge. I'm not an individual life and neither are you. Every single creature or plant or bacteria on our planet is just a different part of the Universe that gives rise to One Life we all share. No wonder our scientists have had such a hard time trying to figure out if some thing or the other is alive. *Every* thing is a necessary part of One Life. That includes rocks, water, air, and all the creatures we think of as alive today. The entire Universe is alive. Then…as I stood there pondering this curious fact of revelation….the most stunning part of it all hit like a ton of bricks. The part that's critical to your happiness and mine.

It's this. If you and I and everything else shares one life, the very idea our lives can be *judged* is nonsense. Why? There aren't different lives to judge. No life can possibly be worth more or less than any other because it's all the same Life. Your life or mine has to be worth exactly the same that of Einstein, Mother Teresa, or the Pope, because it's all the same life. We share the same soul. It doesn't matter if we're rich, poor, smart or handicapped either. No life can possibly be worth less than another. Judging each other's lives is as ridiculous as judging the life of a rabbit's foot worth more than the life of his tail. Anyone who believed that sort of thing about rabbits would be called crazy. So why don't we think men and women judging each other are equally crazy? Right there on Point Pelee that day my three different revelations came together and I saw why.

But We Can't See It

Why don't we realize that judging each other is insane? Back when we began building our Great House of Knowledge, we chose to give the Poem of Life a meaning that makes us think every thing in the Universe is completely separate.

Unfortunately, once we made this choice, our worldview called "Reason" wouldn't let see the truth. Reason stops us from seeing that you and I and all things great and small are different parts of one whole. Reason is what makes us judge each other's souls, even though it is utter nonsense to do so. Reason lets us see that some folks are smarter and richer and stronger of course. It lets us comprehend that bigger or stronger is often better and worth more as well. But this worldview called "Reason" won't let us see that the lives, souls, or Spirits of each of us must be worth exactly the same…..because we all share the same life, soul, and Spirit. Blind to the whole Truth of the Tree of Life, we waste our lives judging each other.

Seeing the Truth Lights up Our Lives

When I returned home that day after Point Pelee, my mind was boggled by the simple truth. Again and again I reflected on the fact that a Law of Nature made my life equal to that of any person who ever lived or would live. Seeing the Tree of Life was like a light coming on in a dark basement I thought was filled with monsters who'd judge me. Suddenly I realized there was nothing to fear. No judging monsters, not even little ones. I was totally flabbergast. Put yourself in a dark place you're afraid of and you'll see what I mean. When the light goes on your fears disappear. That's why revelations are called en-*light*-enment. They're like turning a light on in the darkness to reveal a truth that dispels fear. That much I already knew about "enlightenment". But *real enlightenment*….the kind that takes fears of being judged away…..does something I never expected. It lets those inner voice ideas we spoke of earlier come into our life once more. The only thing keeping them from us…..is fear of being judged. Of course I'm telling you this in hindsight right now. In the beginning I had no idea this would happen as my fears of being judged went away.

Like a Candle in an Ocean of Darkness

Before I begin describing what happened to me as my fears of judgment ebbed, it's worthwhile going back to something I mentioned many pages ago first. The world we live in today is so saturated with judgments that make us fear being ourselves it's like living in a forest so big we can't even see it for the trees. From personal experience I can tell you I had no idea my life was terribly limited by fears of being judged for the first forty-odd years. I didn't realize that billboards telling me to buy this or that were really saying "if you don't have this or that you're a worthless soul". I had no idea the entire fashion industry isn't about beauty at all. It's about being "in fashion" so we aren't judged less worthy human beings. It never occurred to me that I was swimming in judgments putting fear in my heart every day of my life. I thought this was all just normal and sensible. But in reality it made me swim in an ocean of fear. Fear of coming out of my shell, lest people around me pass judgment.

My guess is that you're exactly the same. Right now you probably don't even realize how much your life is being cut down to a shadow of what it can be by these ever-present fears of being judged. If you don't, you're in big danger of never knowing what it's like to see why you're here and what to do with your life. You won't realize these fears are keeping your inner voice from telling you which way to go. You might not even attempt to re-train yourself to set your heart free. Even after my three revelations for instance, I still didn't know what those fears had been doing to me. It was only some time later, after ideas about who I am began flowing again, that I realized what was going on. My final "revelation" then, wasn't an out-of-body experience or trance-like thing.

It was the stunning realization that *this single fear of being judged had literally stopped me from seeing what to do with my life.* The day after my last insight on Pelee peninsula I slowly started to understand this. Here's how it began.

The Light Begins Working

The day after my final revelation, I leaped up and out of bed around five A.M. To say the least, that was a very curious thing for me to do, because I hadn't been an early bird since the days when Ken and I would go fishing together. But on that fateful day, I was eager to get up for reasons were lost on me at the time. After shaving and showering and munching on cornflakes, I still had an hour of free time before heading out to the office. Ordinarily I would have watched T.V. or something to pass the time. But on that day I wandered over and sat down at my study desk. Then I did something strange. I began writing verse. Looking back at it now, it was really bizarre, but at the time I didn't think anything of it. What kind of verse am I talking about here? Well, a rough description might be a long rhyming Alice-in-Wonderland kind of story. A fairy tale poem all written in verse, about a Bee.

Yes. A Bee getting into one kind of trouble after another. So much trouble, it took me something like one hundred pages to spell it all out. Not that first morning of course. Believe it or not, I got up early day after day for weeks on end writing this crazy rhyming tale. What on earth was that all about? I didn't get it myself in the beginning. It took some time before the sheer impossible amazement of it all dawned on me. Eventually I realized that my inner voice had started to speak to me….as soon as those fears of being judged began to go away. This odd poem I called "BEES" was all about myself and what had happened to me. Lucky for you, I won't make you read the thing.

But I'll give you the very first few lines of it here, because it literally sums up the predicament I'd been in for the first few decades of my life. A predicament created by fears of being judged. Here goes. The very first words my inner voice spoke to me….after years of silence.

BEES
"I noted in clover and grasses one day,"
"Mindful of little respect,"
"A fellow all sullen and seized to complain,"
"Of being girded-'round rather than checked."

As My Inner Voice Speaks Up

Before we go on, I'd like to tell you this. Eventually when I looked back on this curious rhyme about BEES, I couldn't believe my eyes. It took me a while to fully appreciate what had been going on. Even today I look at those few words up there in utter amazement. Why? Because they describe precisely what was wrong with me…..as communicated by my inner voice….to myself. It was as if someone was trying to make me start "knowing thyself" by getting messages to me about who I really was at the time. But had you tried to explain this to me then, I wouldn't even have believed it. It took some time before I simply could not deny the obvious. At any rate, in case it's not clear to you what those few words are saying, I'll explain. In essence, that verse describes an everyday bee, sullen and complaining about being himself. Like bees everywhere, he came into the world as a black and yellow striped ("girded 'round") creature, but he isn't satisfied being himself. He'd rather be covered in checker-board squares. That'd be "checked" in rhyme-talk of course. In summary then, he's afraid to be himself, and the next 99 pages describe the endless grief this brings him.

Looking back at it now, it's me describing myself. My inner voice was trying to say to me…."wake up…you're pretending to be something you're not and it's causing you big trouble". But did I get it? No I didn't. Certainly I wrote it all myself and could read the words clear as a bell as well. So how come I didn't even understand what I was trying to tell myself? I wasn't quite ready. I was still a bit too afraid of being judged to listen. But as those fears went away, I slowly began to understand. Slowly but surely I began to hear what my inner voice had to say. Good thing too, because it was telling me how to be myself. Now I'm going to pass on this knowledge to you.

How to Be Yourself

So how do you learn how to be yourself….to get your dreams back? The easiest way is to have your own revelation. If wholeness is revealed to you…..just like that….out of the blue, your fears of judgment will begin to go away to let your own heart-song into your life again. How do you have your own revelation? Good question. For thousands of years Mankind has tried to find a Path that would take us to where we could see the Truth of wholeness ourselves. In fact, there are many Paths that different gurus or cultures have created to bring you or I to revelation. Sadly, not one of them will reliably take you there. I've sketched out a number of these for you below….just in case you want to try some out. If none bring you the peace of mind and authentic success you crave, don't despair. The Rule of Life in later chapters really and truly can do exactly that. But first, here are a few of the most popular classic "Paths to revelation" I spoke of.

"The Tree of Life, in the book of Genesis, is a tree in the "New Jerusalem" whose fruit gives everlasting life". Wikipedia

Chapter Eleven Point Five
(Stop And Think Right Here)

Before you go any further, I'd like you to stop and think and think about something. I've already put a simple fact in front of you that can change your life in miraculous ways. It's this. There's only one soul in the Universe we all share, so it's impossible you can be worth less than anyone. Even so, it'll take a bit of time before the possibilities sink in. You'll have to retrain your brain with Rule of Life exercises to really get it. But let's stop right now and think about what's going on in the world. Millions of people are desperate to know what to do with their lives, and have been for many generations. Violence is the rule today too, because so many folks have given up on having their share of happiness they've turned mean and ugly. People, companies, and organizations of all kinds looking out for number one are destroying the planet. All because we can't see that the world around us is who we are. All because we can't see the world the right way. Because we've made a mistake.

Can you think of anything more grotesque? You and I are really different parts of each other…..but we're willing to kill the other guy off? Your soul and mine are one and the same…..but I hate yours and you hate mine? We spend our lives going without the happiness we were put here to have….because of a mistake? I don't know about you, but I can't think of a bigger, more disastrous mistake. But…..and here's where you better put your thinking cap on. It's just a mistake. Guess what that means? It means it can be fixed. Probably in one generation if we actually *tried* to fix it. A mistake that could be fixed by the time your kids have kids.

Chapter Twelve
8 Ways You Won't Find Your Dreams

"To put the world in order, we must first put the nation in order; To put the nation in order, we must first put the family in order; To put the family in order, we must first cultivate our personal life; and to cultivate our personal life, we must first set our hearts right". Isaiah ch XXXVII v.1

Lots of Ways to Revelation

If you look around right now in bookstores and libraries, you'll discover all kinds of modern self-help books trying to show you and I how to have "authentic success". These books fly off the shelves because millions are desperate to have real happiness in their lives. But here's a curious fact for you. Even the most popular self-help books and gurus hardly ever actually help anyone find what they're looking for. If you don't believe it, just go take a poll yourself. Ask a million folks who've tried a hundred self-help books if the methods showed them why they're here. You'd be lucky to find a single person who found their way. Sounds ridiculous? It is, but it's not a new story.

You can go back as far as you want in history, thousands of years in fact, and find the very same thing going on. People in every Age have known there's a fabulous thing called "true happiness" men and women can have in their lives, but nobody's figured out a reliable way of getting it. Even so, that doesn't mean gurus in every generation haven't tried to find a Way to this heavenly place of real happy human success. There are quite a few very famous Ways in fact, but every single one of them is completely unreliable.

If you're really, really lucky, on a good day one of these Ways might work a little, but they almost never do. Why not? Our misguided way of seeing the world called "Reason" will keep you frightened of being judged. That single fear will stop your inner voice from telling you what to do with your life to get the authentic success you so desire. Unfortunately, we've been looking at the world the wrong way just as long as people have been inventing Ways to find happiness. That's why all these famous Ways haven't worked for us over the centuries. It's why self-help gurus haven't helped many people know their heart's desires….Age after Age. Here's a few popular ones I'm sure you're familiar with. Try some if you'd like. After they haven't done anything for you, come try the Rule of Life. It really can get your dreams back.

Modern Self-Help Ways

At the beginning of the twenty-first century, there are many different kinds of self-help books out there trying to help you and I find what we're looking for in life. Later I'll explain where many of these Ways are coming from, and how to make them work for you. For the moment though, let's step back a bit and get a bird's eye view of the modern "find happy success" industry. If you're at all like I was in my lost years, you may not be familiar with what the happiness gurus are saying.

One of the first things you'll notice about the most popular books out there, is that they speak of "Laws of Nature" that science hasn't discovered and scientists wouldn't agree exist. "Laws of attraction" for example, that make it possible for you to "attract what you want in your life", like you were a biological magnet…. for success. Or "quantum laws" that let you create the world of your dreams that are found nowhere in quantum physics. In other words, many of the modern self-help gurus flatly defy basic scientific beliefs about how things work.

They defy scientific principles, rather like saying you could turn gravity off and let your house fly to the moon. As you might expect then, those-in-the-know often pooh-pooh self-help principles. The fact that the self-help industry rarely helps people find what they're looking for seems to support the idea modern self-help rules and mantras are nothing but hot air as well. How can anyone claim a "Law of Nature" is afoot which, when applied, brings real happiness….when it almost never does? Bottom line? Knowledgeable, scientifically trained men and women call the self-help gurus kooks. So are they? No they're not. For the most part they're people with a Vision of a Truth just outside our worldview.

Therein lies the problem. Science is "inside" the worldview and refuses to go out. Self-help gurus have a fuzzy Vision of the Truth outside alright, but they don't know how to take the rest of us there. They don't know what's stopping everyone from breaking through our sacred beliefs about how things work to get to the Truth. So the scientists and self-help gurus are really *both* right. Inside our worldview the self-help "Laws of Nature" make no sense. Outside they do, but until we all accept the simple fact that we're all part of one whole, hardly anybody is going to get "outside". Gurus who've stumbled outside our worldview by revelation will keep on shouting…. "there's a Truth outside you must see to discover what to do with your life". But those in-the-know will keep on calling them fools.

The Way of Zen

"Learning Zen is a phenomenon of gold and dung. Before you understand it, it's like gold; after you understand it, it's like dung".
- Zen Proverb

When the word "Zen" comes up, most of us immediately think of the strange, absurd, "koans" Zen Masters use to focus their students. Ask a Master how to find the Truth and he or she might say…."seek shelter from rain in the ocean" (little grasshopper) for instance. Or you might be advised to "go where you are not, and the Truth will seek you out". Those odd sounding self-contradictions are "koans". But why is Zen famous for paradoxes that most rational men and women stay as far away from as possible? And what on earth do they have to do with enlightenment? To get an idea what Zen's all about and why it doesn't predictably lead anyone to enlightenment, let's use the Great House of Knowledge analogy once more.

Zen may be thousands of years old, but our mistaken way of looking at the world, and all the knowledge contained within it, began much earlier. This Great House was already many stories high at the time Zen was founded. So imagine an ancient Eastern wise man about to discover the roots of Zen. He's digging deeper and deeper into the fabric of things, trying to understand the affairs of Man. Eventually he gets to the very basement of our House of Knowledge and encounters the Poem of Life. Struggling and struggling with this paradoxical looking feature of the world, revelation eventually lets him break through to see the Truth beyond and it sets him free.

Needless to say, the sage wants to share this Truth with men and women of his Age. But this man does not realize we've given all our knowledge a mistaken meaning that prevents people from seeing the Truth. Don't forget, he dug down to where the Poem of Life is, but it was revelation that let him break through without understanding how he got there. All our ancient sage can say is that he was near the paradoxical-looking Poem of Life when revelation happened. And so that's what he says….in the form of koans. Koans say….."the Truth is close to paradox".

Unfortunately, Zen doesn't tell us that paradox is a kind of approximation of wholeness we must aspire to, to find what life has to offer. As a matter of fact, Zen is famous for its "evasiveness". Zen never directly says what the Truth is or precisely how to see it. Again and again it just boggles the mind with koans. Certainly Zen can take you right to the foundations of our mistaken worldview called "Reason". But it is entirely possible to beat your head against the brick wall of Zen koans all your life without ever being gifted with the revelation needed to break through. Go that Way if you want to, but I wouldn't recommend it. What I do recommend is the Rule of Life coming up later. With it you can reliably train your brain to see wholeness in the world That will convince you your life can't be worth less than any life. Seeing that will set you free.

The Near-Death Way

Near death experiences appear to be Ways of having revelation, because people pronounced clinically dead…who come back to life…..frequently behave just like folks who see the Truth. Men and women who took everything for granted will begin to cherish every second of life for instance, just like people with real Life Missions. Individuals who venture near death slow down to appreciate the roses and begin to discover who they are and what to do with their lives as well. Just like those gifted with revelation.

But of course, near death experiences are just as unpredictable as everyday revelations. They come out of the blue and most sane people wouldn't really want to have this kind of painful Vision of the Truth. Inflicting great pain and suffering upon yourself won't guarantee any kind of revelation either….so don't even *think* about it. In short, I wouldn't aspire to getting near death to get your calling back if I were you.

But I *can* tell you a story about a man I knew personally who had one, and promptly got his Life Mission back. It took decades before I realized what really happened to him though. His name is Jacques, and I worked with him many years ago in Montreal. Here's what happened after Jack died.

Jacques Comes Back?

Jacques was a process operator in a big copper refinery where I worked back in nineteen-73. I'd say he'd been there fifteen years by the time I arrived. Anyway, Jacques had some very, very bad luck one weekend. A humongous dump-truck tee-boned Jacques at an intersection, demolishing his car and most of his body. Needless to say, Jacques was in the hospital when I arrived at work Monday morning. So there I was, joking around as usual, for about two seconds. Soon I realized something was really wrong somewhere, because every single soul was so far down in the dumps the place was like a cold meat-locker with the lights off. It was obvious something terrible had happened and I was afraid to ask.

Eventually I got up enough courage to question someone. Sure enough, there was reason to be bleak because Jacques was in a coma and the doctors didn't think he'd live. But as it turned out, Jacques' time wasn't up. It took many months of hospital and rehab for Jacques to recover, but eventually he returned home, more or less back to normal. It was during this final phase of Jacques' recovery at home that he surprised me. We were sitting at his kitchen table having a coffee and I said….."I guess you'll be back at the plant soon". It wasn't really a question, because Jacques was now fit as a fiddle and I assumed he'd be back any day. "Nope" said Jacques, just like that, like it was so obvious I should have known. "Why's that?" I stuttered, taken aback by his instant answer. "I'm heading to B.C. to train as a mountain guide" he said right back just as quickly.

"Mountain guide?" said I in disbelief. "You heard me" said Jacques with complete conviction. "What made you want to do that?" I asked. "Dying" Jack said. "Pardon me?" was about the only thing I could think of to say. Then he told me.

What Jacques Saw Over There

Jacques then described what I now know to be a classic near death experience. I hadn't even heard of any such thing at the time though, so I could hardly believe my ears. As the dust settled after the truck hit Jacques' car, he found himself floating above the accident looking down on the terrible scene. Then he was drawn up and into a long tunnel that took him to a kind of "being-of-light" that told him he would forever be surrounded by everlasting love. But then he was told he had to go back. Next thing Jacques knew, he was in an ambulance with a man pounding on his chest. Some days later, Jacques regained his full conscious awareness and knew something had changed. He knew he had to go where his heart had always been pointing him. I asked Jacques what he meant by that and he told me.

Suddenly in the hospital he saw why he'd always loved mountain guide movies and why wilderness adventures always fascinated him. Finally he realized why the outdoors had always spoken to him with a siren song. "My purpose in life is to be a mountain guide" said Jacques. "That's what I'm here to do, and that's what I'm going to do". Sure enough, he did it too. He never came back to work with us at the plant. Instead he found a west coast company that trains outdoor guides and went there. I've never heard hide nor hair from Jacques since, but did get stunned by him one day some ten years later. I was watching a nature film on television about the Grand Canyon that day. Being interviewed was a man who owned a tour company that takes folks down into the canyon on mules.

I'm sure you've already guessed who that was. It was Jacques. I could not believe my eyes or ears as he joyfully described how much fun his business is and how many people he's taken down the path to the Colorado river. Right there sitting on my couch I knew for sure that Jacques had had the kind of revelation that brought his true calling back to him. But don't forget. Standing in front of trucks to get your Life Mission back is not a good thing to do. You may well have a Vision of the Truth that will set you free as that big Mack flattens you out. But unlike Jacques, you probably won't come back to tell us about it.

The Wilderness Way

Have you ever heard of folks having revelation in the wilderness? Apparently some people venturing far out into wild places alone see the Truth out there. I'll admit I never saw the Truth that way, and I traveled alone in the woods many times. I never met anyone who did personally either, but I've read accounts of people who have. So how does that work anyway? Actually, it's easy to explain how it works, but the explanation won't help you much. In short it goes like this. The Truth you need to see is that everything around you is a different part of who you are. You and all things everywhere are really just different parts of one whole…..including other people.

But if there's anything that makes it difficult to see this Truth, it's other people, because it sure looks like they have completely *separate* "minds of their own". That seems to fly in the face of wholeness of course, because wholeness means *nothing* is really separated from you. Alright, but if you go way out into the wilderness by yourself, what do you leave behind? Other people. It's not just wild places that make for revelation, it's being left completely alone. That's the key to having wilderness revelation.

If you're absolutely alone in the wilderness, it's possible to begin seeing that everything around you is a different part of who you are. Why? You aren't distracted by those "other minds". That's all there is to it. But like I said, knowing that won't help you have revelation, because it doesn't help you change your basic beliefs about the world. For that you will have to re-train your brain with the Rule of Life.

The Ways of Oneness

"How can we know the dancer from the dance?" (William Butler Yeats)

If there's an "overworked" phrase where concerns having revelation it's "become one with the world". Gurus all over the place offer this advice, sometimes in the form of " getting rid of our ego or sense of self". Back in my own aimless years, I read long and hard about "becoming one with the world", but never found clear instructions for doing it. I often wondered what this would be like too, because it sounded scary. I mean, if you lose your sense of self do you just dissolve into the world …. disappearing completely? Isn't losing your sense of self completely just like dying? Until I'd had my own revelations, I just didn't get the idea of "oneness". I didn't realize that "becoming one" with things doesn't mean vanishing or anything like that. Now I understand it, and it's easy to explain.

To see what it means, first think about a daisy with ten petals. Each of those petals is actually "one with" all the others, because they're different parts of one whole. Each petal *is* the others, because they merge seamlessly together to form a unitary daisy. There's no real boundary between any of the petals. But those petals don't disappear, just because they merge with each other, losing their individual identities in the process.

There are still many different petals even as there is One whole daisy. Wholeness means that daisy is "One and Many" at the same time. Same with you and the world. To "become one with" the world then, all you need to do is change the way you see things. Instead of thinking you are a separate thing-unto-yourself, see everything around you as a different part of who you are....just like your arms and legs are. When you can actually see and believe this simple truth, the power of "becoming one with the world" will be upon you. You'll automatically begin manifesting your potentials once more by coming out of your shell and being yourself. Even better, by courageously exploring the world *your* way, you'll keep on growing until you're fully Human. In case you've forgotten, that will bring you your fair share of Bliss.

The Way of Meditation

As you might expect of a lost soul like myself who liked to read a lot, I eventually discovered books about meditation. Lots of books about meditation. After reading a few, I learned that meditation can certainly relax mind and body, but it doesn't necessarily lead to enlightenment. It didn't lead me to enlightenment for instance, and it rarely takes anyone there. So what's with this meditation stuff if it doesn't reliably deliver what's advertised? Meditation is a method of trying to take Mind and Body to that quiet, peaceful place where we're not tortured by fears of being judged. Ages-old meditative techniques can actually take you or I right up to that wall of fear I spoke of earlier, but won't help you get past it.

On this side of that wall is deep relaxation that can help with stress in today's world. On the other side is enlightenment that lets our dreams flow back into our lives. Unfortunately for too many people though, meditation will not reliably show anyone how to transcend that wall. To do that, you must change your basic beliefs about the world.

If you do, you'll discover the fruits of "transcendental meditation". We call them "peace of mind and purpose".

The Way of Religion

Most people wouldn't say religion has anything to do with the famous "what should I be doing with my life?" puzzle. But it does, because religion is about love, and love is the prescription for discovering why we're here. Why can love show us who we are and what to do with our lives? Because love is wholeness. Just ask two people truly in love what it feels like and they'll describe wholeness to a tee. Some say they feel "complete" for instance, as if they and their spouse were parts of a 2-piece jig-saw puzzle that's been seamlessly fit together to make one whole. Others talk as if their soul mate and they were One Spirit in two bodies. A classic description of "One and Many" if there ever was one. Otherwise called "wholeness". When in love as well, people frequently suggest they share so intimately, it's as if there is no real boundary between them, even as they remain different people. Sure enough, that's wholeness again in the form of love.

So why hasn't religion helped men and women grow Human over the centuries? At bottom all religions preach love after all. Our mistaken way of seeing the world makes it all but impossible to comprehend wholeness-as-love and benefit from it. It's as simple as that. Certainly Religion is a real Way men and women can aspire to seeing the Truth, but it's all but neutered by our selfish worldview. I'm not knocking religion here by the way, just trying to tell you this. Unless you train yourself to see the world differently, religion won't help you find your way.

The Way of Science

Ask the world's leading scientists if Science has an aim and many would say it's to understand the nature of reality. What's reality? Nobody knows. Thousands of years ago, the philosopher Plato said reality was something so absolutely separate from us, we can only know shadows of it…but never reality itself. Even today, scientists would agree with Plato. But to really understand where Plato is coming from here, you must realize what he's saying. Plato is telling us we can't know anything at all about "reality itself", which begs a simple question. Surely we must at least know the "shape of reality itself" by its shadows? If you see a shadow of a man for instance, you can tell if "he himself" is tall or thin for instance. But Plato says reality is a very different thing altogether. Reality is something we can't know anything at all about…..even as we know all kinds of things about it from its shadows.

By now you should be able to recognize this is nothing other than good old wholeness. That means the aim of science is to come to grips with wholeness. Unfortunately for science, its most cherished tool called "Reason" won't let it comprehend wholeness. Reason is a particular kind of "rationality" or way of making sense of the world that has limits. One of the limits of Reason is this. It will not let us comprehend the nature of reality. It keeps us from seeing that very Truth each of us needs in our lives to find happiness. Science really can be a Path to enlightenment if scientists would help us change our way of seeing the world. Give science a try if you want to then, but don't expect miracles. Miracles are on the "other side" of Reason.

My Way

Now that you've had a peek at some familiar Ways people have tried to see the Truth over the Ages, I'll offer you a better Way. The Rule of Life. The Rule of Life is better because it can change your beliefs about the world in a way that will let any or all those other Ways work. Every single one of those other Ways are bona fide Paths to enlightenment. The only trouble is, somewhere down each Path you'll encounter the wall of fear you're familiar with now. Learn how to take away that wall and you'll find the Truth on any Path. This Truth will bring you the true success you were put here to have. What's that? After all this you still just want money? I knew that was coming. I guess I have to hang a mega-carrot in front of your nose first.

Follow This Carrot To Your Dreams

Once again, please don't get me wrong. There's nothing wrong with having bucks, boats, baubles and goats. Like I said before, all that is a byproduct of making dreams come true. Make your dreams come true and you'll "attract an abundance" of it into your life. But that's just second prize. With your own dreams you get a bigger prize. That's the carrot I'm about to hang in front of you. It's called "real, authentic, human happiness".

Are you complete in yourself? [The root] answers, "No, my life is in the trunk and the branches and the leaves. Keep the branches stripped of leaves and I shall die." So it is with the great tree of being. Nothing is completely and merely individual". Edward Everett (1794 - 1865) US statesman, orator. In "Draper's Book of Quotations for the Christian World," by Edythe Draper, 1992.

Big Chapter Thirteen
Still Just Want Money?
(See What Dreams Are Worth First)

"Happiness is the only sanction in life; where happiness fails, existence remains a mad and lamentable experiment". -- George Santayana, 'The Life of Reason'

Would You Like a Dream Life?

Why would you want to make a big, huge effort to train yourself to see wholeness in the world? It gives you a decent shot at what's called "Happiness". Real, true-blue, authentic Happiness is what happens when you learn how to grow yourself *your* way. I can tell you this as well. By working your way towards your dreams, something absolutely amazing transpires. Something people talk about a lot, but rarely have. You'll "get a life". Actually, it's even better than that, because you'll *create your dream life*. So what does a dream life look like? It's a multi-faceted thing, like a diamond or emerald cut to sparkle like starlight. If you'd like a sneak preview of this amazing thing called "Being Human" please read what follows. It's here to make you want true success so badly, you'll work your tail off at Rule of Life exercises to get it.

Two Kinds of Happiness

On this third rock from the sun we live on, there are two kinds of happiness. Little and Big. Anyone can tell you what little happiness is. Money. Itty bitty kitties. Cash. Stuff like that. But Big Happiness is something else. Even ancient philosophers knew everyone wanted it, and wondered why most folks don't get it. As a matter of fact, sages in every generation have called Big Happiness the Holy Grail. Something men, women, and Mankind, has been dying to get for Ages.

But, sadly, they haven't got much because Reason has stopped them. Here you are. "Happiness-101". A primer on "Big Happiness". If you still don't want it after this, beam yourself back to the Mother Ship. Tell the other aliens what nut cases we earthlings are.

Before You Go On

Here's something I learned slowly. It may help you as you read on. All the little pieces of happiness below are like icebergs. When I was young I saw them floating on the surface of the world, but they looked like chips of ice to me. I had no idea how big or powerful they were. Certainly I saw that people wrote about them generation after generation, but I had no idea why. Here's why. Any one is worth more than a lifetime of money.

Happiness is Having Direction.

For the first forty years of my life, I had no idea what real direction was. I thought people with direction picked school courses out of a book, worked hard, and got themselves good jobs. Lucky ones got promoted, creating a terrific career that took them ever onwards and upwards. What I didn't realize was this. These folks are going somewhere alright, but not in the direction their hearts desire. Real direction comes from knowing who you can be. To have real direction, you need a deep insight into who you are, so you know for sure which way to take your life. Thankfully, as we'll see later, this insight called "Vision" returns like Magic when you dump fears of judgment. Once Vision comes back, you'll see your destiny ahead like a mountain peak on the horizon of your life. A mountain with your name on it. Who you can be is there waiting for you, and you'll be absolutely driven to become this person of your dreams.

Just so you know exactly what I'm talking about, here's what my Vision is like. I have a simple message of hope I want to get to as many people as possible, and to do that I must write it and speak it and convince as many people as possible to help me. There are a million different ways of getting this message out of course, and as we speak I don't even know all the ones I'll be trying. Even so, the Way to go is clear, because everything ahead is about spreading the Word. See what I mean? I see the Way with Vision, but not precisely how it will go down. Here's something even better about Real direction to think about too. Real direction gives you an aim in life that never goes away. Unlike direction picked out of a book that can fail when things get tough, true direction will always be there for you.

True Direction is Forever

"Fanaticism consists in redoubling your efforts when you have forgotten your aim".
-- George Santayana

Having a real aim in life is like having an internal compass to guide you if your life gets too dark to see clearly. In essence, you'll be able to look back with your mind's eye to where you came from. There you'll see the arrow-straight path you've been on, pointing to your destiny ahead. In real terms, you'll recognize things done and people and places in the past that were part and parcel of your Life Mission, each pointing you in one direction you'll feel compelled to go in. Now you can move forwards into the darkness ahead, lining yourself up with that Path behind. Eventually you'll break out of the darkness and see the Path stretching ahead forever. This kind of inner guidance is a good thing too, because everyone gets their share of dark days in life.

The death of people close to you can bring deep sun-less days for instance. Financial or other disasters can dim the light and blind you to what's ahead as well. With true direction born of Vision though, you can continue to inch ahead slowly, guided by inner knowledge of where you're going. In a sense, Vision creates its own light to help us through the darkness. On the other hand, people following book-direction are really lost when the darkness descends. Their books can neither comfort nor guide them when bleak days arrive. From personal experience I can tell you what real direction feels like too.

Your Direction Will Feel Like Mine

Real direction makes you feel like you're on a bobsled run. By that of course, I mean you'll be absolutely driven to take one path in life that's meant for you and only you. The Way ahead will be clear and obvious, and no other will make any sense to you. It's like you'd been thrown into a bobsled and pushed onto the course. If you've never seen a bobsled run, it's an icy downhill trail with walls on either side. Once you're on the slippery slope, you're not getting off until the end. Same with real direction. Once you have it, you're headed to your destiny…. no matter what. Certainly there will be obstacles, distractions, setbacks and bumps of all kinds along the way. But as you pick up speed your momentum will carry you through every one. As the gravity of your aim pulls you forward, you'll crash through any barrier.

Take me for instance. When my Vision returned, I had that message of hope I mentioned above to deliver. But friends, acquaintances and those-in-the-know said "give it up…..it's all nonsense". I felt like a guy trying to sell Elvis-on-velvet paintings to art connoisseurs. "What's the point" I'd sometimes wonder, as bleakness and despair moved in.

But then I turned around and looked back at the arrow of destiny in my life. It is an awe-inspiring thing to see a dead straight arrow beginning before birth and pointing ahead to the future you must create. Seeing that Path ahead and behind let me answer the "what's the point" question easily too. The point is, it's who I am. It's why I'm here. I'm destined to *try* and get the message out forever, even I fail for the rest of my life. Destiny is like that by the way. You can't know for sure how far you'll get with your aim in life….but you can know with certainty you'll keep on trying to go there. The world can judge you worthless for your beliefs as well, but you'll know you're following real direction. From personal experience I also can tell you that having direction forever is stunning and awe-inspiring. Not always fun and games. But truly amazing every step of the way.

Happiness is Called Fulfillment

Pretty much every helpful book out there these days promises the kind of authentic success in life that brings true fulfillment. Many can deliver on fulfilling dreams too, but you have to be very careful when it comes to this wondrous feature of being human. Fulfillment is all about that fabulous feeling you get when achieving desires of course, and anyone who's achieved goals has felt some fulfillment buzz. In my own aimless years even *I* had some fulfillment fun by making adopted dreams come true for example. But therein lies a problem with fulfillment. In reality there are two very different kinds of desires, so there are two equally distinctive kinds of fulfillment. Just for fun I'll call them names. One's called paltry, weak-kneed fulfillment. The other I like to call the real Magoo.

Not Week-Kneed Fulfillment

So how do you get a whole whack of weak-kneed fulfillment? By achieving weak-kneed desires of course. Those are the kind you pick from books. Desires to be a doctor, lawyer, or candlestick maker because they sound great. Desires mom and dad have for your life…that have nothing to do with who you are. Goals your teachers say will make you an important person. Dreams picked from the shelf because you have no real idea what to do with your life. And yes indeed, you really can fulfill these paltry desires. You can get yourself as much weak-kneed fulfillment as your stomach can stand. I did. But there's a far bigger kind of fulfillment out there. The Real Magoo. Real fulfillment is so much bigger than the paltry, pretend, adopted kind, it's a totally different animal altogether. Like a sixty pound ant perhaps. Interested? O.K., then listen up.

The Real Magoo

Real fulfillment comes from achieving your heart's desire. Everyone's heart desires exactly the same thing as well. Way down where our heart-song lives, all we want to do is be ourselves. We all want to grow that unique human being inside us until it blossoms. Everybody truly desires making a living by being in sync with who they are, and true fulfillment means following the plan we come here with. I hope that sounds suspiciously like the real Magoo to you, because it absolutely and for sure is exactly that. It doesn't matter if you're destined to be an artist, scientist, carpenter or musician either. Achieve your heart's desire and you'll have as much fulfillment as any human being ever had, because it's a bona fide Law of Nature. But of course, there's a catch. There always is. You have to know what your heart desires first.

By now you should know how to do that, even if you haven't got started on the path to real fulfillment yet. In case you're not sure, I'll tell you. A bit later in this book you will discover a Rule of Life and exercises cut directly from it. Do them religiously and with as much conviction as you can muster. They will change the way you see the world so your very own heart's desires flow back in to your life again. Go after those true desires and the Real Magoo will be yours. That reminds me of a sad fulfillment story, about a guy who never met Mr. Magoo.

Doctor Steve and Mister Magoo

Way back in the seventies, I was still trying to break my small engineering bones. Snap, crackle, pop they went, but I was stone deaf. Anyhow, one year I worked in a huge multi-national firm, churning out chemicals by the truckload. There I met Doctor Steve. Steve was world famous inside our company. He had a hundred patents to his name by the time I arrived, and there wasn't a bigger guru in the place. Born and educated in Germany, Dr. Steve was a real industrial professor. You could tell by looking. How? His office was big as a baseball diamond and twice as high and wallpapered with degrees and awards. Even the biggest bosses treated Dr. Steve like royalty too, so a sardine like me knew he was a big fish.

But curiously, big Steve and little me clicked just like that. Yours truly with donut-sized desk and slightly less knowledge and Steve with fifty plus years of big career behind him. Despite the stunning disparity, we were birds-of-a-feather under the skin, and ate lunch together in the company cafeteria three times a week, jawing about anything but work. Same thing in Steve's big office ten times a day. Not a scrap of work-talk there either.

So what the heck were Steve and I the Mutt and Jeff twins buzzing about? Puzzling, wondrous things about the world. Steve loved biology puzzles, like Darwin's evolution and the magical code of DNA, and would talk endlessly about them at the drop of a hat. The thing is, Steve wasn't a biologist. He was certainly educated to the hilt, but without a single study course in biology. As a matter of fact, Steve had enough Phd's from big ancient German Universities to create his own alphabet. If I recall rightly he had a doctorate in Physics and one in chemistry. But as far as I know, Steve never got close to the biological sciences. Even so, a passion for the natural world of biological things burned way down deep in Steve. A passion he never followed. Sadly, it was the same old story then as it is today, but with it's own twist. In Steve's day, industrial chemistry was big in Germany, but biology wasn't even on the map yet. Everyone in the know told Steve to take chemistry to "get a good job" of course. And biology? That was for nerds. Actually, they didn't have nerds in the early 1900's, but you get the idea. At any rate, Steve listened to Mom and Dad, and everyone else….. except his inner voice…and became a chemist. That brings me to the sad part of the story.

What Steve Learned

Steve retired while I was there. The company had a big party for him of course, but Steve had a little party a week later at his place just for friends, and I got to go. I'd say I was youngest there by forty years and the last to leave. By midnight even the heavy drinkers had gone. At the stroke of twelve, Steve's wife had more than enough nostalgia on rye as well and off to bed she went. That left me and Steve, sitting feet-up in his beautiful oak paneled library, jawing as usual. Suddenly Steve got really quiet and pensive and looked straight at me in a real scary way. Five seconds later he blurted out like an industrial terrorist…. "you'll never be a good engineer".

I was floored. In those days my self-esteem was big as a bee's head button, so I took it personally. I felt like I'd been shot by a howitzer and left to die on the battlefield. Steve saw me deflate like a bad balloon of course, so he picked up the thread and carried on. "Don't get me wrong" he said. "You have huge potential to do something really great…..but it's not going to be engineering". Did that pick me up out of my big dark hole? No it didn't. My poor little mushy ego had been stepped on big-time. So on he went. "If you apply yourself in engineering you'll probably make a big career of it, maybe even rising to the top and winning awards like me". "But I have to tell you something I learned". By then I was confused. Steve just said I could make a big career like his, but ten seconds earlier I was a spastic engineer? That sounded like complete nonsense to me, so I was all ears. I'd always loved absurd nonsense puzzles. Remember? Anyhow, Steve got all my attention with that one. Sure enough, he told me what he'd learned. I understood what he said alright, but it didn't help me at the time.

At the End of His Career

Steve always wanted to be a biologist. Once he had kids and mortgages and moocho other stuff though, he figured it was too late to pack up and change careers. Now that Steve's career was over, he had this to say. Being best at something your heart's not in leaves you half-empty. Steve was telling me it was possible in life to adopt dreams that don't come from the heart, and actually make them come true. Only to discover at the end of it all that they're not *your* dreams. Sadly, even all Steve's accomplishments left him feeling empty. The bottom line is, Steve never met Mr. Magoo. He never had the real sense of fulfillment that comes from following your heart's desire. Steve was trying to tell me I wouldn't either, if I stuck to engineering. It was obvious to Steve I didn't have real engineering bones. It was equally obvious to me too, but Steve couldn't tell me what I should be doing with my life.

Only my inner voice could do that, but at that time of my life I couldn't hear it. Fears of being judged had screwed the tap in my head tight shut. No chance of real fulfillment for me yet.

Happiness is Being Important

"Half of the harm that is done in this world is due to people who want to feel important" . -- T. S. Eliot, 'The Cocktail Party'

If you look around right now, you'll see all kinds of unhappy bad things going on because people don't believe they're important. Violence of all kinds for instance, not to mention folks spaced out on drugs, trying to dull the pain of feeling unimportant. In short, if you or I don't believe our souls have any worth at all, we can self-destruct or go postal and try to destroy the world. Feeling important is therefore important to everyone. It's part and parcel of being happy. That much is obvious to pretty much all of us. But here's something a whole lot less obvious. Every single one of us is absolutely equally important, and cannot be otherwise, because it is a bona fide Law of Nature. The weakest man is as important as the strongest. The richest King has the same net Human worth as the poorest person on the planet. The Tree of Life makes sure of that. If this doesn't seem to make sense to you, you're not alone, but I have something to tell you.

It's not because it isn't true, it's because you can't see the Truth. On the other hand, if you use the Rule of Life to open your eyes, you will see an astoundingly happy thing ahead of you. You can have as much "self worth" as the biggest, richest, most accomplished man or woman on the planet. Because it is already there for you. It's your birthright. As a matter of fact, you always have been worth as much as anyone anywhere….even when you couldn't see it.

So here's something for you to think about. If you've always wished you were a big chief or rich person, so you'd be important, you can stop wishing. You don't have to *wish*. Just train yourself to see the world's whole and your eyes will open up so wide you'll see the Truth. The truth is you're exactly as important as any man, woman or child who's ever lived or will live. Believe me, seeing that will make you really happy, because happiness is being important.

Destiny's a Happy Thing Too

Destiny is something most people simply don't believe in. But when you begin to experience it for yourself, it will more than knock your socks off. Some time after I'd begun manifesting my own potentials once more, the full, awe-inspiring weight of destiny was made apparent to me, and I made up a little story to try and describe what it feels like. This one. Imagine your life is like a Journey down a path. Scattered on either side of the road along the way are millions of different things of every conceivable kind. By the age of five years, you begin collecting bits and pieces in a knapsack and carrying them along with you. How do you decide what to pick? Some things you choose because they're just plain attractive, sparkling away on the side of the road. Others you decide to make your own because friends or teachers tell you to. And on you go, picking and choosing by flipping coins and taking the advice of T.V. gurus. Now let's fast forward thirty years or so. You have maybe five hundred things in your knapsack, none of which seems to have anything to do with any other. In fact, it looks like a big bag of junk to you. Then one day you have a near-death experience and it changes the way you see the world.

It's a Mind-Boggling Thing

Some time after coming back from death you're taken aback by a little voice from somewhere deep inside. "Dump out all those things you've been carrying around in your rucksack" it says, making you wonder if you've gone crazy. You don't feel particularly insane, so you do. So there you are, staring at those five hundred little bits and pieces randomly collected for several decades. Suddenly something begins to dawn on you that stuns you beyond belief. Every single piece is a watch part. In fact, on the ground before you is precisely every part needed to make an exquisite watch. And nothing else. But this just doesn't seem to make any sense to you at first. How on earth is it possible to pick nothing but watch parts from the millions of things along the way….by chance? You didn't even know they *were* watch parts until ten seconds ago. It just doesn't compute. But believe it or not, you are about to get an even bigger surprise.

What could possibly be more surprising? Realizing you're here to assemble that watch will surprise you more. Knowing why you're here won't just surprise you in fact. From personal experience I can tell you there are no words in any language that will adequately describe the kind of surprise being confronted by your destiny brings. Just in case you're wondering, it's a beautiful kind of surprise, and it can be yours. All you need to do to get it is remove your fears of being judged. After some time and with some work, you'll begin to experience the beauty of destiny yourself. In everyday practical terms, you'll look back and see every single thing in your past life is there for a purpose. It's all a necessary part of your calling. A Life Mission revealed with stunning clarity as you learn how to become yourself. Take me for example. In my case I saw all my crazy reading and aimless wandering and absurd questioning as jig-saw pieces I'd assemble to get my Mission message out.

Looking back at my life I finally understood that each day and every trial was a lesson learned. Each was needed to make my dream life real. And so, when you look back at your life and see every part adds up to a single purpose, you'll know what destiny feels like. It's a feeling like no other, and I guarantee you can have it for yourself. Just pay attention to the Rule of Life coming up soon.

The Fountain of Youth Will Make You Happy

I'm sure you've heard the expression "fountain of youth" before, and thought nothing of it. If you're at all like me (and I know you are) you think it's just an old saying or meaningless phrase. I know why too. It's because you think youth has something to do with your age. Why do you think that? Because most people start off life physically, intellectually and Spiritually fit.....and go downhill from there. They begin growing all facets of their being and then give it up. Not everyone of course. Just 95.%. The rest stay young all their lives, because youth has nothing to do with how long you've been here. It has to do with envisioning a dream life and creating it. It's all about enthusiasm, and growing and adventure and being surprised by what tomorrow has to offer. As people in every generation have said, youth is a state of mind and body. It's a way of being, not a clock. People who understand what being young is all about really and truly know how to bathe in a fountain of youth as well. I can tell you how to turn that fountain on for yourself if you'd like.

You would? O.K., but first I want you to remember that fears of being judged are an inhibiting Force that keep your potentials from flowing into the world. To become young, you have to learn how to release your Spirit. When you do, ideas about who you are and what to do with your life will come flooding out of that shell they've been in. Like a river.

Or a fountain. You'll be deluged with dreams of your very own that you'll work to make real. A brand new you will continue to be reborn as you make your way to where your destiny is. All that fun and joy and enthusiasm "youth" is famous for will stream into your life once more. Still don't believe this is the real and true fountain of youth? Go find a real person driven to fulfill a life-mission. Someone in their seventies, eighties or hundreds. Here's what you'll see. They're still as vibrant and enthusiastic about life as any twenty-something. They may be more seasoned and wiser and less inclined to make the same mistakes they made before. But they're still filled with wonder about the world and excited about what each new day might bring. Just like young people are supposed to be. Like we're all supposed to be actually, from birth to death, as we carry out our appointed callings. Like I said. Getting rid of your fears of being judged will literally let you tap into the real, true, mythological fountain of youth. I am not kidding either.

Real Self-Esteem is a Happy Thing

If you take a Journey with me to change the way you see the world, you'll eventually have something I call "Real self-esteem". Real self-esteem is nothing like ordinary self esteem. It is an absolutely mind-boggling and eye-opening experience the likes of which are almost unbelievable. Interested? Alright, I will now explain exactly what I mean. To start off, we'll review ordinary self-esteem. We'll simplify things a bit to get the point across. Let's say you're a monolithic guy or gal with one single talent that defines who you are. You're a great poker player. O.K., so you can feel great about or "esteem" that one talent of yours. You can say "I feel good because I've been gifted with poker playing skills". That's ordinary self-esteem, because you esteem...well....yourself. Authentic, or "Real" self-esteem is stunningly more powerful. To get some idea what it's like, imagine you've managed to begin seeing the world around you is who you are.

You've realized that you and the world are just different parts of one whole. Now you're beginning to see that the talents of other people are flowing into your life like gifts. Gifts meant for you as much as them. You'll see the guy next door is a world class marathoner and the lady down the street is a pianist without compare. But now you esteem *their* talents like you esteemed your own before. Why? Because you see you and they are really just different parts of each other....so *their* gifts really *are* yours. Once you truly see the world this way, you'll be bowled over by a simple fact. You'll esteem the talents and skills and accomplishments of every single soul you meet.....just like you esteem your own poker playing skills. You'll get big joys from your talents and successes, and just as big joys from the talents and successes of everyone around you. You feel first class if you win, and feel just as good for winners if you don't. When you get a prize you'll be happy about it, but you'll be happy to see other people get prizes too. If something good happens somewhere, you'll feel like it happened to you...and it'll bring your sense of worth and value up.

Eventually... as the full idea of wholeness dawns on you, you'll esteem the entire universe, as you literally "become one with it". There you go. Real self-esteem is a universal, infinite, forever sense of importance and significance. That's a different kind of animal isn't it? Like horses that look like goats that look like horses perhaps? It sure is, and it is a wonderful happy part of being human. If you want this kind of amazing self-esteem without end....it's yours. Just learn to see that the world is whole and you'll have it. Like Eddie. His story is below.

Eddie's Real Self-Esteem

Way back in public school, I met a guy with Real self-esteem. His name was Eddie and he was mentally handicapped.

Ed was in grade school with me, because there weren't places for kids with special needs back then. Thank goodness, or I couldn't have learned anything from Eddie. Anyhow, here's Ed's story. Like you'd expect in today's sad world, Eddie was right at the bottom of the social barrel somewhere down by the squashed pickles and flattened eggs. Kids taunted him every chance they got. It would have driven most kids to the nut house, but not Eddie. He just smiled and waved back. Ten kids yelling twenty names at Eddie? No problem. Smile and wave. A whole pack circling Eddie like wolves? Smiley wavey. It made one heck of a big impression on me at the time, because it looked like Eddie knew something the rest of us didn't. He did too, and here's how I found out. One day I was sitting on the school steps waiting for the school bell when Eddie wandered over and sat down beside me. Soon a small flock of mean-spirited kids flew in, like sharks attracted to my chum Eddie. Boy-o-boy, now there's fun and games to play. "Hey Dumbo!" they howled and squealed, like little maniacs in a big padded cell. "Why doncha drop dead!". Guess what? Sure enough. Nice big smile with a fine firm wave of the hand from Eddie.

Eddie Had it But Most of Us Don't

To say the least, I didn't get it, because my brains weren't big enough. Even so, I was very curious about impossible looking things like that, so I just had to ask. "How come that don't bug you Eddie"? I said. Back came the old "sticks and stones will break your bones, but names will never hurt you" thing. But it wasn't Eddie's words that impressed me. I'd heard that old bones and stones saying lots of times by then. It was the way he said it that went to my soul and stayed there. Even me the slow-witted guy could see Eddie knew something about that old fable I didn't. He looked me in the eye and said the words really, really slowly, trying to impress something on me that I was missing.

Ed knew they meant something big and was trying to teach it to me, trying to pass on a gemstone to a fellow human being. But I confess I simply had no clue. In fact, it took me fifty years to get it. Here's what I was too thick to get that day. Eddie knew his life couldn't be worth less than anyone else's life, because he saw the Truth of the world clearly. Why do I say that? He acted just like folks who do. Now I'd like to say thank-you. Thank you for *trying* to tell me the Truth Eddie. What a gift that would have been if I'd really understood it like you did.

Doing Your Best Makes You Happy

When I was a kid, Mom always said…"just do your best son, that's all that's important". I'll bet your Mom did too. The thing is, my best was almost never really best. It didn't really seem to matter what I did, someone was always better. Those real best guys and gals always got patted on the back and blue ribbons too. And we second, fifth and last bests? No one noticed. Does that sound a little bit familiar to you? O.K., so why should you try and do your best if it's not the best? What the heck is the point of that old saying if nobody really cares about your best?

The point is this. Doing your best doesn't mean being number one, or two, or twenty-two. It means "doing your own thing". It's knowing what to do with your life…..and doing it. That ancient piece of wisdom it trying to tell us that growing ourselves *our way* until we flower is critically important to who we are. We won't be happy if we don't do exactly that. If that sounds suspiciously like a calling to you, you're right. It's also why most folks never get fired up about doing their best. For obvious reasons. Which are? They don't have a clue what *their* thing is. It's kind of hard to do your thing after all….if you don't know what it is. Our inner voices are supposed to tell us what our thing is, but when fears of being judged turn the taps off….we're lost.

And you? Would you like to benefit from "doing your best" like mom and dad keep on saying? All you need to do is learn how to let yourself out of its shell. You need to understand what's stopping you from being yourself. Take away the inhibiting Force keeping your reason for being from you and you'll see. Doing *your* best really and truly *is* best…..for you and only you.

Happiness is an Adventure

"The day shall not be up so soon as I…. To try the fair adventure of tomorrow".
  -- Shakespeare, 'King John,' V,v,21.

If you look up the word "adventure" in a dictionary, it'll say it's an "exciting and remarkable experience". With that in mind, I always wondered why so many gurus kept on saying "Life's an adventure", because in my own aimless years there was very little excitement and not much to remark on. In fact, it went something like this. When the alarm went off I'd drag myself out of bed and drive to work I didn't give a parrot's hoot about. As soon as I got there on a Monday morning, I'd begin Thanking God Friday was around the corner. I'd wade into my work and do a good job, but without any feeling of purpose or real sense of heartfelt accomplishment. Because there was zero aim to all my efforts, I didn't have the satisfaction of building anything…..much less a dream life. It all just seemed to add up to one big heap of meaningless projects completed and goals achieved. An adventure? Not even close.

Maybe you can identify with this description of "getting nowhere"? As a matter of fact, even my vacations were dull and lackluster things, because I really wasn't re-creating myself. Why not? For work and play to be an adventure, you have to be engaged in making your own dreams come true.

You have to be inching forward to your destiny to be excited about it all and find every step truly remarkable. When you finally get your very own dreams back though, you'll see what's meant by adventure in life. It's surely not all fun and games....but it really is something to write home about. Here's what I mean. The most amazing thing about life when you have something to do with it is the growing that takes place. You get to stand back and watch brand new parts of who you are come into the light of day. It's a bit like watching some flower grow that you've never seen before. It continues to surprise you with its shape and color. But make no mistake. This is you yourself we're talking about surprising you here. It makes you really wonder who you can eventually be. It is a very remarkable thing to watch *yourself* grow. If you got to travel through some enchanted forest filled with amazing new sights and sounds, you'd probably return to gush over the adventure. When you enchant *yourself* with newness and growth and surprising turns of fate, it's an adventure beyond compare.

I know the idea you can surprise *yourself* sounds a bit odd, but creative folks tell us it happens to them all the time. Songwriters and poets often say the words or melodies "come to them" in ways that take them by surprise for instance. Sometimes the solution to a puzzle will come to we lesser folks suddenly and surprisingly too. Growing yourself is much like that. A brand new you will keep on getting born again and again, in ways that will really surprise you. Having experienced it myself now for quite some time, I can tell you that this kind of adventure is a very happy thing. No doubt about it. Happiness is an adventure. If this sort of life appeals to you, the Rule of Life coming up can make it happen.

Love is Happiness Writ Large

"All work is empty save when there is love". -- Kahlil Gibran, 'The Prophet'

The wall of fear we've been talking about now forever, does all sorts of bad things to you. Here's maybe the worst. It will make it all but impossible for you to have true love in your life. Why? Fear of being judged will keep you from being yourself, trapping you inside that shell of yours. Unfortunately, it's hard to find love if you're scared to be yourself. Terrified of being judged, you'll barely explore the world of people at all. Even worse, Mr. or Mrs. Right could show up on your doorstep tomorrow morning, but you and he or she just won't recognize each other. How come? You have to "know thyself" first….and that's exactly what fear of being judged stops you from doing. But what the heck….let's imagine by some miracle the guy or gal of your dreams gets paired up with you by some computer dating service.

You're still out of luck. Love still won't happen, because real love will ask you to grow…. but you won't. You're too scared. It's going to ask you to become selfless as well, to fuse intimately with another soul. Sadly, you're not going there either… because you're afraid of being rejected. You just won't take a chance….on love. So there you are. If you can't get past fears of being judged to figure out who you are, you'll end up like Tony. Or the millions of similar people in every city. Remember Tony's story? He had no idea who he was either, so he blindly picked the wrong soul-mate off the shelf. Sorry, but it's true. If your number one goal is to find that love of your life, you'd better get your calling back. It'll prepare you to become one with another human being, while remaining uniquely different. In the ultimate expression of wholeness. We call it "love".

When You Get Happy, You Get Peace of Mind

Back before I'd started growing up again, I heard lots of people talking about "peace of mind". I must say it sounded fabulous, but truth be told, I had no idea what it really meant.

After I discovered the full truth, I was shocked to realize how little I understood about this common expression. I simply didn't comprehend that we're all stuck in a huge "war of mind". Here's what I mean. As I mentioned earlier, in today's world, every waking moment is a kind of examination, with everyone judging us all the time. People are looking at our size, shape, color, strength, and appearance, ready to judge us worthless if we don't measure up. Our cars, houses and financial success is assessed by everyone and judgment pronounced. Unhappy is he or she who isn't rich enough. But it gets worse. We're all so inundated with the idea of "being biggest and best" every which way possible, we judge *ourselves*. Billboards and televisions asking us to buy this or that…so we're better than the next person, make us stop and see if we're up to snuff. We pass judgment on ourselves and feel bad if we don't make the grade. Some folks in some places might even find themselves in danger for their lives if judged and found wanting. People of one color will literally kill folks of a different feather for "being different" for instance. All bad stuff that comes from judging each other.

Alright, so let's stop for a moment and think about this. You and I are in a "war of mind" because every which way we turn, we'd better be covering our backs…lest someone judge us and inflict some kind of mental or physical harm. Enemies are left, front, and right behind us…waiting to catch us off guard. It's like being in a real war, because we can be made to believe our souls belong in hell if enough people pass judgment. A very sad state of affairs to say the least. But here's where peace of mind comes in. If you change the way you see the world, you'll understand that it is simply impossible to be judged. Your soul can't be worth less than anyone or anything. Why? Because we all share One Life, One soul, One heart-of-hearts. When you get to this place, you're no longer attacked every moment of your life by fears of judgment and the war-of-mind stops.

You now know what it's like to have real peace-of-mind and why it's so justifiably famous. It's part and parcel of what it means to be truly happy. Here's a real-life peace of mind story for you too. Mine.

A Peace of Mind Story

In my own life for many, many years, my mind was surely at war with the world and itself. Like every soul ever born, I desperately wanted to be myself, but every which way I turned I didn't seem good enough. In the early years for instance, most kids scorned my absurd jokes and some girls wouldn't dance with me. Teachers loved students at the top, but hardly paid attention to me some steps down. Even when it came time go get my hair cut, I'd worry myself silly... because I might not look right when it was all done. As I eventually moved into the corporate world of business I was always pretending to be an engineer or industrialist, neither of which is true down deep where I live. I was always afraid I'd get exposed somehow. But do you know what it's like to live a lie in every aspect of your life? It's like being on the battlefield night and day, hoping you don't get caught out in the open....being yourself....or caught pretending to be something you're not. In short, you're damned if you do (be yourself) and damned if you don't.

That was me for a long time. But after I began to wake up and work towards my very own dream, something astonishing happened. Peace of mind. I just began "being myself" using what I had where I was at the moment to further my dreams. I no longer worried what people really thought, and was surprised to find I was even more effective than ever. I was also amazed to discover that magical things happen when you live your life being yourself. Opportunity and success and reward seems to come out of nowhere as you use the Rule of Life to make your own luck.

It's like having a great calm descend upon you, even as you fight business or other battles. With a quiet confidence born of "knowing thyself" you go into the darkness unafraid to be yourself. This is what's called "peace of mind" and it comes from knowing the Truth of the world.

Happiness is Real Power

"To live happily is an inward power of the soul". -- Marcus Aurelius, 'Meditations'

Why do you think youngsters today want to be "bad boys" (or girls) and spend half their time playing games based on nothing but violence? If you step back and take a look at this sad state of affairs, you should be totally flabbergast, but I'll bet you don't even bat an eyelash, because all things bad and violent are more common than sand on beaches. I don't think anyone could possibly argue about that in a world where there are more handguns than church pews and entire nations commit most of their gross national product to building war machines.

But why on earth would human beings want violence in their lives? It's fair to say that anyone who's experienced violence first-hand did not enjoy it. Would you like to be shot, tortured, blown up or made to watch that kind of thing happen to your loved ones? Are you a big fan of pain and suffering…being inflicted upon yourself? Not likely. In fact, even the most hardened criminals don't like violence…foisted upon themselves. So how come children of all ages take delight in harmful things? For one thing, they can't see they're really harming themselves. Foolish discrimination makes them believe violence inflicted on others is fine but violence inflicted on them is not.

But that's not what makes us violent in the first place. What makes people strike out with force is a deep need to feel important. A feeling of importance that disappeared with their reason for being. Violence is all about having power over others. We do it because we believe power gives us importance. With the power tools of violence, (guns, knives, lies, aircraft carriers etc.) anyone can be strong, rich, and powerful....all synonyms for "important".... by force. Give a teeny-bopper a gun for example and he or she may well take your wallet and maybe even your life if it stands between them and the car they want to look good in. But guns aren't always needed for violence. People in positions of corporate power can take the life-savings of millions too...by abusing the power of their office. Becoming as important as the billions of dollars they stole can make them. Politicians can gain importance (money) by taking graft, and police can make a mockery of law and order by stealing drugs to sell. All in an attempt to gain the self-worth that disappears when we lose our callings. In short, we're violent because we don't have that undying sense of infinite and everlasting importance human beings crave. But here's something for you to think about. Violence isn't necessary. Any man or woman creating their dream life gets as much personal importance as they can possibly handle. To these inspired people, violence is simply insane.

Enough's Enough You Say?

Okay dear reader, by now you've probably had enough "happiness is" stuff, and (hopefully) want some for yourself. So let's get going to do exactly that. Now comes that Rule of Life I've been promising.

Chapter Fourteen
Want To Know Why You're Here?
(Follow the Rule of Life)

"You can come to understand your purpose in life by slowing down and feeling your heart's desires". - Marcia Wieder US writer, motivational speaker

Is It Stunned Cows in Crop Circles?

The Rule of Life comes directly from the deep and abiding Truth of the world, and we're going to cut exercises from it to help you find your Way. But before we carry on, I'd like to tell you how most folks react to this Rule at first. Kind of like three dazed cows caught making a crop circle. What on earth does that mean? It means people don't recognize the cure for their unhappy lives, even when offered it. This is a very scary thing if you think about it. I'll make up a little story to characterize this frightening state of affairs. Imagine a man lost in a desert and dying of thirst. If he doesn't find water soon, he's toast. Suddenly he gets to the top of a sand dune and encounters a water tap on top of a pipe going down into oceans of fresh water.

But this man has a little problem. He doesn't have a clue what a tap is. He doesn't realize that the silver metal thing there on top of a pipe can be turned open to bring life-giving water to him. Salvation is there right in front of him, but it's not going to happen. He wanders away, still looking for water, and dies. Alright, now imagine it's *you* dying of thirst in the desert, but this time someone comes along and tells you what the tap is for. But instead of turning the tap to drink your fill, you call your benefactor a fool and wander away looking for water. Totally ridiculous you say? Yes it is, but if you're not careful, the same kind of thing can happen to you in the very pages of this book.

I am now going to tell you how to use the Rule of Life to let your own life-creating potentials flow into the world. And it is entirely possible you could ignore me.

It's a Rule to Train You (To Get-A-Life)

So what exactly is the Rule of Life anyway? It's a very simple rule that comes from seeing how the world really works. Once you see the simple Truth, the Rule of Life falls out into your hands like you'd opened a box and dumped it out. If you'd like to discover this awe-inspiring potent Rule of rules yourself, I can help you do it right now. First let's review the Truth. In case you've forgotten, it's this. Everything in the world is a different part of you. Alright, so if the world is who you are, how do you think you should be treating the world? The ridiculously simple answer to this question is the Rule of Life. That's it below…in big black letters.

Treat The World Like It Was Part of You.

Disappointed? I hope not, because this Rule is more powerful than anything you have ever encountered and ever will encounter. But I will admit there's not much to it. I'll bet it sounds familiar to you as well. No? C'mon now, think for a second. Doesn't it remind you of the old Golden Rule you were taught in grade school? It should, because the Golden Rule is a watered down version of the Rule of Life. Just in case you live at the center of the earth and haven't ever encountered the Golden Rule before, I'll spell it out for you. It too is big and black, but not even a millionth as powerful as the Rule of Life.

Treat Others As You'd Want To Be Treated

Just to make sure we're both on the same page here, let's compare these two rules for a moment. Here's what the Golden Rule says. "Other people are just like you, so treat them like you'd want to be treated". Yes? Precisely, but the Rule of Life goes two steps better. Here's step one. The Rule of Life doesn't just say other people are *like* you....like the Golden Rule does. It says other people *are* you. Yes....*are* you. You and they are different parts of each other. Parts of One whole. Still with me? O.K. ....here's step two. The Rule of Life doesn't stop with people, like the Rule of Gold does. It says treat everything in the world like it's a different part of you. Because it is. Just so we don't leave anything to your imagination here, the Rule of Life is telling you that everything under the sun is part of you. It's saying in no uncertain terms....."treat everything like it was your own arms and legs and nose and face". Why is it telling you to do that?

This awesome rule wants you to realize, slowly but surely perhaps, that there is only One Life in the Universe that everything shares. It wants you to burn that into your brain until you no longer have any reason to fear being judged. Taking real action according to this rule in the real world is what helps you do that. The Rule of Life is saying...."don't just *think* about the Truth of the world....*live* it every day by *acting accordingly*". Alright, but you should also be able to see that the Golden Rule is simply a watered down version of the Rule of Life. Why would we water down the Rule of Life? I'll tell you the sad reason why.

It's The Golden Rule on Steroids

Way back in the pages of this book I suggested that Mankind chose to see the world the wrong way a very long time ago. Maybe as far back as ten thousand years men and women silently agreed that the world was filled with many different separate things....people included.

In reality, the world is One whole, but once everyone had chosen a selfish way of seeing things, the simple Truth became nonsense. The Rule of Life became ridiculous. In a world where everything is believed to be a separate "thing-unto-itself" the Rule of Life is all but useless. The closest thing to this Rule in our selfish world today then, is the Golden one. The Golden Rule is a pitiful approximation of the life-giving truth, because it continues the belief things are separate. How? It says "treat others like you'd want to be treated". The word "others" means separate souls. Sadly, in reality, there are no "others". In reality we are all One. See what I mean here? The Golden Rule can't help us discover who we are and what to do with our lives, because it doesn't tell us the full truth. It doesn't tell us the world's whole. It can't get us past our fears of being judged. No doubt the Rule of gold been working small miracles for thousands of years, but it's not powerful enough for big miracles.

Why Do We Need a More Powerful Rule?

What do we need a more powerful Rule for? Well, the short answer is to get your dreams back of course, and help millions finally know what their hearts really desire. But in case you somehow didn't notice, we need a better Rule to stop Mankind from going to hell in a missile. It's obvious if you think about it, but frightening. Keep in mind, our mistaken way of seeing the world goes back many generations and starts right at the heart of our collective soul. That makes us treat everything in the world selfishly. Unable to see that we and the world are one and the same, we happily harm different parts of ourselves, with predictable pain.

Take the environment for example. We soil our own nests every day, and wonder why we get sick from the poisons. Then there's what we call "commerce".

People everywhere looking out for number one, greedily destroy people, things or places, all of which are needed to sustain their very own lives. Sounds suspiciously suicidal? It absolutely is. Now we get to bigger and badder things. Entire Nations try to impose their will on other countries and have been doing so for a long time. Ever since we chose to see the world the wrong way actually. Then they wonder why it all comes back as terrorists in the night. And why does this bad Karma come back around to haunt these very same nations? They started off doing harm to what they thought was "others". But it was they themselves all along, so nobody should be surprised that big pain comes back. There are lots of other terrifying things our mistaken worldview is doing to us too, but I'm sure you get the idea.

Which brings us to the Rule of Life. It can stop all this destructive nonsense for very simple and obvious reasons. It's not obvious to you? Of course it is. Once people and nations see the world is who they are, they won't want to harm themselves. It's as simple as that. But until we all comprehend wholeness, everything we do will be fundamentally self-destructive. We will be destroying ourselves without even realizing it, because the truth is the truth, even when we can't see it. And so, unless we have a better Rule of conduct for Human affairs, our mistaken worldview called "Reason" will keep on destroying us. Pardon me? You're not interested in big miracles like saving the world? You just want to save your life? Sorry. I forgot.....it's *your* nickel you forked out for this book....so let's get back to *your* life.

The Rule of Life Will Change Your Life

So what can the Rule of Life do for you? It can get your calling back and give you every ounce of authentic happiness ever made, but only if you use it to train yourself to see the world differently.

Don't forget, even the Rule of Life won't do a darn thing for you if you don't work at it. Yes you have to actually get up and do something, because working, stretching, and trying makes things happen. It's what makes dreams real. That's why all those self-help books have rules, methods and mantras in them. Never noticed? Take a few minutes to look at several hundred. I'll bet you noticed a theme running through pretty much all of them? They're all How-To books. Like…."How to Make Mr. Money Your Girlfriend". Or my personal favorite…."How to Find Aliens in Your Garage". No question about it, how-to means to-do. Those book authors aren't dummies. They know nothing happens without work. You won't even find aliens without looking in your garage. Still not convinced? Ask your self this. Do weight lifters get stronger by reading weight lifting books? I don't think so. How about mountain climbers. Have you ever seen any conquer Everest by watching Everest movies? No you haven't. Whether you want to believe it or not, nothing happens without work. But just in case the mere thought of work depresses you, here's something to pick your spirits up. The Rule of Life will bring you a very different kind of work. I call it "Real Work" because it's the stuff dreams are made of. One taste of Real Work and you'll never ever let it go.

This Rule Offers You Real Work

What the heck is Real Work? It sure isn't "job-work". Job-work is where you put all kinds of effort into doing something your heart isn't in. Job-work is working like hell to make money and things that will leave you feeling half-empty at the end of it all. Real work is making something much more magical and mysterious and miraculous. It's making the life of your dreams. As a matter of fact, Real work is creating life itself as you go. In everyday terms, Real work is making a living being yourself. And don't forget this.

By taking your life in the direction that's right for you, you automatically get a share of authentic happiness that's as big as anyone ever gets. Real work is how a stunningly unique part of the Universe unfolds with explosive potential. In case I lost you there…..that'd be YOU! It's working to make a Human Being flower, by fulfilling your purpose on earth. You have exactly what it takes to make your own life too, so you'll enjoy it all. Yes you'll strain and pain and flounder and sometimes get hurt, but when the going gets tough, you'll get going. Believe me, when you know where you're going in Life, getting going is fun. Even the hard parts. So don't get shy when I mention work. End of lesson. When you're back from recess I'll show you the exercises I made from the Rule of Life.

Chapter Fifteen
Six Rule of Life Exercises
(Will Free Your Soul)

"He who looks outside dreams, he who looks inside awakens." (Carl Gustav Jung)

One More Time

Remember that guy in a desert up there who died of thirst? He didn't realize the tap in front of him was piped into water. Before you read on, I want to revisit this man's predicament, because it could be yours. Unfortunately, I've seen lots of folks stare blankly at Rule of Life exercises and then go looking "outside" for their hearts' desires. Like that poor fellow lost in the Sahara, they just don't understand where their dreams are. They're in that vast ocean of potential within us, that no soul can actually visit. But thankfully, you can let your dreams come to you, by ridding yourself of fears of judgment. As a matter of fact, there's no other way to know what your heart really desires.

Just so you know, here's a few things that won't get your calling back. Becoming an expert at making choices won't do it. If you're still afraid of being yourself, you'll just have too many choices, and no way to decide. Going to the far ends of the earth looking for your dreams won't help either, because your dreams are as close to you as can be, locked up behind that fear. Finally, no amount of knowledge will help you. You can take as many college and night courses as your wallet can support, but unless revelation comes with your diploma, you'll be out of luck. When all is said and done, the only thing you need to know with certainty is this. There's only One Life we all share. If you're ever going to understand your life is beyond judgment, that's what you have to know. So don't waste your time and effort looking "outside". If you do, you'll never know what to do with your life. Pardon me?

You want a real life example of someone who keeps on looking....
"outside"? Here you go. Joe's story.

Joe's Story

Joe is an old friend of mine who's been trying to figure out what to do with his life for a long time now unsuccessfully. But don't get me wrong. I'm not saying Joe isn't successful. Holy pups who woof and wiggle their way out of the pound! That's the last thing you'd say about Joe, because he's accomplished many impressive things. After accounting college for example, Joe worked his way up the ladder to become Chief Financial Officer for a big public company. A "really good job" if there ever was one. Fifteen years later he jumped ship and went out on his own as a real, competent, bona fide consultant. Just so you know, that'd be the exact opposite of yours truly the incompetent engineering non-guru. No doubt about it, Joe had real accounting bones, and helped folks with big bucks keep money from the Tax man. As you might expect, that put Joseph into the income stratosphere himself. In short, Joe had created one of those careers dreams are made of. Hadn't he? Yes indeed he had....but not Joe's dreams. Something was still wrong somewhere, because Joe still knew he didn't have a clue what to do with his life. I know that for sure because Joe and I talked about it endlessly.

But Joe's one heck of a determined guy, so he did the right thing and changed careers. Not because he knew which Way to take his life or anything. All Joe knew for sure was that he was in the wrong place, so he did a switcheroo and became a college teacher and text-book author. As I write this, Joe's just finishing up text-book number three in fact. Now everyone in Joe's neighborhood thinks he's a powerhouse of a guy making dreams come true. But is he? No he isn't. Sadly, Joe knew in his heart-of-hearts that some special power deep down inside wasn't being released.

Joe's soul tried to help him out with this as well, because one day it began speaking to him. Joe explained it this way to me. "One day I had an odd idea I should be writing one of those finance books for dummies" said Joe. "A book that takes everything I've learned about getting wealthy and shares it with the world". As Joe described how this soul-direction came to him out of the blue and compelled him to begin writing, I was amazed. Instantly I recognized Joe's inner voice speaking to him, because it was like the strange BEES message I received from my own heart. Joe actually managed to write a first revision of this book too, before giving up. Why on earth would he give up? Same story over and over. The real, authentic Joe had started coming out of its shell with that book, but like a billion other folks on earth, he was terrified of being himself. His soul had finally pointed him in the right direction, but thoughts of his work being judged stopped him cold and he put the scary unfinished manuscript under his desk.

That's where it was when I noticed it and spoke up. "You know Joe" I said, "working on that book is probably the most important thing you could do." "How's that?" replied Joe with some interest so I carried on. "Because working your dream is what shows you who you really are and what you should be doing with your life." Joe thought about that for a moment, and was obviously intrigued, and I ventured a bit further. "So how come you're just letting it sit there?" I added. "I don't really know" said Joe. "I really want to finish it, but I keep on thinking nobody wants to listen to little old Joe here". With that I knew for sure why Joe gave up....against the advice of his soul. He'd just uttered a perfect example of self-judgment. Fears of being himself had stalled Joe's dream, and I said so. I tried my absolute best to explain and get joe to muster the courage to defeat those terrible fears. And? Joe listened politely and with all his considerable intellect. He comprehended everything I had to say, but that manuscript is still sitting in Joe's office....unfinished.

Now Joe's taking more night courses to develop his interests, hoping they'll show him what to do with his life. Joe simply doesn't realize this kind of knowledge won't help him. He doesn't yet recognize that to live his dream life he has to "know thyself" by making fears of judgment go away so his inner voice can give him direction. No doubt about it, Joe is still looking "outside" for his dreams. But they are just not there. And you? Inside or outside? Your choice.

"Smooth seas do not make skillful sailors." (African Proverb)

You Have to Exercise

I know, I know, you don't want to do any work. You'd rather be an immature, aimless Zombie of a man or woman until you die. No? O.K., then. You have to train yourself backwards and forwards and upside down until you can see wholeness in the world. Yes….that means hard work. Day after day, month after month, doing simple exercises. What exercises? Thank you for asking. Exercises I fashioned from the Rule of Life. A Rule that looks a bit crazy in the beginning, but like my Dad used to say it's really….."crazy like a fox". These exercises will force you to treat the world like it's part of you…. even if you can't see it yet. It's a classic example of "faking it 'til you make it". A real-life practical Way for you to get close enough to the Truth so you can finally see it up close and personal for yourself. Believe me, it is a lot more practical than getting near death, or swallowing Zen kibble….koans I mean….for decades.

If you're athletically inclined, you can imagine you're training for some sort of marathon. Day by day the efforts will slowly add up and your fears of judgment will fade. Slowly but surely you'll begin to know your heart's desires again. I can tell you this for sure as well.

Knowing what your very own heart really desires above all things is a special thing the likes of which you've never known before. Alright....enough talk. Here's the exercises.

No.#1: **Get To Know Your Enemy**

About two thousand years ago, the Chinese general Sun Tzu wrote a famous book called "The Art of War". In it, Sun Tzu says this about "the enemy". *"If you know the enemy and know yourself, you need not fear the result of a hundred battles"*. This advice applies directly to your battle to discover who you are today, and I am now going to tell you precisely why. It's because you probably don't even recognize the ruthless foe surrounding you right now. A foe capable of taking your life from you. But don't misunderstand me here. I'm not trying to say you're stupid or anything. Smarts have nothing to do with it. It's all about beliefs. Beliefs about how the world works we've all been taught form the cradle, for many generations. These beliefs allow the enemy itself to come right into our homes disguised as something we want. Like poison covered in sweet, desirable chocolate perhaps. Or the worst kind of Trojan Horse you could imagine.

Here's where Sun Tzu's ancient advice comes in. If you don't learn how to recognize the enemy in all his disguises, he will....for sure....get you. This enemy will take your life from you as certainly as any conqueror. Now let's get to the nuts and bolts of it. Your enemy is fear of being judged, and you are swimming in fearful messages of judgment 24-hours a day. In today's world, our selfish worldview makes us believe everything we do, say, and are must be bigger and better and best if we're to have self-worth. Everywhere you turn in the world today then, you'll find blatant or disguised messages making you fear being yourself. Exercise number one is getting you to recognize this message coming at you from every direction.

It won't take you long to realize we're so caught up in judging each other, it's pretty much all we're doing. By learning these millions of ways we judge each other, you're getting to know your enemy. Other Rule of Life exercises will help you defeat this insane judging. Here's an example for you . You'll find lots of other real-life examples in the Journal part of the book that follows. Oh yes. Maybe I should tell you this while I'm at it. I'm going to make *you* write a Journal too. Yes I am. We'll get to that later. For now, here's your first example of recognizing the Message of Fear in your life.

Getting to Know Your Enemy

When you're looking for the Message of Fear, you're looking for things that say…"I'm better than you" or "if you don't do this, you won't be good enough". Messages of judgment of one kind or the other. O.K. so let's just travel to your workplace for a moment and look around. What is the boss's ten-piece suit trying to tell you? It's saying "I'm smarter and more powerful than you are". It's one way someone can send the message…"anyone can tell just by looking that I am more important than you". Yes? Of course, but let's now go check out the single ladies in your place of employment. There's usually at least one who believes wholeheartedly she's "it". What exactly is "it"? Good question. You fellows can probably get the answer to that by asking her out. But a word of caution here guys. You'd better look a lot like Brad Pitt or Elvis and have moocho money. Why? Because Miss Big jogs (she's a long distance runner of course) will only dally with the best. How will you know if you're the best? Don't worry. She'll be judge and jury on that one. As a matter of fact, if she's not overly polite, she might even call you a loser out loud. In front of the entire office. A public hanging you might say. Ouchey wouchey!

Get the idea? You won't have to look far to find ways we judge each other worthless. The more you look…the more you'll see. Eventually you'll hardly be able to see anything else, because judging each other is the Sport of Champions. More popular than baseball. But don't forget, you're just getting to know your enemy here so you can get out from under your fears. Lots more examples follow in this book, just in case you lose your way a bit.

No.#2.: **Don't Foolishly Discriminate**

"Discrimination is a hellhound that gnaws at Negroes in every waking moment of their lives to remind them that the lie of their inferiority is accepted as truth in the society dominating them".
- Martin Luther King, Jr.

Here's something about wholeness that everybody has noticed for a very long time, but failed to see the truth behind. Every single thing everywhere is "the same but different". What the heck does that mean you ask? It means you can pick any two different things you want, and, with some effort, find some way they're also the same. Take pigs and petunias for instance. They're pretty different alright, but they're also both "living things". Or maybe you'd like to pick stars and sand. They sound so far apart they couldn't also be the same. Right? Not at all. They're both made of atoms.

Starting to see the picture? It doesn't matter what things you choose, or how different they are, somebody will be able to come up with a way they're the same. Why? Because the world is one whole and everything is simply a different part of the same thing. It simply isn't possible that anything can be so different that it isn't the same as everything around it some way, shape, or form. So what? So this. We Human Beings have got ourselves lopsided where wholeness is concerned.

With our amazing powers of discrimination, we've taught ourselves the Art of seeing how things are different alright, but then we promptly fail to see that they're the same. Why is that? We've been looking at the world through the selfish eyes of Reason for so long, we don't notice anymore. Unfortunately, that's called "foolish discrimination", and it leads to all kinds of grief. You get grief when people of different colors attack each other because they can't see that they're the same. How are they the same? They're people. Foolish discrimination grief happens when you can't see your air and mine are one and the same, so you pollute mine....and we both get sick. Bad things take place if you think you and the world are separate, so you do harm to anything and everything. Your grief will eventually have to arrive back in your lap because you've unwittingly harmed yourself. You can probably come up with all kinds of standard grief to have by foolishly discriminating. But there's a much bigger kind of grief you'll get by failing to see everything around you is "the same but different".

Foolish Discrimination

What kind of big grief am I talking about here? If you foolishly discriminate all your life, you'll never know who you are or why you're here. Never will you know what your Life Mission is. That will bring you as much grief as you can handle. And so, Rule of Life exercise number two is all about forcing you to train yourself to see wholeness. Like all exercises though, they don't work if you don't do them. This might even sound a bit silly to you at first, because it sounds so simple. Even so, I can tell you something from personal experience. Once you discover it's impossible to find things so different they're not also the same somehow, wholeness will dawn on you. Soon thereafter you'll begin to understand your life has the same worth any life does. That will be the beginning of your rebirth.

So go ahead. Try it out. Make a game of this exercise with friends, challenging each other to find any two things too different to be the same. Keep at it until the truth of it is a reality for you. To get you started, I'll give you some examples of yours truly foolishly discriminating with the best of 'em. Believe me, I've done my share, and soon you'll have to admit you have too.

I Catch Myself Foolishly Discriminating

Here's a simple example of yours truly discriminating foolishly. Unfortunately, we've all been so brainwashed to do it, it's like a bad habit that's hard to kick. I guarantee you'll find lots of things like it in your life. Off we go. A few days ago I was slowly driving home from work when a guy zoomed past me at something close to twelve hundred miles an hour. "@#~! Idiot!" said I out loud, like I was a saint myself or sweet buttery guy who never did anything wrong. But guess what? I've done more than my share of idiotic speeding, probably earlier that very same day actually. But wait a minute here, that means I'm calling some guy names for doing what I do. How can me... and millions of other folks.... do such a dumb thing? I'll tell you exactly how it works. There's a big difference between me speeding and anybody else speeding. I'm sure you're familiar with this difference in fact. What difference would that be? He's him and I'm me.

You heard me right. Believe it or not, that's all the difference people need to foolishly discriminate. All you have to do is look around and you'll see people everywhere calling others names for something they themselves do all the time. And why do they think this makes sense? They just can't see other people do the same things they do…..differently. They see the difference between themselves and others, but just can't see how others are the same.

They keep on foolishly discriminating, limiting their lives and causing all manner of bad things to happen. Don't believe you foolishly discriminate? You're foolishly discriminating.

You Can Catch Yourself Too

If you still don't believe you probably foolishly discriminate eight days a week, here's a few simple examples to point you in the right direction. Let's say you're a preacher advising your flock not to kill. But you regularly take deer hunting vacations. Killing animals for fun that is. Guess what? Sundays you say killing people is bad, and for recreation you kill other little beings. Same but different. Truth is, your reverence for Life is shallow, and you don't even appreciate it. Don't like that example? How about this one. Imagine you're sitting down with your son, trying hard to give him some life lessons by pointing out that bragging is bad. "I never brag myself" you say, trying to hammer home the advice. "In fact, in the last thirty years I've seen everyone around me brag like heck….but not me….I've got more moral fiber than that my son". Can you guess what that is? Bragging. You and those nasty braggarts are the same but different.

"Nonsense!" you say? Yes it is, but it's true. All you have to do is look around you a bit and you'll see people of every persuasion foolishly discriminating. Here's a few more ways I've done it myself. I've looked down on pathological liars….ten minutes after misrepresenting something I did to make myself look more important. Yep. Foolish discrimination again. Me and those liars are the same but different. I've laughed out loud at twenty-something kids with soup-can exhausts on their cars, making moocho noise to sound powerful. Then I got on my big old Harley Davidson motorcycle….with noisy pipes I put on to sound powerful. Get the idea? Foolish discrimination is everywhere.

_No.#3_: Learn to See the Tree of Life

This exercise is perhaps the most important of all, because it will eventually lead you to realize it makes no sense to think your life isn't as important as any life anywhere, any time. Before we get to it though, let's review the Tree of Life again. Contrary to what pretty much everyone believes today, there simply aren't all kinds of different lives in the Universe. To crib a few words from scientific philosophers, this thing we call "Life" is an "emergent phenomenon". That means One Life *emerges* from the sum of every single thing in the Universe, exactly like a jig-saw picture emerges from the sum of puzzle parts. One Life means there aren't many different separate lives to judge. It means every single thing in the Universe has equal worth when it comes to making up the One Life we all share as well. There you go. That's the most important part of the Tree of Life.

This great Tree means you and I should not live in fear of being judged…..because it makes no sense. Rule of Life exercise number three is therefore a very simple way of putting wholeness in your head where it belongs. It gets you to look at whole things, seeing time after time that no part of any whole can be judged less worthy than any other. It can change your life dramatically if you get the point of it all. And the point is this. People who say you're worth less than they are because you're smaller, weaker, poorer, or just different, can't see that you *are* them. They're just like that smart-ass puppet hand of mine back a few pages that didn't realize he was calling himself names. He didn't understand the One Life we all share has infinite worth. Just in case you missed my meaning here….that means you have infinite worth….right now. Only people blind to the truth won't see it. O.K., let's sketch out Rule of Life exercise number three and do a few together. There are more for you to look at later in my Journal.

Potent Simple Minded Exercises

You can learn to understand the Tree of Life by looking at any whole thing at all. You won't have to go far to find one either, because everything everywhere is a whole. Like what? We'll start with a clock. Clocks are made of clock parts of course. You don't have to be a missile scientist to realize that each and every part of a clock is equally important to making up the clock either. If you're not sure about that, take out a gear. Now what? It doesn't work, because each and every part is equally important. That was pretty obvious wasn't it? Yes it was, and the same is true of every single thing in the Universe. Take that cake you baked this morning for instance. Next time you make one, try leaving out the sugar and see what your coffee klatch friends think of it. O.K., so here's what I want you to think about while you are taking things apart to see that they no longer work right. Just imagine *you* are whatever part you take out of something. Pretend you're that gear in the clock above or the sugar in someone's cake. Close your eyes, suspend your disbelief…and imagine it.

Now what do you see? Not sure? I'll tell you. Not only are you absolutely important to making up that whole, you are absolutely necessary. You are needed. You are wanted. Without you that "whole" world is really and truly missing something very important indeed. Same holds with your life. Not only does it make no sense to judge your Life less worthy than any Life….because it's all the same Life….but you are NEEDED. We need you just as desperately as the clock needs that gear and the cake needs its sugar. See what I'm getting at? Alright, so every time you do this mindlessly simple little exercise, put yourself in place of the part you removed from some whole and feel needed. Feel the need our world has for your life. And see how silly it is for anyone to judge you….because they're just calling themselves names. Maybe this exercise seems so simple it's not worth doing.

But whatever you do, don't underestimate the power of repetitive training. You can train your Mind, Body, and Spirit to see the Truth this way. All you need to do…..is DO IT! Just to get you started I'll make up another simple little Tree of Life story. It's below.

The Tree of Life Again

Look at the Tree of Life for a moment. See that big, juicy, beautiful apple over there way at the top of the Tree? O.K., now look down. Way down by the bottom. Look for a small, wrinkled, bitter crabby apple. See it dangling just above the ground? So is that gorgeous red apple at the top of the tree better? Sure it's bigger and brighter and has a lot more flavor, you can see the difference for miles. But now let's try to pass judgment on the life of the apples. Is the big apple's life worth more than the little one's? Truth is, it can't be, because both apples are different parts of the same tree. There aren't two lives there at all, because those different apples share the same life. Trying to say one apple's life is worth more than the other's doesn't make sense. They may be different as night and day, but they're really parts of each other. Like Siamese Twins. That's wholeness. So remember …there's only one life….and it's yours and mine and everyone and everything else's. That's why your life just can't be worth less than any other life. Really. It's true. When you've done enough Rule of Life work …guess what? Your sense of worth will rise forever after until you get Real self-esteem. Remember Real self-esteem? Like Eddie had? No? Go back and read it again.

No.#4: Seek Out and Find Guru-truths

I like to think of the Truth of the world, (that it's whole), as a gigantic mountain range in the ocean of our lives.

A mountain so high and wide that it rises above the surface in many different places as islands. Some islands are close together of course, but others are very, very far apart. Over the centuries, dozens of these islands have been discovered by passionate explorers of many different persuasions, roaming the ocean of life trying to understand how the world works. On the surface of this ocean, these islands are frequently so far apart it doesn't look like they're connected at all. They're often so different in appearance as well, even the explorers themselves don't realize they all stem from one mountain rising from the depths. I call these islands "guru-truths", because they're all different aspects of one Truth discovered by different kinds of gurus over the Ages. One Truth presenting itself many different ways. Some of these fervent exploring souls are modern self-help gurus trying to show you and I the Way to true happiness, while others are leading-edge scientists investigating the nature of reality. Still others are mystics and prophets and poets, or priests of various religious traditions. Spiritual leaders are amongst them as well, and even ordinary men and women writing about their experiences of revelation.

Rule of Life Exercise No.#4 is all about visiting these islands of Truth. Once you've visited many different islands, you'll begin to glimpse the singular mountain of Truth below the ocean of your life. The point of it all of course, is to change your mind about the world and dissolve your fears of judgment. The gurus have made it easy for you and I to visit these islands as well, because they've given the islands names we can look up in books. Self-help names like "laws of attraction", "abundance", or "intention". Religious names like "The Tao" and "God". Scientific names like "indeterminacy", "complementarity", or "relativity". All different ways the Truth makes itself known. I'll give you examples to get started and more in my Journal to look at. Then choose your own brand of books and go looking.

It doesn't matter what kinds of books you like to read either, because the Truth shows up in all of them. Here are two examples to sink your teeth into.

The Island of Intention

We'll start by reading about a modern self-help guru's experience of the truth. Wayne W. Dyer. Dr. Dyer has written many books about making dreams real or "manifesting potential" as he calls it. In recent years though, he's given us a book called "The Power of Intention" that speaks directly to the deep and abiding Truth of the world. I'll first try to convey the essence of Dr. Dyer's idea of "intention" and its power. In a nutshell the Power of Intention is:

A Divine Force at the center of all things that can be made to flow through us, manifesting our potentials as it does so. A greater Will that can propel us towards our destiny, differing from the "will power" we exercise in everyday life when trying to intentionally make something happen. A "field-like force" that unites every thing in the Universe and is present in all life before birth and after death. The Source of all creation. A Power that makes we-and-the-world One, allowing us to literally create the world we dream of.

As Dyer points out in his book, anyone inspired by a calling has felt this power of intention. I couldn't agree more. From personal experience I can tell you this as well. When you release this power into your life you will not mistake it for anything else. But of course, you have to know how to do exactly that. If you look closely at that description of the power of intention above, it should be familiar to you. Just in case it's not, I'll spell it out for you my way. The Power of Intention is:

A result of seeing that the world is whole. A Force released into your life when you realize there's One Life in the Universe....so your worth as a human being can't be judged. Divine guidance your inner voice will give you when you no longer fear being yourself. A greater Will that drives you forward on your Life Mission forever as you regain a Vision of who you can become. The blissful, happy, authentically successful life you live when growing human and blossoming.

In short, you get the Power of Intention by being yourself. As a matter of fact, there is *no other way* of having the Power of Intention in your Life. You have to dump your fears of judgment and grow *your* way. That is the single, simple, true and profound secret to releasing this mind-boggling power into your world. In one word, it's "wholeness". When you really do grasp what wholeness means, you'll experience all those facets of "Big Happiness" I mentioned earlier. Dr. Dyer is therefore onto something very big indeed, and you can have it for yourself by taking away that single, sad, and absolutely mistaken idea your life can be worth less than any life.

Heisenberg's Uncertainty

Way back in the 1930's, the famous physicist Werner Heisenberg dug down deeply into the fabric of the world and discovered a form of Dualism. He called it the "Uncertainty Principle" and you can find out more about it in any decent science library. In layman's terms for you and I, here's what Heisenberg discovered. Like all scientists, Heisenberg knew we have to actually reach out and touch the world to know anything about it. Touching the world, or interacting with it to get knowledge is called "measurement" by physicists. That makes sense of course, but Heisenberg discovered something odd about the world when he tried to measure little particles.

He discovered he could know where a particle was or how much energy it had....but not both at the same time. If Heisenberg interacted one way with a particle to know exactly what its position was for instance, he could only know approximately how much energy it had. Same in reverse. He could figure out precisely how much momentum energy it had, but would then only know more or less where the particle was. That's Heisenberg's famous Uncertainty Principle. But this is not the sort of uncertainty you find in ordinary life. In everyday life for example, you might be uncertain where you left your watch, but you can resolve that uncertainty by looking for it. Even if you don't find the watch, you're certain it's there somewhere. Heisenberg's Uncertainty is different. It says there is no possible way anybody can ever know a particle's position and momentum with precision at the same time.

So what you ask? So it raises all kinds of very strange questions about what the world is like when nobody's observing it. The strangest of these questions is whether there's any world at all where there aren't any observers. Sounds completely nuts you say? Yes it does, but don't forget. The smartest and most talented physicists in the world are the ones asking these questions, so who are you and I to call them nuts? Before we get back to what's important about Heisenberg's Uncertainty to *your life* though, let's see just how curiously awe-inspiring Heisenberg's Uncertainty is. A little story will illustrate.

An Awe-Inspiring Uncertainty

Imagine you want to measure the momentum energy of a little particle for a moment. One way would be to shoot it at a little brick wall and count the broken bricks. More broken bricks means the particle had more energy, and you can use that little fact to nail down exactly how much momentum the particle had when it hit the wall. But here's the part that should make you stop and think.

If you know exactly how much energy that particle had, you can't know exactly where it was when the wall fell apart. So? So it's possible the little particle was just in front of that wall when it broke. In other words, it's possible the wall fell down *before* the particle hit it. Don't forget. Heisenberg's Uncertainty Principle says you just *can't* know exactly where that particle was when the wall fell down. Ridiculous as it might sound then, you can't rule out the possibility that the wall fell down before the particle hit it. But how could the wall fall down if the particle didn't hit it you ask? Isn't that absolute nonsense? Those are very good questions indeed, and questions like that are why Heisenberg's Uncertainty is so famous.

What Heisenberg's Uncertainty Means to You

If you're still not quite sure what Heisenberg's formulas are saying here though, you're in good company. Even the physicists aren't sure, but some have ventured "educated guesses". Some suggest Heisenberg's Uncertainty Principle is telling us our most basic and sacred beliefs about what makes sense might just be wrong. And they are right. Here's why. Imagine our view of the world to be like a box we're all trapped inside. Inside this box are all our beliefs about what makes sense and everything we know about the world.

What Heisenberg did then, is explore the box right to its outer limits, to where the walls or ceiling or floor is. There he encountered the Dualism Poem of Life in its "Uncertainty Principle form". Had Heisenberg given this Poem the right meaning (the world is whole), he would have broken through the limits of this box to where a different way of making sense of the world is. He would have gotten beyond the limits of Reason to a "greater reality" on the other side.

Far more importantly however, Heisenberg would have helped you and I discover what to do with our lives, by taking away our fears of being judged. Unfortunately, Heisenberg did not do this, because he was interested in physics, not your life and mine.

Goose Bump Stories

Scientific guru truths should inspire awe and wonder in you because each is like the different parts of an elephant in the ancient blind men and pachyderm story. In case you're not familiar with this old tale, I'll sketch it out for you here. Then I'll tell you exactly what to wonder. Here's the story. Three blind men go out into the jungle one day and happen across an elephant. Each explores a different part of the beast and they return to their village. Back home they explain that three different "leg, tail, and trunk animals" were discovered, because they don't realize that leg, tail, and trunk are all parts of one whole. Even so, these men suspect there might be more to those different creatures out there than meets the eye. They wonder what might be hidden in plain sight in the jungle. Scientific guru-truths are exactly like that. They're different parts of one gigantic thing hidden out in the open in the world that Reason is keeping from us. "Like what?" you ask? That's what I want you to wonder every time you read about a truth of science. Each time I offer a scientific guru-truth, I'll partner it with a goose bump story so you can wonder again and again what's hidden before your eyes in the world. We'll begin with a story designed to make you wonder about Heisenberg's famous Uncertainty. Then we'll get back to Rule of Life Exercises.

"Knowledge is an unending adventure at the edge of uncertainty".
- Jacob Bronowski

Heisenberg's Goose Bumps

Heisenberg's uncertainty principle is telling us it's possible we really don't understand how the world works at all. Take that wall falling apart before the particle hit it for example. There are a hundred million reasons why it can't happen, but Heisenberg's formula says we can't rule it out. That's why Werner got goose bumps. He realized that all one hundred million of those reasons could be wrong. Don't quite get the picture? Here's where the goose bump stories come in. I'll make one up right now that should illustrate how wrong we might be about how the world works. When you finish reading, start wondering.

We're On Shaky Ground

Heisenberg is telling us something like this. Imagine you built a gigantic building on what you think is really solid ground. It's a hundred stories high, twenty miles on a side and filled with all twelve billion of your closest relatives. Plus all your treasured possessions of course. Great, but there's a small problem you didn't notice. As it turns out, that solid ground is really the frozen surface of a very deep ocean. Unknown to you, you've built everything on ice. For many generations that ice has been good and strong, and hasn't given you any trouble. But today is going to be a big day.

Why? You're just about to add one final story on that huge building. The very last one. The one that will break the ice. Then what? Disaster I'd say. You won't even know what hit you. That's why Heisenberg had goose bumps. He realized everything we know and understand about the world might be on really shaky ground if we'd misunderstood the nature of things as badly as his Principle suggested. Still not sure what I'm getting at here? Well then, I'll tell you point blank.

If we don't wake up and see wholeness in the world for what it is soon, our mistaken worldview called "Reason" may break the ice under our feet, destroying everything around us. If that doesn't give you goose bumps, not much will.

No.# 5: **Put the Truth in Action**

"Even if you're on the right track, you'll get run over if you just sit there." (Will Rogers)

One time-tested way of bringing beliefs into your life is putting a truth in action. In essence this means getting on-board with some program you're still not quite sure of, and letting the results convince you. It's suspending your disbelief so you can give truth a chance. To give you a concrete idea what I'm getting at here, just think about lifting weights for a moment. Imagine you had no idea you could train yourself to lift gigantic weights. You just don't realize your muscles can grow and grow if you start small and work up slowly. Then one day you come across a guy who can lift 500 pounds. This fellow says you too could lift this kind of weight if you trained. But it makes absolutely no sense to you. You can't lift 50 pounds, much less five hundred. The idea you could lift hundreds of pounds is impossibly unbelievable.

But let's say the weight lifter somehow convinces you to begin slowly lifting more weight every day for a month. He's managed to get you to suspend your disbelief and give the truth of muscle growth a chance. Then what? You can hardly believe it yourself, but it's true. A month later you're lifting 100 pounds. And here's what I'm getting at. If you hadn't suspended your disbelief, you never would have known the truth about muscle growth. You'd still be thinking weight-lifters were aliens of some kind. See what I mean? Sometimes you have to take a chance on Truth and start living it….so you can believe it.

In the case of the Truth we're talking about here though, acting according to it will do more for you than make you strong. It will literally heal your Mind and Body. "But I'm not sick." you say? Yes you are. Here's why.

Destroying Wholeness Creates Disease

When you can't see the world is whole, you'll think everything is separate, including yourself. You'll shatter your life and everything around it into pieces. The result is called "disease", because disease is nothing more or less than a loss of wholeness. If you're not sure about that, go look it up in a good dictionary. By definition, all disease results from destroying wholeness. If a flu bug gets at you for example, it screws up some small part of you, compromising the wholeness of a critical system and making you run a fever. If cancer destroys a part of you, you're in big trouble because your body needs every part to work properly. Same holds with any thing you care to mention. Families become diseased or "dysfunctional" if mom or dad don't work the way they're supposed to. Mom, dad, and all the kids suffer from this loss of wholeness. Even inanimate objects work this way as well. Take a spring out of a watch for instance, and it'll be "diseased" because it isn't whole any more. Unfortunately, your life will also be badly diseased if you don't treat everything around you as if it was who you are. You'll be just as sick in Mind and Body as you would if attacked by viruses or cancers or other bad things.

Live the Truth

Living the Truth is a lot different from reading about it and understanding it and then doing something else. You can't be like the man or woman who goes to church on Sunday and commits every sin known to Man for the rest of the week.

The Truth I'm speaking of here isn't a book-learning truth you memorize to pass a test and then forget completely either. This is a Life-enhancing, all encompassing, inspiring kind of truth that must be part of your Mind, body and soul if you want authentic Human happiness. You must learn to believe from the depths of your heart, that everything around you is a different part of who you are to get your calling back. Once you do, you'll automatically live this truth for obvious reasons. In case you aren't sure what these reasons are, let me tell you. From the depths of your being you'll want to treat the world with care and compassion…because the world is who you are. Here's a few ridiculously simple examples of living the truth. Let's say you're at dinner with your spouse, and he or she is recounting some little tale of the day. If you're living the Truth you won't be interrupting. Why? Deep down you know *their* fun telling tales is *your* fun, and you won't want to spoil it for either of you. "Deep down" means you know for sure your heart and theirs is one and the same, so you do the right thing for your shared heart.

Here's another "living the truth" example. This time you're driving along a country road having just eaten a fast-food hamburger on the run. If you're living the truth, you won't toss that burger bag out the window. Why not? You see the world around you as a different part of who you are, and you're not about to pollute yourself. From the core of your soul you know that kind of thing makes no sense. Alright, one more example and you can go find millions on your own. What's the chance a man or woman living the Truth would inflict pain on some other creature. Not sure? Zero. Nobody who knows the Truth is going to inflict pain upon themselves, because it would be a sad kind of insanity. Unfortunately, this kind of insanity is being played out all over the world countless times every minute, because hardly anyone sees the Truth, much less lives it.

No.#6: **Look For Signs of Truth**

More than just gurus roam the ocean of life of course. Men and women in different lands of every color and inclination have voyaged together there for Ages. Some have discovered smaller truths, and left them behind as gems of wisdom or oft-quoted guides to daily life found in quotations books so popular today. I like to call many of these wise old sayings "signs of Truth", because they're like little billboards telling you and I where to find far bigger islands of Truth. Not full-blown outposts of wholeness perhaps, they're helpful nonetheless because so many exist and all point to the mountain of Truth beneath our lives. You'll find them in the writings of prophets or oral traditions of mystics. Woven into folk tales and enshrined in the myths and legends of native peoples, these little signs are everywhere. The more you find, the sooner the full Truth of wholeness will bring your dreams back. I'll share a few with you here right now, and more in my Journal later.

"A short saying oft contains much wisdom". - Sophocles (BC 496 - 406) Greek poet

Karma is a Sign of the Truth

I'm sure you've heard people say "what goes around comes around" many times. It's our way of expressing what ancient Indian philosophers called "Karma". So what exactly is Karma anyway? Most of us believe it means if we do good or evil, good or evil will come back to us. Folks really into Karma then, will want to sew seeds of goodness to reap a harvest in kind. These men and women will do as much good as possible, hoping good will "come back around" to them. But there's a hitch here people who believe in Karma don't often like to point out. Namely, bad things often happen to good people.

Men or women doing nothing but good have been killed by terrorists or struck down by terrible illness for example. You may even know some good, decent soul yourself whose family has been taken by tragedy or who's been felled by cancer. All their life they did good, but what did they get back? Sorrow and sickness. So where did all the good go? It sure didn't seem to "come back around". Doesn't that mean Karma is just wishful thinking? Not at all, but you have to change the way you see things to understand Karma. To see what I mean, let's first look at Karma through the selfish eyes of Reason, that makes us think everything is completely separate. I believe in Karma so I give you a hundred dollars, hoping my investment will pay back at least as much. Ten minutes later I get run over by a truck. My surprised soul flies off thinking "so much for Karma". Alright, that's the selfish view of reality for you.

Now let's change the way we see the world and look again at Karma. This time you and I see very clearly that we're different parts of each other. Different parts of One Life. Now when I act with generosity and kindness towards you by giving you that gift, guess what? There's no waiting. I just did that good to myself, because you and I are really One. I discovered why giving is as good as receiving too, because it *is* receiving. Now I can understand Karma. What goes around came back around to me, even before I got hit by that truck. Unfortunately, until you give up the selfish way of seeing the world called "Reason", Karma will only be a sign of the truth.

A Backwards Sign

Some signs of the Truth are backwards . They tell you to run the other way as fast as possible.

Here's one for you right now, but there are more in my Journal. Look hard at this, and then go the other way. I call it the "wrong sign", but it's the right one to help you find yourself. Here's what I mean. If you live anywhere on Mother Earth you'll hear people yelling "*you're wrong*" at you most of your life. No sooner do you make a little mistake for example, but someone will treat you to that brow beating advice. Even so, these misguided folks can do you a big favor by reminding you there's nothing wrong with being wrong. As a matter of fact, making mistakes is the only way to learn and grow. Truth be told, being wrong is one of the hallmarks of success. Anybody who does anything with their life always does ten wrong things for every right one. Take Abraham Lincoln for instance. He failed miserably time after time in politics until, eventually, he got it right and became President.

Same with any person who's achieved anything. Just ask them and you'll discover hundreds of mistakes they made you never knew about. Mistakes are how you work your way from little seedling to gorgeous blossom of a mature man or woman…..as long as you learn from them. So every time you hear somebody calling you names for making mistakes, remember this. They're *wrong* for thinking less of you. They're dead *wrong* for not applauding you. They're holding up a big sign that says "It's Alright to Be Wrong". Follow those wrong signs to your dreams.

You'll Need Help to Stay the Course

Now you have six exercises that will help you discover what to do with your life, but who will make you do them when I'm not here? I know for sure you want your very own passionate dreams back…..who doesn't? But if you're like me and pretty much everybody else I know, you might just give up on the Rule of Life before your Mission dawns on you. Can you think of anything worse than that?

You've been put on the Road Less Traveled to your dreams, but soon you take a crossroad leading nowhere again? That's like getting hung twice for a crime you didn't commit. Believe me, you do not want to be given one chance at an authentic life, and toss it overboard. That's why I've also given you Mission exercises. They're designed to help you stick to your guns long enough to begin hearing the Divine voice of destiny in your life again. Think of them as Life-Purpose Police if you want to. They'll make you walk the straight and narrow ....to all you can be. Here they are.

Chapter Sixteen
Mission Exercises
(Keep You Chasing Your Dreams)

"Permanence, perseverance and persistence in spite of all obstacles, discouragements, and impossibilities: It is this, that in all things distinguishes the strong soul from the weak". Thomas Carlyle

What Are Mission Exercises?

Having a mission is like trying to get to a mountain top on the horizon of your life. There will be stumbling blocks, tough times, and people trying to stop you every step of the way. You'll have miles to go before you blossom, so it'll take quite a while to get there. All your life for example. That's more than enough time to get lost or give up. Enter Mission exercises. Some are there to keep you on track, by reminding you what you're after. Others help you get the courage you need to keep at it, until you've tapped into that great ocean of encouragement within you. That inner Force will sustain you forever once you've got it flowing, but until you do, you'll need a little help. We all need help along the way. There's even an exercise to assist you in believing impossible things. I recommend you believe in a few impossible things every day too, because everybody will tell you the world can't possibly be whole. If you don't want to take *my* advice, listen to what the Queen said to Alice in Wonderland.

"Alice laughed: "There's no use trying," she said; "one can't believe impossible things." "I daresay you haven't had much practice," said the Queen. "When I was younger, I always did it for half an hour a day. Why, sometimes I've believed as many as six impossible things before breakfast."

MX No#1: A Seeing-I-Dog

In the beginning of your Journey, you won't see what to do with your life no matter what, because you're still blind to who you are. You'll need a two hundred pound seeing-I dog that smiles like a Cheshire cat. But don't worry, it doesn't bite, it's just an exercise that keeps you on a firm heading.... when you can't see which way to go for yourself. Just follow this puppy to those "Happiness Is" things in chapter thirteen. Pick one-a-day and think about it. Google about it. Talk to friends about it. Mull it over and over and over again, dreaming about how great it would be to have in your life. See folks on T.V. who have it and say to yourself....."*I don't want to go to my grave without having this*". And the point of it all is simple. Coveting happiness every day, will remind you what you're missing right now and what your calling will provide you with. Here's an example.

What Being on a Mission Feels Like

Go back to chapter 13 and find where I described what having a Life Mission feels like. It's the story about picking watch parts in the Journey of Life. Now stop and think about it for a minute. How awe inspiring would it be if you could look back at your life and see everything you ever did is a part of one astonishing project you're drop-dead passionate about? Imagine each life-experience adding up to a single purpose you were put here for. Now you know for sure why you're here and your life feels like part of a Divine Mystery. Every single day you have a glorious reason for being. Every morning you have a huge electric desire to get up and greet the day to get going on your Mission again. Just think about being able to inspire yourself with thoughts about who you can be. Believe it or not, real, true Missions let you do that every day of your life. Still not sure what I'm getting at?

When your Vision finally clears enough to show you which way to go, you'll begin to see what all those gems of wisdom and inspirational sayings really mean. You'll know what it means to have a "place in the sun" for instance, and what the "Freedom song" is about. Expressions like "having it all" and "doing your thing" won't just be nice sounding words motivational speakers use. They'll ring true as life to you, because they're part of your life. As a matter of fact, all kinds of old wisdoms will begin to resonate with fire and passion, as you discover their full meaning in your own life. Instead of wishing for these amazing things you never thought you could actually have….they'll be yours. You'll get to know them inside out and intimately, and revel in the glory they come with. If that sounds like something you might like to have, your Mission exercise is working. Now remember you're doing Rule of Life exercises to get these Joys of Being in your life. Don't forget to actually go and do them either.

MX NO.# 2: **Real Leaders Can Help You**

When you get Vision back, you'll be a bona fide leader yourself, because real leaders are just men and women being themselves, doing their thing and growing their way. That's something to look forward to isn't it? No question about it, real leaders in your life can help you get there as well, because they radiate courage like light-bulbs. They radiate the light of leadership like raging forest fires or the sun itself. Get close and you can soak it up like a towel sops up water and it'll help you past fears of judgment. But watch out, because only real leaders will make you toasty and fearless. Sad to say, not all leaders are real leaders. Lots of men and women in big offices or positions of leadership aren't leaders at all. Certainly they're smart, capable people who have adopted dreams and made them come true. But unfortunately they're doing things they weren't put here to do. There is absolutely nothing wrong with these individuals of course.

Many are high achievers using skills and talents to go somewhere. Curiously as well, these people will be doing all the same things they'd be doing if they really were real leaders. They're making things happen and building things and out front breaking trail, like real leaders. But they're not, because they're breaking someone else's trail. Down deep, their souls know it too. Ask them if they know why they're here for instance, and they won't have a clue. So how do you find a real leader to encourage you to be yourself? Here's what to look for.

They're CEO's, Housewives, Bosses or Bricklayers

Real leaders are authentic people going about their lives being themselves. They can be CEO's, bosses, bricklayers or brothers, but all know in their hearts every soul is equally important. This inspired knowledge makes real leaders stand out in any crowd, because they won't be doing anything to put themselves above the rest of us. Authentic Human Beings won't look down on you for example, even if their skills and talents are a million times greater than yours. True leaders will make you or I feel significant because they believe wholeheartedly that we are. Without a need to inflate themselves, real leaders radiate compassion, respect, giving, cherishing, courage, generosity, kindness, and love. They easily and openly admit their weaknesses too and won't call us names for making mistakes. Empathy, consideration and care are hallmarks of real leadership.

When all is said and done then, real leadership is nothing more or less than Being Human. Yes real leaders are strong, forceful and relentless and sometimes do tough things that cause pain for others. Bona fide pathfinders don't just hand out gold medals and ribbons.

On occasion it'll be the tough, painful lessons men and women need. Frequently people need to be pushed out of jobs to where the right opportunities for them are for instance. Many eventually realize it was the best thing that ever happened to them, although it didn't seem like it at the time. People often get forcefully stopped from doing bad things by true leaders also. Driven by dreams and a passion for life, real leadership is obvious to anyone with eyes to see. Just look for these signs I've mentioned and go there.

A Real Leader

One place I worked, I was a head honcho and Gualberto was an hourly guy in the factory. The very first day I met Gualberto, I knew he was different, because he was absolutely driven to do something with his life. Four days a week he'd finish work and head off to night courses studying computers. Like a combination of moon rocket and sleep deprived puppy, Gualberto was on a mission following his dream. It didn't take me long to discover Gualberto was a real leader either. Here's how.

At the time I was still struggling daily with this book, and it was beating the living daylights out of me. Because we were birds-of-a-feather Missionaries, I told Gualberto many times how I felt like flushing the darn thing down the toilet to put me out of my misery. Every time I'd finish writing it, I'd have to start again. Needless to say, this was exasperating, frustrating, infuriating and sometimes depressing. But every time I related my tales of woe to Gualberto, it brought the brimstone and fire out of him as he encouraged me to go on with my work. Always he inspired me with stories of triumph, because Gualberto emigrated to Canada from Portugal, and began here with nothing. No work. No education. No language. But this slow start and all the setbacks along the way did not stop Gualberto from following his dreams and his stories of success never failed to perk me back up again.

Every single time, Gualberto would pick me up and send me back into the land of the living, because he was a real leader. He still is, but these days he's a computer guru, living his dream and inspiring everybody around him. If you'd like more examples of genuine leaders you'll find them in my Journal later.

MX No.#3: How to Believe Anything is Possible

"So many of our dreams at first seem impossible, then they seem improbable, and then, when we summon the will, they soon become inevitable." (Christopher Reeve)

To discover who you are, you only have to see one thing clearly, not two, ten, or thirty. All you have to see is that every thing, person, and creature in the world is a different part of you. Sounds like a piece of cake doesn't it? I wish it was, but this simple truth has been made all but impossible to understand by our misguided way of seeing the world. Even so, here's something you might want to think about. Time after time, impossible things have been made possible. It's been going on throughout history in fact. Every Age starts off knowing what's possible and what isn't, but Age after Age what's possible has changed. You'd think by now we'd all realize that all "impossible things" will probably become possible sooner or later. But it sure doesn't look like it. In our Age for instance, millions will tell you it's impossible the world around them is who they are. That's where this Mission exercise comes in. It's a simple-minded exercise that makes you look for "impossible things" that, with time, became possible. If you keep this exercise up long enough it will eventually dawn on you that "nothing is impossible". When that simple fact settles into your brain, it will help you believe the impossible truth and get your dreams back.

Examples of Impossible Things

"Man who say it cannot be done should not interrupt man doing it." (Chinese Proverb)

Here's a trick for you, to help you find impossible things….that became possible. Think of "impossibilities" this way. "Impossible" just means we can't figure out how something works. With this in mind, you'll begin to realize pretty much everything you see around you was once impossible. Take everyday cell phones today for instance. Five hundred years ago, nobody in the world would have a clue how it was possible to talk to someone on the other side of the world using a little lump of metal. Your cell phone would have been an impossibly magical, mysterious thing a few centuries ago. Was it really an "impossible thing"? Yes it was….to men and women hundreds of years ago, because they simply could not have figured out how it worked. It would have been as impossible to ancient people as walking through walls or aliens are to most folks today.

Same holds with thousands and thousands of things in the world today. Go back far enough in time and i-pods, refrigerators, nylon jackets and genetically cloned sheep will be impossible things that eventually became possible. My suggestion to you is therefore this. Take any everyday thing you want right now and go way back into the mists of time with it. Imagine what men and women in the stone Age would have said about plastics, metals, glass or laptop computers. Keep on doing that until you start to believe "nothing is impossible".

MX No.#4: Multiply Your Chance of Success

*"I have never met a man so ignorant that I couldn't learn something from him." *(Galileo Galilei)

Learning to see the world is whole is a bit like going to the moon. It's a lot tougher to do by yourself. Perhaps it's possible, but I really wouldn't recommend it. Here's what I do recommend. Look around and find friends to work on your exercises with. The old saying "two heads are better than one" has stuck around for a long time because it's true. When you collaborate with other Human Beings, they always come up with all kinds of things you'd never in a million years think of yourself for example. That brings to the table all kinds of different perspectives, experiences and insights you just wouldn't have on your own. It's like having a gigantic toolbox to assist you in building something, instead of one single monkey wrench.

In this case however, what you're trying to build is your dream life. If I were you then, I'd accept as much help as I could get for that special project. If you've ever brainstormed with a group of people trying to solve some puzzle or job-related problem you'll know exactly what I'm getting at here. Every person present contributes different little sparks of knowledge and the result is often a firestorm of inspiration. Problems that looked completely insoluble get solved, and participants have a great time doing it to boot. This particular Mission exercise then, has huge potential for explosive progress being made. This is precisely how men and women put Man on the moon after all. Guys and gals working together overcame every single obstacle confronting their impossible Mission of going to another planet.

Now that I think of it, I'm going to change this exercise from a recommendation to an imperative. If you're not quite sure what that means, I'll spell it out for you. Don't go it alone. Don't even *think* of trying to find your Way in Life by yourself. This is a very serious project you have here, so pull together some people to work on it with. Here's a real-life example of what I mean.

Len and I Brainstorm About Destiny

Here's a real-life example of a man called Len working with Rule of Life exercise number four to find his Way. I have to tell you that Len hasn't yet freed up his inner voice much, but one day our brainstorming took him a step closer to doing it. Here's how it went. Like pretty much everybody I've met, Len initially pooh-poohed the idea of an "inner voice" speaking to him about who he really is. "How will I know my inner voice when it speaks to me?" he asked me more than once. "If this special voice speaks to me in ideas, how can I tell them apart from regular ideas?" Len wondered out loud many times. Then one day as I was probing Len for evidence of his soul speaking out, I heard it weakly crying in the wilderness. As it turns out, Len has the soul of a real runner, so our explorative talks stumbled into experiences Len has had with jogging over the years. Back when Len was a kid, he naturally gravitated to school sports because his heart was in it. Track and field was a big fun thing for Len and he joined up with his highschool running team. Unfortunately for Lennard, he wasn't the absolute best on the team, so his coach spent heaps of time putting him down for it.

As you might expect, being called names for who you really are is painful, so Len gave up his treasured sport. But later on in college something deep within him told Len he should give running another chance, so he ventured out onto the track once more. This time his peers looked down on him for being middle of the pack, so Len's jogging spirit went back into hiding again. Until he graduated. Then, for reasons Len couldn't explain, the road began to call him once more and he took up jogging on his own for sport. In fact, Len began racking up "fun runs" in the 5 and 10K range, and accomplished dozens by the time of our talk. And so I turned Len's attention to these experiences. "Look back in your jogging life and what do you see?" I asked Len.

At first he didn't see what I was getting at, but slowly it began to dawn on him. Something within Len had been calling out to him to get back out there and run. This "calling" came as desires and feelings and heart-felt needs Len had for jogging. Suddenly Len recognized his inner voice. This voice speaks to us about who we are, and with the heart and soul of a runner, Len's spirit-voice spoke to him this way. Time after time it was saying…."you're not the winningest marathon runner in the world, but a special, unique kind of runner nonetheless". Year after year this inner sense of who he was spoke to him. It said…. "You need to run because it will bring you great joy….it's part of who you are". But even though Len's inner voice had been right in front of him for a long time, it took "working with others" to let him see it clearly and understand how the authentic soul within communicates.

Len therefore learned something really important about wholeness from our conversation and so did I. I learned yet another example of something I already knew. We're all the same down deep, even when we're dramatically different people. We all have the same soul that speaks to us these ways. So how about it? Do you want to learn how to get your own dreams back faster? Do your Rule of Life and Mission exercises with others. Work together to grow Human.

Now What?

Now you have ten different exercises to do, but exactly what will happen if you do them? You'll get a very special thing called "Vision" back. Vision lets you see who you are again and which way to take your life. But there's more. Vision lets you see something else. Thousands of tools, lessons and opportunities all over the place that will help you become all you can become. Books, people, and every life experience you have will become like a teacher to you, assisting you in your personal growth.

When Vision returns, you'll see personal gurus and guide-books everywhere you look. I am not exaggerating either. Eventually you'll come to see that every single thing in your life is an amazing lesson to learn about Being Human. Whether you want me to or not, I am now going to tell you precisely what Vision is and what to expect of it.

"Champions aren't made in gyms. Champions are made from something they have deep inside them-a desire, a dream, a vision".
Muhammad Ali

Chapter Seventeen
The Rule of Life Will Restore Your Vision

"True philosophers are lovers of the vision of truth". -- Plato, 'The Republic'

What is Vision?

Vision is ideas about who you are and what to do with your life that come to you like Magic when you remove your fears of being judged. Slowly but surely these little ideas and parts of ideas go together and add up like a sort of jigsaw puzzle. Eventually they let you see exactly why you're here. So what does it feel like to have Vision come back? It can be a slow dawning of your Life purpose that sneaks up on you over time, fuzzy at first, but clearing up as the days and months go by. Or it can arrive suddenly all-of-a-piece like the solution to a puzzle sometimes does, after many ideas have competed for favor in your mind for a while.

Don't Want Vision?

Maybe you're smugly sitting there right now amongst your two cars, three kids, and the Big House and don't think you need a Visionary Plan for your Life. That's fine, but just so you know, here's what'll happen if you don't have one. You'll still get lots of ideas and wishes and dreams in your four score and fifty years. They'll be like a big box of parts you can make something with. But, sadly, without Vision you won't see what you're supposed to make. Certainly you can make a fabulous petunia planter out of all those bits and pieces, and your petunias will love the little home you've built. But guess what? You're not *supposed* to make a petunia planter out of your life. You're supposed to see what to make of it with Vision. See what I mean? No?

Gee....I got another piggy who don't want to swim the Atlantic here eh? O.K., I'll spell it out. Without Vision you can still make a life for yourself.......but it won't be yours.

Vision Isn't Supposed to be Rare

Between you and me, I always thought Vision was a special, magical thing Marco Polo and men who went to the moon had. Something you get if you have a big brain like Einstein, or a big heart like Mother Teresa. The reason I thought that is simple too. It's because people with real Vision today are rarer than hens' false porcelain teeth. In fifty-odd years I've met perhaps three people with the kind of true, bona fide Vision dreams are made of. That includes myself. And you? Can you really say the lady next door has Vision because she's driven by heart-song to go somewhere only she can see? A woman who radiates courage, greets each day with stunning optimism, and is hell-bent for leather to carry out some aim her soul needs like air? No? How about Mom or Dad then? Have they always accepted you for who you are, encouraging you to go *your* way even if it is absolutely opposite to theirs? Because they know who they are and want you to as well?

No again? Okay....so have you ever meet a real live Visionary? Anywhere? Anytime? I'll bet you haven't, because Vision is a special thing for saints or world-class sinners. Isn't it? I'm sorry, but it isn't. Vision is supposed to be for absolutely every single soul on the planet. In case you aren't sure, that means you and I and at least ten billion others. If we all weren't so terrified of being judged, everyone would have Vision. Vision is simply the kind of natural insight each of us needs to grow human. It's a standard sense like hearing or touch we're all supposed to nurture from our baby days until it guides us home.

This thing called "Vision" is not....I repeat...NOT... just for a few special folks at the top of Everest like you see nowadays, or for those few far-sighted gals running companies you read about in magazines. Each man and woman amongst us is born with a real Vision of what to do with our lives and we're all put here to follow it to our dreams. Yes it is and you can have it by following the Rule of Life.

You Need Vision to Grow Up

Here's something that comes right from the news flash I just delivered to you in the note above. Vision being really rare in the world today means something sadder than sad. Hardly anyone grows up, because every single one of us needs Vision to grow up. It is just not possible to grow up if you don't have a Vision of who you can be. In case I haven't made myself clear here.....mature Human Beings are stunningly rare things in the world today, because Vision is absent. Maybe one in many hundreds of thousands grows anywhere near fully Human. I know, I know. You thought all those aging folks around you were grownups. Me too for a heck of a long time. But I have some bad news for you. Once you begin to understand what it really means to be Human, you'll change your mind. You'll have a very hard time finding "grownups" around you.

What Does it Mean to Grow Up?

So what does it mean to grow up? Overall you can say that growing Human means becoming less selfish, and becoming selfless means a lot of good things. Mature people don't need to be told "right from wrong" or study the idea from some book for instance. A Divine sense of what's "right" flows freely from their hearts.

The "right thing" to do comes automatically from following the Rule of Life, because this rule makes us treat everything in the world as if it was a different part of us…..because it is. As a result, grown Human beings aren't violent towards each other or the world, because they know in their hearts they'd be committing sins against themselves. Authentic human beings derive great joy from helping others grow as well, and make excellent partners of all kinds because they don't shy from responsibility or commitment. Everyone growing Human soon sees responsibilities and commitments as opportunities for more personal growth, and seeks them out instead of running away. In practical terms this means taking care of children, pets, parents, and spouses, even when things go badly wrong like divorce, financial disaster or infirmity.

You won't find deadbeat dads amongst the grownups for instance, and mature people will not hoard wealth at the expense of family. Authentic growing individuals identify strongly with other people as well, because the Rule of Life lets them see themselves in others. If you're lucky enough to meet a man or woman working hard to grow, you'll recognize the maturity as a deep and genuine interest in you that will make you feel good. They will speak directly to your heart and you'll know it. Those are a few ways you can distinguish grownups from children, however old they might be.

 On the flip side, you can easily spot childish people of any age too. Un-grown men and women love receiving for example, but don't give much because they lack the maturity that makes giving a joy. Immature human beings don't stop at refusing to give either. Most often they're taking as much as possible from everyone….."looking out for number one". Children aren't limited to taking our possessions either. They take life too, without noticing it's making a mockery of theirs.

It starts with bullying and torturing small creatures of all kinds, and escalates into homicide, genocide, terrorism and the like. All sad character traits of immature men and women. All stemming from a lack of Vision in the world. If you look around you right now therefore, I believe you'll begin to see hardly anyone is growing up because we're stuck in a worldview that won't let it happen. This is one good reason you and I should be crying out for help to change things.

Why Vision's Called Vision

Vision is called Vision because it's ideas that make you say "I see". There's nothing at all surprising about that of course, because lots of ideas make you say the same thing. Puzzle solving ideas for example. When someone shows you how to solve a puzzle, the first words out of your mouth are…"I see". But you don't mean you're using your eyes. You've just had the ideas you needed to solve the puzzle. And what do you say when you discover Kitty Katty won't come to your party? "*I see*…..my party isn't good enough for you".

Once again, it's not your eyes that are making you say that, it a simple *idea*. What idea? Katty's a snob. Vision is exactly like that. As you become less and less afraid of being yourself, ideas will flow into your mind, giving you a special insight into the meaning of your life. There's no better word than "Vision" to describe that kind of insight either. But don't forget this. You simply will not get Vision ideas if you're afraid of being judged. That single sinister fear will keep Divine ideas about who you can be from you. It's that simple. You won't get the right ideas for your life. I should add this however, from my own experience of Vision. When *your* Vision really matures and becomes clear, it will *feel* a lot like seeing with your eyes. You'll be able to turn your Mind's eye to the horizon of your life and *see* who you can be there.

There you go. The full-blown experience of Vision, really is *seeing*. Just a different kind of seeing than you're used to. A fabulous kind of seeing.

Vision Is Not Visualizing

Here's something worthwhile pointing out to you about Vision as well. Vision isn't the "visualization" you've probably heard of or read about. It's a stunningly different thing altogether for a very simple reason. In essence, Vision is real and visualization isn't. But don't misunderstand me here. I'm not saying visualization isn't a good tool. It really can be, but you have to understand the difference between Vision and visualization to make the latter work for you. Here's what I mean. Vision is seeing who you are supposed to become, so you can work your way there. Vision is a special kind of insight into who you are that lets you follow your destiny.

On the other hand, visualization is imagination. It's imagining you becoming something or having something or doing something. Anything you can imagine can be visualized too. For example, using visualization techniques, you can imagine yourself rich and famous or climbing Mount Everest. With effort, you can make your Mind conjure up images of you with a huge bank account or movie-star spouse or humongous boat. If you visualize "something you want" with enough ferocity, it'll help you seek out and achieve the goal too. Yes you can do exactly that. But now I'd like to direct your attention back to Dr. Steve. Unless you skipped all the previous chapters you should remember Doctor Steve's advice to yours truly several decades ago. Steve told me to go after things my heart was in…or I'd feel half-empty at the end of it all. Thirty years ago there wasn't as much talk about visualization as there is today, but Steve was reflecting on it anyhow.

Steve had learned the hard way that you can make your brain visualize any kind of "wants" at all, and use your native smarts to go get them. But if they aren't *your* true dreams coming from *your* soul, they'll never be worth much to you. In short, visualization has nothing to do with that authentic person at your center that wants to be set free. But here's something interesting about visualization. If you use the Rule of Life to get your very own Vision back, visualization becomes a fabulous tool you can use to go after *your very own* true-blue goals. You can let your Mind take snap-shots of your own Vision and hang them out in front of you to keep you trucking in that direction.

As we speak for example, I routinely imagine myself speaking my message of hope to a crowd of millions…because it is really in tune with my Life Mission. I visualize different facets of my dream life too, that came from my Vision of who I want to be. Right now I have a whole bunch of these "snapshot visualizations" arranged in front of my Mind's eye to encourage me to make them real. But don't forget. These pictures weren't picked from a book or put there because someone said they were great things to aspire to. They came from my heart when I lifted the fears of being myself from it. See what I mean? Visualization is a good thing for sure. But only if your heart tells you what to visualize.

Nothing Motivates Like Vision

If you've been out in the working world for a while, you will have noticed a big lack of motivation out there. By that I mean this. Most folks aren't getting up and going to work every day because they absolutely love what they're doing. A few are of course, but they're rarer than velveteen pig feathers. By far the vast majority are motivated by a paycheck that helps them pay bills, get toys and gets them the heck away from work on vacation.

If everyone in this vast crowd won the lottery tomorrow, the entire North American continent would grind to a halt, because nobody would be show up for work again…ever. Sound familiar? Even so, this sad state of affairs is good for business. Not the businesses the unmotivated people are working in of course. The "motivation business". In case you haven't noticed, a gigantic industry has grown up around the fact most people must be prodded with something pointy to do a great job. Vast numbers of gurus make big bucks advising employers how light fires under their employees. The bottom line goal of these gurus is to show men and women how to make the aims of their company their own. When that happens, people will move heaven and earth to get any job done. But it only happens to people with Vision.

Vision Moves Heaven and Earth

Real Vision motivates like this. Imagine you and I and two friends have a Vision of pooling our resources and building a cottage together that we'll time-share for vacations. Each of us absolutely loves the idea of a couple weeks on the lake every summer with the kids, fishing and boating and picnicking in the sun. And so we divvy up the tasks according to our individual talents. Belinda the super-star talent scout and dance mom pulls together all our schedules and connects all the dots of the project for us. Jim the whiz with carpentry does framing and decking and stuff like that. You take care of real estate matters because that's your thing. And me? I'm the money guy, making sure we don't get in trouble.

Alright, so now we have a group of very different people with very different skill-sets who happen to have a shared aim in life. Do you think Belinda has to beat me with a stick to get me up and at my appointed task in this matter? Not at all. I'm up early in fact, because this work really and truly means something important to me.

Me and everybody else is truly a "self-starter" when it comes to this project. The motivation gurus will go broke trying to sell us tips and pointers about how to get going, because our hearts are better at that than they could ever be. Yes? No doubt about it. But what I just described ain't happening much in the working world today. And here's something else you may or may not have noticed. The motivation gurus aren't making a dent in the great Sea of un-motivation. Not even a deaf pony's whisper of a dent. There is a really simple reason for this too. Hardly anyone has a clue what their aim in life is, because they're lacking Vision. If people in the working world knew what their aim in life was, they could go find a similar minded company to align themselves with. In fact, a kind of musical chairs would happen as like-minded people with similar aims hooked up in the proper organizations. Each company would become like the cottage building crew I just described. Every one would be populated with people with a shared aim in life. And? Talk about motivation. Each person would be passionately motivated to make their dreams come true. Heaven and earth would be moved daily because nothing, I repeat …..*nothing* ….motivates like Vision. And so. If you want to experience the motivating force that comes from the heart, the one that cannot be stopped or denied, be sure to get your Vision back.

Vision Isn't Always Grand

The word "Vision" is almost always used to mean something big. CEO's are said to need "Vision" to guide their companies for example, and Spiritual leaders with "Vision" are supposed to be inspired by a great power. In my own earlier life in fact, I didn't think the word "Vision" applied to anyone but the rich and famous or powerhouse leaders. I was very wrong about that, but also right in a certain way. In many cases, rich powerful and famous people really do have true Vision.

This legendary thing called "Vision" is surely what has shown the greatest people of all time which way to take their lives. No doubt about it either. Real Vision really is a staggeringly powerful experience worthy of being enshrined in myth and legend. But here's the thing. Everyone can have it. As a matter of fact, we're all *supposed* to have it from birth to death, because it's the only way we can see who we are and can be. That brings me to the way I was wrong about Vision. For every single one of us, Vision is nothing more or less than the right ideas we're supposed to have about what to do with our lives. That means each person's Vision is uniquely different, but uniquely great whether big or small. The greatness comes automatically from the Tree of Life after all. Don't forget that Tree. It guarantees your life and mine are worth the same, even if you're King of the world and I'm…well….just me. It cannot be any other way because there's only One Life and we all share it.

So what kinds of Vision can there be? Your Vision might be to become the best stay-at-home mom on the planet, caring for your children every which way possible. To make that dream come true then, you might learn how to home school your kids and read up on all the children's books to tell them great tales every night. Maybe you'd research nutrition as well, to make sure they grow big and strong on your creative meals. There's all kinds of things you might do to create the life of your dreams, all stemming from your Vision of who you want to be. And what's great about that you say? Everything, because every single Vision leads to a unique blossom on the Great Tree of Life. If your Vision is to lead our world out of the mess it's in…..that too is equally great….for the same reason. And so here's one final thought about this I'll leave you with. Vision is always grand, even if it isn't. In case you didn't recognize it, that's the Poem of Life once more.

A Little Vision Story

Speaking of little Visions of staying-at-home ... I know someone as we speak... with a small dream. A Vision of who she is and can be. Carrie. Carrie's dream is to be a bona fide home-maker and always has been. From childhood, Carrie dreamed of growing her nurturing, home-making self until it blossomed. She's been doing exactly that for the last twenty-five years. She's been teaching her two kids how to be human beings.... and learning along with them. Carrie's made her home an inviting, safe, comfortable oasis any lost soul would be happy to find themselves in. There is no plastic wrap on Carrie's couches or cats kept off the coffee table. Every room in Carrie's house is a living room, because you can sense real life in them all. Carrie gets excited every year by different veggies in her teensy little postage stamp garden as well, because she's all about growing this and growing that and growing everything. Family and carrots and kitty cats for instance, and...of course .... herself.

Go to Carrie's place and you'll feel the sunshine bursting forth, even on a rainy day. I know. I've been there. It's like stepping into an enchanted forest Carrie grew by Magic there, with kids and pets in a heaven all their own. It's a house filled with peace of mind and people happy to be themselves. No doubt about it, Carrie is making her Vision real. A real Vision of Being Human. But here's something else really neat about Carrie's family for you. Last week I spoke to Carrie's son Justin on his twenty-first birthday. "After I graduate (biology) next May I'm off to make my dream come true" he said. "What dream?" I asked, slightly stunned but delighted to hear it. "I always wanted to be a professional scuba diver" said Justin. "And I got an offer to train as a diver with an Adventure tour company starting June".

Why did that tickle me pink?" you ask? Carrie's Visionary home kept Justin's dream alive. Probably the only dream still living on Carrie's block.

Your Vision is Easy (For You)

Have you ever heard someone say…"each of us is an absolute genius at something"? I heard it many times, but between me and you I always thought it was a crock of chicken spit. I didn't see any big genius in me or anyone around me actually. Once and a while I'd see some famous dude on T.V. who looked like it might apply to them. But they were one in a few million. So I thought. But eventually when my very own Vision began to clear up once more, the full and amazing truth of it dawned on me. It's a very simple truth too, and I can tell it to you in hardly any words at all. Every single one of us is an absolute genius at one thing and one thing alone. Being ourselves. Nobody in the known Universe is as good at that as we are. Or at least we're supposed to be.

Unfortunately, millions of us are so inhibited by fears of judgment, we never get to be ourselves and feel like a genius for doing so. But it's true. You and I and every soul born is a one-of-a-kind person that needs absolute genius to perfect and blossom. Lest you think something less than genius is needed for that job, let me remind you. Each of us is an infinitely complex creation capable of feats that boggle the mind any way you look at it. Imagine being the pilot of a Starship for instance, filled with stunning technology and the means to go anywhere. That's you right now. You are the Captain of a life with astounding potential, that can be filled with amazing experiences and mind-boggling adventures. You are also the world's biggest expert at piloting that ship to its destination. A genius beyond compare at growing that portion of the Tree of Life.

And here's something equally stunning to think about. To feel like the genius you really are, all you have to do is learn how to have those Vision ideas I keep on harping about. But….listen close now….getting the ideas of a genius…..your kind of genius….will be as easy as falling off a log to you. Why? You were *designed* for them. However simple or complicated your Vision ideas are….they'll fit you like a glove. They'll suit you like that great pair of jeans you bought last week. Better even. See what I mean here? You have a stunningly unique talent for exactly those Vision ideas that will make you a genius at creating your dream life. But don't forget. Being your kind of genius doesn't mean you can do any old thing at all. There's another old saying out there you can be fooled by. Here it is. "You can be anything you want to be". I'll bet you've heard that one before, because it's thrown around these days like a Frisbee. And sure enough, this ancient wisdom is absolutely correct. But you better understand it correctly.

Because You're A Genius at Being Yourself

You really *can* be anything you want to be. But the operative word here is "want". You sure as heck better know what *your* "wants" are. You can't just pick some "wants" out of a book and expect to become that. It has to be your heart's desires you want. In case you have forgotten already, your heart wants you to be yourself. Picking something out of a book to make yourself feel important won't cut it. And so, strive to become yourself, and you'll be a true genius at it. You will be able to write like Shakespeare….if you really are a Shakespeare writing kind of guy or gal. If not….you'll never be hailed for your amazing playwriting, nor will you experience the Joys of Being Human. You can become a brain surgeon or astronaut or world's best spider-man too…..if that's who you really are. On the other hand, if you still think you can become any old thing at all, just go try. Try to become an auto mechanic if you have zero mechanical aptitude.

Try window washing fifty stories up if you're terrified of heights. Try becoming a piano player if you're a tone-deaf guy or gal. Get the picture? You can "be anything you want to be"....*but you have to want to be yourself.* That brings us to your lot in life if you don't choose to be a genius. Keep on pretending to be something you're not and you'll be very badly handicapped. Rude people will call you an idiot.

Vision Makes You Gifted

"Every good gift and every perfect gift is from above, and cometh down from the Father of lights".... -- Bible, 'James' 1:17.

When I was young, I thought "being gifted" meant being supremely skilled at something, like gifted piano players playing Carnegie hall, or gifted mathematicians winning math prizes. Like pretty much everyone, I believed "being gifted" meant being the absolute best at something, or close to it. But the truth is, it doesn't mean that at all. Yes the best people in every contest, trade and profession really are gifted, but so too are the rest of us. To see what I'm getting at here, let's go back to that "inner place" I spoke of earlier. The one I encountered in my trailer room at Rainbow Lake. Do you recall what I said about that special hidden place?

No? I'll say it again then. This famous place at the "center of us all" is absolutely and completely out of bounds to you and I. We simply cannot go there. Nobody has ever been there. But that doesn't mean you and I can't know it. This stunning place of potential at our core is really like an infinite ocean that just happens to have a pipe going down into it....with a tap on top. Thank goodness too, because you and I can get our hands on that tap. If and when we do...and we learn how to open the tap, guess what happens. That ocean of potential gets made real, by flowing into our lives.

Every idea we need to figure out who we are and which Way to take our lives comes from this profound place of potential "within" us. Those are Vision ideas I speak of. They come to us when we the tap is opened. By now you should know what that tap is too. It's fear of judgment. Take that single fear away and out comes what you need for your life. That brings us to what "being gifted" is all about. Absent fears of judgment, ideas about who we are flow to us from the ocean within, like gifts from some far away place. There you go. That's what "being gifted" really means. It's being gifted with precisely those ideas that let us "know thyself"…so we can create our very own dream life. As it turns out then, the gurus were right all along. We really do have to "look within" to find our dreams. But there's a twist the gurus don't mention. To be gifted with this self-knowledge, you and I must understand that the gifts must *come to us….we can't go to them.* There's only one possible way to be gifted as well. You must understand how to open the Tao. Did I say Tao? Sorry, I meant tap, but this faucet really does tap into a very famous thing called the "Tao", so I didn't really get it wrong. As a matter of fact all those gifts you and I are desperate to have in our lives come from the Tao. Gifts like peace of mind and purpose and everything that makes for true Human happiness. So here's some advice to you where the Tao is concerned. Work as hard as you can at the Divine Rule of Life for living and you too will be gifted.

Tao-101

I know I've dropped the Tao on you by surprise with zero notice, and now I've got some explaining to do, so let me give it a try. If you look up the Tao on the net, you'll probably find references to it in the Tao Te Ching, written by Lao Tzu. In this book it is written:

The Tao that can be told is not the eternal Tao;
The name that can be named is not the eternal name.
The Nameless is the origin of Heaven and Earth;
The Named is the mother of all things.

If you look at what Lao Tzu is saying here, two things should stand out. The second one is obvious because Lao Tzu flat out says it in plain words. In the third and fourth lines above he says that the Tao is the origin of all things in Heaven and Earth. It's where everything *comes from.* Like I said above, all the gifts of Being Human come from the Tao. That much is easy, but it's that first thing Lao Tzu says about the Tao that's boggled many minds over the Ages and he says it in the first two lines. To grapple with this part, first imagine something somewhere called the "Tao". Lao Tzu is telling us nobody can ever go see the Tao itself…..but there are thousands of books written about it we can read. But it's the part between the lines Lao Tzu left out that will twiggle your mind.

Ready? If nobody has ever seen the Tao itself, how on earth can there possibly be any books written about it? Does that mean all those books are pure fiction and the Tao doesn't exist? No it doesn't. It means we know the Tao, even though we can't know the Tao. That is the fundamental mystery of the Tao. Now that I've put that on the table, does it ring any bells? No? Gee doggone whiz then. Go back and start at the beginning of this book again. By the time you get back here you should. It's the Poem of Life. The Tao is nothing more or less than the Dualism Poem of Life that has two meanings. Give that Tao Poem of Life the correct meaning and you'll discover the real significance of what Lao Tzu is saying as well. It's this. See the world is who you are and all your true dreams will flow from the Tao. That's Tao-101 for you.

Knowing Thyself

In my former life, I saw myself as a kind of continent in the great sea of the world, and "knowing thyself" meant looking on this island for my unique strengths, skills, and character traits. Certainly this is true, but there's more to it than that. To really "know thyself" you have to look "offshore" as well. By that I mean you have to realize that who you are doesn't stop at the edge of the island. Once you begin to see yourself and that ocean as different parts of one whole, returning Vision lets you "find yourself" in the rest of the world around you. A few simple examples of what I mean will suffice. If you think you're an island unto yourself you won't find yourself in those big famous career books. You simply won't recognize yourself there. Same holds with all kinds of opportunity. If you don't have a Vision of who you are, the right sort of deal could knock on your front door tomorrow …..but you won't answer it. You won't recognize it. You won't see yourself in it. You won't *find yourself* there. In modern-day terms, you won't have the "recognition software" on-board (Vision ideas) to know that deal has *you* written all over it.

If that makes you a little nervous, how about one more to push you over the edge and go do some Rule of Life exercises. You won't recognize your own soul mate without Vision either, even if you stumble over each other at the grocery store six times a week, dropping bags of carrots and T.V. dinners in the process. Without Vision the love of your life will look like a stranger to you. On the other hand with Vision you'll *find yourself* everywhere, because you've finally understood how to "know thyself". You'll see signs all over the place, showing you how to get to the promised land.

Signs of the Promised Land

It's easy to understand why Vision lets you see signs all over the place that will point you to your destiny. Just recall that Vision is ideas about what to do with your life. Once you know what to do with your life, it's easy to see things around you that can further that aim. I'll give you a few examples from my life to illustrate what I mean. My aim in life is to get my message of wholeness to as many people as possible. So imagine me driving down the freeway and seeing a billboard advertising the Toastmaster club. If you're not familiar with Toastmasters, they're groups of people getting together to practice public speaking. No question but public speaking is part of my Mission, so I might call a local club up that very same day and start practicing giving talks myself. In short, I found myself in that billboard. But here's the thing. Twenty years ago that billboard would have held no interest for me, because I had no clue what to do with my life. For it to become a sign showing me which way to go, I had to have an aim in life.

Same kind of thing could happen at a cocktail party, if I stumbled into a local president of an environmentalist group. With Vision I'd see this man or woman as a potential ally. In essence, they and I are both on Missions to change the world for the better, and I happen to believe making the world whole could achieve their goals and mine. And so this person would be a living sign on which it is written…."perhaps we could work together to benefit mutually". A final example could be business challenges showing up in my day job. The need to become a proficient salesman in a tough economic environment is like a sign that can be read with Vision. This sign tells me the better I get at selling, the more it will help me with my Mission. Without the kind of Vision that comes with a calling however, all these signs are blank.

Create Your Own Signs

Speaking of signs, here's something that might shuffle your mind backwards a bit. Something you won't fully appreciate until your own Vision returns. In essence, every thing you do or say is a kind of sign you can learn something from that will help you on your Life Mission. To see where I'm coming from, imagine everything you ever did or said was written down in a Big Book. You're the author of this Book of Your Life, so presumably you know what the story means. But give this book to ten people and you could well get ten different meanings back. So? So there is not any fixed or absolute meaning to the book of your own life. But contrary to what you might think, this doesn't mean it has no meaning. It means it can have more and more and more meaning all the time. It means you can keep on revisiting what you say and do yourself, and learn new things all the time from them. As if your very own words and actions were curious signs you can keep on reading between the lines of to learn amazing new things about yourself.

A perfect example of this is BEES. I was surely the author of this poem, but at first I thought it was just an interesting kind of exercise in rhyming. Later I saw it had far greater meaning to me, because it was describing how fears had limited my life. BEES was a sign I created myself, and yet I could not see what was written there until my Vision returned. I can tell you this as well. Nowadays I know everything I say or do is a sign I can revisit again and again, seeking out deeper meanings. This is one way I continue to "know thyself" with greater and greater depth. The more I "know thyself" the more able I am to carry out my Mission. Same holds for you.

Vision Comes Before Choice

Here's something you'll hear a hundred times a week. "Life's all about choices". Successful people of all kinds offer that advice because it's absolutely true. But there's a great big trick to making choices the gurus don't often point out. To make the right choices in life, you can't be blind to who you are. A little story can illustrate what I mean. Imagine you're a blind man or woman in a store, trying to choose a pair of shoes to match your outfit. Nobody's there to help you either. So how can you choose? You can go "eenie, meenie, minie moe" and pick one. Will the shoes match? Probably not. Your blindness won't stop you from choosing of course, but it sure will make it difficult to make the *right* choice.

Unfortunately, the same sort of thing holds for making life choices. If you're blind to who you are, you simply won't recognize which careers, or soul mates or other important things are meant for you. You can still make those famous choices all day long. But your chances of making the right choices will be slim to none. There's a real easy way to know if you're making the right choices too. If you are, you'll be luxuriating in all the happiness stuff in chapter 13. If you aren't, you'll still be thanking God for Fridays. And the bottom line? Choices really are great things, but Vision comes before choice. Below is a real example of a real man who made many good choices without having Vision. His name is Jeremy.

A Real Expert Decision Maker

Jeremy is an old friend of mine who'd probably be considered an expert decision maker. He's a senior executive getting paid a whole lot of money to make choices for his organization. As a matter of fact, Jeremy is a gigantic fan of that "life's all about choices" expression.

I've heard Jeremy parrot that one out many times as he recounted goals achieved and missions accomplished. "You have to be strong-willed and capable of making the right choices to get anywhere in life" Jeremy said to me just the other day as he surveyed the money he'd made and possessions acquired. But right after that Jeremy lapsed into his "wistful mode" and began wishing out loud. "You know John" he started off, "I've sure made lots of money and climbed a lot of corporate ladders, but I've always felt I could do something bigger and better with my life. I've always felt I had the potential for doing something more important". Keep in mind of course, five seconds earlier Jeremy had just trotted out his "life's all about choices" mantra. Yours truly saw the opportunity and grabbed it with both hands. "So why don't you just choose something Jeremy" said I, as innocently and pure as wind-driven snow.

"Pardon me?" Jeremy asked, suspecting something was afoot here. "Well, life's all about choices isn't it?" I answered. "So choose what important thing you want to do and go do it". Silence from Jeremy's end as his brow wrinkled up, making him look like a pug dog pondering the meaning of life. In a few moments Jeremy responded. "But I don't know what it is" he said. "So what's the point of that life's about choices thing if you have no clue what you're looking for?" I submitted. That seemed to hit Jeremy like a ton of bricks, because he had no answer for it. But….of course…I had one for him. I first explained the "Vision comes before choice" idea and left it there until Jeremy had no choice. He had to ask "how do I get Vision?". "That's quite an interesting story" I said, and told it to him. In fact, Jeremy looked long and hard at the Rule of Life and decided to give it a try.

And here's the kicker. That little talk Jeremy and I had was about two years ago now and about a month ago I got a call out of the blue from Jeremy.

He wanted to thank me for helping him get his own Vision back. Here's why. Jeremy called to tell me he was quitting his job to follow a dream he'd all but forgotten about. He and his wife are opening a Bed and Breakfast in Ireland. I was struck dumb by the news and almost cried.

Vision Gives You The Journey That Counts

"A good traveler has no fixed plans, and is not intent on arriving." (Lao Tzu)

How many times have you heard people say…"in life it's the Journey that counts"? I think I heard it ten times last week alone. But like all things in Life, there's a lot more hidden meaning to discover in that particular truth. To tease some more meaning out of that old saw, look around you for a moment and you'll see everybody is on *some* kind of Journey. So let's ask some if their Journey really counts. Push a few to be honest and they'll admit they're not ecstatic about their lot in life. Back some into a corner and they might just tell you their life is "the Journey that sucks!". A few rude people might even describe their Journey this way: "Life's a bitch and then you die". Ask a thousand folks and you'd be hard pressed to find one passionately recounting stories of purpose and fulfillment on their Journey. Like I'm trying to do here for example. In short, they might *say* "It's the Journey that counts". Chances are they understand all the words of this famous saying as well. But you won't have to look too closely to realize they aren't behaving like they're on any kind of Journey that *really counts* to them.

So what's up here anyway? Something seems to be amiss. And it absolutely is. That old saying is perfectly and completely true and always has been, but it's not just *any Journey* that counts.

The Journey that counts is the one you embark on to make *your* dreams come true. Making dreams of wealth and stardom picked from a book true won't count at the end of it all. To find the Journey that really and truly counts then, you must learn how to let your very own heart-felt dreams flow from your soul. Blissful passionate Visionary dreams that light up your life and give you a bona fide reason for being here. Only if you follow your destiny will you take a Journey that counts. The only Journey worth taking is the Journey of your heart. Believe me, I've been on both kinds and can tell you this. Ordinary treks to get money and status are puny little things beside the Voyage your soul wants to take.

Vision Takes and Gives Courage

Here's something interesting for you about Vision. It may take courage to get it, but Vision also brings courage with it. Here's what I mean. To get Vision, you need courage to start you working on the Rule of Life, and real leaders can provide you with enough to get you going. But wonder of wonders, Vision returning will encourage you to work harder at the Rule of Life which will give you more Vision which will give you more courage. What an amazing thing. Starter courage gave you courage which gave you courage which gave you courage! This chain reaction of encouragement is akin to what happens in atom bombs, and it will release never-ending strength of purpose from within you. So be prepared to get drowned in torrents of bravery and valor when the truth of wholeness dawns on you. But don't forget. When you finally have the courage of your own convictions, start giving it away to people who need it. That's the rule. When you're a real leader you have to lead, by courageously being yourself.

Being Courageous Does This

Some time after I began to have the courage of my convictions once more, I noticed something odd. People seemed to be attracted to me, as if I had something they wanted. At first I didn't realize what was going on, but later it dawned on me. What people everywhere want above all things, is to be themselves. In essence, that is exactly what I was doing as I worked my dream and went about my business trying to further my Life Mission. I was a living example of someone with no fear....of being myself. And here's the thing. Any authentic soul radiates a kind of sunshine and warmth from within. I call it the "light and heat of leadership" because that's exactly what it is. There are many chilled souls desperate for this kind of spark everywhere too, and when you wake up to who you are you'll discover this about them. Automatically they'll turn towards you for warmth, because they want your inner fire for themselves. In the beginning then, as I took up my own calling with gusto, I felt like a little campfire, with a few folks circling around. As my Mission picked up steam, I felt like the sun itself with legions of lost souls orbiting, hoping to rekindle their passions. As you get your life-purpose back then, don't be surprised when it happens to you.

You Came With Seeds of Vision

Believe it or not, if you know what to look for, you'll find seeds of Vision in you as we speak. You arrived in this world with them, and you've probably stumbled over the darn things a hundred times....without knowing what they really are. That's what the next chapter is all about. I'm making it possible for you to see seeds of Vision circling your soul since you were born.

Seeds that surely sprouted way back in childhood when you were still growing *your* way. Sure enough, those seeds are patiently sitting there right now, waiting to get growing again. As I point out one after another to you, you'll begin to realize they're still capable of growing into a spectacular Human blossom. The only thing stopping them is that ever-present sinister fear of being judged. No doubt about it. Fear of being yourself is stalling your growth. Take away that terrible inhibiting fear and your soul will leap for the sunshine and sky and become capable of flying to the moon. So pay attention. These seeds of Vision can show you what to do with your life.

Chapter Eighteen
Seeds of Vision
(Are In You Right Now)

"The seed of God is in us. Given an intelligent and hard-working farmer, it will thrive and grow up to God, whose seed it is; and accordingly its fruits will be God-nature. Pear seeds grow into pear trees, nut seeds into nut trees, and God-seed into God".
Meister Eckhart (c. 1260 - 1327) German Christian mystic

Let's Get Acquainted (With Vision Seeds)

Let's not forget that you came with a Plan for growing yourself into a unique Human Being. That's why the DNA part of the plan had no choice in the beginning. It had to put together the right people parts first, so you didn't become a unique rabbit or horse. Only later is this Plan for your life supposed to show up as Vision ideas that tell you which way to grow. But even before your Vision has grown enough to let you see who you are, you will find it in your life in seed form. If you know what to look for, you'll recognize these little nuggets of your own potential waiting to be nurtured. You'll know them as funny feelings, hunches, inklings and ticklish suspicions that make you think there should be more to Life than you have now. They're the very first little sign posts on that famous Road Less Traveled you have to take to who you can be. So listen up. Here's a hitchhiker's guide to the Universe of Vision seeds for you. I put it here so you know for sure you have real true Vision just waiting to be grown.

Wanting to Make a Difference.... is a Seed of Vision

I'll bet pretty much everybody has said they want to make a difference in the world at one time or the other.

Everyone wants to be recognized as a Human Being who has value and real worth. But when all is said and done, making a difference means finding the meaning and purpose and significance you were put here to have. Making a difference doesn't mean doing something that everybody says is important. It doesn't mean getting the Nobel Peace Prize, or finding a cure for AIDS, unless that happens to be your destiny. It means doing the most important thing you could possibly do in the world. Being yourself. No doubt about it, that famous need to make a difference is huge need to be yourself. It's about that desperate desire we all have down deep to grow Human. Wanting to make a difference is a real true seed of who you can become. If you really do become yourself, you'll make a difference, whether you invent a new scientific theory or fix your pickup truck so it's the pride of your life. And here's the good news. You really CAN make a difference, because you really can learn how to be yourself. Just pay attention to what I'm saying and that authentic person at your center will flow into the world again as you get your calling back. Believe me, when you get your very own Life Mission back, you'll know what this famous difference is about. It's about the difference between real life and the life of a Zombie.

The Difference I Wanted to Make

Here's a true story about me wanting to make a difference from fifty years ago. By then I'd already lost my Way. One day on the way to grade school I saw a dog chained to a pole by a doghouse. An empty water bowl sat nearby and the chain was just long enough so he could get in and out of the tiny makeshift shed. He and I looked at each other and our souls met. He was desperately sad and so was I, but not just because I felt bad for him. When I looked into his eyes, I recognized myself. I knew his sadness and imprisonment first-hand, because he and I were in the same prison, both being stopped from being ourselves.

Me by bad ideas I was fed from birth about who I am. He by people who'd accepted the same ideas. Then and there I wanted to make the world a different place, so he and I didn't have to be in prison. I didn't know it then of course, but that desire to make a difference was a seed of Vision in me. A seed I could grow to get out of that prison and maybe….just maybe…..get a few other people and creatures out.

Wanting to be on the Team

Are you crazy as crackerjack about team sports? Not really? O.K., but maybe you'd like to be part of the team that makes things happen at work. No? Wow. You really are one in a million. Everyone else wants to be some kind of team member. Being on a team is so desirable, even becoming unofficial mascot in front of a T.V. will do. Armchair quarterbacks and Wednesday morning quilt bee captains for example. But why is it that people everywhere watch teams, join teams, or pretend to be part of teams? Well, the short answer might be that everyone wants to be a winner to make themselves feel important. If you play on the right team or even cheer for the champions, you might think you got what you were after. Your heart-of-hearts won't agree of course, because you can't get self-worth that way and it knows it.

But there's something more to all this team stuff than meets the eye. Something about team membership that really does resonate in our souls. It's this. Wanting to be on a team is a seed of Vision in all of us. A hint of something wonderful that can happen if we grow up. It works like this. If you're lucky enough to be part of a real team, you'll know what it's like to be bigger than yourself. You'll have an idea what it's like to lose your ego and become one with something. Why? On real teams, each player gives and takes and gives up selfishness for the common good. They give up their individual identities to become one with each other.

Becoming one with things is what wholeness is all about of course. That's what team membership gives you a small taste of. But remember this. That need for wholeness in your soul is a just seed of Vision. A hint of a far greater wholeness you can have if you grow yourself the right way.

Becoming the Universe

Can you guess what I'm talking about here? By now you probably can. Grow this seed of Vision in you and you'll become the Universe. You'll see clearly that everything in the world is a different part of who you are. Far more importantly though, you'll discover what it's like to truly become whole. As your Vision matures and it tells you which way to take your life, you'll begin to experience that deep and profound healing wholeness that comes from discovering who you are. It's like joining the biggest, most astonishing team you could imagine, whose goal is to let a brand new consciousness emerge and change everything. A consciousness called "Being Human". I call that "Team Universe". If you'd like to join up, just follow the Rule of Life.

That Deep Need to Help

"Teach this triple truth to all: A generous heart, kind speech, and a life of service and compassion are the things which renew humanity." (The Buddha)

Lots of guys and gals have a deep need to help people, or creatures, or the environment, because deep down we all know the truth, even if it hasn't risen up into those brains of ours. The truth is, everything around us is who we are. People. Creatures. Our environment. It's all *us*. In our heart of hearts we know we should be treating ourselves with respect, compassion and care.

That's why so many folks have a need to "be of service", or help the world. Their souls know this desire to help is desire to help themselves-the-world. I hope you noticed I didn't say "help themselves *to the world*" by the way. I said…help *themselves*….who just happen to *be* the world. I'm talking wholeness here, not selfishness. And you? Ever felt a need to become a big brother, or to donate to charities, or join a helping organization like the Red Cross? Are you a part-time environmental activist ….trying to help the earth survive? Guess what? That's a seed of Vision in your soul to grow. It's a seed of Being Human, so go ahead and grow it into something amazing. You.

Wanting to Change the World

Here's another very famous seed of Vision in all of us. That ancient wish everyone has to change the world. Have you ever caught yourself wanting to do that? I have, but I used to think only a few rare people like the Wright Brothers actually did such a thing. The world is a pretty big place after all, and most of us can barely change our own backyards. Right? Completely wrong. When you begin to come to grips with wholeness, you'll see that this desire to change the world is really a desire to change ourselves. Why?

Well, it's easy to see if you think about it for a minute. If everything around you is a different part of one whole, then changing yourself changes the whole. Changing yourself by growing changes the whole world….the entire Universe actually…just like that. If you don't believe it, just try this out. Say you have a gray sweater you'd like to spruce up a bit. So you sew a nice big red heart over the heart. Now ask yourself a question. Has your sweater changed? Yes it has. The whole sweater changed when you changed the part over your heart.

Same thing applies to you. Begin to grow yourself *your* way once more and you'll change the entire world you're part of. There's no way around it. The only reason we don't see it clearly every day of our lives, is that we've separated ourselves from the world. Today then, it doesn't look like growing ourselves changes the world. But it does. And everybody is desperate to change the world today, because deep down they know we're supposed to. Our souls know each of us was put here to change the world all the time....by growing ourselves our way. So don't forget. When you catch yourself wanting to change the world....you just saw a seed of Vision nestled down by that authentic person of yours. Now go do it! Learn how to see the world correctly and you'll feel the kind of power that changes the world flow through you.

There Must Be More to Life

Remember that "must be more to life" sign of losing a calling? That famous saying you've been repeating endlessly now for years? O.K., but how come you're so sure something is missing? You didn't say "*maybe* there's more to life than I've got now". Or "*perhaps* something is missing somewhere". Not at all. You used the word "must" to tell the world you had absolutely zero doubts about it . But have you ever wondered why everybody is so sure there must be more to life, even when they can't say exactly what's missing? When all is said and done, it's simple. It's because they're looking at a seed of who they can be. A seed of Vision buried within all of us.

Alright, but what is it that we all know with absolute certainty about seeds? They have potential. Potential for growth. Just add food and water to any ordinary seed and you'll see what I mean. Unless it's dead, you can be absolutely certain something will grow from it.

Maybe you have no idea what it will grow into, but you'll be *sure* it has potential to grow into some kind of interesting plant. Right? Exactly, and the same holds with that "must be more to life" feeling we all get now and then. The certainty comes from knowing deep down we can grow ourselves into something spectacular ......because it's our *potentials* we're feeling. See what I mean? If you've ever said "there must be more to life" you were looking right at a seed of who you can become. You are in touch with your potential. If you grow that seed of Vision within you, it will show you what to do with your life. Eventually, as your life begins to fill up with happy things made possible by growing up, you'll also realize there really was way more to life than you had before. In fact, you'll realize your life was only a mere shadow of what it has become.

Seeds Can Get Stifled

Now you've had a peek at Vision seeds, and I hope you can hardly wait to get them growing again. But here's something I should warn you about right now. The Road Less Traveled you're about to head out on has many roadblocks on it that can stop those seeds from growing. But don't worry. I am now going to point out these pitfalls and show you how to get past them.

Chapter Nineteen
Seven Roadblocks
(On the Way to Your Dreams)

"One who gains strength by overcoming obstacles possesses the only strength which can overcome adversity". - Albert Schweitzer (1875 – 1965)

Roadblocks on the Path of Life

Roadblock Number One on the Path of your Life is fear of being judged. That barrier can keep you in your seed-shell forever, but it isn't the only stumbling block. Over centuries we've put lots of nice brick walls, grease pits and quicksand patches smack in the Road. The one we're all supposed to be going down, making it less traveled every generation. Soon nobody will be on it. Here's a few.

A Roadblock Called Common Sense

To see that the world really is whole, you have to give up common sense. If that sounds like the biggest roadblock you ever heard of, you're probably correct. But trust me, I am not going to ask you to pull the whiskers off tigers or play blindfolded in traffic. All I'm going to do is ask you to give up common sense. To get an idea what I mean, let's first make it clear what common sense is all about. The words "common sense" mean "basic beliefs everybody has about how the world works". It's a sense of how things work that we all have in common.

And here's the most basic belief we all have in common about how the world works. Essentially everyone believes the world is filled with many different, separate things. That's the root sense of how the world is, that people everywhere hold to be true.

And that's precisely what you have to give up if you want to discover who you are and what to do with your life. You have to give up thinking the world consists of many different separate things, and see those things as different parts of who you are. Different parts of One whole. As I said before, once you give up this "common (but mistaken) sense of how the world works", you'll begin to realize we all share One Life. From there it's but a short hop, skip and a jump to realizing your life must be worth as much as any life. Once you're there, your life will never be the same again, as you begin to see who you really are once more. Unfortunately, if you can't get past this common and misguided sense of things, it will be all but impossible to see why you're here. But don't despair, because you can climb this barrier with me. The Rule of Life will show you how to re-train your brain to see the Truth. The Truth is, you are the world. People with common sense might not believe it, but it is absolutely and unequivocally true.

The Barrier of Selfishness

The next barrier is called "selfishness". Sad to say, the world today is absolutely and fundamentally….right from the core….selfish. No question about it. Our selfish ways begin with our mistaken view of the world. But the real gut-wrenching, soul destroying, pain inflicting aspects of selfishness don't just come from believing things around us are separate. Not at all. It comes from making sure everything we do is selfish. Individual people take from others to get more "self worth", as selfishness rises to new heights for example. Billboards on every street corner scream "do this or get that and your life will be worth more" as well. Do we buy the argument? Of course we do. We spend most of our lives trying to feel more important by having more or being better than others. We pay teachers to teach our children selfishness too. We believe wholeheartedly in selfishness from the depths of our souls to the tips of our fingers.

And it is destroying us. And so, the barrier of selfishness is in your face right now. If you can't get over it I'll tell you exactly what will happen. You'll never know what your own dreams are, much less make them true. Not a chance.

Bogus Individuality

"In order to be an immaculate member of a flock of sheep, one must above all be a sheep oneself". – Albert Einstein

It's fair to say that "individuality" is a prized thing, at least in the Americas and Europe. People with "character" stand out in a crowd and are praised for their distinctiveness. Pretty much everyone wants to be "different" to get kudos for it too. Nobody wants to be one white sheep in a big flock of identical pristine snowy looking animals. Unfortunately, individuality is something that can be so badly misunderstood, it becomes a barrier to growing up. As it turns out, there are two ways to "be different", only one of which will be of any use to you. I call these "real and bogus" individuality because that's exactly what they are. One is an expression of authentic "difference", and the other is fake. Human Beings are "authentically different" when being themselves, because that's the only way their amazing uniqueness will flow into the world.

On the other hand, people terrified of being themselves often simply do weird things or look strange…*trying* to be different. That's "bogus individuality" and to get it you could set your hair in concrete or keep Tasmanian devils as pets….because nobody else does. So how can you tell if you or someone else is an "authentic individual"? Easy. Ask he or she (or yourself) if they know why they're here. If they don't, it doesn't matter how odd looking they are or weirdly they behave. They aren't "true individuals". Same holds in the other direction of course.

Real individuals might not look peculiar or behave abnormally. They could be mild mannered, conforming, or even outright boring….if that really is who they are. That reminds me of a real life story of a guy called "Puck" who really did look different. Here's Puck's story.

Puck's Story

One company I worked at, there was a guy in the plant they called "Puck". I never did learn why they called him that, and wasn't about to ask the man himself, because he was about seven foot thirteen high by four feet wide and topped the scales at three hundred pounds. Puck would have looked different standing there in his birthday suit, but this guy went way out of his way to look even more different. He sported a big goatee beard…..dyed orange and a Mohawk haircut…..dyed blue. Like most fellows Puck's age, he wore a big nose ring as well, but this one had a small skull on it that gave me the creeps. Then there was the leather. Mr. Puck never wore anything but ancient beat up leather that looked like it had been abandoned by the cow at death. I'm talking vests, pants, shirts and who-knows-what-else hidden behind the scenes. You name it, and it was gritty black leather, studded with steel rivets like you see on bulldog collars. You could see Puck coming for miles, giving you lots of time to get out of his way.

The thing is, Puck wasn't the big dumb tough guy he looked like at all. If you could get past his shocking appearance, you'd discover he was an extremely bright, considerate man. I did, and I learned something from him. One day I asked …"what's with the colored hair and leather Puck?". "I'm supposed to be different" he said. "What do you mean…*supposed to be*?" I said. "Dunno" said Puck…"I just want to express myself". "You want to be a bad-ass biker?" I said. "Not really" said Puck…"I don't know what I want to be….but I know I'm different".

That's when it hit me. We all know deep down we're astonishingly different. But most of us never figure out how to let that difference out. We're never able to really be our truly unique selves, so we just *try to look different*. But, like Puck, we know in our hearts it isn't the real thing.

A Pitfall Called Abundance

"Every increased possession loads us with a new weariness". -- John Ruskin, 'The Eagle's Nest'

If you'd care to visit a local bookstore, you should be able to find quite a few books advising you how to "attract abundance" into your life. Better yet, just check out any on-line bookstore. I found something like 6,700 books on "having abundance in your life" on Amazon for instance. Many of these books are fabulous additions to your library of things that can help you create the life of your dreams. They certainly describe an abundance of things you can have too. But you should be very careful about attracting an abundance of things into your world. You might just attract a wrong abundance.

Take me for example. When I was still astonishingly immature, at the age of forty-five for example, I too wanted an abundance of things. I actually thought I was doing pretty well at attracting abundance, because my money was multiplying and everything was getting bigger. Houses, properties, cars, and toys for example. Bystanders probably looked at me and said….."that guy sure knows how to attract an abundance". But the truth was, I didn't have a clue what real abundance was about. I was just hindering my growth by focusing on a "dumb abundance". Thankfully, I now know what the difference is, and can spell it out to you with gruesome clarity.

To do that, I'll just make up a little story to illustrate what a "real abundance" is. I'm sure you'll get the point real quick. Imagine planting an acorn in fertile ground, and coming back fifty years later. What do you think you'll see? Thousands of branches and millions of leaves. Birds nests old and new and perhaps a tree house built by children who have gone on to become men and women. If you look more closely you might see this giant tree is home to many small creatures as well. Mice have burrowed by its roots for example, and hundreds of different insects call this tree their Universe. If you took a tally in fact, you'd discover an astonishing abundance of things, all part and parcel of the life of this oak tree. That's what is called a Real abundance. A huge diversity of things relevant to the unique life of that oak you planted so long ago. Real abundance is everything that follows from growing something. Anything that grows *the way it was meant to grow*, attracts a real abundance of things necessary to the creation of its life. As we'll see in a moment, this applies to your life as well.

But now let's explore what I call a "dumb abundance". To do that, we'll go back to that acorn you planted, but this time imagine the acorn doesn't grow at all. It's fallen on barren ground perhaps, and nothing happens. Fifty years later you return to find nothing but the place where you put your acorn. Now what? Now you can "attract a dumb abundance", by piling a bunch of things in a circle around the hole in the ground where the acorn used to be. So go ahead, line up coins and cars and stuff of all kinds. Make a big pile of things surrounding the acorn's grave. There you go, you've now got a "dumb abundance". A dumb abundance is just an abundance. It has nothing to do with the growth of some unique life. See what I mean here? No? Alright, let's give some real and true living examples in terms of human beings. That should do the trick.

Real Abundance

Let's say you're a business lady at heart, and have a real dream you want to make true. Here's what bystanders will see. Day by day, year by year, you'll be exploring business ideas and trying to create the business of your dreams. As you grow your dream life of being in that kind of business, you'll fail more than once before you succeed. Part of the abundance of things germane to your life could easily be a bankruptcy or two, as you learn financial lessons necessary to running a business. In fact, you'll probably find an abundance of tough things like this, before things smooth out and your dreams really get going. Certainly there will be an abundance of money in your life too, but mostly debt in the beginning. The gurus talking about attracting abundance rarely mention these parts of your abundance jig-saw puzzle. But they are just as necessary as the toys and riches made possible later by your successful business.

When all is said and done then, the abundance you attract will be a many faceted thing. It will consist of joys and hardships and challenges, as well as physical stuff like the machines your business uses and the cash it needs to operate. Your real abundance will be really diverse and it will make your ever-growing life a thing to behold. On the other hand, other unique lives will attract a radically different looking abundance of things. Farmers, poets, peace activists or firemen will all attract a "different looking abundance". But here's the most important thing to know about "real abundance". Every single soul who learns how to grow *their way* and create *their dream life*, gets an equal share of Bliss. Bliss is another word for that abundance of things I called "Big Happiness". So don't forget. When you see the abundance barrier coming up, attract the right abundance into your life or you will regret it.

"A man's life consisteth not in the abundance of the things he possesseth" – Luke 12:15

A Barrier We Call Parenthood

This little roadblock will probably throw you into defensive mode right away, if you happen to have kids yourself. I've been called dicey names many times for just bringing it up. But it only sounds mean-spirited and selfish if you don't fully appreciate it. I'll try to help you appreciate it. If I fail, feel free to call me names. Here it is. I believe it is pretty much accepted wisdom that you can't really follow your dreams if you have kids. Most people don't have a clue what their own dreams are of course, but they believe this gem of wisdom also. For the sake of argument however, let's assume you're one of those rare birds who actually does have a real dream….but you have kids. Like pretty much everybody else, you believe it would be selfish to spend money or devote time to your dream, because your kids need both. You are absolutely right of course, but also absolutely wrong. It's true you need enough money to feed, clothe, and care for your children. And it's absolutely the case your kids need time with you.

But if you do not understand that your children are Human Beings, you could easily withhold the biggest, most powerful and valuable gift imaginable from them. Here's what I mean. When all is said and done, the only thing of importance to your children, is figuring out what to do with their lives and doing it. Why? Because that is what brings authentic success. If you are teaching them by living example how to make a dream real….infusing them with courage in the process, they will at least have a decent shot at having that happy life you so desire for them. On the other hand, if you teach them that dreams are nothing but "luxuries" people can't afford to have if they have kids, guess what? They will teach the same to their kids who will go on to pass this travesty on generation after generation. You will have committed a crime against unborn Humanity.

In case you think I'm blowing smoke here, just go ask a few social workers or psychologists. They'll tell you that parents can start off an endless chain of sad behavior by being bad examples to children who keep on passing the lessons on. Now let's return to the money and time thing again, and get our priorities straight. It's certainly true that you can give your kids five more video games if you don't spend any money following your dream. You can also play five more video games with them if you're not spending time working your own dream.

But if you have a real dream, your kids will be *part* of it. You and they will work together to create a life of many dreams. Yes it will sometimes be a challenge to make ends meet, but challenges are what growing is all about, and you will all learn from them and grow even faster because of it. Certainly your time with the kids will be limited…but you will learn first-hand what the expression "quality time" means. Your times together will be worth more than they ever could be if you weren't living an authentic life. I hope you really do appreciate what I'm saying here, because it really is a big truth your family cannot live without. So don't let generations of people get stopped by the barrier of parenthood, like a lady I know personally. Here's Sue's story.

Sue's Story

I know a woman called Sue, who started off her own long chain of lost souls some time ago. She doesn't know it, but her children are being home-schooled in the Great Art of Getting Lost Forever. They'll almost certainly pass the lessons on to their kids as well, and so on for a long time to come. Here's Sue's sad story. Susan is a thirty-something lady with a good job and three kids. Twins plus one. Sue has a hard working husband as well and they can lay claim to a pretty good standard of living, including a nice house, two cars, and hundreds of toys for the kids.

The thing is, Susan's always wanted to be a doctor. She's had this dream all her life and several years ago decided it was time to make that dream come true. Signing up for pre-med courses, Sue began her studies. Then came familiar obstacles all dreams have tied to them. Parents, friends and colleagues laughed out loud at her for example. "*You ... become a doctor?*....HA!....tell me another one!" said pretty much everyone. But Sue didn't let that barrier slow her down. She kept studying, getting great grades, and loving every minute of it. But friends and parents aren't done yet. They have bigger ammo in reserve. It's called the selfishness cannon, and here's how it goes. "Are you telling me you're going to take useless toys and extra junk food out of the kids' mouths to make your dreams come true?"...said her closest advisors. "You're going to deprive the tiny waifs... just to show them how to get-a-life?" said mom and dad. That did it. Suzie just plain broke down and cried over the thought of taking ice-cream bars out of the mouths of her little babies. And so she gave up her dreams, and those of all her grandchildren.

Robotic Naysayers

I know I'm repeating myself talking about naysayers, but it's for your own good. I have to train you to use them to your advantage, so you can leap this hurdle with ease. All set? Let's get at it. Have you ever met a robotic naysayer, stuck in the "on" position? Sure you have. It's the guy who has a million reasons anything you come up with can't be done. Or the gal who laughs knowingly when you suggest anything new. What does she know that you don't? It can't be done of course. These amazingly consistent men and women are programmed pessimists. Thinking of changing jobs maybe? "You're too old, young, small, big, black, white or green" say the naysayers. Trying to get your own dreams back are you? "Six ways from Sunday it's dumb!" they say. O.K., but who are these guys anyway?

Not sure? I'll tell you. They're people who don't know what to do with their lives. Wait a minute here. Is there something wrong with this picture? People who have no idea why they're here are trying to stop the rest of us from figuring that out? Isn't that a lot like a deaf man advising you on ring-tones for your new phone? Yes, as a matter of fact it's pretty much like that. So how are you going to get past this endless barrier of people bound and determined to stop you from getting ahead? You can actually make the naysayers work *for* you, by remembering what the Russian psychologist Ivan Pavlov learned about reflex training. In case you've never heard of Pavlov, he discovered he could train dogs to drool when he rang a bell. Once the dogs were trained, all Pavlov had to do was ring a bell and they'd slobber all over him, as if dinner was around the corner. But Pavlov's discovery can be used to your advantage. You can train yourself to slobber at the mere sight of a naysayer. Sorry. Only kidding. But you really can train yourself to see these folks for what they are.

It works like this. Every time you hear a man or woman say "can't, don't, won't and it's impossible"… say this to yourself. "There's someone going nowhere… and I'm not going with them". When confronted by someone dragging their feet, learn to recognize that scraping sound as naysaying and go find someone else to have adventures with. As soon as someone calls you names for trying and failing and aspiring to greatness….hear Pavlov's little bells ringing and say this out loud: "*I must be on the right track, because naysayers are experts at recognizing people chasing dreams*!". If you think this is just some kind of silly exercise I made up to add some padding to the book, think again. I have literally trained myself to love naysayers. Every time I hear one now, a little bell goes off in my head. I know for sure these people have missed the boat, and can't come with me to the promised land. Here's something a little spooky for you to look forward to as you start training to push past the naysaying barricade as well.

Eventually you'll notice the naysayers following you around. Why the heck would they do that? Deep down, every naysaying human being knows they're well and truly lost. Each naysayer also harbors a passionate desire to be set free. When these cynical pessimists dimly perceive that you are well on your way to true Freedom, they will automatically begin to follow the light you cast upon them. Yes they will. I guarantee you'll have your own followers.

A Real Robot Story

The story you are about to read is absolutely real, but recently modified. In its original form it was just a plain naysaying story about a fellow I worked with in one of my day jobs. But this story has dramatically changed of late, so I have come back and updated it. It's a bittersweet kind of story actually, but real life is often like that. Many years ago when parachuted into a company on a rescue mission, I inherited a manager by the name of Barry.

Barry had been there for decades and was famous for his pessimism. You might even say Barry was an *uber naysayer,* because his native smarts let him see the half-empty side of the half-full glass in an instant. No sooner would I suggest some improvement project or another but Barry would trot out fifty obstacles, six pitfalls, and three good reasons we shouldn't even bother. He was so quick in fact, it often made my head spin. Just so you know, really smart people make the best naysayers. They can come up with reasons to quit right now that you can't deny. To avoid quitting and actually make dreams come true when they're around, you have to put earplugs in.

Anyhow, Barry was so good at this game it sometimes made me laugh and sometimes made me want to cry out loud for someone to shoot him!

Luckily for me though, I'd already trained myself to see naysayers for what they are, so Barry didn't really bother me. In fact, I took on the challenge of trying to take the cause of Barry's naysaying away. Namely, his root fear of being himself.

The Story Changes

At first my efforts yielded absolutely nothing. But Barry's powerful intellect and broad multi-faceted soul was not asleep. Silently it watched and listened as yours truly delivered messages of hope. After some time I realized that Barry had actually trained *himself* to see his own naysaying behavior, and try to tone it down. Barry hadn't actually changed his stripes yet, but he had taught himself to "keep his naysaying mouth shut". That in itself was quite a remarkable thing, considering Barry had decades of foot dragging behind him. As time went on however, I began noticing that Barry wasn't just keeping his mouth shut. Slowly he began taking other naysayers to task for throwing cold water on things. I could hardly believe my eyes, but sure enough, Barry's soul had been responding to my talks about wholeness all along…without saying a word. Eventually Barry regained the courage of his convictions and began making big life changes on the way to his dreams.

A Miracle Happens

Then routine surgery left Barry paralyzed from the waist down. At first the docs said he wouldn't walk out of the hospital. Tests indicated he had no nerve function below his navel, but miraculously, a day later, Barry began wiggling his toes. Still grossly impaired at this stage, Barry slipped into a natural deep dark depression and began grieving. What happened next was like a burst of sunshine. Barry's soul flexed its muscles and burst out fighting.

He took on this challenge with stunning optimism that would have bowled over naysayers at fifty yards. In one huge flash, Barry grew more Human and literally passed yours truly on the Road Less Traveled. Barry has not simply abandoned naysaying, he has become an inspiration. I myself am absolutely inspired by this man's courage and determination to carry on and make his dreams real. So don't forget this when you stumble into your share of naysayers on the way to your dreams. At the heart of every pessimist is a strong soul who might even help you find your own way some day.

An Obstacle Called "Blindness"

Here's an obstacle that is really tricky to get past to say the least. It's the kind of blindness you're afflicted with if still terrified of being yourself. An absence of Vision that makes it impossible to see which way to take your life. Here's why this obstacle is so tough to surmount. Chances are, if you're reading this book, you'd give just about anything to really see who you are and what your true passion is. Correct? Alright, so I'm here to tell you there are signs all over the place with exactly that written all over them. Signs at your workplace, in your family life, and out in public where everybody can see them. These signs are like billboards plastered along the freeways on which it is written: *"This is who you are and here's your very own authentic dream"*. Televisions are broadcasting these signs too and you'll even find them on your ipod. Yes they're in books of all kinds and newspapers and magazines. If you had Vision you'd see them.

That brings us to the obstacle. I'm saying you have to follow the Rule of Life and get your Vision back to see them. But how the heck do you know I'm not just pulling your leg here for fun and profit?

It sounds a bit like someone saying...."if you learn how to wiggle your ears and toes at the same time you'll see leprechauns all over the place you never saw before". Yes? Absolutely. Except for one thing. It doesn't matter if you see the leprechauns or not, but seeing what to do with your life is very useful. Useful enough to take a chance on getting Vision back. Worst that can happen is you waste some time. Best that can happen is you find everything you're looking for in life. There's one of those famous choices for you, and I hope you make the right one. Just to help you make it, I'll ask you to recall your experience with new words. Remember what happens when you learn new words? You discover you were blind to them because they show up today in books you read yesterday...but didn't see them. Same kind of blindness.

"There is a magnet in your heart that will attract true friends. That magnet is unselfishness, thinking of others first... when you learn to live for others, they will live for you". Paramahansa Yogananda (1893 - 1952) India swami, teacher

Ready For More?

Let's stop and review for a minute. One you've started working the Rule of Life daily to recover your passion in life, you'll want to know what to expect as seeds of Vision begin growing again. This part your Journey needs some little flags to mark the trail because it's easy to miss signs of progress in the beginning. When Vision begins to stir once more, it does so in very subtle and unfamiliar ways. Ways you could easily miss completely or simply disregard, if you hadn't been prepared for them. Destiny must have been with me in the early stages of my own rebirth for instance, because I didn't ignore the odd feelings of Vision returning, even though I had no idea what was going on. What follows then, is a guide to the feelings you'll have as your very own Vision begins to come back into your life. Signs of Vision seeds stirring.

Chapter Twenty
How to Know
(Vision's Returning)

"Our consciousness rarely registers the beginning of a growth within us any more than without us: there have been many circulations of the sap before we detect the smallest sign of the bud". George Eliot

Nothing Happens at First

Heartfelt seeds of real Vision are a lot like ordinary seeds. They don't spring up full grown instantly or even grow quickly. It takes a little while before they'll make themselves known in your life. In fact, you might even say they're a lot like carrot seeds. Think you'll have carrots for dinner tonight because you planted carrot seeds at eight A.M. this morning? I doubt it. Same thing exactly with seeds of Vision nestled by your authentic soul. You won't see who you are and what to do with your life day one. In the beginning very little happens, but take heart, and don't give up on your Rule of Life work. All kinds of good things are happening beneath the surface, just like in the old story about a Chinese bamboo tree. Ever heard this tale? No? It's below.

Like the Chinese Bamboo Tree

Imagine someone gives you a Chinese Bamboo Tree seed for Christmas. "Wow …thank you very much" you say…"that sounds like a fun thing for the garden!". So off you go in the spring and plant your little seed. Year one you water and fertilize and weed your seed six times a day. And? Nothing at all. O.K., but you know some seeds take a bit of time to grow, so year two you make sure it has lots of sun and space.

You cover it completely with Panda poop too....but nothing happens. Now what? Well, you're persistent, so you repeat the same thing again next year and year four. Still nothing. By the fifth year, you're getting sick and tired of tending this stupid seed. But wait a minute....what's that over there. A tiny little shoot is coming up. Then.....miracle of miracles your bamboo tree grows NINETY FEET in the next six months! You can hardly believe your eyes. You can hardly believe you didn't give up on it as well. Same thing applies to seeds of Vision. Virtually nothing happens in the beginning, but if you don't give up on them, they'll begin to stir. You'll know this astonishing renewal of your own passion by many different feelings. I've outlined some below for you to watch out for.

Funny Feelings

One of the very first "odd feelings" you'll get as Vision seeds stir is hope. Hope comes back into your life when you start believing in possibilities again. Just so you know, when you have no idea who you are, possibilities are nothing but vague, unreal, taunting things that never have the ring of truth to them. Even worse, you won't even realize you don't believe in them. You might think you do, but trust me, you don't. If you did you'd be busy making possibilities real right now. But you aren't. Are you? I didn't think you were, so to give you an idea what rekindled belief in possibilities feels like, I'll present two stories. One is made up and the other is from my own experience with hope coming back.

We'll begin with the little fabrication. Pretend for a moment you're a really poor child, living on the wrong side of the tracks, with parents who hardly have a nickel to their name. You don't have toys or pocket money or things the other kids have. To make matters worse, on the way to school, you have to pass a candy store that displays its wares in a huge window.

There in front of you every day are dozens of different candies you'd give anything for. But you don't have a single penny, and have given up hoping for candy money. Then one day something very strange happens. As you approach the candy store you see a big sign out front. The sign says…"owner won the Lottery and has retired to California…..so take whatever candy you want….it's free". Stopped dead in your tracks in complete disbelief, you stand there in front of the store staring. At first you can't believe your eyes, but the door's wide open and nobody's there. At first you think it must be some kind of trick. Surely the door will be slammed in your face if you go for candy. But nobody's there and that door is open wide as the Arizona sky. Back and forth your head goes between disbelief and small hope. You take a step or two towards the door and begin to feel dizzy as Joy grows in your breast. Your head starts to spin as you get closer and nobody's stopping you from making your dream of candy come true. Standing in the store you have feelings of exhilaration, wonder, and flat-out amazement. Gigantic hope for candy fills your heart like sunshine. You can barely believe it's possible. Even more amazing, you finally realize you can have as much candy as you want, and can come back tomorrow for more. Hope coming back will feel something like that as a warmth from within bursts into your heart and lights up your life. I know for sure, because it happened to me. My very own real-life story is below.

Hope Comes Back

It was maybe fifteen years ago now that I began to have hope once more. Hope I could find what I was looking for in life. I remember that day very well indeed. It happened in my place of employment. It was one of my very first experiences with how Vision shows you what possibilities can be made real. I was chief of a manufacturing firm at the time and had dutifully created some goals for my managers to achieve.

By then my fears of being judged had been pared down and some Vision had returned. Enough that I could see clearly what achievements were possible for my company. Just to make sure you understand what I'm getting at here, without Vision you don't really see what is possible at all. You're just making up goals that seem to make sense. On the other hand, Vision lets you see the what's really possible in your own future. At any rate, I'd seen some goals with Vision, and my management team had actually achieved them. Then came my odd experience. After a meeting, one of my managers came to me with a puzzled look on his face and a question. A graph he'd created showed his department slowly but surely moving towards an efficiency goal I'd set. Over a period of twelve months the curve made a bee-line to where I wanted it to be. But I've never forgotten the question he asked. "How did you know a year ago that my department would rise up to exactly this efficiency?" he said. He couldn't figure out how I could see into the future.

At first I told him I'd just set a goal and he'd achieved it. But then I realized something and corrected myself. The truth was, I really was seeing into the future. With Vision I saw what was really possible for that particular company and how to achieve it. I therefore explained to him how Vision lets you "see into the future", and he was amazed. So was I, because that little conversation made me realize something important. Suddenly I knew for sure that possibilities I was imagining for my own life would be made real…..just like that. And to say the least, it brought huge hope into my life. Hope I might achieve what I thought was possible for me. I felt pretty much like that kid in a candy store we just met.

Old Memories Come to Life

When Vision begins to stir within you again, you'll also be stunned as old memories come to life. Ancient recollections will have meaning they never had before. Vision doesn't just let you see the future, it makes it possible to turn back the pages of the book of your own life and discover yourself there. As a matter of fact, the more your Vision matures, the more amazed you'll be when looking back. Eventually you'll see every single thing you ever did was part of the Plan for your Life. A Plan you'll take up with huge passion again. Here are two of my memories that meant nothing to me until I had Vision. The first is really and truly strange. I thought it was strange at the time, but with Vision it became ominously so.

One night back in my college days, I was heading home late from studying at the library. On the way was a gigantic oak tree at the top of a hill I was plodding up. Granted I was all but exhausted from marathon studying, and maybe I was hallucinating. But whatever the heck was going on, I recall it clear as a bell some thirty odd years later. Suddenly I looked up at the tree silhouetted against the sky and saw something odd. You know how you can see animals in clouds? Well….here's a better one for you. I saw words written in tree branches. They said: "Write the Book of Life". I can still remember stopping dead in my tracks and rubbing my eyes. In an instant the words disappeared and I assumed my brain had played a trick on me. Even so, those words in the tree were just as clear as animals in clouds and I pondered them all the way home.

Needless to say, I had no idea what the "book of life" was, or what those words were telling me to do. By the next day I'd put the experience out of my mind, but I never forgot it. Many decades later, that memory suddenly surfaced as seeds of Vision began to stir within me.

Suddenly as this scrap of new-found Vision tingled, I turned my Mind's eye backwards in time and stopped dead in my tracks again. I saw those words in the tree had been speaking about this very book. At first I refused to believe it, because my experiences with Vision were few and far between at the time. But eventually I simply could not deny the obvious. This book really is a "book of life" and those words in the tree were a kind of sign pointing me somewhere I would eventually go. I'm sure you don't believe a word of it, because it's strange as strange can be. It also happens to be absolutely and completely true. When you get your own Vision back, you'll come to believe in this kind of thing, because it is a bona fide experience of growing Human. The next Vision stirring story you might even believe right now.

A Vision Stirring Story

Here's another example of newfound Vision creating meaning in my own early life. This time stirrings of my inner sight pointed me way back to when I was about fifteen years old. By that age it's fair to say I was absolutely entranced by light. The way colors and shapes sprang alive in its presence intrigued me no end, and I was fascinated by the way light would make things appear and disappear. To completely sane people, turning out all the lights wasn't exactly a puzzle. But yours truly the oddball wonderer wondered what was going on. I'd point a dim bulb at something (uh…no.. not me) and turn the brightness up. And? All kinds of little details were revealed that I couldn't see before. Light seemed to conjure them out of nowhere like magic.

Same in reverse as well. If I turned the lights out, it was as if everything disappeared. "Does light somehow create and destroy?" I asked myself when no one was around to laugh at me. One time I even ventured to say out loud "light's a truly magical thing".

To which my mother replied…."No son it isn't, it's a bulb on a wire". I have to admit though, I didn't believe her. For reasons I just couldn't fathom at the time, light remained an awesomely real magical thing to me. Now let's fast forward a few years. Say ten. By now I've read a whole lot of science books and discovered that light has puzzled and intrigued virtually every scientific mind since Aristotle. I've also discovered that the mystery of light has only deepened over the Ages, as we've come to learn more about it. Not only has light inspired artists of all kinds to create their works, it's motivated the most modern quantum physicists to study its ways. By twenty five years of age then, I'd come to realize that light really was a magical thing.

Now we have to let another twenty years go by, to where I'm recovering my own Vision. At the age of forty-five, I'm beginning to see that light in all its magical forms is a kind of Divine guidance men and women and Mankind needs desperately to find the Way. I'm starting to understand that the light of the world has been speaking to us for many generations, in religious, artistic, and scientific ways, trying to show us who we are. Slowly I'm beginning to see that light and love are one and the same and necessary for our salvation. But with this inner sight of mine growing, I also can see back to those teenage years and the mysterious way light made itself known to me. With Vision I saw those profound feelings of awe and mystery were there to push me on my Mission. It would take decades before I "knew thyself" enough to be able to say this with confidence. But as seeds of Vision stirred within me some years back now, the essential truth of it began to dawn. In essence, I could clearly see the emotions light kindled in my soul were signs on my own Road Less Traveled. Signs I couldn't read until I could See.

Old Memories

Yes, I agree. Those examples of how Vision can show you who you are in your own past life are stone crazy kinds only a demented soul like myself would have. So maybe I'd better give you some sensible examples. These fall into the category of "interest memories". Guru counselors are always telling us we can find what we're *really* interested in back in our childhood years. Apparently our very own passions in life can be found there more easily, because they're not all cluttered up by adult baggage. Accordingly then, all we have to do is look back and see what really turns us on, fires us up, or passionately inspires us. It certainly makes a whole lot of sense, and there's a whole lot of truth to it as well. But if you're anything like I was, you can look back at the pages of your life all you want without any kind of "Eureka" experience. I desperately combed the book of my own young life many times looking for the Bliss I was told should be there. Every single time I found nothing of particular interest. Now I know it's because I simply didn't have the eyes to see.

As Vision began stirring in me once more however, I began to look back again…and was floored. All kinds of memories of who I really am were sitting there right out in the open. Here's one for you. Back in the "good old days" when I was about ten, we had what were called "library classes". I believe these classes have gone the way of the Dodo since, but back then they were staples in our educational diet. There we were taught how librarians organized libraries via the "Dewey decimal system" and wrote "book reports" on books we had to read. I don't remember a lot about my library lessons, but one thing has stuck with me ever since. The library teacher kept on picking me to read my book reports, and made a big fuss about my silly little stories. At the time I thought she was, well, just picking on me.

But thirty five years later with burgeoning Vision, I looked back in time and saw something very different. I could see very clearly I was naturally inclined to scratch out thoughts on paper. As a matter of fact, I've kept on doing this very sort of thing in various ways all my life. In terms the gurus would use, one of my core interests or passions has always been "writing". At heart I'm really an exploring soul, but writing is my way of sharing my explorations. Some explorers communicate their discoveries by mathematical means and others by literally singing them out. There are as many ways to reach out and touch the souls of other human beings with our life-adventures as there are people to do it. And writing is an intimate friend of mine, because it's who I am. But do you think I could see that part of me before Vision came back into my life? I could see my various forays into the written word alright, but it didn't hold any significant meaning for me. For the real and true soul within us to stand out like a beacon of light, we need Vision.

The same sort of thing will happen to you too. As your Vision stirs, you'll start seeing who you are in old "interests" of yours where you saw nothing of importance before. Here are a few simple examples. Let's say you're a musician-at-heart turned accountant to make money. Early joyful days writing small songs and learning to play the guitar may come back to you and you'll recognize your true self there. A person you looked at for years but didn't know. An authentic soul, calling you from afar to be yourself. Or maybe you're really a farmer way down in your heart-of-hearts, who became a lawyer to please mom and dad. Stirring Vision may make you remember joyful days planting little veggie gardens. The feel and smell and taste of Good Earth may flood back into your life again, making you see your destiny. Truth is, you're destined to be a man or woman of the earth. See what I mean? No? You will. Just work the Rule of Life exercises.

Sad Memories

When Vision begins to stir again, there's a good chance sad memories will come back. The story goes like this. That little soul of yours started off on its long Journey to grow itself way back at the beginning of the Universe, so you'd come a long way by the time you were born. But soon thereafter you were confronted by a world full of people bound and determined to keep you from being yourself. You were taught beliefs that keep you down, and filled you with fears of being judged. If you've managed to fearlessly run this gauntlet since birth, being yourself all the way, you're one of the very, very rare lucky few. For most people however, it will be much more like this. Imagine you came here with the soul of a singer, and you have real dreams of being a country music star. By the age of five you're belting out tunes you've heard on the radio and by ten years you'd sing on the street corner for nothing. Singing is your true passion in life and you can't get enough of it.

But unfortunately, your parents have other ideas. Mom and Dad and Uncles and Grandfathers are all physicians, and doctoring is a sacred family tradition. Singing is fine in your family too of course….as a hobby. But becoming a doctor is where it's at and nobody is going to let you forget it. And so, in a five act play acted out in every town in America, you become a medical practitioner to please the powers that be in your home life. No doubt you discover it's a great and honorable profession, and even enjoy what it has to offer. But way down deep there's still a country singer stuck inside its shell.

Now let's move ahead to somewhere in your early forties. You've built up a great medical practice by now and pretty much "have it all" according to everyone you know. By some kind of miracle however, you've began to discover who you really are and your very own Vision is returning.

Looking back at your own life, the authentic soul of a country singer is staring back at you. But sadly, you also see how everyone has unintentionally steered you away from your Life Mission. Now you have no choice but to take up your calling again, because it's who you are. If you don't you'll live a lie all your life. Here's where we get to sad Vision stirring memories. At first you'll be saddened that you grew any way but your own for so long. You'll be depressed giving up the light of your life. Despair will creep in from all directions at first. But soon a happier thought will dawn.. Now you know which way to take your life. With passion and hard work you can make up for lost time as well. Beginning to realize all is not lost, you'll dust off your signing shoes and get growing once more. Making your own way again, the sadness will eventually vanish. I know for sure because I've been there.

The Freedom Song

If you look up the word "freedom" in a dictionary, you'll discover it means being released from restraint, prison, slavery or other bad things that hold people back. With that in mind, I want you to know this. Dissolving your fears of judgment will give you the most potent sense of Freedom you've ever had….or could have. As this terrible inhibiting fear goes away, your soul will be set free. Your heart will break out of the shell it's been imprisoned in and soar to the heavens above. You'll discover this about true Freedom as well. It isn't easy or fun and games. It's work we must do to grow human. Here's how I discovered the Freedom song for myself, as my Vision emerged again. Well do I remember that day my first feelings of true freedom came to me.

I was out jogging in the winter at the time and plodding down a desolate country road. My Vision had been coming back for maybe six months by then. Suddenly I realized something that should have been obvious decades earlier.

With startling clarity I saw that I wasn't any kind of management guru. Certainly I'd been pretending to be one for years, but truly I'm an explorer-at-heart in love with the deep and abiding mystery of things. A man smitten with beauty and wonder and the Divine nature of reality. Now what? By this time I'd managed to haul myself way the heck up the corporate ladder where birds with feathers like mine were few and far between. Where I needed to go to fulfill my Mission was in some other world completely.

At first I felt like a Dolphin who's awakened from a deep sleep to find himself in a desert. He can see the ocean dimly on the horizon, but how does he get there? For a moment a wave of depression flooded over me as I jogged along that isolated road. But suddenly the reality of Freedom hit me. In an instant I realized I was Free to work my way there. With Vision I could see a mountain ahead with my name on it, so I knew which way to go. So what if there were several other mountain ranges between me and my fully grown self. Big deal if swamps and tigers and who-knows-what stood between me and my aim in life. Freedom means freedom to struggle and work and fail and succeed…in the great Journey to become human.

Freedom doesn't mean the prison gates open up and that's it. It means we have the Freedom to make those possibilities that are "right for us" into realities. We have the Freedom to choose destiny over makeshift goals and to follow our calling instead of being called by selfishness. Once I realized I had the Freedom to make my way from where I was to where I wanted to be, I was elated. Finally I really understood what the Freedom song is all about. It's about manifesting our potentials for Being Human. You too will see what the Freedom song is about, and feel what I felt, when that special insight into who you are called "Vision" stirs.

What Freedom is Like

Just so you have a really good idea what kinds of feelings to expect of Freedom, here's a story that illustrates what I mean. Imagine you've been falsely imprisoned, all locked up and forgotten in some dark forsaken place. Then one day a little miracle happens and you notice a tiny crack in one wall. What's miraculous is the little ray of sunshine coming through, because it tells you the crack leads outside. Tentatively at first you scratch around the edges of that crack, and a few small grains break off. The wall is tough as nails of course, but with every clawing effort you're making the tiny hole bigger one fleck at a time. Then it dawns on you that it's possible to get out. Maybe it will take you a year of fingers torn raw and eyes strained in the dark. But nothing is going to stop you now. As a matter of fact, you're already free.

You're free to work as hard as you possibly can to get somewhere you absolutely have to be. That's what Real Freedom is all about. It's about working your way to where you want to go from where you are. Way out on that icy road by myself that day, I knew I was Free. I guarantee you'll feel that sense of freedom when your Vision comes back. Why? Because the essential ingredient for Freedom is seeing where you must go to become all you can become. If you don't have that Visionary ability, you will never be Free. Believe me, true Freedom is one of the most potent, mind-blowing experiences you can have in life.

"Freedom is a possession of inestimable value". - Marcus Tullius Cicero

Vision Starts With Suspicions

Unlike you, I had no one to guide me in my Journey. As a matter of fact, in the earliest stages of my rebirth, I didn't even *know* I was on a Journey. I am very thankful therefore, that destiny was hard at work in my life, pushing me forward even as I had no idea where I was going. I say that because some of the earliest signs of Vision stirring are so subtle and unfamiliar, it's a wonder I didn't just plain ignore them. But something way down deep told me I needed to pay attention to these curious feelings. Now I can describe them to you, so *you* don't ignore them either. Ignore them at your peril, because they're the beginnings of a brand new and amazing life. I call these first feelings of "self knowledge" *suspicions of authenticity* because at first that's what they are. All you have is suspicions something is happening deep within you, as if something is moving about, ready to make itself known. It feels a lot like when you have a word on the tip of your tongue for example. You *suspect* it's about to arrive, but you still can't quite recall it. It's a kind of "restless, nervous, vague feeling of anticipation". Something is going on for sure, but you don't know what it is. If you start feeling like that it's good news, because soon those vague suspicions will turn into a kind of knowledge that will stun you with its certainty. An example from my life will explain what I mean.

Vision Becomes Certain

It's fair to say I've known "pretending" is a bad thing for a long time. Even when I was pretending to be something I wasn't, I could have written a decent essay on how ridiculous it was. Like everybody else, I'd been taught this lesson back in public school. What I didn't realize was that I had "secondhand knowledge" of this particular wisdom.

As a matter of fact, virtually all my wisdom was secondhand knowledge cribbed from books. I had no idea there was a firsthand kind of knowing I could have that's dramatically different from the indirect "intellectual know-how". But I sure as heck found out as my Vision came back. As this inner sight stirred and grew and tentatively made itself known, suspicions of something happening suddenly crystallized as I began to have the kind of knowledge that flows from "Source". "Source" is that vast ocean of Tao potential at our center, that provides for us in times of need and shows us how to align our hearts with our dreams. "Source" is the fount of all true knowledge that mystics and poets tap into. This kind of knowing begins with fuzzy intuitive suspicions and then arrives with complete conviction. It is so doubtlessly certain it is beyond question.

As the inhibiting fears of judgment went out of my life then, I began to *know* pretending is a travesty in a way I never knew before. My soul was telling me it was so, and I did not doubt it. In fact, I *could* not doubt it. I had a deep need to avoid pretense. I was overcome by a profound desire to cut away every scrap of it from my life. But not because someone was telling me this was the right thing to do. Not in the least. I knew it firsthand in a way that could not be shaken. The entire world could tell me "pretending is the way to go" for example, and I would turn around and go the other way. I would stand alone before the world and defy everybody on it. Why? I have certain knowledge of it from Source. And so, when those odd feelings that something is happening around and about your heart, let it be. Let it be and soon you too will hear your heart speaking to you from Source. You will get absolute, doubtless knowledge of who you are as suspicions of authenticity show you how to become real.

Vision Ideas Add Up

If you've ever done a jig-saw puzzle, you'll know that the little pieces eventually add up in a remarkable way that lets some beautiful picture emerge. Exactly the same happens as you dissolve your fears and Vision ideas begin coming to you. Certainly it takes some time and effort before you get to see who you are and can be with clarity, but inevitably a wonderful picture will appear like magic. Many of the pieces of this puzzle will actually be known to you as well. They'll be old ideas you had that have far greater significance as your Vision comes back. I'll give you a personal example so you know what I mean. Even way back when old buddy Ken and I used to go trout fishing at six-mile creek, I knew there was something about getting out there in the woods and exploring rivers that was near and dear to my heart. Later on in my life as a lost soul, I even wondered if maybe I shouldn't aspire to becoming a fishing guide because of it. It seemed to make sense because I really loved the art of fly fishing and adored the outdoors. Even so, I was never driven to go that way like real and true fishing guides are. It was certainly one of my "interests", but knowing that didn't help me find my way in life.

As we speak, I'll bet you've experienced this sort of thing yourself. You look back in your childhood and find things that turn you on, but you're no further ahead with "finding yourself" having found them. Right? Been there, done that. Alright, let's let that old idea sit for a minute while I find another that didn't do anything for me until Vision returned either. As I mentioned earlier, I've always been passionately curious about how the world works, reading anything I could get my hands about the subject since day one. Profound scientific puzzles have always fascinated me in a way that made me think they were sacred. For a while then, I thought I might be a professor kind of person who'd gain joy from learning for the sake of learning and teaching.

I even dropped out to pursue graduate studies in physics and philosophy....just before my trip to England. Surely I wanted to explore the world of the intellect, and venture where no man has gone. But my heart wasn't in it, and I gave it up. For reasons unknown to me at the time, my soul pushed me right out of that profession. It was another example of finding a passionate interest....that lead nowhere. Alright, so now we have two "ideas about who I might be" just sitting around gathering dust, because I don't know how to put them together. They (and quite a few more) sat on the shelf for a heck of along time, until fate allowed me to see what they meant. Destiny eventually let them add up so a picture of who I really am could emerge. Here's how it went.

Vision Emerges

Eventually those and other ideas fused in my head, as Vision gave me the eyes to see. First I saw what it really was about fishing trips I loved so much. It wasn't catching fish, or seeing animals or even the fabulous fresh air, although I was a big fan of them all. It was the exploration. I was always entranced by the wonder of what might be around the next corner or under some log in the creek. Sometimes ducks would come racing down the river out of the blue at face level for example, whistling wings startling both Ken and I as they flew inches over our heads. Other times a "lunker trout" would shoot out from behind a rock to grab our baits, scaring the pants off us as if we had been attacked by the predator ourselves. Always we were probing the unknown and half breathless in anticipation of what was going to happen next. These are the things exploration is about. Surprise, excitement, and wonder.

Same thing held for the scientific and philosophical puzzles I loved so much. I was always mesmerized by the mystery and magic of the unknown behind them.

From my earliest days I knew there could be amazing discoveries right out on the surface of the world, for those who could change the way they saw things to make them stand out. O.K. so now we can add the ideas up. With Vision I can now see I'm an explorer-at-heart with a profound love for the sacred nature of the world. More to the point, I can see that all my exploring of the natural world and the world of ideas was for a purpose. It was to get a message of hope out. A message that can show others how to find the Divine purpose of their lives. As it turns out, each of my old ideas of "who I might be" contained a kernel of passion for being human. Eventually as they added up, they formed the contents of this book, and my Mission of spreading the Word. But to see this picture of the Being-within-me I had to take away my fears. I had to let them add up to give me Vision. The same thing will happen to you. Tear away your fears of judgment and wonder of wonders, all those old "interest memories" of yours will magically coalesce into a real dream. A true dream of who you are and can be.

*"The Master observes the world
but trusts his inner vision.
He allows things to come and go.
His heart is open as the sky".-* Tao Te Ching

Feeling Gifted

Do you recall what I said about being gifted before? Very special ideas about who you are and what to do with your life….come to you…like gifts from some distant and inaccessible place. But what exactly does it feel like to be gifted? Well, there's an old expression you sometimes hear people using that describes what it feels like.

You'll feel "comfortable in your own skin" because being gifted is nothing more or less than being yourself. It's the feeling you get when you're being human. And here's why that will feel so good. It doesn't matter what your "gifts" are, using them to become all you can become will bring you an equal share of Bliss. Each of us receives many different "gifts" too, because Being Human is a multi-faceted thing. We all get intellectual, physical, spiritual, emotional and other gifts for instance. To get your share of Bliss and feel gifted, all you have to do is grow them. Let's take me as an example. Physically speaking my gifts are very modest indeed. I can't lift giant weights like some can, and I can't run long distances very quickly either. But if I run *my way*....slow and steady....I get huge, wonderful physical joy out of it. I feel just as gifted running five miles in fifty minutes as the world class marathoner does in doing it in fifteen. I know I'm getting the same fabulous physical feelings as I feel the strength and conditioning in me and revel in the way the body moves.

The same holds for all my other gifts. I might not be a rocket scientist, but I derive special pleasure from exploring the intellectual world my average brain is capable of exploring. I can feel gifted by wondering, although what I wonder about might not make the history books. Feeling gifted is that great comfortable feeling you have when practicing the Art of being yourself. You do not want to miss out on it. When you start to feel this Divine comfort of being in your own skin then,   it's a really big sign Vision's coming back.

Unconscious Direction

If you look back in the book, you'll find a description of what destiny feels like (picking nothing but watch parts on the Journey of Life). But there's another kind of feeling you'll get once your Vision begins to come back.

It's really and truly kind of spooky-scary in a way at first. Eventually however, as you realize there's nothing to be frightened of, it just becomes awesomely beautiful. In essence you'll begin to feel like there's some Great Hand behind you pushing you somewhere, even when you had no idea it was there. Let's go back to that destiny story again and think about it. In this story a near death experience caused you to dump that knapsack out on the ground. Suddenly you discovered you'd collected nothing but watch parts and your reason for being here was to put that watch together. So what exactly was it that steered you relentlessly in that singular direction, somehow guiding you each step of the way? Was it just a lucky coincidence you picked up nothing but the parts of an exquisite watch, giving you something to do with your life? Lots of people would say that's exactly what it was. Just lucky happenstance….one watch part at a time. But when you actually get your very own Vision back, you'll also see something you didn't expect. You will see it as clear as day.

With Vision you'll see without any doubt at all that you'd been receiving unconscious direction…all your life. Everything you did and said was motivated by an unseen Force guiding your life towards a particular purpose. When you awaken to who you are once more, you'll have no doubt that destiny is a Divine power in the Universe meant to show each of us the Way of our lives. On the other hand, if you never use the Rule of Life to restore your Vision, unconscious direction will be nothing but nonsense to you. You'll go to your grave never knowing who you are. I don't know about you, but I'd rather have Vision.

Doing Something

Back when I was maybe ten years old I began to make that famous saying "there's nothing to do" my theme song.

As a lost teenager I trotted it out millions of times, and by the time I was an adult I'd become an expert at "doing nothing". Even as an executive, outside my job I had "nothing to do". Now I know what that oft-heard expression is really about. It means "I'm not motivated to try and try and finally succeed, because I'm afraid of failing". Actually it means "I'm terrified of being judged". When you're all but paralyzed by fears of judgment, that's the way you see the world. It's a dull, gray, lackluster kind of place because you aren't engaged in it. You aren't out there exploring and adventuring and playing and living, because you're afraid of being yourself. And here's the thing. If you aren't being yourself, you aren't reaching out and grabbing hold of the pull-chain of the world. You have to actually pull the world's chain to turn the light on so you can see what to do. Once you learn the trick of being yourself again however, you'll be astonished. Turn the light of the world on and there will be more things to do than you could possibly do in a million lifetimes. You'll be motivated like a herd of demented beavers to get out there and cut down some trees. As a matter of fact, erasing those root fears of being yourself is the magical motivation tap all the gurus are looking for. Take them away and you will have huge motivation to create your dream life. Not to mention drive, persistence, energy and huge hope for a future filled with Joy and Happiness. Never again will you hear yourself saying…."there's nothing to do".

More Obstacles?

The next chapter describes things that can stop your Vision from growing, once you've got them sprouting again. But don't despair. You can get past them too. I did.

Chapter Twenty-One
Why Vision Stops Growing

"Obstacles cannot crush me; every obstacle yields to stern resolve". Leonardo da Vinci

There are lots of obstacles on the path to becoming yourself. Some try stopping you before you start. Others make growing Vision tough, even after you get going. Like these. But don't worry, you can get past them. I did.

Immaturity

Here's something that will certainly happen when you resume growing *your* way. Another big rock to climb on your path. You'll begin to see just how immature you really are, and it can be depressing at first. One way to look at it is like this. Imagine you're a kind of flower that's supposed to have ten very different mature petals when it blooms. For the sake of argument we'll call these ten petals physical, emotional, sexual, intellectual, social, spiritual, creative, adaptive, explorative and ethical. All different ways of being in the world. By the age of eighteen then, a fearless human being should at least have all ten petals unfolded, even if they're all undeveloped. Three out of ten might be half grown by this time, with others reaching for the sunlight to find sustenance.

This same person by his or her twenties could expect two to be mature, and the rest still growing gangbusters. By the mid-forties he or she would be a flower with perhaps five petals mostly grown. With continued courage, this person could expect as many as eight petals to be fully developed by their fifties. By the age of seventy or eighty then, a fully grown human being could be ready to die. On the other hand, here's what you can expect to see if you've had no idea what to do with your life for years, no matter how old you are.

At best one or two petals will be stretched out slightly. The rest will be stunted. In essence, fear of being judged will have kept most of you from growing. Don't forget this either. If you've been pretending to be something you're not, you may look like a grownup with lots of achievements. But, in "flower talk" you've taped someone else's petals on your stem. A "rose at heart" may festoon him or herself with lots of daisy petals for example, but they don't count. To anyone with eyes to see, an un-grown rose sporting daisy parts just looks silly. Take me for example. Before resuming growth in the right direction once more….in my mid forties…. pretty much all my petals were juvenile to say the least. Oddly however, most people around me didn't even notice because they hadn't an eyelash of Vision. To similarly lost souls I looked normal. Believe me, I wasn't even close. Not one of those petals had seen more than the slightest light of day.

Now I know this with certainty the size of mountains of course, but back then I didn't even have a clue. But here's some good news for you, especially if you're about to resume your Journey later in life (40's or older) like I did. Your time on earth does have some benefits that can be applied here. Chances are you've learned all kinds of things that can accelerate your growth. Hunger for true success, clear knowledge money doesn't buy happiness, and a true idea how short life really is for instance. You'll have all kinds of colleagues, contacts, friends and acquaintances to turn to for help with the Rule of Life as well. Skills learned on the job might also assist you big time as your Life Mission dawns. In short, older folks often know more than younger ones, and this hard-won knowledge can help you make up for lost time. But only after you've added one fiercely critical ingredient. "Self-knowledge". And so, you'll absolutely be confronted by your own immaturity as the Rule of Life opens your eyes to who you really are. When that happens…don't sweat it…just wake up to who you are and become who you can become. You'll soon catch up.

Immature Me

As mentioned above, I woke up to find myself a grossly immature human being at the age of forty-five. Even my writing persona was badly stunted. As you might expect, resuming my life as a "toddling writer" made for a very long period of slow growth, a lot of which was depressing. For years, every time I looked back at my work it was bad as bears in the henhouse. Certainly I could tell I was improving, but how many times would I have to re-write the entire book? (Answer? Ten). With such a long uphill climb, you'd think I would've given up long ago. But it's impossible to give up your Life Mission once it's come back, because it's how you create yourself anew each day. Giving up would be slow motion suicide. I might have been depressed about my immaturity many times, but suicidal I wasn't. Same will hold true for you. It won't matter how immature you are when waking up to your life's purpose. Passion for your own cause will make you put your shoulder to your mountain and keep pushing.

You Might Not Like Yourself

Here's another chasm you might have to cross on your Journey. Seeing your authentic self for the very first time…..and not much liking what you see. It works like this. Throughout your life you will have been taught that some people are better than others. Those with bigger jobs, more money, fancier toys and so on for example. Chances are you swallowed that wholesale. In your mind maybe bankers, businessmen and stock brokers are the little cat's big meow for instance. You might even be all three. But now you've discovered your soul shines with the heart of an artist. Unfortunately, your brain has been hard wired to consider starving artistic souls riff raff. Now what? Now you learn a famous lesson called "accepting yourself".

Thankfully, Vision gives you what it takes to do that. because it lets you see something important. Bliss. Vision lets you see how to get the Bliss everybody wants. Once you get a taste of your Bliss, you'll have no problem accepting yourself. As a matter of fact, discovering yourself is a lot like winning a lottery. Once you've won, you aren't giving the prize back. It may be a shock to discover you weren't who you thought you were. But that wears off quickly as Joy comes back into your life. Accepting yourself soon gets better too. It's only a preview of something bigger. Poets call it "loving thyself". When you enter this region of Being Human, you ain't going back. Guaranteed. Here's what it was like for me as I worked past acceptance to love.

Acceptance and Love

All my life I revered scientists for their profound insights into how the world works. Had I enough brains, I might even have become one myself. But truth be told, I didn't and my soul is really quite different from that of most scientists. It's fair to say my heart is closer to that of a poet or artist, even as I'm passionately curious about the nature of things. As I awakened once more to my Mission, it became clear being a scientist wasn't me at all. Having always harbored secret thoughts of becoming one then, I had to give them up and accept myself. At first I had to do a little grieving for the loss of my "false dream". But soon this acceptance turned into a kind of "love".

It happened suddenly one day and I remember it very, very clearly. It took place on that bridge near Kingsville where I'd had my revelation, but a few years later. As usual, I was cooling down after a hard run, reveling in the sheer beauty of the morning. I was thinking how amazing all the dewy sunlit leaves and tinkling sounds of water keening gently around my feet were. It was a truly beautiful scene, filled with wonder and mystery.

Then another thought soon arrived. It occurred to me that lots of people would love to get inside my head to see and experience this way the world was to me. Then it hit me. This was my soul I was talking about people loving. I had just realized that the soul within me was a beautiful thing, worthy of love. Suddenly I recognized what poets mean by "loving thyself". They mean deep within each of us is a wonderful soul that anyone could love. This is the same soul we all share by the way, and it's in you as I write these words. That means you and I and all creatures great and small are worthy of great love. Once I'd had this insight into who I am, acceptance of myself blossomed into "true love" for Being Human. As you begin to accept yourself for who you are then, be prepared for love forever after.

The Paradox of Leadership

Anytime on your Journey you can benefit from the paradox of leadership. If you're not familiar with it, I'll describe it for you. First let's review paradox. Paradox is two opposite things hung together in the same expression, like an oxymoron, absurdity, or Zen koan. Seeking shelter from rain in an ocean filled with water for instance. Paradox is something most people steer clear of because it doesn't seem to make any sense. A sign that says "go left and right at the stop sign" might be an example, because it's hard to see how you can do both. When it comes to the paradox of leadership though, I want you to run *towards* it...not *away* from it. Here's how it works. Real leaders often tell us we're every bit as great as they are. But should we believe them? The reason we believe leaders is because they're greater than us isn't it? Isn't this greatness what gives them their authority? If it is, we have a problem here don't we? If we believe them we'd be as great as they are, which would take away their authority....so we shouldn't believe them?

What kind of nonsense is this? It's not nonsense, it's the paradox of leadership. When all is said and done however, it isn't really paradoxical either. It's wholeness. Real leaders are trying to tell us the One soul we all share is fabulously great. They're trying to say this singular greatness manifests itself in as many different ways as there are people. Each of whom is equivalently great, and worth exactly the same. Don't forget this either. Real leaders get their authority *from Source* to tell you and I we're as great as they are.

Bad Characters

The more you grow, the more you get to "Know Thyself". Unfortunately you'll soon begin to know "thy unseemly self". In essence, you'll start to realize there are islands of all the different characters known to Man within you. Including the bad ones. Little outposts of spite, dishonesty, hatred and violence for instance. Look long enough and you'll find all the good and bad in the world "in thyself". This is a bit disconcerting at first, but soon you'll realize something that will make you feel better. You can grow all the good parts of you and let the bad parts wither up to where they're no problem to anyone. Take violence for instance. Violence only becomes bad when it's grown huge. Tiny violence is, for example, is raising your voice in anger at someone or pushing someone out of line at a sale to get goods for yourself. But if you grow that violence it can go to shouting and then physically assaulting and even killing. Let that kind of violence starve for fuel however, and it settles back down to where it should be. Namely small, inconsequential parts of being human.

The same holds for all the "bad characters" you can come up with (and will find in yourself). Concentrate on growing the positive, life-enhancing traits within you to get your share of Bliss, and these "bad characters" dwindle down into small annoyances no one is bothered by.

Teensy hatred is simple dislike for instance, and miniscule greed is just having that second piece of pie. All the "bad characters" can be put in their rightful place by being eclipsed by good. So there you go. Yes you will find all the good and bad known to Man "in thyself", but if you grow Human by following the Rule of Life, you'll learn how Good can triumph over Evil.

How Good Triumphs over Evil

Here is a personal story of how Good began triumphing over Evil in my own life. It's how I managed to take a "bad character" called "pretentiousness" and pare it down to a benign form that actually does good. As related earlier, my past life was dominated by pretending to be something I wasn't. A lot of people call this "living a lie" and yours truly had it perfected for decades. I pretended to be smart. I pretended to be a businessman at heart. I pretended to be anything that would make me feel "important". But as my Life Mission returned and I put heart and soul into being myself, my pretending shrank down to a mere shadow of its former self.

Now it shows up as "putting on a good face" to my employees for instance, when fighting business battles. I may "pretend" to be absolutely confident of the outcome of some adventure for instance, when I'm only sixty percent sure it's going to work out. This kind of "benign pretending" actually does some good, because it lets me worry about which way things are headed, while sparing countless others the burden. Keep this in mind however. I'm not outright lying about anything here. I'm just "remaining positive" in the face of adversity and it's actually a small sort of pretending that has redeeming value. It's one small way Good can triumph over Evil. You too can make all the "bad characters" in your life into these stories of triumph.

The Rip Van Winkle Effect

Here's something that can slow you down on your Journey at first that takes a bit of getting used to. I call it the "Rip Van Winkle Effect". Probably you've heard the story of Mr. Winkle who slept somewhere for many years, returning to a village he hardly recognizes. Interestingly however, this story about awakening is centuries old and found in many cultures. Just Google about Rip Van Winkle in Wikipedia for example, and you'll see what I mean. You'll see what I mean in your own life when awakening once more to who you are as well. It will go like this. When you're reborn to the path you should be on, you can easily discover you're in a land as foreign to you as Mr. Winkle's village was to him. You can find yourself in the wrong friendships, places of work, and even marriage. As if you'd stumbled into them when sleepwalking for instance, which is pretty much what has actually happened. In essence you've surrounded yourself with similarly immature people, like any good sparrow might flock together with others of its kind.

When you wake up again and start growing again however, you might just notice something else. You're not even a sparrow at heart, and you've flocked with who-knows-what other kinds of bird! This is the most disconcerting part of an awakening, because you discover what's sometimes called "irreconcilable differences". In other words, if you turn out to be a flamingo, but friends, co-workers and…unfortunately…your spouse, really are sparrows, you have a little problem. You're like a fish out of water or someone where they shouldn't be. It's another one of those sad-at-first things you'll have to contend with on your Road Less Traveled. You will contend with it too, because your Life Mission will make you. To become all you can become, you'll have to grow away. It won't be easy, but you will, because the Bliss will be calling you to do exactly that.

Growing Away

Let's review why you're here on earth for a moment. You're here to be yourself. To grow that unique flower called "you" until it blossoms. Once you've got that straight and know which way to grow, nothing will stop you. Even the predictable pain of growing away from stifling friendships, partnerships and unfulfilling marriages. Don't forget that working the Rule of Life releases courage from within and encourages you to work harder to release even more. You'll need that wellspring of courage to grow your way, especially when you must depart from an old, familiar life of many years. We human animals aren't big fans of inflicting pain upon ourselves of course, but with courage we can get those tough and painful jobs done when we have to. With hope for an authentic life in our hearts, we can know deep down that it's right to go this way as well.

There is one other thing you should know about this painful part of growing. Those improper friendships, partnerships or marriages I spoke of aren't just one-ways streets. It's not just you or I suffering a superficial life by staying in these relationships. These inadequate pairings inflict pain on both parties in equal measure. Friends, partners and spouses are prevented from growing *their way* by *our* failures to make the break. Failing to pack up and grow elsewhere is a sin committed against ourselves and our various life-partners. Understanding this helps us negotiate the pain of these necessary separations. We can be rest assured we are doing the right thing for all concerned. Not that this knowledge makes it any less painful. But eventually it makes it right.

Growing Away: A True Story

As you might expect of a man who got lost early in his life, yours truly eventually woke up in a Life-partnership that was not right for both parties. It had never been right of course, but absent the courage that comes with a Life Mission, it had never been made right. By the time separation happened, a full twenty five years of marriage had gone by. From first hand experience I can therefore tell you that growing away from a long term partnership, however unfulfilling, is exceedingly difficult and painful. But here is something anyone facing this kind of thing should know. It's not possible to become all you can become if you continue in a partnership that's wrong for you. If you want to fulfill your Mission in Life, which is to grow fully Human, you'll have to make the break. You'll have to feel your share of pain and suffering to go your Way.

Waking up Alone

One last obstacle to watch out for is a lot like the Rip Van Winkle thing, except lonelier. Any guy or gal waking up to who they are in today's world will soon notice they're alone. Not a soul in sight who "knows thyself". No one nearby driven to carry out a life-mission. Certainly there are lots of people in the world who do have their very own Mission to carry out. There are guys and gals with real callings in every land and people driven by Vision all over the place. The trouble is, they're one in a million. They're so rare, you probably won't ever run into a real live one…..maybe not even a dead one. The thing is, when you get your Vision back you'll want to meet these kindred spirits to exchange "war stories" about growing Human. You'll want someone to share tips and pointers about exploring this Great Journey of personal enlightenment.

But good luck. Until the world changes, people with real Vision will stay rare as rabbits on the moon. You'll be surrounded by people completely blind to who they are and more or less alone on your Journey. But know this. Every single man or woman who ever discovered why they're here is cheering you on….. RIGHT NOW! There are real growing human beings in every town and country on earth, hoping for your authentic success and pushing good Karma into the void for you as we speak. Why do I say that? Because this great community of Being Human does exactly that for a living. Each of us who awakens is bound by a sacred trust to give growing vibes to the world and help a greater consciousness emerge. Part and parcel of growing up is building a better universe. As a matter of fact, one of these supportive souls is very close to you as we speak. Who might that be? It's a secret. But here's something else to think about. If you don't have Vision right now, all of what I just said will sound silly. Draw your own conclusions.

And Now For Something Different

Let's fast forward a bit here now and suppose you've managed to get seeds of Vision within you stirring and a few have even started growing. You've battled the obstacles I've mentioned and now you're on your way. Fears of judgment are getting smaller day by day and your Vision is clearing up. Now you're like a blind man or woman who has suddenly been given the gift of sight. Now it's time to really start working on growing yourself. Now it's time for the dreaded Journal.

How Much Have We Grown Up?

How much do you think Mankind has grown Human in the last few million years? One hundred years ago, North Americans actually kept Human Beings as slaves. In case you didn't know, slaves were considered "sub-human", animals, rather like pets. So let's think about that for a minute. After several million years of evolution, men and women can't recognize other Human Beings....because they have different colored skin? Surely this must be some kind of terrible joke. If it isn't we'd better hope it's just a temporary insanity, because it would mean Humanity hasn't even gotten out of the cradle yet.

Chapter Twenty-Two
A Journal Tool
(To Help You Grow)

"To be without learning is to be without eyes" – Lithuanian proverb

Why Do a Journal?

If you look around at books written to assist people with life changes, you'll find Journals. So what's with these things anyhow? Why do so many authors recommend you and I put thoughts on paper or record our experiences with personal growth? Well, the short answer is, it's a way of learning. When you were in school for instance, you probably took notes and practiced writing out answers to questions before exams. This too is journaling, even if it doesn't normally go by the name. In the case of school-work however, all this repetitive writing is to test yourself for right answers. There aren't "right answers" to worry about in your Rule of Life Journal. Right or wrong, everything you put there can help you find yourself.

The Journal I'm asking you to begin here is very different from school journals in one other significant way as well, because it asks you to practice being yourself. Schoolwork journaling is more about practicing winning or being best or pretending to be something you're not. So don't forget. Being yourself means writing from the heart. It means saying what's on your mind and describing how you feel. In this Journal you must be honest with yourself and "say it like it is". When trying to rid yourself of foolish discrimination for example, you must tell the world (your Journal) you called someone names for doing what you did yourself yesterday. You have to look yourself in the eye, screw up your courage, and spit it out.

When all is said and done, the Rule of Life Journal is all about "outing" yourself. (Getting out of your shell). This is not a schoolwork program where you artfully fabricate all kinds of good stuff, and plagiarize from the net to fool your professor. If you play these games in your Rule of Life Journal, the only person being fooled will be you. You'll think progress is being made and be disappointed when you discover it's not.

Why Not Do a Journal?

If you're like 90% of the world out there, you won't want to write a Journal. I would have called it a complete waste of life fifteen years ago for example, and found ten good reasons why not to. To me at the time, Journals were New-Age, self-help crap. Actually, I would have used far less socially acceptable words to describe Journaling back then……but you get the idea. There were two simple reasons why. One was belief. The other was fear. First the fear thing. From first-hand experience I can tell you that no lost soul wants to put his or her authentic being right out on paper where somebody might actually catch them. Why? They might be judged and found wanting. Expressing ourselves, even when it's a tiny bit, on paper, in public, is scary in today's world, because pretty much everyone out there is ready to pounce on us. That's one reason you'll have to be cajoled into doing a Journal. You're afraid. You probably don't believe it will do anything for you either. This second reason can stop you just as fast as the first one. As a matter of fact, if you've stopped authentically growing a long time ago you won't just think Journaling is stupid. You'll have completely forgotten what real growth from the heart is about. It'll be impossible to you, so you won't even bother trying. Take the guy in one of my engineering departments for instance. He literally forgot the *idea* of growing. Before I carry on with my plea for Journaling then, let's visit Kyle.

Kyle Forgot About Growing

Kyle was an engineer in a factory I ran, who was certainly competent....but slow. Unfortunately, this particular manufacturing company was engaged in what's called "mass customization". That means every single product made in the plant was custom engineered. It also meant the engineers had to produce designs as fast as the plant could make them, or everything came to a crashing halt. Which brings us back to Kyle. Kyle needed to be speeded up big-time, so my engineering manager and I gave him tips, pointers and daily exercises that would improve his productivity. My decades of experience improving productivity told me Kyle could double his output by following our examples. But the look on Kyle's face told me he did not believe it was possible. I knew exactly why he didn't believe it too. Kyle didn't comprehend the idea the exercises would change him. He was trying to visualize himself doing twice as much.....the way he was right then....which was impossible.

Kyle didn't quite understand the fact that he would eventually do twice as much....just as easily as he did half of it now. He saw nothing but pain and suffering as he tried to double his output without doubling his ability. He'd forgotten the essential thing about growing that makes miracles happen. Change. Kyle had so little experience with personal growth, that he no longer even believed in it. If you think this is a ridiculous, made-up story, I can assure you it is not on both counts. I have seen it time and time again in all walks of life. People give up growing until they no longer even believe it is possible. That could easily be one reason you're about to reject the idea of doing a Journal yourself right now. Before we head off to my Journal though, I'll give you a real-life example of someone refusing to Journal for the other reason. Fear.

Fear Stopped Len

In another company I worked at there was an I.T. guy by the name of Lennard. Soon I discovered that Len was one of those people who knows deep down they're lost, but has no idea how to find the Way. He knew he had potential to do bigger and better things, but no idea what that might be. Eventually Lennard came to know that yours truly was actually writing a book about that very thing he was desperate to know. Namely….himself. Over time I convinced Len that fear of being judged was the culprit deep down inside him, limiting his life and keeping him from knowing who he was. I managed to make him understand those fears had go away to hear his inner voice. I actually got Len to comprehend Rule of Life exercises and how they could train away his fears as well. Then we got to the nitty gritty. Now I asked Len to actually do the exercises and write them up in a Journal. Guess what? Ain't happening.

Keep in mind here, Len is dying of thirst for knowledge of who he is…and I am offering him water. Shouldn't he at least be taking a little sip? Just in case it slakes that thirst of his? He's suffering from a parched soul and I come along and offer a cool, refreshing drink. But he won't take it. What can I do? I know he won't find what he needs to save his life in the direction he's headed. But like every horse known to Man, I could lead Len to an ocean of life-giving water, but not force him to partake. In this case I knew why too. I recognized the fear on his face as I suggested he put his soul on paper. I'd been there myself, and knew the look. I asked Len a few times if he'd started Rule of Life and Journal work. But he got more fearful with every such chat, as if I was backing him into a corner. I knew he wasn't ready yet. Something like a painful mid-life crisis or experience "hitting bottom in life" is often needed to get people ready. Years later when Len left our company, he still wasn't ready. I still don't think he is today. And you? Are you ready? You can start small like I did.

I Started Small

I didn't have anyone telling me to start a Journal, because I stumbled into it myself. But make no mistake. I was terrified of having my thoughts and feelings and emotions being seen by anyone at first. Back in the beginning of my Journaling, I hid my paper notes so friends, acquaintances and spouses couldn't possibly find them. When I graduated to computers, I password protected my files at so many levels, it's a wonder didn't lock myself out! But eventually my closet Journaling reduced fears of being myself to where I could actually do it out in the open. Now I'm unafraid to bare my soul in the pages of this book. Start small if you have to then......but start. If you don't you will regret it as you take your last breath in that old age home.

Chapter Twenty Three
My Example Journal
(Will Show You How)

"A journey of a thousand miles must begin with a single step". -- Lao-tzu, 'Tao Te Ching'

It's Not My Original Journal

Looking back now, I can see I began Journaling back in 1973. That was when I started scratching out notes about how the world works, authoring my first "big book of goofballs" as a colleague called it at the time. Don't forget, "Journaling" isn't just writing out poetic thoughts about how your day went in a store-bought, leather-bound writing diary. It's expressing yourself any which way you want to. That first "goofball Journal" of mine has disappeared completely now, but the second Journal I still have. This series of writings took place in England circa that first revelation I shared with you earlier. Three or four dusty, yellowed notebooks containing those thoughts sit in a box somewhere in my basement right now. Along with them are about a thousand loose leaf pages of Journal number three. That Journaling effort was the ground-work, underpinnings, call it what you will…beginnings of this book. It began after my third revelation on Kingsville's little bridge.

If you were so inclined, you could follow threads from this page all the way back. As a matter of fact, this very book is one of my Journals. *This* Journal differs in an important way from all the others however. It distils out the important points of those other Journals to help you climb your own personal mountain. The "example Journal" that follows is a kind of "study guide" to doing Rule of Life work and Mission exercises. A sort of "Cole's Notes for finding yourself" you might say. It's filled with real-life examples, little stories, and hard-won advice.

My experience becoming Human has been boiled down to where it resembles stiff nasty black coffee in an old rusted out can. Just like the kind Norm's dad made for us at Tilley lake fifty years ago. Stiff enough to wake the dead I hope.

It's Four Seasons Just For You

By writing this book I came to realize I'd been through four distinct seasons of awakening. Therefore I patterned the Journal below on how the earth turns from winter to spring and continues through summer to autumn. Each season is there to show you what to expect in that phase of your own Journey. Every season has its own character as well. Take Winter for example. Winter is the season of being lost. It's when you'll still be struggling to kick start the Vision you've left behind. Everyone who finds their dreams again starts off in this cold and dark winter place, but take heart. I was once on this lost part of the path myself and pushed through the icy terrain. I've added lots of stories to keep you company and guide you past this part of your life. There's lots of little vignettes about how lost I really was at this stage too, before the Rule of life gave me hope and light and took me out of the darkness. If these tales remind you of who you are now, don't worry. By Autumn you'll have made yourself over into a driven man or woman yourself, enthusiastically carrying out your own calling.

But of course spring follows winter, so spring is what you'll find next in the Journal. Spring is when Vision begins to stir again, and you'll want to know what it's like in real life. That's why part-two of the Journal contains lots of Vision-stirring tales. There you'll find dozens of real-life stories describing what it *feels like* to begin waking up.

Then comes summer. Summer arrives when your very own Life Mission begins to dawn on you. As ideas about who you really are get released into your life once more, you'll be stunned to realize you really do have a purpose. You'll be even more amazed to look back at your Life and discover that purpose was always there. In the summer part of the Journal you'll see what I made of my own memories as well, once I had eyes to see. I've added lots of examples of what it's like to see your authentic soul staring back at you from day one….where you saw nothing and no one before. I guarantee you'll begin mouthing that famous saying…."I can't believe I didn't see myself there before". By now you'll know why you couldn't find yourself in your own life however. It's because you didn't have the Vision to see.

Finally you'll get to the Autumn portion of this book. Autumn is when your purpose on earth is fully revealed to you and you're bound and determined to carry it out. It's when you begin to blossom and know what you're called to do. You'll want to know what it feels like to have a real live Life-Mission of course. True stories describing exactly that abound in this part of the Journal. Each will give you an idea what it'll be like to be driven to follow your heart's passion again. Just follow my examples and follow your destiny. By this time of the book you can look up and see the promised land too. If you listen you'll hear everyone there singing the Freedom song. Your song of Freedom. So let's go. Watch me transforming from lost soul in a shell to growing Human in the following pages….and go do the same. See me become happy to stand before any crowd calling me names…..and follow suit. Let's travel together and meet up with Eddie. Remember Eddie? He could take on a whole world of people calling him names for being himself….with a smile and wave. I don't know about you, but I'm following Eddie the leader.

Chapter Twenty-Four
My Own Real Winter Exercise Journal
(Examples of What It's Like to Be Lost)

"I am a part of all that I have met." *(Alfred Lord Tennyson, 1809-1892, English poet)*

What Is It?

What follows is a real Journal written by yours truly in the hollow dark hours of early mornings. All the dates and times and places and people are all real as can be, although a few names have been changed to protect the guilty. For those of you who can't believe anybody would be up and writing by four A.M. every day I submit this. When you get your own calling back, don't be surprised if you too are "early to bed, early to rise", making yourself healthy, wealthy and wise. In your very own way of course. If what follows looks like it wanders all over place and time to you as well, you're absolutely correct. I wandered back and forth through the pages of my life, distilling nuggets of hard-won knowledge so you wouldn't have to spend decades trying to re-invent this wheel. In case you didn't know, it's legal to do this kind of thing if it helps people get their dreams back. So let's get going here right now. Watch me getting transformed by the Rule of Life from lost soul to man with a Purpose. If you religiously follow the Rule of Life and Mission exercise examples, you too will soon be chasing your own dreams. On the other hand, if you're far too skeptical to follow me and discover your destiny, that's O.K. You can just read it for fun if you want. But if you do, I can promise you this. You'll set yourself Free.

Thursday January 3rd, 2008, 4:15 A.M.

Wow..... minus twenty degrees F. out today. Looks like I'll be done jogging even before the sun comes up again. Bummer. I never was a fan of darkness.

How Lost I Was

Looking back at my life takes my breath away because I was lost so early and stayed that way so long. Now I see I was completely aimless, even by the time I joined boy-scouts. Interestingly though, lost as I was, I remember being puzzled about my own scouting behavior. Here's what I mean. Scouting's a great thing for young boys for all kinds of good reasons. You meet new friends, get to play physical games that keep your heart ticking along nicely, and go camping way out in the woods. Boy-scouts get to do all sorts of things that are pure fun, but there's another part of Scouting that's even more important. Merit badges. Boy-scouts are encouraged to explore the world and earn badges for what they've accomplished. There's badges for bug collecting, fire-starting, and wilderness survival. Learning astronomy, building a stamp collection or becoming an amateur geographer will also get you little official patches to sew on your uniform. Some kids eventually look like Admirals of the fleet once they've got badges up one arm and down the other.

The point of it all is learning and achieving and "seeing the world" of course. Which brings us to yours truly. Back in my own Boy-scout days I recall being mesmerized by the Big Book of Boy-scout Badges. Like a kid peering into a candy store, I lusted after every single one of them. But I didn't get hardly any. Why not? Sad to say, by this time I was already so afraid to fail, I just wistfully looked at them all, as if they were impossible dreams or wishful thinking.

No doubt I could have gotten every single one of those badges, and had a whale of a time doing it….if I wasn't so fearful of being myself. Even in those days I knew something was wrong somewhere though. My heart told me all those badges were well within my reach, but my fear of being judged said "don't go there…because you might not be best or might even fail". My soul was saying "go for it John", but I heard all the potential naysayers shouting even louder…."be careful sonny, because we're ready to call you worthless". To this very day I remember wondering what was holding me back, because I felt the reins halting me so strongly. Okay, so the point of this opening tale is this. I stopped growing as a Human Being even before Boy-scouts, but eventually managed to find my way. I stayed stunted for a very long time, but used the Rule of Life to get my passion back and get growing once more. There is absolutely zero doubt that you can too, regardless of how long you've been lost.

Missionary Zeal

The whole point of Mission exercises is to cajole yourself into sticking to the Rule of Life long enough to begin getting results. They're supposed to be carrots you hang in front of your own nose to keep you moving in the right direction, even if you can't quite see the Promised Land ahead yet. Alright, so let's get one done right now. Just follow me as I make my way through it. Step one is going back to Chapter Thirteen to choose some true Happiness, so I'll pick "real self esteem". Real self-esteem is all the self-worth or personal value in the Universe. It's the most astonishing feeling of worthiness possible. So how do I do a "real self-esteem exercise"? I'll pick two real live people I know who have amazing skills, and esteem them. Bob D. and Mary G. Actually, Mary has two astounding talents I can enjoy.

One is "mirror writing". Mary can sit down anytime she wants and write upside down and backwards …..about as quickly as you or I can write right-side-up. If you don't think this is an amazing skill, just try it. By the time you've laboriously scrawled out your own name, Mary will have written you a five page mirror-letter. O.K., so leave that talent sitting for a moment while I go get Mary's other talent. This will boggle your mind backwards. In short, Mary can read the mind of mechanical machines. It goes like this. In Mary's home town, there's a gambling casino, and she visits it now and then for fun. But one fateful day, Mary discovered something absolutely astounding. A kind of "Rain Man" skill you might say. Believe it or not, she could tell when the mechanical one-armed bandits were about to pay off…..by the sounds they made. According to Mary, these machines would make some kind of subtle sound she couldn't describe in words, about three or four spins from the payout. Impossible as it sounds, Mary learned how to make them cough up cash. As far as I know, she made something like $500 a month off those machines for years, until newer bandits were installed that didn't have gears and springs to make the tell-tale noises. At any rate, this is clearly a talent to be in awe of. Now to Bob D.

Bob's Talent

Bob was a guy I worked with some years ago who had uncanny computer skills. He could figure out what was wrong with astronomically complex business software, by staring at three small clues nobody else had a clue about. Bob could peer under the surface of oceans of these programs, and see where the anchor was stuck. It was like someone figuring out what picture a thousand piece jig-saw made up, by looking at several pieces. Bob's talent was head-twisting like that. Now for the "real self esteem" exercise. To get real self-esteem, you esteem the talents of other people as much as your own.

As if they were gifts sent from afar, meant for all of us. In my case I can revel in the talents of Bob and Mary, as if they were meant for me. I can tell you this as well. As you train yourself to appreciate the talents of others as much as your own, the skills and abilities of friends, strangers and persons of every stripe become wonderful. Eventually you'll be esteeming people everywhere and even pets for what they can do. Once this education in how to esteem the world around you sinks in, you'll begin to know what "real self-esteem" feels like. In my little exercise here for instance, I multiplied my own "self esteem" by three. But over the years I've managed to compound it like money in the bank. Why? Because I can see that everything and everyone around me is who I am. So I'm esteeming myself every single time. Now I can esteem the gifts of everyone everywhere. Believe me, real self-esteem is a wonderful thing.

My First Rule of Life Exercise

Time for a Rule of Life exercise, so I may as well start with the first one. Getting to know my enemy. Before I get going on this though, it's probably worthwhile to repeat something I've said before. As a race of beings, we spend pretty much all our time judging each other, and we don't even notice. Just about everything we do or say is geared to putting ourselves higher up one totem pole or the other, hoping it makes us worth more than the next person.

But unfortunately, most of us have no clue we're dog paddling way out in this terrible sea that's keeping our dreams from us. That's why you absolutely *must* do this exercise. You must see what kind of challenge having authentic success is all about in today's world. So let's start. As we speak, I'm sitting in the Toronto airport, waiting for a shuttle bus to take me home from a trip.

Every second person I see here has one of those "smart phones" that do everything the kitchen sink will, plus send e-mail. But for most people they're nothing but "status symbols". Here's where you can get to know your enemy. Look around and see how many status symbols you can find. Now remember this. Every one is sending you the Message of Fear. It's saying you can't have worth as a Human Being without those things. Every single status symbol is like another barrier between you and your dreams, because it's sending the wrong message. The right message is this. It is impossible your soul can be worth less than any soul. After you've found a million status symbols out there, you'll begin to see how big your enemy is. But you can defeat him with the Rule of Life.

January 3rd, 2008, 4:00 P.M.

Home early today from getting my front tooth fixed. Darn bridge got loose, wiggling in an old root canal, making an ancient abscess above it flare up. I sure hope the antibiotics kill off my little friends the bugs. Nothing personal of course, but I have to have teeth.

Seeking Signs of Leadership

Time for another Mission exercise, so my fire doesn't go out before I get both feet planted on Destiny Road. Number two on the list is soaking up courage from a real leader. So where can I find one? Lucky for me, these inspirational people aren't just big gurus on television or in the pages of books. They're everyday men and women with the courage to be themselves. Certainly some are famous stars, but many others are people we never hear about, who take on huge challenges and continue to grow, however hard Life gets. As it turns out, I know someone like that personally. For privacy purposes I'll change this man's name….but the story isn't altered. I'll call him Glen.

Glen was a senior executive about seven or eight years ago, in a job that paid big bucks and supported his happy family very nicely. Glen also loved what he was doing, because he'd managed to discover who he was, and find a way of making a living being himself. Then, out of the blue, the family owned company he'd helped build was turned over to the kids....who didn't want Glen in the inner circle. Like lightening striking from the sky, Glen suddenly found himself out of a job. Did that faze him? Not at all. Out Glen went and started a business on his own. Like all real leaders, Glen saw adversity as a challenging opportunity. He took that half-empty glass and flipped it right over. "For every door that closes another one opens" said Glen at the time. And sure enough it did. Glen's new consulting business took off and he was having more fun than ever before.

Then cancer made it's ugly presence known in Glen's life. It made him slow down and cut back his business, but it didn't effect his optimism. He took on the cancer like any other challenge. It looked like Glen had won this battle too, until a few months ago when suddenly the cancer showed up in many other places. And here's the leadership lesson for you. Glen told me recently he didn't really think he was going to win his latest medical battle. He's a an "optimistic realist" who knows some things are just outside our control. Even so, Glen's still trying to learn something new from every painful lesson, growing himself.....his way....right to the end. Listening to Glen tell me what this terrible disease was teaching him, even as he suffered, blew me away. A firestorm of white hot courage flooded into my own life directly from Glen's soul, telling me never to give up on myself and my own Mission. Here's something you should know as well. Glen isn't the only true-blue Human leader out there radiating courage like a Super Nova. There are unsung heroes out there on every street corner if you look for them.

I'd suggest you do too, because these real people can help you discover the most important thing of all. Who you are.

Friday January 4th, 2008, 5:30 A.M.

There's so much ice out there this morning, I'd better watch my step out jogging. I better be careful on those cold black roads. Most drivers aren't expecting joggers out like lights before the sun.

Rule of Life Exercise…..Foolish discrimination

No question about it. I've been taught to foolishly discriminate for so long, I can catch myself doing it anytime I want. Here's an example. Last week I had a sales meeting, and brought in enough donuts for the entire office to have one or two. It's a monthly tradition played out in sales offices all over the place and ours is no exception. At any rate, I was making my way to the boardroom this day and had to pass through the engineering cafeteria where the mountain of donuts sat. Rounding a corner, I saw an engineer… who will go un-named…. take four spicy little confections, wolfing two on the spot and escaping with two more to his desk.

"What a greedy little fat-faced pig!" said me to myself, conveniently forgetting my own decades of sow-like behavior. Truth be told, when I was a kid, I used to take more than my fair share of pretty much everything, trying to make my little brother lose out. Particularly speaking, I recall a box of chocolates Brian and I were supposed to share one Easter. A beautiful box of maybe twenty little chocolate bunnies and chickens it was. My chocolate addiction is making my mouth water just thinking about it as we speak. But here comes the sow story. I believe I snaffled off fifteen sugar filled delights for myself before Brian had the smallest chance of getting one.

Gone like the wind they were, and I probably would have eaten the entire box if Mom hadn't caught me. As usual therefore, me the dirty old pot was artfully calling the donut-eating kettle names. Forgetting on purpose that he'd done more than his share of taking more than his share. Foolishly discriminating with great aplomb and efficiency like, well, a fool. There you go….I've admitted I've foolishly discriminated all my life. Now it's your turn.

Mission Exercise Number Three

The third Mission exercise is practicing seeing impossible things becoming possible. Once you've gotten good at believing impossibilities, it won't be any stretch to see that everything around you is a different part of who you are. Here's an example everybody's heard of. One day in the dim past, the earth went from absolutely flat-as-a-pancake, to round as a golf ball. Pretty much overnight. Just like that. How on earth is that possible? Let's just think about it for a moment. Back when the earth was flat, nobody had flown to the moon or even managed to fly with the birds. In short, they were absolutely earth-bound. In case you haven't noticed, the earth up close and personal is flat. Go north, west, east or south, and you'll find nothing but flat. People in these flat-earth days were just as smart as we are today of course, so they asked themselves the duck question. If it walks flat, quacks flat and looks flat everywhere, what is it? It's flat.

How could it possibly be anything else if it's flat everywhere? Gravity hadn't been invented then either, so there was at least one good reason it couldn't possibly be round. Namely, everybody on the bottom would fall off. Every soul on the planet agreed it was impossible the earth could be spherical. Then somebody had some new ideas and it changed. Now everybody believes it's impossible it could be flat. Same holds with wholeness.

Maybe you can't believe Mount Everest is a part of you, like your own knees and manicured nails. But some day the world will change again, from all broken into pieces to One amazing whole.

A Guru-Truth

Here's a beautiful little guru truth for you, discovered by the physicist Erwin Schrodinger in the early 1900's. An island of pure wholeness rising above the ocean of our lives. Like all scientists, Schrodinger knew we have to touch the world to know it. But Erwin was a true blue *mad* scientist, so he wondered what the world is like *before* we touch it. Being a mathematical genius as well, Schrodinger invented a formula to tell us. Then he did an imaginary experiment to test his equations. It went like this. Erwin imagined a cat in a box with a machine that could kill the poor creature in a way that was unpredictable. He set his experiment up so it was possible the cat was dead....but also possible it hadn't been killed. Schrodinger made sure there was no way to know whether the cat was dead or alive except by opening the box to see.

Then he asked his formulas what was going on in the box when he wasn't looking. And what did they say? His formulas told him there was a mixture of live and dead cat in there. Not a live cat or a dead cat. A "live-*and*-dead-at-the-same-time" cat. A bona fide impossible feline. But how can Schrodinger be sure his formulas are correct? A live-and-dead-at-the-same-time cat on paper is one thing, but Schrodinger is swearing on a stack of Bibles this odd feline is really in there. There's only one way to know. He'd have to open the box to check it out. But this turns out to be something of a problem, because Schrodinger's formulas told him something else. They said there was no possible way to get a glimpse of the strange living-and-dead creature. According to his equations, that live-and-dead cat will collapse into a live cat...or a dead one....faster than he can open the box.

How fast are we talking here? It's all over *before it starts*. Yes, you heard right. So what's wrong with Schrodinger's equations? Nothing. It's not Schrodinger's math that's wrong, it's our entire view of the world. Like many brilliant mathematical physicists, Schrodinger had dug right down to the very foundations of our worldview called "Reason", to where it breaks down. He'd managed to uncover the Poem of Life with its absolutely incompatible parts absolutely fused together in an impossible way. This great Poem showed up in Schrodinger's equations as that instant collapsing of the impossible kitty, into a real live or really dead cat. It should have told Schrodinger we've been mistakenly thinking we're separate from the world. But it didn't, so our selfish view of reality is still keeping you and I down.

Monday, January 14th, 2008, 4:00 A.M.

Why Schrodinger Got Goose Bumps

It's easy to see why Schrodinger's own equations would have given him goose bumps. In short, he knew full well there was nothing wrong with his formulas. He also knew nothing is supposed to be over before it starts, according to what makes sense. At bottom then, Erwin Schrodinger had to suspect something was very wrong with our most basic beliefs about the world. Not being able to figure out what it was would have made the hair on his neck stand up. His spine-tingling feelings would have been well founded too, because his famous work with collapsing cats points to Man's salvation. That key is wholeness, and it is sometimes known by another name. Love.

Lost Looks Like This

Let's not forget that this book has two basic parts.

One part is providing that kernel of knowledge you need to discover who you are. The other part is showing you how dramatically I changed from lost soul to Man with a Mission by doing what I'm asking you to do. This next page belongs to that latter part. It harks back to when I was not above grossly misrepresenting myself to try and gain the self-worth I'd lost with my calling. Here's my embarrassing story. One day in my late twenties, someone asked me how I did in college. Sure enough, lost soul that I was, I invented an earth shaking accomplishment. I told that trusting person I'd won the President's gold medal for academic prowess, achieving unprecedented marks and setting new records for blinding brilliance. So did I? Sure I did. The Queen of England made a special trip over and gave the prize to me herself personally as well.

Alright, so maybe I didn't actually win any such award. Maybe I placed second or third and just stretched the truth a bit? Not even close. At best I'd clawed my way right up to the middle of the class. In fact, my school didn't even *have* a "President's medal". Boy, that's a really sad little story isn't it? Yes it is, but it's played out all over the place every day of the week. Otherwise sane and decent people will fake resumes, pump up their accomplishments like balloons, and lie through their teeth if it makes them look more important. Bragging by lying is a time tested way of propping up terribly low self-esteem. But here's something you can look forward to. When you get back on the Path of being yourself again, presenting a fake person to the world will become completely ridiculous. You'll have no use for it whatsoever, because being your authentic self is so wonderfully heart-warming, anything else is a non-starter. I can tell you for sure because my Life Mission erased all that kind of behavior like a big gummy rubber eraser.

Tuesday January 15th, 2008, 5:00 A.M.

Gee...my little Kittsen cat has been snoozing away beside me as I write for ten years now. Every morning he suns himself under my banker's lamp. The little creature started off about the size of a teacup, but now he's fifteen pounds of wool on my desk.

Losers: A Sign of the Truth

Here's a sign of wholeness in the world that's so obvious it's ridiculous. Pretty much everybody sees it every day of the week, but they still don't get it. Losers. Nobody misses the obvious fact that winners need losers. I mean, there can't *be* any winners unless there are losers. Take away the losing team and there is nobody to play with. I've known that all my life and it's fair to say the whole darn world knows it. So how come no one thanks losers for making winning possible? Simple. We're stuck in a selfish worldview that separates winners and losers. We can't see that winners and losers are just different parts of the same game, or competition, or race. We can't see that it's taking our dreams from us either. So every time you or I win, we'd better thank the losers for our prize and when we lose, we should be thankful we've had the privilege of people helping us grow. We should be reminding people that winners and losers really need each other to get their dreams back.

A Sad Snapshot

Here's another sad snapshot of yours truly in the late fifties, which goes to show how early I lost my Way, and how far I've come. It's mid July 1957 or so and once again I'm at our annual cottage lake fun-fest. The very same summer games I would try to drown myself at about six years later.

This time I'm too young to head out across the big waters, but there are lots of things for little kids to do as well, like the twenty-yard dash for tiny tots. And so off I go with ten other little tykes, racing my heart out for the finish line. Right from the start I'm in front and running like the wind. But a few moments later another little guy catches up. Soon he's ahead and I'm running second....then third. Then...suddenly... I tripped and fell and bystanders big and small rushed in to help the poor little soul up. What a terrible piece of misfortune. Wasn't it? Embarrassing as it is to admit it, there was no bad luck to be found there at all. I pretended to fall. I tripped myself up. I threw myself down on my own face.

Why on earth would anyone do that? I'd already been taught my soul would be worthless if I lost, and it sure looked to me like I was about to become a loser. By this time of my life I'd do just about anything to avoid being judged a loser. That is one heck of a painful little memory to me now, but absolutely true. So how about you at an early age? Can you recall hiding behind shyness or trying to blend in to avoid being asked to answer in class? Same thing. You were afraid to be yourself. But don't worry, because you can grow out of it at any age. When you do, you'll be able to admit how lost you once were....right out in public.....just like I did.

Tuesday 7:00 A.M....Jan 15, 2008

Five minutes before I head out to London for lunch. Enough time for a Tree of Life exercise.

The Truth in Action:

Here's something you'd better understand if you want to see why you're here.

If you don't actually get up and work at seeing the Truth, nothing will happen. You have to take action to get anywhere. That's why the old sayings "if in doubt…DO something" and "fake it 'til you make it" are famous. Reading about the Truth may be good, but putting it in action is better. Here's a simple way you can put the Truth in action too. By giving. There are lots of ways you can "give" as well. If you don't have time, you can give money or vice versa. There's a simple rule you can apply if you're stuck trying to figure out "how much". Give what you can afford. Take time for instance. Maybe you're so busy from dawn to dusk you can barely find fifteen minutes a day to eat lunch. Fine, but you can invite someone to lunch *with* you and listen to their life-stories. Listening is a kind of giving and there isn't anybody that can't take a few minutes a day to listen. Same kind of thing holds with cash. If you can only afford to give a single penny, go to your corner Milk Mart and look for that little dish they keep there for spare change. Put your penny in when getting your daily bread and you'll be putting the Truth in action. Acting like you believed the world around you is who you are will make you believe it eventually. Getting your Body to do something will change your Mind. Mind and Body are hooked up together like that for a reason. To help you see the Truth.

Thursday January 24th, 2008, 8:00 A.M.

Wow….what a winter wonderland today! The old bird feeder is swimming with birds this morning. Four Juncos. Two hairy woodpeckers at the suet block. A gorgeous half-pink house finch swilling seeds like there was no tomorrow, and three fuzzy little nuthatches! Good thing I put out lots of food yesterday.

Positive Thinking: A Self-Help Guru-Truth

Browsing my favorite book-store yesterday, I came across a granddaddy of self-help books. "The Power of Positive Thinking"....by Norman Vincent Peale. Originally published in 1952, it's been on the shelves for more than fifty years. In the "Power of Positive Thinking" Peale suggests that we can have faith that every difficult situation contains a small positive thread that can lead us to victory. According to Peale, every dark cloud has a grain of silver in it we can profit from and any half-empty glass is always half-full. Peale's heart-warming stories of triumph illustrate how men or women overcame hardship with this kind of faith. But why did Norman Peale have such undying faith in his "Positive Principle"? Because it is founded on the Truth. Right at the center of Peale's inspirational works is what we call "God, love, or wholeness". Wholeness is why that tiny grain of silver is always found in the darkest of clouds. There is nothing in the Universe that is not a mysterious Yin and Yang mixture of darkness and light. But let's not forget this. That tiny spark of light in the darkness is there to remind us that the world is whole and we are each other. When we see this simple Truth for ourselves, Being Human or "God" comes into our lives and makes us happy. Norman Vincent Peale gives us hundreds of beautiful stories to illustrate the amazing way wholeness can change our lives. That's why his work is virtually timeless.

A Silver Lining Story

Speaking of silver linings, I have a real true story about them for you. Some years ago, I happened to see a inspirational speaker on T.V. who was born without arms. To say the least, this man was truly amazing. He'd taught himself to do pretty much anything you and I can do...only using his feet where we would use our arms or hands.

He went to college, married and raised a family, and built an inspirational speaking business that motivates people all over the world to get out there and use what they have to make a life for themselves. It is absolutely mind-blowing to see this man in action. By sheer luck and impossible chance one day I actually managed to meet Alvin Law personally. One afternoon I was fueling up my car in Toronto, Canada, over by the airport, when Alvin himself drove in......one foot on the steering wheel. He then got out and proceeded to grab a gas hose with one foot and fill up right beside me....like it was nothing. To the rest of us standing around the pumps it was more like a miracle. There was no possible way you could mistake this guy for anyone else either. No question about it, it was the one and only Alvin Law of AJL Communications.

Having just recently seen Alvin on television, I spoke right up and told him how much he inspired me to follow my own dreams. Alvin thanked me for saying so of course, but then said something that stuck with me ever since. "Every cloud has a silver lining"....he said with conviction that struck me forcefully ...."and I've been mining mine all my life". Immediately I thought of Norman Peale's books, but Alvin gave me a profoundly deeper appreciation for how deep that vein of silver goes. When you are faced with a real live example of what Peale wrote so much about, it stuns you with the reality of wholeness and "positive thinking". Alvin then gave me his business card that I have in my wallet to this day. I keep it there to remind me that silver is everywhere. If you ever get a chance to see Alvin speak....grab it. He'll inspire you as much as he did me.

Friday January 25th, 2008, 4:41 A.M.

Here we go again. Mr. pussycat likes eating computer cords, light bulb chains or knick-knacks. But as soon as I try stopping him, the giant fur-ball rolls around on my desk, scattering books, pictures and coffee cups. Cat lovers everywhere will recognize this picture.

Sun Tzu's Exercise: (Getting to Know My Enemy)

Little signs of people judging each other are everywhere of course. Bob will turn his nose up at Jerry for example, because Jerry's house is smaller. Mary will turn her back on Gillian because Gill doesn't have pearls. But there are lots of big signs. Really big signs our enemy might just be winning the war, taking our dreams from us forever. Signs so big, you might barely see them for what they are. Entire nations judge other nations less worthy because they follow different religions for instance. Countries will topple foreign governments at the drop of a hat to install their own as well, because they believe theirs is better. Complete races of people will proclaim other races inferior too, and enslave them if they can. Mobs of sports fans will judge other clubs worthy of death and inflict violence upon them. These gigantic signs of our enemy are all around us all the time. But today we think it's "just the way it is". "It's always been this way"…. say the pundits…."it's just Human Nature". Isn't it? No it isn't. It's people everywhere giving up Being Human. It's signs our enemy might just defeat us, if we don't wake up soon.

Tree of Life Exercise

Let's see here, what exactly is the Tree of Life anyway? It's One eternal Life that emerges from the sum of everything in the Universe, when all things become one.

It's like the One picture that emerges when all the different jig-saw puzzle parts blend together, giving up their separate identities to make up a whole. But if we keep on thinking everything in the world is a separate thing-unto-itself, we can't have eternal life. Certainly we'll see that everything in the world is connected, but until we change our worldview, we won't take the next step and let everything become One. Why? Sadly, we believe "connected" means any two separate things are connected by some third separate thing. We're so selfish, we don't even realize that all these kabillions of separate things-unto-themselves in the Universe can only *be connected*.... because they're different parts of one whole. In essence, as a race of beings, we've been staring at the jillions of trees around us for Ages, without seeing the Forest. So here's a Tree of Life exercise for you.

Look around and see how individual things *are connected*. You and that elephant in the London Zoo *are connected* by planet earth for example. You're both standing on the same Terra Firma. But that connection, is only possible because you and he and the earth and I are all different parts of One whole. If you can *make the connection* then, you are looking evidence for wholeness in the face. Same with some butterfly in the Amazon rainforest. He and you are swimming in the same ocean of air. If you can *see the connection*, it's because you share the same life. Even those faraway stars you look at each night are part and parcel of who you are. Just look up tonight and the starlight shining on you will *make the connection*. When it does, know your soul is worth as much as any soul. See what I mean? Get out there and play the "make a connection" game again and again, until it dawns on you that you and the world are one whole.

Selflessness: A Backwards Sign

"When the ancient Masters said,
"If you want to be given everything,
give everything up,"
they weren't using empty phrases.
Only in being lived by the Tao can you be truly yourself". – Tao Te Ching

At the dawn of the twenty-first century, most people think selflessness is a sign of weakness at best. At worst some think selflessness is a slippery slope that begins with giving away things and ends up giving up everything, including your life. But true selflessness has nothing at all to do with suicide, or even giving things away. Real selflessness is simply seeing that all "selves" have the very same human worth. It's nothing more or less than recognizing that there is a level playing field for all the different parts of our one collective soul. It's the opposite of selfishness that tries to take things from others to feel important. Selflessness is all about just being yourself and attracting that abundance of things necessary to your life around you. You don't have to give those things away to become selfless either, because they're necessary to who you are. You can share with other less fortunate souls of course, or give as much as you can afford to others. But the most important part of selflessness is just valuing others around you equally, whether they are richer than you or not. And here is why I call selflessness a "backwards sign of the Truth". In today's world, pretty much everyone will tell you selflessness is stupid and not to go there. If you want your share of Bliss, you are best advised to go in the opposite direction. Run there if you can. Why? That's where your dreams are.

Monday, February 4th, 2008, 6:00 A.M.

I am at war in my day job these days, and will have to turn the company upside down and backwards to become competitive. I won't be winning any popularity contests doing it either.

A Guru-Truth For Today

Browsing the web this morning, I found something the ancient Chinese philosopher Confucius wrote. About 2500 years ago, Confucius said..."before you embark on a journey of revenge, dig two graves". That sure is a scary little saying, but what is Confucius trying to tell us here? It sounds suspiciously like he's saying "killing your enemy kills yourself", but it's not often taken literally. Even so, many people have seen a glimmer of the Truth buried in Confucius's wisdom. Most of us realize that hatred is a caustic emotion that does as much harm to we-who-hate as to those hated for instance. Generations of men and women have discovered that forgiveness is a liberating thing as well, as if revenge was a kind of imprisonment. But let's not forget that Confucius was a man of deep insight into how the world works.

Perhaps he was trying to tell us something more than meets the eye. Personally I believe he was, because, difficult though it is to believe, your enemy is really a different part of you. By killing he or she you are diminishing your own life. You are killing part of yourself. Really and truly then, you should be digging your own grave when contemplating revenge. If you and I and all the warring peoples of the world could see this Truth more clearly, revenge would be a very silly thing to pursue indeed. I therefore submit Confucius's famous saying as a bona fide guru truth exemplifying wholeness in the most profound way imaginable. A way that makes enemies become different parts of each other and stop the violence.

Tree of Life Exercise

The Tree of Life is so huge, pretty much everybody misses it. Forget missing forests for trees, we've been missing One Life in the Universe Age after Age. Here's a simple example that's been staring us in the face, ever since the science of biology got going a hundred years or so ago. Every single, solitary person and creature on earth has the same ancestors. Even today's kindergarten students know this little fact. Everyone would agree the divine spark of life in you right now is the same one passed on to every living thing on the planet. My greatest possible grandparents and yours are one and the same. It doesn't matter what color you are either, or where you come from. In fact, your ancestors and mine are the same even if you're a cockroach or crocodile. (Nothing personal…but it's true). As a matter of fact, if you look hard, you'll realize even the rocks and plants are far flung relatives of ours, all stemming from the same ancestral chemistry set. Every one different fruits and leaves and branches on one Tree of Life. So what does all this mean? There is only ONE life in the universe we're all part of. Far more important to you and I though, it means no life can possibly be worth less than any other life. Even the life of that fly you took yesterday without thinking.

A Very Big Surprise

I am now going to tell you something that is really and truly astonishing, in two parts. You'll need to stop and think about this to fully appreciate what it means. Here's part one. If you're caught up in any kind of substance abuse, getting your own dreams back is the absolute cure. That includes, alcohol, cocaine, speed, glue, or whatever. Nobody who really has a mission to carry out in their life wants any part of it. Just to make myself absolutely clear, I'm telling you that our mistaken way of seeing the world is the absolute cause of every kind of drug abuse known to Man.

But of course, we aren't even looking in the right direction for the "cure". The root cause of all this sorrow and pain is fear of being judged...but all we do is pass judgment on sickened souls by calling them derogatory names like "alcoholic" or "drug addict". Can you guess what that accomplishes? To put out this inferno, we throw gasoline on the fire and fan the flames.

A Personal Surprise

Here's the very personal second part of the story. In my own aimless years, I could have accurately been called an alcoholic, because I passed the simple test. I drank to get drunk and did so pretty much every weekend. Alcohol had a magnetic pull on me. Come Fridays, off I went to the wine store right after work, and nothing could stop me. Once and a while I would try to stop myself, because *even I* knew it was sad and destructive. With super-human willpower, straining mightily against the pull of it, I could stop for a short time. But it was like hanging onto a tree in a hurricane. I did not have enough strength of will to give it up.

Now let's fast forward to where I've managed to start growing Human again and have a calling to carry out. For a little while into my Mission I'd still been boozing on weekends. But one day on the way to the wine store I felt a revulsion for what I was about to do. Ordinarily I "looked forward" (a very bad description but true) to getting drunk, but this day I had a bad feeling about it. Even so, I got the booze and headed home. Soon I had my first glass poured and half downed. As the alcohol buzz began, my mind and body started to rebel. It did not want it. I almost gagged trying to get it down. It was as if I was attempting to drink paint thinner. My Mind-Body knew it was poison and was trying to keep me from taking it. I could not drink it. I had never experienced anything like this before and did not know what to make of it.

I thought I must be getting the flu or something and reluctantly left the booze alone that night.

Something Strange is Going On

Next day, hoping I was feeling better, I tried sloshing down the booze again. This time I could not even get past a few sips. A bottle and a half of wine was left untouched in my house that weekend…..an impossible thing in any alcoholic family. By the following week, I had awakened from some kind of fog. Now the very *idea* of drinking until I passed out was unbelievable. I remember thinking "what would possess me to do such a thing". Now I know it was fear of being judged. As more time passed and I continued being occupied with various facets of my Life Mission, the full truth of my experience was made clear to me. I knew with certainty that I had turned to alcohol because I lost my reason for being here. I also knew with the same certainty getting my Mission back had cured me of the need to medicate myself.

It is now many years after that fateful last day with wine, and I have no use for anything that reduces my consciousness, much less puts me to sleep. If I'm offered a beer or glass of wine these days, I consume it so slowly my consciousness of this stunningly beautiful world is not impaired at all. My aim in life now is to *increase* my consciousness, not decrease it. I now know this too. Getting dreams back means tapping into that huge ocean of potential at our center. It means tapping into a far greater Will that makes our individual puny willpower look silly. As we learn how to "know Thyself" to release our callings back into our lives, we begin to understand what "Thy Will Be Done" means. It means the great hand of Fate is behind us, helping us go our own Way. When this happens, you will realize that the hurricane has stopped and willpower isn't needed to hang on anymore. No longer is there any storm.

Having experienced this first-hand, I know it to be true. You can experience it yourself by working at the Rule of Life until your dreams come back.

Wednesday February 6th, 2008, 5:15 A.M.

The anniversary of my brother Brian's death just went by. It's been a year now since air got into his dialysis tube by mistake. This sure makes me realize how quick things can change for the worse. The truth is, I don't really know if I'll make it home alive for dinner tonight, so I better appreciate what I have while I have it. Amen.

The Truth in Action

The Rule of Life says I have to *act* like the world is who I am. It doesn't say…."*think* about it or…*read* about it". It says….."get out there and *do* something". Putting the truth in action means *action*. It's ridiculously easy to start acting like the world is who I am as well. In essence I have to start taking care of the world like I take care of myself. That means doing simple things like feeding the birds, recycling, and being a good Samaritan if the chance presents itself. It means conserving energy for tomorrow and behaving kindly towards my neighbors. You don't need to be a student of language to realize all those words I used are *verbs* and verbs mean……*taking action*. Each little everyday example is an example of taking care of business. Just in case you forgot, *your life* is *your business*, and it will be enriched by treating the world like it was who you are. Don't be pooh-poohing all these simple minded ways of putting the Truth in action either, because they're cheap and easy ways you can invest in the life of your dreams. They'll eventually help you discover your very own purpose on earth, as your way of seeing things is changed by them.

A Seeing-I Exercise

Any kind of exercise is easy to give up on too early, before real results show up. That's why the seeing-I exercise is so helpful. By continuing to focus on the happiness I'm seeking, I'll keep on working to get my dreams back. So let me go back a ways and remember what Dr. Steve told me about the kind of real fulfillment I want for myself. I have to do *my* thing in life to get it. It does not matter how much I achieve while I'm here, if they aren't my own authentic heart-felt goals, I'll feel half-empty at the end of it all. O.K. so I'll make up a little story to help convince me I want authentic fulfillment before I die. I'll revisit this tale every day to keep me working at the Rule of Life until it's mine. Here you go. Fake fulfillment is what a partridge gets if he pretends to be a rabbit. If this creature stays true to himself, he'd fly like a bird when need be. But something is very wrong, because he's pretending to be something he's not. He's running around like a very slow rabbit. Soon he'll get his share of fake fulfillment from Mr. Fox, who will have him for dinner. On the other hand, if this sad soul learned how to be himself, he'd get *real* fulfillment, by flying away. Real fulfillment by another name is Freedom.

Knowing my Enemy

In Sun Tzu's day, the enemy was pretty obvious. A huge herd of Huns would come riding over the horizon to wage war, and nobody could miss them. It's relatively easy to study the habits of your enemy when he stands out like a sore thumb. But in the world you and I live in, the enemy is more like poison covered in chocolate. He's disguised as anything but an enemy and made to be so desirable you'll invite him right into your house. Messages designed to fill our hearts with fears of being judged abound in today's world then, but we accept them as friends. Take automobiles for example.

Why do you think car makers put out new models every year? Is there something wrong with the old models….year after year? Are the manufacturers just exploring possibilities like scientists, so you and I can enjoy the discoveries? Are auto makers like poets, inspired to create for your enjoyment and mine? There must be some good reason we'll suck the earth dry of resources to put out brand new cars all the time. But what could it be? It's too obvious for words really. It's so you and I can pretend we're worth more than the next guy or gal…by having the newest, biggest, best car on the block. In case you aren't quite sure what I'm saying here, let me summarize it for you. We think new cars will give us the self-worth we've lost with our callings. Even worse, we're all but hard-wired to think we're worthless if we don't have the newest best car.

Car manufacturers are in luck then, because you and I are motivated by a deep fear of being judged to buy their products. But let's stop and think about that for a moment. Let's try and put it in perspective. New cars are pretty much like cocaine if you think about it. Both are consumed to dull the deep pain caused by losing our reason for being here. Neither can cure the disease, but we-who-consume them are convinced more of the same will help. So what do you think happens to a Man who spends all his resources on drugs like this? Soon he runs out of capital and turns to violence trying to feed his habit. Eventually he descends into hell. Don't think this is a very good analogy? You had better get to know your enemy a whole lot better.

Sunday February 10th, 2008, 12:00 noon

A Quantum Guru Truth

Many twentieth century guru-scientists have discovered wholeness masquerading as paradox, but Neils Bohr's complementarity interpretation of quantum physics takes the mask off. Boy…that's quite a mouthful if you say it that way….like scientists do. To scientists, quantum physics is a very complicated business, all about light in its many forms of matter or energy. But Bohr's complementarity is the most important part of it all, and it's simple enough for me and you. Here's what it's all about. Imagine quantum physics is a thousand page story about Man's great Journey to grow Human. Bohr's complementarity comes from asking a simple question. How much can the quantum physics story tell us about Man's Journey? A "complete" story would tell us absolutely everything, as if we'd actually been to the destination ourselves, instead of just reading about it.

If you stop for a second and think about it, that's a pretty potent question. Actually going somewhere is always a heck of a lot different than just reading about it after all. If you've ever been to the moon yourself, you'll know what I mean. Books about it pale in comparison to the real thing. That's why Neils Bohr wanted to know what a "complete" quantum physics story would be like. One that would tell him everything about Man's great Journey. Bohr's complementarity is the answer to this question.

Bohr Wants to Take Us There

Bohr wanted a complete theory of reality that'd actually "take Man there", and he discovered it. Bohr figured out the correct meaning, or interpretation to give the quantum physics story that really *can* take Man to the promised land.

Bohr told us a complete story would be an absolute fusion of absolutely incompatible ideas. That's "complementarity", but it's just another name for wholeness. It describes how different things merge seamlessly together so a whole can emerge. It's all about how one thing can be many at the same time. And here's what's important about Bohr's discovery. Neils Bohr explored to the very limits of Reason itself where its foundations are. He laid bare the deepest parts of our House of Knowledge, where wholeness is. Wholeness we mistakenly tore apart Ages ago to create our present, potentially fatal, view of the world. The sad one that keeps our dreams from us…by making us think one life can be worth less than another. Bohr should have realized our whole House of Knowledge is built on the mistaken idea that every thing is completely separate. But he didn't, so we're still rushing headlong towards disaster. Even so, Bohr's Truth is still there, like a spectacular key we can use to unlock the door to the promised land. A land of peace and purpose and happy freedom. And how do we unlock this door? Each of us has to see the world around us is who we are, so every one of us has our own dreams to follow.

Neils Bohr's Big Bumps

Read Neils Bohr's work and you'll see he got more than goose bumps over complementarity, because complementarity is the Truth of the world, and it gave Bohr angst. Angst means "anguish, torment, anxiety, trouble, sorrow, worry, and fear". Bohr had angst over complementarity, because he knew deep down it was the key to something big. And it is. It's the key to Man's salvation, and a scientific key to unlocking big secrets to the Universe. But Bohr didn't see how to use the key. He didn't realize complementarity was where we can change our mistaken view of the world called "Reason" before it's too late. No wonder Bohr's goose bumps burst into angst.

Tuesday February 12th, 2008, 4:30 A.M.

My old Welsh friend Andy's art-work reminds me of how much time has gone by in a heartbeat. Thirty years have flown under the bridge since we shared a house in England. As a matter of fact, 1975 was when I began my first Journal that would eventually morph itself into this very book. Andy's brown trout wood-cut on my wall is now three decades old.

My Enemy

Yesterday I saw my enemy on the road. Have you ever been on a busy freeway where every gal in her big V8 just has to pass you? Did you ever wonder why? No? Think about it. It can't be because she's getting there faster. She won't get more than ten car lengths ahead all day. Too much traffic. Alright, but maybe she's about to deliver a baby? Probably not. O.K., so maybe she's so late for work she'll get fired if she doesn't hurry up? Not likely. So why the heck is she risking her life and ours to get ahead? She's programmed, like you and I and everybody else. In today's world, we have to get ahead to be important, any which way we can. We're so well-trained to "get ahead" we'll do it one car at a time on the highways.

Don't buy it? Haven't you seen some guy darting in and out, climbing the traffic ladder to get somewhere fourteen seconds earlier at great risk to his health? Or the lady who changes lanes every ten seconds, trying to get ahead….but doesn't…because she ends up in the slow lane anyhow? Why would anyone attempt to pass in an endless stream of traffic, when the best they're going to do is get one car ahead? It's because our enemy has turned us against ourselves. People everywhere will try to regain the self-esteem they lost with their dreams, even if it kills them.

That's why our enemy is so sinister. Our enemy has dug in so deep we don't even know what we're doing anymore.

Foolish Discrimination

Human beings have become experts at foolish discrimination. We've learned a million ways to say "what's good for the Goose isn't good for himself". As far as we're concerned *we* can do just about anything.....but other folks better not be doing it. Why? There's a difference. Remember that difference? They're them and we're us. O.K., here are three ways I caught myself foolishly discriminating recently. If you can't find three of your own, you have your eyes tightly closed. I gained twenty pounds and still looked down on the fat guy next to me. Ridiculous? Yes, but absolutely true. I've spent money on fancy cars as well, and then promptly called people with fancier ones names for being greedy. Stupid? That was me alright. I wanted to kill terrorists because they wanted to kill us too, but thankfully …..now I can see the folly of foolish discrimination more clearly. If you don't think it's folly, just ask yourself why we'll never end the war on terrorism. It's because we think killing terrorists is A-O.K., but terrorists killing us is terrorism.

Friday February 15th, 2008, 7:00 P.M.

Home early today. I've got time to do a couple Rule of Life exercises

Finding Folks To Grow With

Here's a little story that will give you an idea why working with friends and strangers to see wholeness is so powerful. Imagine you live in a city surrounded by a very high wall with only one door in it.

Unfortunately, that single door is locked and nobody has a key. There is absolutely no way to get out of this place. It would be a kind of prison if there wasn't something special going on in this city. What's special is the rivers. Within the confines of this town are many rivers boiling up out of the ground, bringing with them everything inhabitants need to nourish their lives. Toys and joys and food and sustenance of every possible kind are carried into this walled abode. Men and women who have learned to go to these rivers find a feast of things to build their dream lives with.

On the other hand, people who don't realize what the rivers can do for them live sad, shallow lives, starved for things they need to grow. That's the little story. Here's the point of it. In our world, other human beings are those rivers we must meet to help us grow. Other people are rivers of invention and inspiration and helpful hands where concerns growing ourselves. Every time two or more heads are put together for purposes of growing, an explosive waterfall of power is generated. And so, if you don't work with other people to see the world differently, you will have a very hard time going it alone. Like men and women in that little town above, your life will be a shadow of what it could be.

The Yin Yang Truth

Unless you're a very, very sheltered soul indeed, you'll have seen the Yin Yang sign many times before. Usually it's a black and white circle with an S-curve down the middle, but I'll bet dollars to donuts you never thought it had anything to do with you. It surely does. You might even say it's the key to the meaning of your life. As a matter of fact, you could say the Yin Yang sign is the real and true formula for authentic success. Here's why. The famous Yin Yang sign is a picture of that vast sea of Tao-potential at your center. That very same potential you've always known you have down deep, but haven't been able to get at.

The Yin Yang sign isn't the Tao itself of course, only a picture of it. But thankfully, this famous sign also tells you precisely how to release your potential. All you have to do is understand what it's saying, so let's spell it out in simple black and white. The Yin Yang sign is like a two-part jig-saw puzzle you must put together to see who you are. It has one white part and one black part, so let's assemble the puzzle. Slide the two pieces together so their "S" sides match. Now what? To release Tao potential you must let the white piece and black piece blend together seamlessly to become one. If you don't let them become one, all you have are two separate parts sitting closely together.

On the other hand, if they become each other, a *whole* emerges from the sum of those parts. This "whole" emerges from the sea of Tao potential. It's a brand new and completely different thing from the separate Yin and Yang pieces you made it from. And so, this ancient symbol of wholeness is trying to tell you this. If you see that the world around you is who you are, your "authentic person" will emerge into the world and it will make you happy. That is all there is to it. This fabulously simple little picture really is the secret to discovering who you are. It is a stunning picture of the Truth.

Monday February 18th, 2008, 6:30 A.M.

Hope I don't run into any nut cases out there jogging today. Yesterday some guy pointed his pickup truck right at me. A sad soul who thinks running joggers off the road gives him power.

A Real Leader

Some years ago, I hired a corporate coach to help me make over our company. This was an executive lady who'd given up a six figure income to go out on her own.

As a single mom with teenagers at home however, starting a business was risky, not to mention unpopular. Friends, family, and strangers alike offered a million good reasons why she shouldn't follow her dreams. By far, most of these reasons had to do with dollars. In today's world dollars win over dreams nine times out of ten. But Gwyn was one of those rare people with the courage of her convictions, so off she went into the wild blue business yonder knocking on doors and selling her coaching skills. Eventually, listening to her inner voice, Gwyn soon discovered a Spiritual side of herself she didn't know she had. When all is said and done, spirituality is about growing Human, because the Spirit of Man emerges into our lives when we grow. So Gwyn's consulting business began to change from growing profits to growing people. Instead of teaching business skills, she started coaching men and women in the Art of being human. Personal organization and time management training were replaced by lessons in integrity, truthfulness, and meditation.

As Gwyn re-oriented her business though, she soon discovered that building a Spirit coaching business is even harder than growing a business consulting practice. In fact, I'd say it's ten times harder, because so few people are in touch with their Spirit. But that did not slow Gwyn down in the least, because she's a real leader, fed by courage from within and able to stand alone before any crowd. An example to all of us who need that kind of courage to go our own Way. If you want to find a real leader like Gwyn in your own life to encourage you, here's what to look for. A person going their own way regardless of what anyone else thinks about it.

Competition: A Backwards Sign

In today's world, competition is a backwards sign, pointing away from the truth, because most people by far compete for the wrong reason.

The truth is, competition has nothing at all to do with winning. Lotteries are about winning, but competition is supposed to be about *growing*. Unfortunately, we've misunderstood the world so badly, pretty much everyone competes just to win. Most men and women enter competitions to be feted and lauded and pronounced important when they come in first, to make up for what they've lost with their callings. They will lie, cheat, steal, or destroy themselves with performance enhancing drugs to do so as well. So what exactly is the misunderstanding here? Competitions are supposed to be ways people can collaborate to stretch and try and fail and succeed in growing Mind, Body and Spirit in the direction they came with. Sports competitions can take large numbers of athletically inclined men and women and give them opportunities to hone their skills for instance. Businesses competing can do the same for people with heads for numbers and talents for making things happen.

Any kind of competition is really supposed to be a way of challenging human beings to grow like flowers in the direction that's right for them. There's nothing at all wrong with one team or person winning a game or new customer and the other losing either. It's simply part and parcel of the process of growth. Winners can be lauded too, but in a world made whole again, even losers feel good about those placing first, and winners will applaud the competition for helping them grow. But keep in mind something very important here. Each competitor is supposed to know what game to get into to grow him or herself *their way*. Someone with athletic talents then, whose Mission is to teach arithmetic, shouldn't be spending their life running road races....just because they could win. But in today's world, a person with the soul of a teacher may well dedicate themselves to running, to gain artificial self-esteem by being a "winner". Sadly, this kind of person loses, even when they win, because they're just pretending to be something they're not.

The next time you're watching some competition then, and see that it's about nothing but winning, remember this. Go the other way. Compete to grow. Don't forget to figure out first which way you should be growing too, or you'll never know who you are.

Wednesday Feb 20, 2008, 4:40 A.M.

Looks like it's time to order mail-order plants for the garden already. It's nice to live in the middle of an old apple orchard, surrounded by acres of rabbits after so many years of big city life. Some might say there's way too much lawn to tend, but I don't mind a few Saturday hours on the old tractor each summer.

What's Impossible?

Everything in the world is a curious mixture of absolute familiarity and absolute mystery. The familiarity part is easy to see. Take the buttons on your coat for instance. No doubt you recognize them as buttons, however odd they might be. You might even have a reasonable idea what they're made of and who made them. But if you start digging into those buttons, you'll eventually run into a mystery. In short, you won't be able to figure out where they really came from or how they're made. The ancestry of those buttons on your coat is so long and complex, there's no way you can get to the roots of them. Every machine making buttons has parent machines that have parent machines for example and so on right back to before the industrial revolution.

Same for the parts in button making machines or the materials they're made of. Even if you spent your entire life trying to fully understand where your buttons came from and how they were made, you wouldn't be able to. That means the buttons you know so well, you don't really know at all. It means something else too.

This way every familiar thing in the world sits on a complete mystery makes everything impossible, miraculous magic. The way to have this kind of magic back in your life is to become whole once more. Becoming whole is an impossibly magical Journey filled with wonder and the deep and abiding mystery of Life. If you don't believe it, it's because you haven't been there.

Saturday February 23rd, 2008, 8:00 A.M.

Today one of my old supervisors called to chat. Carlos is a guy who knows in the meat of his bones he has huge potential. I do too, but like most people Carlos is waiting for bosses, friends, mentors or magicians to tell him what to do with his life. Carlos has no clue he's blinded by fears of being judged and doesn't even believe it when I tell him. Unfortunately, if Carlos doesn't wake up and "get it", he'll be doomed to a life of personal mediocrity.

I Was Like This

Are you one of those people who takes way too many things personally? Constructive criticism feels like terrorism to you perhaps? Silly little jokes about your car make you want to cry like a baby? Not to worry. When you see your life is worth as much as any life, it will all disappear…..even if you take everything personally right now…like I used to. I'll give you two examples of what I was like to identify with, but here's something to think about. Now that I have real self-esteem, ten Federal Judges could pronounce my soul useless every day and put it up on billboards on the freeway. My response to this giant assault on my inner being? Smile and wave. Like Eddie. Alright, so here's some painful pictures of how I was. As a teenager, I was so afraid to ask the girls to dance it was probably record-breaking. It would take me forever to pluck up enough courage to ask an American Sweetheart to waltz.

And what happened when she said "no thank you, I'm waiting for the Captain of our football team to ask"? I thought she'd handed me an order of execution I was supposed to carry out myself. Good thing we didn't carry guns in those days too or I might have. I felt like a Salamander run over by a steamroller. Guys with normal self-worth would have just moved on to the next fish in the ocean. Me? I asked Mom if I could move out of the State. Compare yourself to that sad case but don't forget. The Rule of Life can help you leave all that kind of shenanigans behind.

Like This Too

Here's a second example of how personally I used to take things. When I was in grade eight, the teacher loved to read final exam marks to the class, from the top down. I believe he was a sadist. At any rate, at the end of the year, we all looked forward to this event. Finally the day comes and Mr. teacher stands up there with his list and starts reading….slowly….pausing now and then to stretch out the pain. Number one on that list was read with a flourish and asked to stand up for applause. Number two got slightly lauded with "and a close second is…..". Then came yours truly in number three position. I must have swelled with some pride at that little accomplishment…. right? Are you kidding? At that time of my life I believed winners were worth everything and everyone else was a real loser. I was acutely embarrassed. I can still remember my name being called out and the very sound of it stabbing into my heart like a knife into vermin. Looking back at it now, it is hard to believe, but it's absolutely true. When you cannot see it's *impossible* your soul can be worth less than any soul, the smallest thing can make you feel like that. Thankfully, you can learn to see the Truth and put that sad silliness behind you.

Karma is the Truth

Most folks know Karma as "what goes around comes around". But if Karma was real, you'd think good people would get good back and criminals would get what they deserve. Trouble is, bad things often happen to good people and criminals get away with murder every day of the week. So Karma must be nonsense. Right? Not at all. We just can't see what Karma is telling us, because we've separated ourselves from each other and the world. Here's how to understand Karma properly, and realize it is the full and unadulterated Truth. To start with you must see that the world around us is who we are. Now take a person doing good to the world. It "comes back" instantly, because the world is who they are. Same with a person doing bad things to the world. Instantly the bad is done to them, because they and the world are different parts of each other. The Truth is, criminals don't escape Justice…because their crimes are committed against themselves. So here's what Karma has been trying to tell us. When we all see the world is whole, no one will want to do bad things to themselves.

A Foolish Discrimination Story

Foolish discrimination is everywhere. Here's an example an old friend told to me one day that I'll pass on to you. Many years ago, my friend was out golfing with a big-wig. Some VP, CEO or other big letter guy I believe, trying hard to get ahead. O.K., so Norm and this man are coming up on the fifth hole beside a farmer's field and there picking tomatoes are Mexican migrant workers. Sure enough, Norm's partner pipes up. "What a bunch of losers!" he says, chuckling away like a golfer with foggy glasses on, laughing at a tiger in the woods. To which Norm replies. "Maybe they're not so dumb."

But Norm didn't get too far with that one, because this man raised his nose as high as possible in great disdain and said...."and what would *you* know about winning?". Needless to say, that chilled the golf game down a wee bit. So what was Norm getting at? Simple. Those migrant workers were doing exactly what Mr. senior manager was doing, in their own way. Traveling to America they worked for six months to take back a year's worth of money in Mexico. Bottom line? They lived like Kings and had half the year off. As a matter of fact, they were getting ahead faster than Mr. Big. See what I mean? I hope so, but that particular executive didn't because he was too short-sighted, foolishly discriminating with the best of them. When all is said and done however, he and those enterprising Mexicans were exactly the same....but different. Sadly, this man's life was being limited by foolish discrimination, but he was unaware of it.

Tuesday February 26th, 2008, 7:00 A.M.

On my desk is an old charcoal sketch of my brother, done by a traveling artist back in the late fifties. Brian was about seven years old at the time and the look in his eyes haunts me, He's already lost his Way in Life, and it shows. Sadly, Brian died before he could find the Path again and now speaks to me from Heaven through that picture. "Don't give up on that book of yours brother John".... he says. "Help people find their Way...for me". I will little brother....for you.

Affirmations are a Popular Self-Help Sign

"Affirmations" is a sign of the Truth you'll find on any bookshelf these days by the hundreds. They're positive, inspirational, optimistic things you can fill your mind with to give you hope for a better life. Some folks believe they're magical wishes that will deliver good fortune if repeated daily.

To become rich and happy then, you say "I'm rich and happy" to yourself every day. But does saying you're happy make you happy? Can you motivate yourself by saying…"I'm motivated" out loud? Well, it's true your brain thinks it's a little bit happier when your mouth is smiling. Optimism is also a lot better in life than pessimism. But the kind of affirmations on the bookshelves today is only a sign pointing to True affirmation. *Real* affirmation isn't just hoping and wishing or choosing a mantra to repeat endlessly. It's seeing.

But They're Not the Real Thing

If you look in a dictionary, you'll find that affirmation is all about knowing something is true and saying so. Here's a simple example. Imagine you want to affirm your neighbor cut his lawn. How would you do that? You could look out the window. If the lawn next door is neat and tidy, you can affirm it by saying…."Bob cut the lawn". There you go, you affirmed Bob cut the lawn by seeing. Alright, so here's what real, true life-affirmation is all about. When you restore your Vision (by losing fears of judgment), you'll see your own brand of happy success ahead of you. You'll see precisely the way to go to have all those amazing, wonderful things the "wishing affirmations" mention.

Now you can affirm your own success in life. You can say…."I see peace of mind and purpose and all kinds of other happy things in my future life". What you mean is you *see* what to do with your life and that's where you're going. Say you love welding for example, and realize you want to do it forever. With Vision you might see your own big or little welding business ahead, that'll bring you great satisfaction. Or maybe you see yourself working for a company welding things that spark your imagination. Parts for a Mars expedition welded in exotic materials perhaps.

So every day you say out loud…"I'm rich and happy and glad to be alive". But you're not just wishing for it. You know where it is, and how to get it. You're affirming it by seeing it on the horizon of your life. That's Real affirmation. Real affirmation is affirming you know where to go to get authentic success. It is millions of times more heart-warming than ordinary affirmation as well. If you hear someone "affirming riches and happiness" out loud then, ask if they know why they're here. If they don't, they're just hoping and wishing. Their affirmations are just signs of the Truth….not the real thing.

Thursday February 28th, 2008, 5:00 A.M.

Another sad day. I have just learned my aunt has cancer. Her husband, my father, and my old friend John G. died of it. The world is losing wholeness faster and faster every year and cancer is one consequence.

Lost Again

Fear of being judged can keep you trapped in your shell so many ways it's hard to believe. Only after you get the courage to be yourself again will you see how this fear has kept you from trying and exploring and taking interest in the world around you. This was really brought home to me recently when seeing a friend's daughter in action at college. This fire-brand of a young lady by the name of Jasmine is so "connected" with life it's inspiring. As a University don, she flexes her leadership skills by helping youngsters in residence get the most out of post-secondary school life, without getting in trouble. As a student herself, she's built a fabulous social and academic network of friends, teachers and other students. In short, she's in the loop big time and it will serve her well. Now let's compare that to yours truly the non-starter back when. I loved reading but joined no book clubs.

I was fascinated by language but never became part of any debating team. Swim teams big and small I passed by too, although I loved the sport of swimming. Being interested in science, art, poetry, hiking, fishing, music and writing, you'd think I'd be found in one or two groups of birds of a feather. But you'd be wrong. I did not join a single one. I just stood silently on the sidelines looking in. In fact, you name it and I didn't pursue it, even though I had a passion for it. I was a person with a huge hidden passion for life, who simply let life pass him by. Decades later I know I wasn't the only one either. In fact, maybe I'm describing someone who sounds suspiciously like you. If so, here's some good news. When you get your calling back, all that passion for "your things" will come rushing back to you….but this time you won't let them pass you by. You'll be right up there with "Jazzy", as her equally jazzy mother calls her, living life to the fullest.

Chapter Twenty-Five
A Spring Journal
(How You'll Feel When Waking Up)

Saturday March 1st, 2008, 4:00 A.M.

March 1st is Dad's birthday. He would have been 90... if cancer hadn't shown up to claim him. Happy birthday up there Dad! Just so you know Dad....I still have many wonderful early trout fishing memories. You and I eating beans and bacon at Blend creek off the back of the old family station wagon for example. Remember that old Coleman stove that used to spit and fizzle and flame out before the beans were hot! You'd have to pump up the gas again, so all that bacon grease wouldn't freeze solid! And how about the exquisite little speckles at Strawberry creek! Dark mysterious creatures hiding under the old wooden bridge, with gorgeous little crimson spots surrounded by bright blue rings. Don't forget Bucket creek either. That special place marked by an ancient bucket upside down on an even older tree stump always fascinated me. The specks were so silvery grey there you thought they might be crossed with lake trout. "Splakes" I think you called them. Now that I'm reminiscing, how about the time we climbed the mountain to fish upper Pass Lake on a raft we built. We drifted around like Tom Sawyer and Huck Finn that day didn't we Dad! Do you recall that monster fish I caught that day too? We both thought it must be a world record trout until it surfaced. Ten pounds of sucker was a big disappointment then, but a fabulous memory now! Thanks a million for those good times Dad. Happy birthday again!

Tree of Life Exercise

Tree of Life exercises help me see how crazy it is to Judge one life less important than another.

So here's something to think about. Imagine you and I share one well, but something is surely wrong with me, because I don't realize there's only ONE source of water and it's ours. For reasons nobody can fathom, I think your water is separate from mine. Unfortunately, that makes me a very bad neighbor, because I don't hesitate to dump *my* cans of paint into *your* water. But surprise, surprise. It doesn't take long before we both get sick. That is exactly how dumb it is to think your life and mine can be separated. And the sickness we both get if I judge your life less worthy than mine is just as bad as well, because it takes happiness away from both of us.

The Fountain of Youth: A Mission Exercise

Back in Chapter-13, I suggested there really is a Fountain of Youth that comes with every man or woman's calling. Unfortunately, we've failed to take care of ourselves and the world for so long, few of us can hardly imagine what it's about. Even fewer can imagine that it's real. To help me aspire to a life of real youthfulness then, I'll stop and mull it over. It's easy to see how men and women could be "youthful of Mind" by taking up their Missions in life with passion and enthusiasm. Most of us have met people of all ages like this and watched them take on the world like wide-eyed kids.

But a real Fountain of Youth would presumably keep our bodies in shape and fill us with energy. Would it make you and I in our eighties look like we did in our twenties? It would make us as physically fit as we could be throughout our lives, as we took care to exercise and ate right. It would also keep hundreds of diseases from us because we'd stop throwing poisons into the environment and ingesting them daily. All this would make men and women in a New Age of Wholeness profoundly healthy all their lives.

But would the real Fountain of Youth make an octogenarian look like a freshly minted twenty-something like most people want it to? No it would not, but it would do something far better. It would take away the stigma of getting old. As young people began to profoundly see themselves in old men and women, age would reveal its own varieties of beauty. The simple-minded silly desire to stay stuck in early life would be replaced by a deeper more awe inspiring need to grow Human. And so, the real Fountain of Youth would make old and young alike equal in value and worth, and each of us would look forward to the various times of our lives. That is exactly what the Rule of Life would bring to the world. A real, bona fide and far more joyous Fountain of everlasting youth.

Working With Others

Here's something my old friend John G. taught me, about how other people can help us grow. In short, it taught me to learn from differences I see around me. Here's one of those differences that really surprised me when I first saw it. John came from Italy when he was a kid, so his entire family was culturally different from mine. One huge difference I couldn't help but notice was mealtimes. In our family, dinner was for eating. It was a practical matter of fueling up for the day, and anything else just got in the way. There was little talking, sharing, or communication because everyone was busy getting the job done.

Then one day I was lucky enough to be invited to John's place for supper. To say the least, I was stunned by the difference. John and his mom and sister spent so much time gabbing, laughing, or sharing little secrets of the day, they almost forgot to eat. Half the time you'd see a fork-full of food suspended in mid-air as someone got lost in conversation! Right away I began to wonder why John's family was so animated. I'd never thought that meals could actually be some kind of entertainment.

You could have taken away the meat and potatoes at John's home, and nobody would have noticed! I can't say that having supper at John's changed our family's way of doing things, but it did show me something was missing. It did make me seek out and find this kind of communion too. Many years would pass before I finally found it, but John taught me it was there to be found. That's the kind of thing I mean by "working with others". Other people can show us entire universes of new adventures to go after.

Vision Stirring Again

When Vision stirs, you'll begin to see things about yourself you didn't see before. Vision won't just let you see who you can be in your own future. You'll see who you were in your past as well, whether you want to or not. Here's an example of what newfound Vision revealed about myself. I was out one early weekend morning in April or May for long jog. Spring had really and truly sprung and I was pondering the amazing scene of rebirth around me, feeling reborn myself as my own Life Mission dawned. Suddenly somewhere along the road something hit me like a ton of bricks. I'd already begun to understand I'd left off growing very early on, but I hadn't really seen the full truth of it. There on that country road however, it dawned on me. Between the ages of ten and forty, I thought people were "who they are" right out of the box.... from birth.

To get an idea how ridiculous this really is, let's apply the idea to a few of God's other creatures. If I believed this about whales for instance, they'd be several tons at birth and a hundred feet long. If giant Redwoods followed this impossible rule, they'd spring up a hundred feet from seed overnight. Eagles would leap straight out of the egg to soar over mountains and ancient tortoises would look the same as their newborn children. In short, my brain did not get the very idea of growing.

I had no clue we all must transform ourselves again and again to become who we can become. That's why I never studied or trained or worked to learn new things. I didn't get the idea we all have potential, but must work hard to develop it. But how could I be surrounded by things growing every day of my life, and fail to understand? It wasn't because I was mentally handicapped. My brain might have been undersized at birth, but it wasn't missing completely. The reality was, I was just too afraid to be myself to go there. Unable to venture out of my shell, my Mind simply rejected the idea of growing up. Out on that road that day, I can tell you I could hardly believe what I was seeing. Thankfully though, I focused on my Mission ahead and didn't dwell on the past.

Young People Better Know Their Enemy

We've been looking at the world the wrong way for so long, entire countries preach against the Truth. As a matter of fact, all cultures have artificial classes that imply some souls are worth more than others. There are Lords and Ladies and Aristocrats and Royals for instance, in places too numerous to count. Castes of various kinds are common too and nobility is considered a birthright all over the world. The idea one man or woman can be of greater worth than another is virtually enshrined in law and order in every land. So how are young people going to get their dreams back? How will they ever be able to believe the soul within them is beyond judgment with millions of misguided people around the world are saying it isn't so. Giant crevasses between men and women are being cultured everywhere. Great divides are being maintained in every land that make wholeness a lie. How on earth can anyone pursue a dream of Happiness against this huge crowd trying to stop them. Here's how. When we see all this mistaken judgment for what it is, entire Nations will be disarmed. Our enemy may be bigger than thought possible, but we cannot give up on defeating him. Before Man dies, he must know who he is.

Tuesday March 4th, 2008, 6:00 A.M.

My little ceramic "believe in Magic" Wizard has been looking down at me from the bookshelf since '97 now. The further along in my Journey I get, the more I see everything in the world is a magical miracle.

Magnetic Attraction: A Sign of the Truth

I'll bet there are a hundred books out there right now about attracting everything we want into our lives. According to the authors, "Like attracts Like" and filling our heads with ideas of riches will attract riches to us. Apparently these ideas will vibrate into the Universe, attracting riches with the same vibrations. It certainly sounds attractive, but where does this idea come from, and does it work? It comes from authentically successful people, and it does work, but you have to understand this kind of success to see how and why. Here's how it goes. Truly successful people have filled their heads with ideas about their accomplishments from childhood. They've been focusing and concentrating and brainstorming about those goals 24-hours a day all their lives. And sure enough, their dreams have come true, much like a giant magnet attracted success to them. But there's something the attraction books aren't telling us. To turn that magnet on, we must know who we are.

It Works if You Know Who You Are

To really understand "magnetic attraction", we have to look more closely at truly successful people. What looks like riches being attracted by a magnet is really destiny. To see what I mean, let's imagine an authentically successful person. A lady who's dreamt of being a pop music star all her life perhaps, right from the cradle.

This woman will have been obsessed with singing from the time she began talking. She will have spent every waking moment thinking about everything to do with pop music. Her head would have been filled with ideas about success in the music industry. And, of course, she will have done everything possible to go there. Certainly her success will have been a long time coming. But this person didn't just pick a dream off the shelf and fill her head with it, hoping it would come true. She knew what to do with her life and was doing it. Bystanders might think it was just those ideas of success that attracted success….but they would have been wrong. You can put those same ideas in somebody else's mind and vibrate them out into the universe….but little or nothing will happen. Only the ideas spoken by your inner voice can act like a magnet, bringing your own unique brand of success to you. That's the key to understanding "magnetic attraction". It only works if you learn how to let your very own ideas of riches and success flow back into your life. But it really does work.

When you begin to manifest your own destiny once more, things necessary for your success will come out of nowhere at you, like you'd attracted them with a magnet. Things you need for your dream life will show up in ways that look like coincidences, or just plain luck. But in fact they're synchronicities you've "magnetically attracted" into your life by following your own real dreams. In case you're not familiar with the term "synchronicity" it's a coincidence so improbable it defies common sense. Here's a kind of example for you. Imagine you've rediscovered who you are and are doing everything to make your dreams come true. Part of your dream is finding your soul mate. O.K. so one day you miss the train to work, and have to catch the bus instead. The bus breaks down so you take a taxi but have to share it with a lady who gets out before you do. This woman drops her purse on the taxi floor by mistake, so you pick it up and deliver it to her that evening on your way to an art show.

As it turns out, the lady is going to the same art show, so you give her a ride. To make a long story shorter, she turns out to be your soul mate. What's the chance of that? Zero. It wasn't chance at all. It was synchronicity. You and she were destined to find each other since the beginning of the Cosmos and you found her by working to make your dreams come true. You and she were attracted together by the magnet of destiny. So what happens if you don't know who you are and can't manifest your destiny?

But it Doesn't if You Don't

If you can't release your own dreams into your life, you can vibrate any ideas into the void you want, but you won't be attracting anything useful. My own departed brother Brian is a good, but sad, example. Like far too many people, Brian had absolutely no idea what his own dreams were, but coveted money and prestige with the best of them. One day someone introduced Brian to a multi-level phone service marketing scheme that promised huge success (money). For a while Brian tried to pitch his product and sound inspired about a future filled with riches. But sadly, I knew it wasn't who he was. There was no doubt in my mind his heart wasn't in it.

By then I'd already learned you can't just pick dreams of fortune off the shelf and pretend they come from your soul. And, sure enough, it wasn't long before Brian gave up, because there was no passion behind it. It's true Brian could have force-fed himself those bogus dreams and made money off them. Lots of people actually do. But when all is said and done he would have regretted having "attracted" that kind of success into his life. From personal experience I can tell you that kind of success is hollow. Very, very hollow. If I were you then, I wouldn't forget the key to "magnetic attraction". Magnetic attraction without discovering who you are is only a dim sign of the truth.

The whole truth is this. If you learn to let your inner voice speak to you again, you really will become a magnet for authentic success.

Tree of Life Story

You know the old saying…"everybody can't be wrong"? Well, sadly, in today's world, pretty much everybody is wrong, about who they are, because they can't see the Tree of Life for what it is. Everybody being wrong about this Great Tree is also scary, because it makes millions of people look like something I saw one day. I wish I hadn't seen it, but I did. A word of caution. This isn't nice. One day I was heading to Michigan for a sales meeting and drove past an abattoir. Just in case you didn't know, an abattoir is a slaughter house, where they kill animals for food. Unfortunately for me maybe, it just so happened that a big herd of cattle was being driven between two fences set close together like a chute, into a building. Thirty or forty cows forced to walk single file….to their death. I couldn't see into the building from the freeway, but I could see what was happening to the cattle.

At one end of the line of animals a man with a stick was pushing them ahead and they were all moving quietly along. But right up at the door I could see cows trying to stop and back up. Some were even rearing up on their hind legs. All in vain of course, because cows from behind were pushing them ahead. Even from the freeway I could see the panic and fear in those cows at the head of the line. They'd been lead somewhere they didn't want to go, but had no idea until it was upon them. And here's the sad thing. When you get your own Vision back, you'll see that millions of human beings are just like those poor cows, heading to the end of their lives without ever knowing who they are. When that great life review at the end happens, they'll see something equally frightening too. They weren't supposed to go that way, and it made them miss the life they were put here to have.

Sounds scary? Good. Maybe it will make you learn to see the Tree of Life before it's too late.

A Spirituality Story

When you get your very own dreams back, something unexpected will happen to you. You'll become a spiritual person. Don't buy it? You think spirituality is some kind of irrational New Age voodoo, with no value to your life? So did I, until I woke up to see how wrong I was. Spirituality is all about loving life, and people of all stripes and persuasions practice it. I have a spirituality story for you too, that illustrates a small part of what being spiritual is about. To kick it off, we have to go all the way back to my England days in the early seventies. In those days I was living in cheap rooms along with several other guys. Did I say cheap? I meant five pounds (ten bucks) a week, complete with mice, roaches, and other small animals I didn't recognize. There was running water too… somewhere down the hall. Anyway, one of my roomies was a guy there by the name of Sean. Sean was forty something, worked in a pub, and rode a bike to work. If you haven't already figured it out, Sean wasn't rich. There was something really odd about Sean too. Believe me….everybody living there noticed it. We called him "Mr. Slow-Moe" because of it.

Mr. Slow Moe

Don't get me wrong here though, Sean wasn't called Slow-Moe because he moved slow. This man was a half decent runner. It wasn't because Sean was stupid either. He was an avid reader and had stacks of books in his room. So where did the "Sloe-Moe" moniker come from? Sean was absolutely un-flappable in a way you had to see to really appreciate. Here's what I mean.

Every once and a while one of the guys would go off half-cocked at Sean for leaving his socks in the hall or spilling sugar on the table, because Sean was a wee bit messy. So messy in fact, it riled the heck out of pretty much everyone. But any anger towards Sean hardly lasted more than a second or two, because he countered with carefully chosen words and calming ways. In fact, Sean could throw cold water on any fight between the other guys, just by whispering something soothing. This guy was like a human sedative for unruly macho men. That's where Sean got the "Slow-Moe" name from. He could slow hot-heads down like they'd been mired in molasses. The rest of us totally lost souls all thought that was really weird. One day, after a few (dozen) beers, I flat-out asked Sean about this molasses thing. "How….burp… come you never flysh off the handle Sean?" I slurred through the booze. And he told me. It took me a few more decades to fully understand it, but I sure as heck remember his words. "I'm thankful for the Gift of Life" he said. Then he added…."and good or bad, it's all Life….so I take 'er easy and enjoy it all". It sounded crazy to me at the time, but it stuck with me to this day. Now I know it's not crazy at all. It's spirituality. Sean was a spiritual man, thankful for everything he had, and finding Joy in it all….good or bad. Sean knew Life really was a Gift. Unfortunately, Sean didn't know how to show the rest of us how to receive this Gift of Spirit. He didn't realize that to have Spirituality flow into our lives, we have to become whole.

Thursday March 6th, 2008 9:00 A.M.

Looks like my mega-bucks Cross Pinnacle pen needs polishing. The one employees gave me when I left my last company. Even years later that big send-off is still heart-warming. I Hope some of my Rule-of-Life lessons are still sticking. I suspect not though, because the powers-that-be there preach exactly the opposite 24-hours a day. Just like everywhere else in the world.

Putting an I Into The World

I have to admit, "putting an I into the world" seems very strange at first, but after a while it starts to make sense. A different kind of sense that can stop you and I from foolishly discriminating. It's designed to remind us that every dumb thing we see other folks doing….we've done ourselves…in our own way. If you keep at this training to see yourself in others you'll find it's a sobering exercise. Speaking of sobering….here's a drunken example of me "putting an I into the world". One of my engineers got himself in a pickle jam recently. He was caught drinking and driving so fast they actually took him to jail. Later a Judge threw the book at him and he had to spend weekends in the clinker. As a matter of sad fact, he even had to spend Christmas behind bars.

As soon as I heard about it, my old selfish lost self kicked in and I said to myself …… "what a disaster and fool that guy is.". But it didn't take long before my authentic soul spoke up and reminded me of my own past follies. Sure enough, yours truly had narrowly escaped the same fate many years before. Driving home from a company party polluted, I'd crashed my car into a curb late at night. Somehow I summoned a taxi and made it home before the gendarmes nabbed me. There you go. I've been a foolish disaster myself. But here's the thing about this kind of exercise. The more you can identify with other people, the more you realize we all have the same soul. That makes you less and less afraid to be yourself….because you know nobody's better or worse than you are. In a very practical way it also lets you connect with other Human Beings to help you do in life whatever you really want to do. This exercise pays big dividends.

Vision Stirs in Funny Ways

Here's a Vision-stirring story that happened just as I was head-hunted out of Kingsville in the late '90's. Off to the big city of Toronto I went, and this time I got a little bit of insight into who I am out on the road while jogging. It went like this. In the last few weeks before taking up the new job, my knees started giving me trouble. At first they'd just ache like green apples after a long run, but soon the little devils began protesting a few miles out. Finally they hurt like hot potatoes as soon as I put my running shoes on. Alright, so you'd think I would have got the message and slacked off….right? Not at all. I just tried to alter my gait. I actually thought I could tell my body how to run, by putting my feet down this way or that to smooth things out. Fine, but have you ever tried taking your body off the auto-pilot it comes with and operating the thing in manual-mode? No? Well let me tell you, it doesn't work, because your body knows how to do its thing a lot better than you do. I proved this to myself too, by making my knees a heck of a lot worse. As a matter of fact, I kept at it until it became impossible to jog anymore and concluded my knees were letting me down. But the truth was, it was exactly the other way around. I just didn't get it yet. What I did get was a small flash of Vision. It went like this.

As soon as I decided my jogging days were over, a little voice from within spoke up. "There's nothing wrong with your knees" it said….."you're just pretending to be a better runner than they can stand". In short, unable to see I was a slow-poke jogger at heart, I'd been beating my knees up trying to run further and faster than my body could handle. I was letting my own knees down. The thing is, I didn't listen to my own inner voice right away. I actually gave up jogging for more than a year before giving up pretending to be something I'm not. Looking back now though, it's clear that a Vision of who I am stirred within me that day. A fuzzy insight into the real me.

Dharma is a Sign of the Truth

Somewhere back in ancient India, the law of "Dharma" was discovered. In modern words, Dharma means there's a Divine order behind the Universe, that helps all life align itself with what's Right. In essence, Dharma is the path of Righteousness each life on earth must follow. But what exactly is the path of Righteousness? There's only one such path, and it's exactly the same for all of us. It's that way of life that always "does Right by the Universe". By now you should realize there's only one way to follow that path as well. Treat the world like it was who you are and you'll be on it. When you finally see everything around you as part of yourself, you'll treat all things with kindness and care, because it's the only sane thing to do. Anything else would be destroying *yourself*.

This way of living "does Right by the Universe" because you *are* the Universe and the Right thing is to take care of yourself. Anyone understanding wholeness fully takes the path of Righteousness, and Dharma is a huge sign pointing us all that Way. The only reason few people benefit from the law of Dharma is Reason. Reason keeps us from treating the Universe "Right" because it's made us think were separate from all things great and small….keeping our life's purpose from us in the process. What a sad state of affairs. Indian gurus many generations ago knew which way we should be taking our lives, but we've been prevented from going there by our selfish worldview. Thankfully, the Law of Dharma is still in effect, and you can still have the Divine beauty of it in your life. The Rule of Life can get you back on the path of Righteousness.

Saturday March 8th, 2008, 7:00 A.M.

Only four weeks left before I pick up my new Harley-Davidson motorcycle!

The Truth in Action Again

Here's something nobody should forget about the Truth of the world. We need to actually get out there and put it in action to truly believe in it. Thankfully, there are all kinds of simple things we can do to "treat the world like it was us". One of the most obvious is taking care of our bodies. Who on earth doesn't understand we should treat our own bodies like they were who we are? The short answer is untold millions, including yours truly for some period of his life. Just look around and you'll see vast crowds who aren't taking care of themselves. If you stop and think about it though, this is a very bizarre thing, the strangeness of which can be highlighted by analogy. Imagine a man about to take a driving vacation to see the wonders of the world. His car is surely a very important part of his vacation plans, so why is he putting water in the gas tank? How come he's letting the oil get way too low for the engine to work? What the heck is he doing trying to drive on two flat tires? Doesn't this man realize he needs his car to take him where he wants to go? It doesn't make any sense.

I'm sure you can see where I'm going with this story, but what's going on in the real world right now is even crazier. Our selfish worldview has even made us separate "ourselves" from our physical bodies. Millions obviously believe they can treat their very own physical bodies any which way they want with impunity. Just like the guy in the car story. This is so crazy sounding it's hard to believe. But all you'll have to do is look around to see people everywhere treating their bodies like they weren't part of them.

Even so, you and I don't have to follow these short-sighted men and women to early graves. We can begin putting the Truth in action to start healing ourselves right now. All we have to do is treat our bodies like our souls want to be treated. With kindness, compassion, and care. If you don't believe it's worth it, ask a thousand men and women who've taken up eating right and exercising regularly. They'll tell you it makes a world of difference. As a matter of fact, I've been on both sides of this fence, so I can tell you what a difference it makes myself. A familiar difference actually. The difference between slothful Zombie and energetic, vibrant, man or woman on a Mission.

An Amazingly Courageous Leader

Talk about bravery and brimstone. I just read an amazing little book about a man so courageous it defies belief. To say the least, it makes anyone's struggle to find themselves a walk in the park. It's called "the Man With a Shattered World" by the Russian brain doctor A.R. Luria. Sadly, Dr. Luria's hospital was filled with brain-damaged soldiers coming in from World War II battlefields. Mr. Zazetsky was one of them. The book is all about his epic struggle to regain life after a bullet tears through his brain in 1942. Letter by letter, word by word, the story is painstakingly written by Zazetsky himself after his injury shatters his senses. Day after day, year after year, Mr. Zazetsky tries to make his world of jumbled impressions whole. Like trying to put together a billion-part jigsaw puzzle with millions of missing pieces. How much courage must it have taken for this man to stay the course? How many people would've given up on this impossible task within weeks….sinking into depression and death? This is the stuff real leaders are made of. Pure Human courage. Zazetsky would be pleased to know how much his struggle can inspire others. He inspired me to do Rule of Life exercises until I too could be reborn.

Tuesday March 11, 2008, 8:00 P.M.

The anniversary of my old friend John's death is coming up. Sadly, he died a day before his birthday. Can you hear me up there old buddy? I'm thinking about you. Remember that night in '67 when we walked miles home in the pouring rain? We'd missed the last bus after dropping our girlfriends off and waded up to our ankles in puddles....good shoes and all, laughing like hyenas all the way! Crazy kids eh? And how about that time I drove the family car into Lake Superior. You were sure my Dad had to be a Saint.....because he didn't shoot me right away! Disasters then, but fun memories now. I sure wish you were here so we could reminisce over those olden days together. Take care Botcha, and I'll see you later.

A Tough Foolish Discrimination Exercise

Foolish discrimination is calling people names for doing what we do, and it's not too hard to practice giving some of it up. If you think less of people for throwing garbage around for example, just remember how many times you tossed gum wrappers out the car window. When shouting at the kids for having messy rooms, think back to when you were their age. Chances are you were just as sloppy. These are what I call "easy" foolish discrimination exercises, and doing enough of them can really change your perspective. But there are also much tougher ones we'll all need to do eventually, if we really want to change the world for the better. Tough foolish discrimination exercises are where we stop foolishly discriminating against criminals. Here's what I mean. In today's world most people think criminals are bad and the rest of us aren't, so we separate them from us in prisons. Judging them "worthless human beings", we treat them with the same disdain that made them criminals in the first place.

But criminals are no different from you and I. The truth is, we all come with "seeds of bad" and "seeds of good". When the bad seeds aren't grown and cultured, they're just petty annoyances. Small greed is taking a little bit more than your share of pie for example, and un-grown dishonesty is telling a white lie to avoid hurting someone's feelings. On the other hand, big greed is CEO's taking the life savings from millions, and big lies is adultery or identity theft. All the bad seeds are tolerable things in their original form, and everyone will find all of them "in thyself". Luckily for most of us, we grow the good seeds and let the bad ones fall on barren ground. Criminals on the other hand, put all their efforts into growing the bad, to strike out at a world that denied them value and importance. Even so, everything criminals do, we do too, albeit in a dramatically different and far less onerous way. If the world cannot see this simple fact of life, we will continue foolishly discriminating against criminals. Unfortunately, this is very foolish indeed, because it will make criminals want to strike out at the world even more than they already are. Foolishly discriminating against criminals is a formula for growing crime.

Old Folks Homes

"Sure, I'm for helping the elderly. I'm going to be old myself someday". - Lillian Carter (1898 - 1983) US nurse

Here's something everybody sees, everybody knows, and everybody ignores. How "old folks" are treated in North America. If you're not sure what I mean I'll tell you. Imagine you're an 80-something lady with huge achievements stacked up behind you for decades. You've built a business, raised a family, and created a charity that's still helping thousands every day, amongst many other things. So there you are sitting on a park bench one day enjoying the sunshine when along comes a twenty-something man with absolutely no clue what to do with his life.

A young man with zero accomplishments and none on the horizon. Seeing you relaxing there, he speaks up in the child-like patronizing voice he reserves for kindergarten children. "Hi sweetie" he says, while patting you on the head...."are you lost?". "He must be looking in a mirror" you think to yourself. You don't *say* it, because you're far older and wiser than that. But you see clearly what the world thinks about "age". Here's precisely what you see. People are so blind to the Truth, they can't even see half of it. Half the Truth would be that old folks are just like us, and we should be able to identify with them. Even so, men and women everywhere can't see themselves in aging people, so they treat them like children or "has beens". But the full Truth is almost scary. Old people aren't just *like* us......they *are* us. We are looking at ourselves. We are looking in the mirror of the world and can't even recognize who is staring back at us. And here's the moral of the story. If you can't identify with older people, you are in big trouble because you're still way too selfish to get your dreams back. If you don't believe me, just wait a few decades. Old age will make a believer out of you, even if it's too late to discover who you are.

Thursday March 13th, 2008 5:00 A.M.

My old friend Norm's birthday is coming up soon now. It seems like a thousand years ago we seven year olds made salt green in his basement, by mashing it up with pine needles. Norm's mother suggested you could see green salt on potatoes a whole lot better, and we boy scientists were eager to oblige. Sure enough, Norman's Mom was stunned by that green sticky, salty stew! Norm and I boiled eggs in test tubes in those days as well, making them growl and rumble and pop like volcanoes. I'd better go get Norm one of those specialty birthday cards. One that celebrates making green salt in the dim light of an old cellar. I'm sure I can find one.

A Sinister Enemy

Perhaps the most terrifying thing about our selfish view of the world is how it makes us sick and then keeps us from seeing we're diseased. Completely oblivious to our declining health, we don't even seek out a cure. If you think this sort of illness sounds ridiculous, I have news for you. There are many kinds of sickness that do this very thing, some we're all familiar with. Alzheimer's disease is one of them. This terrible decline of consciousness often creeps up on people so stealthily they don't even realize what's happening. Frequently it advances to where men and women no longer can imagine that they're ill as well. Brain damage by car accident can also leave victims in a fog about their trouble. In short, there are many ways the brain can be damaged that takes away a person's awareness of the damage. One of them is our selfish worldview. It literally stops us from seeing how sadly diseased we really are. A couple of examples are in order here, but be warned. Chances are your view of the world will make you think these are absolutely normal and nothing to worry about. I can assure you they are nothing of the kind. They are graphic and stunning symptoms of a disease that is going completely unnoticed all over the world.

I will begin with money. If you look around just a little, you'll see something surprising about money. People everywhere will give up love, family, fun, charity and life itself to get rich. Not only that, they will do something they hate to get it. This reminds me of a story I once heard that I'll bastardize a bit to make my point. Imagine a job ad in the paper for ten people to cut down trees with a sledge hammer. The job pays two hundred bucks an hour so there are thousands of applicants. Ten lucky fellows make the cut and get sent out to get started. Needless to say, this is a frustrating job, because it's not possible to cut trees down with a hammer.

At $200 an hour though, all ten guys are prepared to sweat all day for nothing. In the story as originally told to me, one after another man eventually gave up the job because it was so mind-numbing and pointless. But in my version of the story, everyone sticks to the ridiculous work……because of the money. Why am I changing the end of the story? Because it is much like what is going on all over the world right now. People everywhere will do any kind of work that has nothing in it for them….for the money. Like I said, they will abandon family, give up even looking for the kind of job that would grow them *their* way, and forsake every kind of happiness I wrote about in big chapter thirteen. For money. Sounds O.K. to you? It probably does, but if you were awakened to who you are and can be, you'd think the world had gone mad. Because, in a very real way, it has. I have one more example for you that is maybe even worse than the first one.

Violence. We cherish it. We glamorize it. We make it fun to practice in video games glorifying death and dismemberment. Millions of otherwise sane people actually believe arming themselves to the teeth is a "God given right" as well. Many of these decent human beings think it makes sense to manufacture military grade weapons and sell them on the streets too. It's fair to say most of these people would not want to be the targets of the kind of violence they so love. Any man or woman even witnessing the horror an AK-47 can do to a human being would not want that happening to them. But it's not so bad if it just happens to others of course. If this sounds like something out of a horror film to you, maybe your brain hasn't been irreversibly damaged by our worldview yet. If not, it will take some work to let the Rule of Life heal you. All in all then, I have this to say. Our enemy has damaged us pretty badly already. So badly we accept these few examples as "just the way it is" and "fine by me".

I do believe there is still time to bring this disease under control, so the world can be healed by a belief in wholeness. That is why I am asking you to Cry For Help.

The Truth At Work

What do you think our selfish way of seeing the world does to our working lives? Apart from making most of us into zombies waiting for retirement that is. Today we take it for granted that business is all about killing off all the competition and dominating the world if possible. "Do unto them before they have a chance to do it to you" is the mantra of most businessmen and women. Exploitation and greed are the rule in commerce today. I know for sure, because I've been there and done that for a long time myself. I bought into it with the best of them for decades and was as ill as I could be. I've been trying hard to heal myself for some time now, but I'm not yet out of the woods. I have become whole enough to see something clearly however.

This. Business selfishness has really and truly gone so far out of whack it borders on insanity. No. I take that back. It crosses over the line into insanity. Why? Because it's lead to privately run health care companies who routinely let folks die to improve their profits. Believe it or not, men and women receive bonuses for denying other human beings life-giving medical treatment. They get promoted based on the amount of care they keep from people in need. Would the CEO's of these organizations let their own children die to keep profits up? Of course they wouldn't. So why would they do this to others? Our worldview lets them believe some people are worth so little, they don't even have the right to live.

It lets them decide the fates of Human Beings, just like Nazis in the death camps of WWII. In those terrifying places, concentration camp profits were measured in man-hours of labor. You were sent to your death there too, if you couldn't deliver to the bottom line. Then there's fraud, theft and greed. Recently we've all begun to see how deeply and broadly selfishness has infected the business world in other ways as well. Not only have fraudulently criminal CEOs been showing up all over the place, but people in power have risked the entire financial system with their greed. One after another gigantic financial institution is now collapsing from deals designed to make money by people who would break any law to get it. Do you think a man or woman is sick if they'd destroy the lives of millions to get more money for themselves? No? Do you think there is anything wrong with you and I then, if we think this is just "the way capitalism works"? No? That's why our enemy is so slickly sinister. Our view of the world lets us stare at the festering illness in the body of Man and shrug it off. This is what our selfish way of seeing things is doing to our working lives.

Superman is a Real Leader

Last week a very brave man encouraged me to fight on with my Mission….however hard it gets. I'm sure you know this famous guy by his real name. Superman. His stage name is Christopher Reeve. If you haven't heard about this amazing man, I'll tell you about him. Chris was just launching a huge career in show-biz when a horse-riding accident left him paralyzed from the neck down. Anyone but Superman would have been knocked into a huge depression and stayed there, but not Chris Reeve. Not at all. His books, "Nothing is Impossible" and "Still Me" radiate courage like a super-nova at the very least. When I screw up my eyes and imagine myself in Chris's place….I'm floored by his stunning inner strength. Before reading his books, I thought Superman was a comic-book character.

But he isn't. He's real people like Mr. Reeve. Now I know what Christopher's trying to tell you and I. Each of us has a superman within us, just like the philosopher Nietzsche said. A sea of strength to be used for whatever Life throws at us. To let this kind of courage flow into our lives though, we must see the Truth of the world. Chris Reeve saw this truth without a doubt and helped teach me to see it more clearly. Go read Chris's books and he'll help you see it.

Saturday, March 15th, 2008, 7:00 A.M.

The Hot Air Balloon Ride Company will be flying again next month. Maybe this year my wife and I will get our ride. It's been two years since we signed up and paid our money, but every time our turn came up….it was too windy, or cloudy, or whatever. Six times we've been cancelled so far. It started off as a birthday present for two April birthdays, but at this rate, both candles might burn out before we fly.

The Biggest Surprise

Getting Vision back will probably be the biggest surprise of your life. It was certainly the biggest surprise of my life, for one simple reason. I had no idea I'd lost anything….. much less the most important thing I could possibly lose. There's really no way to accurately describe what it feels like to finally see what you're here to do…..after years of being totally lost. But I can give you some idea by making up a little story. Imagine you buried a thousand big gold bricks in your backyard…..and then completely forgot you put them there. Ridiculous? Maybe, but bear with me. So there you are with millions of dollars dug into your own back yard…..and you don't even know it. Some strange disease has made you forget those riches.

To make matters worse, you've suffered for the last twenty years or so, not having enough to eat and barely keeping a roof over your head. Poor as a street cat all these years, you couldn't afford to go past your front steps to see anything of the world either. Then one day, your memory comes back. Suddenly you recall burying the gold. At first you can barely believe your own brain of course, because forgetting something like that should be impossible. Even so, you suspend your disbelief and start digging. Sure enough, three feet down you discover gold. At first you're stunned. But stunned doesn't describe your next emotions. When you realize those riches were sitting there every poverty stricken, starving day of your life, you're bowled over backwards. Same thing for me when Vision began to return. I was knocked for a loop when I realized what I'd lost for so long. Every single thing Human beings covet in the world was lost along with my Vision…..but I hadn't even realized it. Maybe there's a better way to describe what getting Vision back feels like, but you probably get the picture.

Tears of Joy

When Vision comes back, it can bring with it a big rush of positive emotions as well. Believe it or not, it can make you cry "tears of joy". Here's a personal example. As my own Vision returned, I saw I was here to try to help people past their fears of judgment by writing books and getting my message of hope out. To do that I had to first put this book together from the million little pieces it began with. I also had to learn how to write clearly enough to make the message ring like a bell in readers' ears. That turned out to be a lot tougher task than I expected. To make a very long story short, I had to give up trying to make my writing look like other authors first, and speak as simply as possible so the message wouldn't get lost. Finally, I had to organize, edit, and present my work in an authentic "voice" as they say.

All this took many years, but one day as it was beginning to come together, something took me by surprise. Editing my work one morning, I began to cry. To say the least, I was taken aback by the outpouring of feelings. Eventually, after this had happened a few more times I finally began to understand what was happening. My soul was trying to tell me I'd found the key to setting myself free. I'd been venturing out of my shell to become myself, and this amazing experience caused great tears of joy to flow. Big happy emotions flooded out, as I realized I wasn't lost any more. Don't be too surprised if it happens to you as well. If you've been cooped up inside your shell for years, you'll probably shed tears of joy when coming out.

Unconditional Love: The Truth Writ Large

"The greatest gift that you can give to others is the gift of unconditional love and acceptance".
- Brian Tracy US author, motivational speaker

Have you ever wondered what "unconditional love" is? I once had a conversation with a lady who believed unconditional love was ridiculous. "If I give someone love" she said, "I expect love back". She went on to add…"It makes no sense to love someone who abuses me either". At the time I thought maybe she was right too, because loving someone who hates us or even maybe wants to kill us just doesn't seem to make a lot of sense. So why do poets and philosophers speak of unconditional love as if it was the best thing since sliced bread? The short answer is because unconditional love *is* wholeness, and we need it in our lives to discover who we are. Here's how to understand this potent version of the Truth. Imagine a mother who continues to love her son, even after he has become a murderer. Is she loving his murderous ways? No she isn't. Is she condoning murder? Not at all. But how can she love someone who's turned evil?

Mothers know something the rest of us might not. A mother's heart knows there is no possible reason or "condition" to separate the world into pieces. Every mother understands this intuitively, because her children begin as part of her and she knows deep down they are forever. Mothers therefore know that failing to love their children would be failing to love themselves. Each woman who gives birth realizes that the most evil child must also be loving and good, as long as there is any good at all in the world, because he or she is only part of One whole Universe. Never can there be nothing to love in anyone as a result. But there is yet more to unconditional love that Mothers can teach all of us. Unconditional love is a prescription for rendering evil benign. When we treat the world as if it was part of us, good grows and evil shrinks. Evil reduced to where it should be is small pettiness and white lies. Small evil is rather like a tolerable speck of dirt on the tail of your beautiful white shirt. On the other hand, treating the world selfishly grows evil into the monsters of hatred, murder, terrorism and genocide. Motherhood makes this lesson about unconditional love available to all of us, and it's about time we learned it.

Another Vision Stirring Story

Somewhere back in the cement jungle of Toronto my knees tried to tell me I was letting them down, but I didn't listen. I completely ignored those feelings from my body, telling me who I was, until forced by injury to give up running completely. At the time I had no idea feelings of all kinds are alternate ways our inner voices speak to us, trying to help us go our own way. But now I know this. The Vision we need to guide us in our lives is composed of ideas and feelings of all kinds. Think of Vision as a tapestry woven of concepts, ideas, feelings, intuitions and hunches if you like, all adding up to a special insight into who you are. With that in mind, here's another story about Vision stirring as feelings from my body make themselves known to me.

This time I actually listened to what my body was saying. Here goes. At the time I was working in the Mississauga suburb of Toronto, and living in Bolton, some 25 miles distant. We were right on the Humber river with a gorgeous conservation area kissing our back door. In fact, right off our deck there was a jogging path out through the woods to the river and back again. Sure enough, I heard jogging sirens calling, and couldn't resist. I'd been off jogging for more than 12 months by then, so I had to start off slowly, keeping a wary eye out for knee problems. This time I slowed down at the merest hint of an ache and listened closely to what my body was saying. Hard to believe maybe, but I was keeping myself in the comfort zone. Then one day out amongst the dewy spider webs and glossy leaves I started thinking I should be gearing up hard and pushing myself. For decades I'd always tried to run twice as long and hard as my body would take after all. But something was very different this time.

This time what my legs were saying dawned on me, like a dim bulb coming on in a dark place. They were telling me I wasn't a professional athlete. Slow jogging is who I am. My legs and knees and tendons and bones had been trying to tell me that for a long time too. And here's the wonderful thing I learned that day. I can keep on jogging all my life, as long as I pay attention to my inner voice and stay within my limits. Maybe when I'm eighty, my inner voice-feelings will tell me I can only walk a block every hour. That will be perfectly alright too, because an authentic 80-year can't really be expected to do anything else. Vision is all about authenticity.

Wednesday, March 19th, 2008, 5:00 A.M.

Sad day today. Buddy John died on this day some years ago. Miss you botcha.

John Shows Me the Way

In honor of my old friend John G. today, I'll tell a foolish discrimination story. Back in my sallow, short-sighted youth, I'd hear men and women from other countries talking with an accent and laugh at them. Every time I heard someone speaking broken English, I'd say to myself "listen to that dumb loser". You've probably thought that yourself, because we're all trained to think that way. Then, back at the end of highschool, I met my old friend John, and English wasn't his first language. John spoke Italian until he was fourteen or so, in Italy, like he was supposed to. And soon I began to notice something. Maybe John didn't speak perfect English, but he was nowhere near dumb. In fact, John was a lot more capable than I was, which pretty much destroyed my idea people speaking second languages were stupid. Then John taught me some Italian and I received a second life lesson. Sure enough, I spoke bad Italian with the worst of them. But did I notice? Of course not. I actually thought I was pretty smart because I spoke a fractured, shallow, dull-witted smattering of a second language. So why were Italians looking at me as if I was a dumb loser? All I was doing was massacring their way of speaking and maligning their heritage?

At first I was perplexed. Surely they can see I'm a hero for knowing ten Italian words? Then it dawned on me. Those people I used to laugh at *are* heroes. It takes courage to emigrate to a different country and start all over again after all. It takes big smarts to take on this kind of challenge and come out ahead too. But why couldn't I see this obvious fact of life before? Getting way off track in life makes you blind as a bat to the simplest things you can imagine. Now I realize John taught me something about being a real Human Being long before I really became one. He taught me to see myself in other people. Thanks again old friend, for another gift you gave me.

Tree of Life Exercise

Why do we think Einsteins, Popes, Billionaires, and Presidents are more important than we are? It's because their theories are smarter than ours and their faith is bigger. Their riches are greater, and their power reaches further. Anyone can see that just by looking...can't they? Absolutely. But let's not forget something here. If all these other people are different parts of us, it's your life and mine we're talking about. If you think all these people are important then, you and I *must be* equally important. Not only that, but you and I can esteem and enjoy the accomplishments of these human beings like they were gifts sent from afar meant for all of us. That's how Einstein can be smarter than you and I…..but our lives are all worth the same. It's how Mother Teresa can be more saintly than us, while having a life equal to ours. When all is said and done then, the One life we share makes sure of it. So don't forget. When you hear men and women trying to pretend they're more important than us, there's something important you should know. They're absolutely lost.

In the Spring of My Life I See….a Tiny Spirit

Here's something that happened to me somewhere in the Spring of my metamorphosis. It was back in 1998 if I remember correctly. I was stepping into the shower one morning when I looked down and saw one humongous spider the size of two horses! My badly trained brain immediately tried to get me to flush it down the drain. I was about to do exactly that when my inner voice whispered. "Hold off" it said, "don't forget what wholeness means". At that I stopped and stared at the little creature for a moment and pondered. I stood there watching for about five minutes. Finally it dawned on me. He and I share the same life. If I ended his, I'd take a small part of my own away.

By that I mean the amazement of seeing such a remarkable little animal would have been removed from my experience of the world. Then suddenly something else occurred to me. I realized why Zen Masters or other Spiritual people don't hurt flies. It isn't just because they think life is sacred…...although it is. It's because it's *their* life….and they don't want to diminish it. Mindlessly taking lives around us would eventually lead to the most dull and drab existence imaginable, with nary a sight of bird or bee and none of the cricket-sounds of insects everywhere. Silent springs would turn into silence forever. When my mind finally settled down from this amazing revelation, I helped that little spider onto some Kleenex and let him go outside. I can tell you this as well. It made me feel absolutely super, as I watched him amble away.

A Sign of the Truth Called "Now"

For many years I heard people talking about "living in the moment" or being able to find the "power of now", but couldn't figure out how to do it. On the surface it's obvious what these men and women mean of course. They're thankful for what they have now, because it could soon be gone, and they're taking time to smell the roses. Finding joy in every moment of everyday life is the *power of now*. That much is clear, and pretty much everyone understands what living in the moment is about. So why is it that only a few lucky people seem to be able to do it? After I'd resumed my calling I began to understand why. I'll put it to you this way.

When you resume growing yourself *your way* every thing you do becomes part of your Mission, because your Mission is to grow every aspect of your being. Your Life Mission is growing all the potentials of Mind, Body, and Spirit you came with. When taking up your Mission again therefore, you'll be on a Journey that counts….*every single moment of your life.*

If you stop and think about it for a moment, you'll discover that's what "now" is. "Now" is every single moment of your life. As a matter of fact, "Now" is *your whole life,* and the power of "Now" is all those Joys of Being Human we've labeled "happiness". The power of "Now" is had by becoming whole. Unfortunately for too many people, the "power of now" is only a small, shadowy sign of the full Truth, because they can't release those Joys into their lives. Those joyful, happy ways of being are stopped cold by fears of being judged.

The Power of Now

Here's a few ways I personally experience the "power of now". Several times a day I stop and ask myself if what I'm doing is growing my Mind, Body or Spirit. If out jogging for instance, every moment I'm nourishing my physical being with the kind of exercise it's designed to handle. I feel the physical Joy from moment to moment, but also know the exertion is keeping my body fit for writing books and speaking messages of hope. When - problem-solving in my day job, I know the mental gymnastics are helping my Mind stay clear and supple for future things, and revel in this particular Joy of Being Human. As I go about my daily business then, I can see clearly that each and every moment is contributing to my growth as a Human Being, and I derive great Joy from it. I feel this power of "Now" as it flows through my whole life.

A Tortoise Story

Slowly but surely as I worked the Rule of Life, my fears of being judged evaporated and I began growing again. Like many things that change slowly though, it was hard to see progress day by day. Then one day out jogging I knew with certainty I was getting somewhere.

I was plodding along at my normal slow speed on a Saturday morning when long line of bicycle racers overtook me on space-age bikes and outfitted in Tour-de-France gear. They must have been cooling down or something, because they weren't going particularly fast. At any rate, as they went by I heard one say to another "that guy's not a real runner", obviously commenting on yours truly. Here's where we see how far I've come with "self-worth". In years gone by I would have shrunk into a sobbing puddle on the side of the road, having been judged and found wanting. But in this case my very first thought was…"they have no idea what they're looking at". I thought that, because I knew for sure I was as real as real can be. I was just being my real, authentic slowpoke kind of jogger. I knew I wasn't pretending to be something I'm not anymore, and it brought me great joy. It was clear to me as well that those racers still had lessons to learn about how the world works.

Friday March 21st, 2008, 7:00 A.M.

I wonder whether the old lawn tractor will fire right up again this year after being frozen solid all winter in the shed. I think it's the seventh straight year frozen solid all winter too. I'll soon find out.

She Served Up Leadership

Real, true leaders come in every conceivable size, shape, color and job, because leaders are just people being themselves. They aren't necessarily running companies, winning medals, or preaching from high-priced pedestals. Here's a story about an unlikely leader. A cook in the cafeteria in that same company I met Dr. Steve at many pages back. At the time I would not have called her a leader at all of course, because I had no idea how the world works. Even so, this woman stood out so brightly, she attracted everybody's attention and has stuck in my head ever since.

Here's what you'd see if you and I went to lunch together back then. This lady was unquestionably happy with who she was and it showed. She radiated sunshine all the time, like some sort of heat lamp or shining star. It was impossible to get past this woman without feeling better about your day. She obviously loved her job and herself, and pretty much everyone everywhere for that matter. This lady jested and parried and played with her customers. She'd smile and laugh and reach out to you like a long lost friend. How she did it I do not know, but she remembered the preferences of hundreds of people. One day she reminded me I liked shepherd's pie for instance, although it hadn't been on the menu for weeks. To say the least, that surprised me. When someone speaks directly to you as an individual like that it is very impressive. What was even more impressive was her sincerity. When this woman gave you a compliment about your tie or inquired into your weekend, it had a ring of sincerity to it that could not be denied. This was not any kind of institutional "greeter" like you see in big department stores, mandated by job description to "be happy". She *was happy,* and only a brain dead person would fail to see it. That's the key right there. This lady had learned the art of being herself and that is the Art of leadership.

Saturday March 22nd, 2008, 4:10 A.M.

Today I tripped over a half dozen fly-rods and reels I haven't used for so long, it's hard to believe. Oddly enough though, I still consider myself a fisherman. I guess when you start your trout-fishing career at the age of five, it's in the blood for life.

A Story About Courage

"All our dreams can come true, if we have the courage to pursue them". - Walt Disney

It's fair to say the "authentic me" is, well, slightly "weird". Bizarre jokes lurk within and peculiar impossible thoughts hide beneath my surface. I'm one of those people everyone says "how did you ever come up with that?" to. Having no clue myself I've resorted to saying I subscribe to "Strange Ideas Magazine". Most folks seem satisfied with that. But here's the thing about being authentic. When fears of being judged abound in your life, whatever kind of authentic soul you are won't come out much. In my case, those fears inhibited me grossly for many years, but not absolutely completely. Some "weird" stuff has always leaked out, despite the fear of being myself. As I retrained my brain with the Rule of Life however, the inhibiting force of fear began to let more of my authentic self out, sometimes in places where it was not particularly appreciated. Even so, as time went by I had more and more courage to be myself, critics around me be damned. Here's a story about me being me no matter what.

At the time I was working in a billion dollar company owned by a single man. He was quite an imposing character too. The Godfather of Godfathers you might say. In fact, he was the kind of fellow who would drop half a horse in your bed overnight if you didn't toe the line. To set the stage for this story I have to tell you his sense of humor was a bit lacking too. He was about as humorous as a guy on death row I'd say. So there I am one day in the plant when Mr. Mega-bucks shows up. I'm standing beside a machine we'd kind of jury-rigged backwards to do something differently, for good reason, when mister money says …. "fix that….NOW!"…(or die?). Most sane folks would have tried to explain why the darn thing was running upside down and backwards. Truth be told, it was more efficient that way. But not yours truly. From somewhere down where my authentic soul lives came a joke. In the past, fears of being myself would have stopped this bomb dead in its tracks. But by then I'd already opened the tap to let myself out.

And so, without a second's hesitation I said…."Don't have to…..works good broken". The damn thing was out before I could even think in fact. And there we stood. Me and the boss of bosses staring at each other. Him wide eyed like he'd seen an impossible sight. Me wide eyed waiting for the execution. And then….wonder of wonders….he broke out laughing. Then me. For a full minute we laughed our guts out together there on the factory floor. Finally he asked me to explain and I did. Then he put his big boss face back on and said…."keep up the good work". After he left I was dazed over what had happened. I do not believe anyone had ever seen this guy even smile before. It was a stunning lesson in what can happen when you have the courage to be yourself.

Programming Yourself: A Dangerous Guru Truth

Here's a Guru Truth you've probably heard about, but had better be careful with. Some people call it "modeling" or "programming yourself to be successful". It's a simple idea and it really does work. What you do is this. Find yourself a really successful person and copy them as closely as you can. Act like they act, do what they do and chances are you'll be successful just like them. You can teach yourself to be a businessman, real estate mogul, or carpenter this way. Many men and women have done precisely this, and there are lots of good teachers of the art of "programming" out there.

But of course, there's a small problem with this method of becoming successful. I'm sure you've already guessed what it is, but just in case you haven't, I'll refresh your memory. You can program yourself to become pretty much anything you want….but your heart had better want it. If it's not who you really are, it'll leave you empty at the end of your life. Just to flesh it out with a concrete example, imagine you have no clue what to do with your life.

But one day watching T.V. you see a real estate guru who says she can program anyone to make millions selling houses. Three weeks and three thousand dollars later her course of instruction arrives and you set off with determination to make your millions. You can't say you have any real passion for it, but you stick it out for five years and….lo and behold…you've made your first million. The trouble is, something is surely still missing from your life. It sure isn't money, but its absence is felt nonetheless. So what's missing? You. You've simply programmed yourself to be something you're not, and it hurts. If you don't figure out what's gone wrong with your life, you might have some advice for others at the end of it. This advice. Don't program yourself to be someone else.

My Enemy is Like a Trojan Horse

Remember the old Trojan Horse story? Way back in ancient times, an army figured out how to defeat an enemy hiding in a walled city. First the army built a huge wooden horse, and later they hid soldiers inside and pushed it to the city gates and left it there. Finally the rest of the army made a big noisy retreat to make it look like they'd gone. Sure enough, curious people in the walled city eventually ventured out to inspect the strange wooden sculpture. Fooled by the innocent looking Trojan Horse, they brought it right into the heart of the city. That was obviously a big mistake, because enemy soldiers soon destroyed the city and everyone in it from the inside out. Unfortunately, the same kind of big mistake is going on right now in the world. We've brought an even bigger enemy inside our lives called "Reason". In case you've forgotten, "Reason" is our selfish way of seeing things that makes us think we're separate from the world and each other. If anything, it's worse than any Trojan Horse, because we don't even suspect it's making us destroy the air we need to breathe and all the drinking water there is.

We don't have a clue Reason is making people and nations destroy each other. As a matter of fact, we believe Reason is what will save us, by inventing technology or other things to stave off disaster. But it won't. It's a fatal way of seeing the world we're dragging deeper and deeper into our lives. It's just about the worst kind of enemy imaginable, because it's infected our hearts.

Another Reason to Work the Rule of Life

In my old, aimless, pointless life, I heard gurus talking enthusiastically about challenges on T.V., in books and sometimes even in person. These people seemed to actually enjoy hitting brick walls or tripping over stumbling blocks in life. When the going got tough, these enlightened folks really did get going. There was something about their enthusiasm that intrigued me too, because I couldn't honestly say I had it myself. Certainly I'd managed to climb over a few obstacles and accomplish some tough things. But something was missing somewhere. I just couldn't identify with those gurus until I began growing *my way* once more. Then the simple truth of it dawned on me. Everyone on a real Life-Mission encounters difficult obstacles along the way, just like any lost soul does, but every time they get past a rough patch, they get a bit closer to their dreams. All the pain and suffering has a purpose for people with a calling.

That's why fully alive, growing human beings call all the painful, hard, and sometimes frustrating work an adventurous challenge. They're getting closer to their heart's desires with every difficult step, and even the bad stretches are fulfilling because of it. It's a bit like jogging home in the rain, knowing a nice hot shower and dinner is waiting. The discomfort is superficial and more than bearable. On the other hand, folks who don't have a clue what to do with their lives are very different indeed.

Unfortunately I can attest to this sad fact of life personally, because it applied to me for so long. We who are lost also run into hard, painful slopes in life, but getting past them has no purpose. It doesn't push us closer to our life's final goal. It's a bit like a man lost in the wilderness who tries to jog around the trees to keep his spirits up. All he does is get cold and return to some pitiful lean-to in the woods that might eventually function as his grave. This simple fact is precisely why people with real dreams see challenges as challenges, and not disasters. Challenge means "pain with a purpose" to those of us lucky enough to be following our Bliss. If the word "challenge" means "nothing but pain" to you then, chances are you're completely lost and without an aim in life. But here's something for you to think about. The Rule of Life can change your perspective so dramatically about everything, you'll begin to take on challenges with gusto. You'll become one of those souls who shout to the world……"bring it on baby!". How can I possibly say that? It happened to me. If you'd like a real-life example, read what's below.

How I Learned What Challenge Means

I learned all about "pain with a purpose" first-hand by writing this very book. If you think what you're reading right now came easy….think again. Between start and finish was discouragement, depression, and endless hours….make that years….of hard work. Learning the ancient craft of writing brought confusion, delusion, naiveté and disappointment in equal measure for a long time. Not to mention being endlessly trounced by literary agents, book publishers, and all other inhabitants of the book writing world. Including friends, parents and acquaintances whose advice was… "give it up and do something realistic with your time". But these words you're reading now were part and parcel of a very real dream of hope I had, that simply could not be denied.

I was driven by something beyond me to continue through what sometimes looked like forever. Setbacks, re-writes, and starting all over again came and went with shocking regularity, but somehow satisfaction was there too. Somewhere along the line I really and truly understood a stunning facet of true Mission challenges as well. Some years into it, I realized I couldn't know for sure if I'd ever make my dream real. One day it dawned on me that maybe the reward of seeing my message spreading in print was two thirds up my mountain…..at a spot I'd never get to. I could get run over by a truck before making my dreams come true. I might fail to convince the powers that be in publishing to Cry Out For Help with me. At first I was a bit dismayed by these scary questions, but, thankfully, real Life Missions have answers. By then I'd already felt the fulfillment following a calling brings. I'd experienced the joy of growing by struggling and stretching and pushing past my boundaries. I knew for sure I was on one of those "Journeys that count". No matter if I never got where I wanted to go then, because I was becoming myself all along the way. All those tough challenges are needed to make me blossom into a unique Human Being. Once I really and truly "got it", I was at peace with the painful difficulties of my Voyage. You will be too, as long as you embark upon *your* Journey to make *your* dreams real.

Religions are Signs of the Truth

All the world's Religions are signs of Truth in the world. At the core of each is a joyous wholeness that can allow Mankind merge with the Divine if we would all act in accordance with it. But there's something very sad about every single one of these ancient spiritual traditions. It's this. Our faulted way of seeing the world makes it all but impossible for people to comprehend what religions preach. If you don't think so, just stop and think about it for a minute.

Every Religion known to Man speaks loudly about unconditional love, respecting life, and treating our fellow men and women with equal respect. Strip away superficial differences between religions and you'll see they all have the same message. Now take a look at the world. Do you think we're getting that message? Not sure? Let me tell you then. Not even close, and the reason is Reason. Our selfish worldview makes all the important spiritual features of religions look like nonsense. Still don't believe it? Look around you. Does it look like the world is filled with love, hope, respect and caring? How come the clergy has as many sinners in it as the rest of the population? Why is it that you and I will probably lie, cheat or steal if we think nobody will catch us? Don't get me wrong here though. I'm not saying there aren't fabulously caring, giving, loving Human Beings all over the planet. I'm saying that Religions have been preaching a Truth that could fundamentally change the world in miraculous ways…..if even a small majority of folks could believe it. But there's no way more than a tiny minority will ever see the tiniest glimpse of this Truth as long as we're mired in our fundamentally selfish worldview. Even worse, religious organizations themselves are corrupted by it. That's why Religions are, at best, a sign of the Truth….but not full Truth.

Tuesday March 25th, 2008…6:00 A.M….Happy 56th Birthday Norm!

Today is my oldest friend's 59th birthday. Norm and I go back fifty five years now, having met when my parents moved our house by truck, right up close to close to his. That makes for a whole lot of very early memories. Hunting clams on the Kakabeka River for example, twenty miles from home by bike. Twenty miles more than Norm told his mom we were going! I can still remember staring in wonder at those baby clams hatching out in a bottle when we got home.

James Clerk Maxwell's Guru-Truth

Back in the early part of the twentieth century, the physicist James Maxwell discovered another place wholeness is disguised as nonsense. He stumbled into it when trying to break the law. Pardon? Uh….no….James wasn't a criminal, he was trying to break the Law of aging. Scientists call it the second law of thermodynamics, and it's an iron-clad Law of Nature no one's ever broken. The 2nd law says any thing you leave alone will cool off, run down, or get disorganized with time and stay there forever, as long as you leave it alone. Take a glass of hot water for example. Put it on the table and it cools down and stays cold. You can heat it up with a blowtorch if you want, but that isn't leaving it alone. Don't forget you have to leave it alone. If you do, the Law of Aging says that glass will never heat back up again on its own…..even though nothing is stopping it from doing exactly that. Yes, you heard right. Nothing is stopping it from warming back up all on its own. It works like this. Even in that old cold glass of water, there are fast moving "hotter" molecules and slow "colder" ones, but all mixed up so the average is as cool as a cucumber. They're all wandering around like chickens with their heads cut off too. O.K., so once and a while you'd think all the hotter ones would wander over to one side, leaving all the colder ones on the other side, making a hot spot and a cold spot. Say once in a few hundred gazillion years. Yes? Nope. Never happens. The Law of Aging won't let it. Why is that? No one knows.

Maxwell Wants to Know

James Maxwell wanted to answer that question, so he conjured up an experiment designed to break the law of Aging. Here's how it went. Maxwell imagined a wall down the middle of an old cooled-off glass of water, with a little door in it.

Then he pretended a tiny demon was in there who could open and shut the door. James' idea went like this. Imagine ten slow and ten fast molecules wandering around in the glass with the little door wide open. When the demon sees a fast one go from right to left then, he stops it from going back by slamming the door in its face. Same in reverse with the slow ones. Eventually then, by keeping track of their movements, James' demon will get all the hot molecules on one side and cold ones on the other, breaking the Law of Aging. Right? Not exactly. Once Maxwell pondered his imaginary experiment a bit, he had an "ooooops" moment. He realized he wasn't leaving the molecules alone like he was supposed to. Here's why. At the very least, Maxwell's demon has to see molecules coming, to know when to open or close the door. But he can't do that without interfering with them, breaking the "leave 'em alone" rule. Even if he just shines a tiny light on molecules to see who's coming they'll get pushed around by light pellets for example. So Maxwell didn't break the Law after all. He did get within shooting distance however. All James' demon had to do was know the habits of those molecules without interfering with them. James believed that was impossible so he gave up. But it isn't.

But He Doesn't

To carry on where Maxwell left off, imagine Maxwell's demon staring off into the inky darkness of his glass. To break the Law, he has to know whether molecules are coming without influencing them any way at all. But according to philosophers, we can't know anything about the world without reaching out to touch or influence it some way, shape, or form. That's what our senses do after all. Fingers touch, eardrums vibrate when touched by airwaves, and our sense of taste needs chemicals to trickle over and tickle our taste buds. So how can Maxwell's demon possibly know anything about his molecules without actually touching them?

To break the Law of Aging, he'd have to "know the molecules without knowing them", like a Zen Master. That's the key right there. As it turns out, scientists have always known what they need to know to break the law of aging. For thousands of years, philosophers and scientists have realized that each of us has a private soul within us that's kept absolutely apart from the world, so there's always a "knower" to know the world. So separated from the world is this soul of ours in fact, people have always wondered how it's possible to know anything. Your soul and mine is like an absolutely isolated island in an ocean for instance, and the world is another island we can't get to. But the puzzling thing is....our souls have always known absolutely what's going on over there on that other isolated island...without ever going there or having any way of communicating with it. Curious men and women have always wondered how on earth that is possible.

As it turns out, the solution to this ancient puzzle shows Maxwell's demon how to break the Law of Aging. Here's the solution. Your soul and mine knows that isolated island world because it's simply a different part of us. We and it are different parts of each other. We *are* the world. Had Maxwell's demon understood this, he could have broken the 2nd Law, by changing our most sacred beliefs about how the world works. Breaking the second law means changing our worldview. What happens if we break the second law of thermodynamics? Changing our way of seeing the world makes it possible for men and women everywhere to discover who they are and what to do with their lives. It stops people from treating the world and each other badly as well. Breaking the 2nd law would usher in a New Age of peace and happiness for Mankind as we began to grow Human again. I don't know about you, but I believe this is one law we should be breaking.

Thursday March 27th, 2008, 8:00 A.M.

Maxwell's Goose Bumps

Here's a little story I made up that should make you get goose bumps like James Maxwell did when wrestling with The Second Law. Imagine you came across a building on the shores of an ocean one day that's three hundred stories high, one room thick, and a mile wide. It looks like a gigantic sail sitting there in the wind. Unfortunately, this building is located in the middle of hurricane territory and dozens of two hundred mile an hour typhoons hit this piece of the coast every year. To say the least, that building sure must be well anchored down, or it would have blown away long ago. In fact, it's foundations must be something to behold, so let's dig down and get a look at them. After a month of digging, we haven't found any foundation at all. It looks like the building is just sitting there on top of the ground with absolutely nothing anchoring it. But this doesn't make any sense. Hundreds of hurricanes have hit the building over the years, but it hasn't even swayed in the wind. Nothing is keeping it from falling over when pushed by gigantic forces and it looks like one huge hand clapping.

What bizarre thing is this anyway? It is a very big and ancient sign of wholeness in the world, just like the Law of Aging is. The Law of Aging has withstood hurricane winds of inquiry now for a very long time as well, and nobody has found a foundation for it either. There's only one reason we haven't realized what this sign is trying to tell us too. Our mistaken way of seeing the world won't let us comprehend it. That's why Maxwell and many other scientists get goose bumps over The Law of Aging. Deep down their souls tell them this enigmatic puzzle has been trying to tell us something important that we just aren't getting. It's trying to tell us Mankind is heading the wrong Way, to a place where there is no happiness at all. If this doesn't make the hair on your back go up, I'm not sure what would.

Chapter Twenty-Six
A Summer Rule of Life Journal
(Discovering Yourself is Like This)

For souls that get lost like yours truly, Winter's a long cold scary season, because it looks like it will never end. But eventually the Rule of Life works its magic, and Spring arrives. Spring is when the Truth dawns like a morning sunrise, and...suddenly the very idea one person's life can be worth less than another's is nonsense. That brings with it a staggering idea. Summer's around the corner. Summer happens when we see who we are again, and what to do with our lives. Summer is the most astonishing New Age of your Life imaginable.

Friday, March 28th, 2008, 4:30 A.M.

Aunt Viola's 100th birthday's coming up soon. It's amazing to think she was my age when I was born. She's still going strong too. Should I send her new rollerblades this year or skydiving lessons?

Other Souls On the Tree of Life

Today the Tree of Life scared me. After many Rule of Life exercises, I'm truly starting to see that the world around me is who I am. It's not just an idea anymore, it's becoming clear and real, and sometimes scary. Here's how. On the way to work today I saw a farmer beating pigs with a stick, herding them into a big truck. These creatures were being sent on a freezing cold journey to the slaughter house, where they'd be terrified before being killed. Having started to become whole again to identify closely with the world around me it was suddenly me in that cold dark truck, filled with fear and pain and suffering and scared for my life. I didn't just momentarily identify with these poor animals either....I *was* them for a brief moment, and it was awful.

I cannot tell you how bad it was. It made me sick with grief and sadder than words can express to know no one gave a tinker's damn about these creatures. Six miles down the road I settled down, but I couldn't forget what I'd seen and felt. Then the true horror of it dawned on me as I looked around with Vision. Here's what I saw. Millions of blind men and women can't see what they're doing to creatures everywhere. They think they can torture them at will, because they're dumb animals or completely separate soulless creatures. But I have bad news for them and all of us. That pain and torture and suffering is going to come back around to haunt us. It has to, because we're doing it to ourselves. It's already started. The terror we're inflicting upon the world is beginning to spread out into our homes and hearts as we speak. And it will not go away until we change our beliefs about the world.

A Spirituality Trick

"Meditation is the dissolution of thoughts in Eternal awareness or Pure consciousness without objectification, knowing without thinking, merging finitude in infinity". - Sivananda (1887 - 1963) Indian physician, sage

Growing Human is spiritual, because giving up selfishness lets us become one with all things. It lets us "transcend" our individual, separate selves, to join the Spirit of Man. Seeing your own past, present and future as one seamless life can help you do exactly that too. Some people call this art of becoming one with things "transcendental meditation". Here's a simple way I practice it out jogging. You can think of it as an extra Rule of Life exercise or another tool to help you become yourself. My way goes like this.

When I'm way out running on a country road in the beautiful summer heat, I first hark back to when I was a kid, remembering the smell of hot tar on old roads and long-gone summer leaves. Focusing on those old memories, I imagine I'm actually back in my youth again, running along the road to Silver Islet. Eventually it really feels like I'm back there again. Then I go back and forth between now and then, until I'm not sure whether I'm here or there. Losing myself in the now of things, I feel like no particular person in no particular place. Relaxing and going with it, I begin to soar in that peaceful place where the Spirit of Man is. It might not work for you, but you won't know until you try. So go ahead…give it a shot…..but watch out for cars. Don't set your Spirit free by getting run over.

My Ancient Manuscript of Life

When I was a boy, I was mesmerized by the look of the little childish laboratory Ken and I assembled in my parents' basement. But why on earth would I just sit and stare at glassware like it caught my eye with a three-pronged hook? Was it because I was just a spaced-out kid with nothing better to do? Did those hobby-store chemicals melt my brain down? Not at all. I was simply bowled over by that magical mysterious feeling called "wonder", that brings awe and majesty into our lives. Back in those days I wondered what Ken and I could do with our odd twisted glass flasks and little brown bottles of strange powders. I'd wonder what kind of amazing little creatures we'd find tomorrow in the big jars of swamp water lined up on our lab tables as well. Maybe the nature of the world would be revealed to us by Friday. Perhaps we'd make some big discovery after breaking six more test tubes or filling the basement with chlorine gas one more time! Who knew what strange goop might be made to corrode the floor, or what new bomb might be exploded! But, sadly, decades would go by before I knew why that experience was so important.

It's because wonder is in the world to get all of us exploring... to answer the "who am I?" question. Sitting on those basement steps many years ago then, I was staring my potentials, but was too blinded by fears of judgment to see who I could become. Now with Vision restored, I realize my heart-of-hearts saved that memory for me to help me find my way....if ever I had the eyes to see again.

Criminal Factories?

It's fair to say our world today is very much like a criminal factory. It's obvious if you think about it, and lots of people have, coming to the same conclusion. Unfortunately though, the real solution to this ridiculous problem has eluded us. Once we've visited the factory together, I'll ask you to figure out the solution for yourself. Let's start off with a worldview that makes all of us believe everything in the Universe is absolutely separate. That will allow many people to treat their own children badly, making them feel absolutely worthless. If you ask those parents why they behave like that, their worldview gives them a good answer. "It's no skin off *my* nose" they say, describing the way we see things accurately. Unfortunately of course, children made to feel worthless often grow up and strike out at the world, committing unspeakable crimes. If you ask these criminals how they can steal from their mothers or kill people for sport, our worldview will come to their rescue right away. "It ain't me who gets hurt" they'll say, repeating what they learned at daddy's knee. Obviously we have a kind of criminal machine going here now, because even criminals have children who are taught to be criminals from the cradle. But our crime machine is a lot more efficient than this. Why? Our worldview makes us try and cure criminals by feeding them the same poison that made them sick in the first place. In short, we judge criminals to be worthless and treat them that way. Does it help? Of course it doesn't.

Granted, many human beings are so badly damaged by people calling them worthless all their lives, they can't be fixed with love. But the real cure for crime isn't punishment. It's changing the way we see things so people don't turn to crime because they feel worthless. At bottom it's that simple. Sadly however, changing the worldview of an entire planet is not simple. In fact, it is so difficult, it may mean our enemy is winning his battle against us. It may mean our selfishness will make things a billion times worse as suicide atom bombers take us all out. Now it's your turn to guess what the cure is. Hint. Think Rule of Life.

It's Happening

"There is no such thing as a 'self-made' man. We are made up of thousands of others".
- George Matthew Adams

One day after I'd been exercising according to the Rule of Life for a while I noticed something odd happening. Here's how it went. For many years my day job has been running businesses. For those of you not in that line of work, it means trying to get large numbers of different people all moving in the same direction, even if they don't want to. That's what I was doing one morning by getting all my troops together and preaching. So there I was, talking about taking on tomorrow's challenges and climbing distant mountains. I'm trying to warm all these people up to the idea of competing and winning and making things happen. Sure enough, they're all listening politely and pretending to be attentive, mostly because that's what people do when the boss does his thing. Then it hit me. Suddenly I stepped back and saw myself in action and got a bit of a surprise. There I was, striding back and forth in the boardroom, pointing to charts and waxing eloquent about battles won and competitors beaten.

For a second I was taken aback by the sight, because that guy looked just like the success stories you read about in books. He was all fire and brimstone, lighting up his happy campers sitting in a circle at the table. What the heck? It almost looked like this fellow was going somewhere. And wonder of wonders, one or two bystanders actually wanted to go with him! Then out of nowhere came a little revelation. I realized I wasn't just *like* one of those get-up-and-go guys you see on T.V.. I *was* one. I was actually becoming who I could become. For a moment I was slightly dazed by this amazing idea. But it was absolutely true, and it has gotten a lot more so in the time that's passed since. Believe me, it is really an amazing thing to see yourself growing and changing and making your dreams of who you can be real. There is a kind of Magic to it that has to be experienced to really be appreciated. When I think what kind of wooden plank I was in my lost years, tossed about by the ocean of life, it is even more amazing. You too can look forward to feeling this kind of Magic.

Monday, March 31st, 2008, 6:00 A.M.

Well I'll be darned, there's my old college slide-rule in the back of a drawer. A nineteen sixties bamboo computer. People designed rockets to the moon with them. I wonder if I can still make it work. Let me see....two times two equals.....uh....four point three. Still works perfectly!

Summer Vision Works Like This

Vision lets you see where you're destined to go, but that doesn't mean you'll get there. As it turns out, destiny doesn't come with guarantees, and it's easy to see why. Seeing who you can be with Vision is just like looking at the ordinary world with your own two eyes. You can see which way to go, but details ahead will always be fuzzy until you get there.

In fact, distant things can be mistaken for something else. To set the stage for understanding why destiny doesn't come with guarantees then, let's think about ordinary vision first. Say you're making your way up a mountain and see sheep on the path way ahead. When you finally get there they turn out to be white rocks. It doesn't matter though, because they marked the path ahead just as well as sheep could have. Alright, now let's turn to seeing where you're destined to take your life with Vision. Suppose you've awakened to your life's purpose and it's to become an opera singer. With Vision restored, you see yourself getting rich and famous singing Italian love songs. So off you go, learning and practicing and growing into a singer.

Now let's fast-forward fifty years to see what happened. It wasn't opera you ended up singing. Instead you became a piano-bar singer in your home town. You didn't get really rich either, but you found a way to make a decent living doing what you love. Did you get famous? Not really, but lots of local people recognize you from all the singing you've done. What the heck? It looks like your Vision let you down and you didn't fulfill your destiny after all. Did you? Yes you did. What you saw with Vision early on was true, but just a bit fuzzy. You went the right Way alright, and just mistook popular songs for Opera. What you thought was big money, was making a living doing what you love, which really is big riches. Finally, the fame you saw ahead turned out to be a smaller variety. But here's the real truth of it. You got the Way of your life right, just getting a few irrelevant details wrong. Vision and destiny are like that. They really do make a miracle of your life, but leave lots of surprises for you. Destiny makes your life a story you'll want to read…. right to the end….to see how it actually turns out. By the summer of your life you won't want to put that book of your life down either.

Engineering Bones

Remember those engineering bones I don't have? Until my own Vision returned, I couldn't see signs as big as the moon telling me not to go anywhere near engineering. In fact, even the infamous, awe-inspiring and useless bird-house I made in sixth grade shop class failed to tell me I should steer clear of anything technical, mechanical, or requiring tools. You'd have to see that gem of a project to really believe it. Thankfully, there are no photos, so I'll have to describe it in words. Imagine a birdhouse with four walls, each of which is a slightly different height. That little shortcoming made it really difficult to put a roof on. But I tried anyhow, and failed. I created so many cracks, birds would have been better off sheltering under a sieve. I failed to realize birds can't get through quarter inch holes as well, and started off with a teensy little entrance meant for caterpillars. Then I attempted to make it bigger by drilling five little holes together. Chickadees would have shredded themselves trying to sneak in through that jagged mess of peaks and spurs.

I still recall the frustration and dismay as my meager skills failed to make anything looking like an apartment for small feathered animals. It was those strong feelings of me and mechanics being mismatched that should have told me I wasn't suited for anything like that. Truth be told, I'm so mechanically deficient, I can't read a blueprint to make a plywood square. A perfect candidate for engineering school. Not. And you? Is your life failing to take off as we speak, but you don't know why? Do you know you've got great talents somewhere, and it's a mystery that they're doing nothing for you? You're blind to clues about who you are, in your very own life. Just like I was to that bird-house. But take heart. You can teach yourself to see those clues again. Eventually, as your Vision comes back, they'll help you see who you really are.

Your Mission Pilot Light

There's only one point to Mission exercises. They're meant to keep you going until the fire in your belly lights up again. When it finally does, in the summer of your life, you won't need them anymore. But how will you know when the light goes on? There's a very simple and time-honored test you can take, that will tell you for sure if you're on your Way or not. Let's try it out on an imaginary calling. Imagine your Vision returns and you discover your true Mission in life is to play the piano, so off you go to learn your trade. There you are one day serenading friends on the ivories when someone comes along and offers you money to give up playing your instrument. I'm not talking small money here either. Sixty six million dollars to be exact. Crisp new American made bills, each of which stares back at you like a long-lost friend. That's the test. Here's how to score yourself.

Would you give up your dream for the money? Yes? I hate to say it, but it wasn't *your* dream. Playing the piano couldn't possibly have been your Mission in life. Why? Real true blue callings are all about making your *Life*. Remember? Your purpose for being on earth is all about making *you* blossom. In case you somehow strayed from the point then, that means you can't give up a real Life Mission without giving up your life. It's absolutely as simple as that. Truth be told, if you really *were* a piano playing soul, you wouldn't be able imagine a life without your piano. No doubt you'll want to be just as rich as chocolate covered grease balls, but you won't want to be a rich Zombie. Bottom line? You'd choose your life over any amount of cash. So let's stop now and take stock. Can't imagine giving up big bucks for any Mission? Sorry. You failed miserably. Your Mission pilot light is down and out for sure. Believe me, when you get fired up again about being yourself you'll know something with absolute certainty. Believe it or not, life is better than money.

Tuesday April 1ˢᵗ, 2008, 4:00 A.M.

Time to start a count-down. Nine days until I pick up my brand new Harley Davidson motorcycle. Maybe I should be getting a paste on tattoo? Mother Theresa scowling at me for lusting after such a thing maybe? I'll see if my local ink-shop has one.

Another Memory I Didn't Get

Back in my twenties something odd happened to me that I didn't know what to make of at the time. Many years later, when Vision returned, I realized I'd been assaulted by soul thoughts trying to tell me who I was. Here's how it went. In those days I was still attempting to design chemical plants with the only engineering skill I had. Patience. So there I am with a *real* engineer out working on a project in the middle of a big oil refinery. We had a little experimental chemical plant going on out there and were off to check it over. My colleague was hell-bent for leather talking engineering, but I wasn't listening. As we wound our way through the refinery, I was bowled over by the amazing appearance of that processing plant. I was astonished by zigs and zags and curves and big bulbous machines all tied together by thousands of pipes and wires. It looked like a huge modern art painting made of metal to me .. and I said so to my colleague.

"Are you crazy"? said my technical partner, looking at me like I was….well….crazy. And so, afraid to speak my mind further, I shut up. Even so, I was wondering why I should care more about how that equipment *looked* than what it *made*. My engineer buddy was all excited about our equipment and equations…..but I was entranced by questions about beauty. Even then I knew there was something profoundly important about beauty…but I wasn't sure why or what it was. I couldn't figure it out at the time, but now I can.

Each of us has a profoundly beautiful Truth at our center that can speak to us if we let it. It's there to tell us who we are and what to do with our lives. Way back in my own lost years, my inner voice would speak the Truth to me on occasion, hoping upon hope that I'd listen. It was trying to tell me I shouldn't be pretending to be an engineer. Only after my fears of being judged went away did I understand what the beauty of Being Human at the core of me was saying.

I Really Am a Winner

Back when I was really lost, I kept on beating myself up trying to be an Olympic athlete. Torn muscles, ligaments, joints, bones....you name it and I hurt it. But something inside me kept on bringing me back to jogging once I'd healed up, and I always wondered why. Once my Vision came back, I knew why. Every single one of us is supposed to love "being physical" because we all come with physical bodies. We're all supposed to experience this special joy our biological heritage affords us. It's part and parcel of Being Human and nobody should miss this facet of life.

But there's a simple trick to having these joys. Each of us must discover what kind of "exercise" is meant for us. I might be a slow jogging kind of guy for example, but you could be a Yoga person or swimming man. Some people are walkers, and others Tai Chi women. Vigorous gardening or lots of dancing can let you or I "be physical" too, and bring this fabulous kind of joy into our lives. Here's something you might want to think about then. If you're going to the gym every day, and absolutely hate it, but do it to "look better", you're on the wrong track with your life. You're missing the point completely. You aren't supposed to "be physical" so others will applaud you for how you look. You aren't supposed to get your body moving because somebody says "it's healthy".

You're supposed to be "loving thyself", by taking care of the body you came with. You're supposed to be bringing *your kind* of physical joy into your life, exercising because it is a wonderful thing to do. Exercise is a really good example of "it's the Journey that counts". You shouldn't be doing it because it will put you in that size six dress or get you that six pack of abs. It's supposed to be done for the Joy it brings. I can tell you something for sure about exercise therefore. If you're reluctantly doing it as a "means to an end" (so people judge you more worthy because you're thin and strong for instance), you haven't learned to "love thyself" yet. You are still wallowing in fears of being judged and it is limiting your life in ways you don't even realize. It doesn't matter if you're a millionaire and figure you've got that success thing down pat either. If you are "being physical" for any reason but it brings you great joy, you still don't get the meaning of your life. That brings me back to me. Nowadays I know for sure I could never win any kind of prize for my jogging prowess. But I also know for sure I'm a real winner, because I know *my slow jogging way* of being physical brings me great joy.

Don't Follow Fake Leaders

There are two kinds of leaders in the world. Real ones, and fake ones. Fake leaders tell you where to go to get what they have. Real leaders show you how to be yourself. Fake leaders promise you acres of land. Real ones lead you to the promised land. Lots of folks follow fake leaders, but nobody can follow a real leader, because real leaders give you the courage to go *your* way…not theirs. These simple little facts of life are signs of the Truth. The truth is, real leaders help you be yourself.

A Big Enough Enemy to Defeat Mankind?

As Vision returns, you'll begin to see your enemy in a much more dramatic light. So much so that it might just scare you. Here's what I mean. Imagine from the very beginning of time Mankind's only aim in Life has been to figure out who he is. That's what he's here for, and everything he does is supposed to help him in his quest. Every question he asks and way of exploring is another form of the "who am I?" question, because the world is who Man is. So picture Mankind sailing oceans and digging into mountains for thousands of years, exploring to answer this single question. Generation after generation he invents new machines, and writes new poems, trying to figure out who he is. All of it "who am I?" cast a billion different ways. By the twenty-first century Man even ventures into space looking for himself.....without success. After many generations, Mankind still has no idea who he is. Now comes the scary part. Right now, at the dawn of a new millennium, Man is headed the wrong Way, with very little chance of ever discovering the answer to his question. Why? Our enemy called "Reason" is keeping the answer from him. Our mistaken way of seeing the world is making it all but impossible for individuals and Mankind alike to discover who they are. Can anything get more scary than this? Yes it can. This enemy is dug into our lives so deeply, it might defeat all of Mankind. Our selfish way of seeing things could make Man destroy himself and the world around him. If that doesn't frighten you, it's because selfishness has soothed you into thinking everything will be alright. But I can assure you it is not and it won't be made right along the path we have taken.

Saturday April 5th, 2008, 5:25 A.M.

With sales meetings in America today, I might be spending hours on the Blue Water bridge waiting for border guards to interrogate people. All this terrorism has made folks wary of travelers.

Foolishly Discriminating...Against Myself

I learned foolish discrimination in the cradle and practiced it for decades before I realized the folly of it. Even now I keep on catching myself doing it. Here's an example. Sometimes I catch myself thinking... "I'm worth more as a Human Being than that guy, because I have more money than he does". Ring a bell? It should, because everybody is taught to think like that. But it's really very silly, because of how the world works. To see what I mean, you have to understand one simple fact about the world. This fact. "Who you are is who you were and will be". Your past, present and future you are all different parts of who you are. That means somewhere in your past life you were poor....and still are. Call someone names for having less than you do now then, and you're calling yourself names.

For sure this applies to me, because when I left school, I didn't have a house or car or even much furniture. Let's face it, I was poor as a pound puppy. A lot poorer than that guy I looked down on above. Maybe you think this doesn't apply to you because your family had been rich going back to the Dark Ages. If so, you'd better think again about that little fact of life above. Who you were goes back to the beginning of the Cosmos. Your chimpanzee ancestors and mine didn't have two cents to rub together. Go back far enough and you'll discover you were poorer than church mice could ever be. There's no way you can get off the hook, so stop foolishly discriminating against yourself.

Obesity...an odd kind of Vision story

Look around and I think you'll agree that obesity is a problem in North America.

Not only are people getting fatter and fatter, but years of excess weight is crippling health care systems. That's great news for profit-minded people however, because it creates a gigantic market for diet books and diet products of every kind imaginable. In fact, from a business point of view, fat is fabulous, because dieting causes more obesity. You couldn't ask for a better product than one that causes folks to need more. Cigarette makers and diet book authors discovered this kind of money making miracle a long time ago. So how the heck are we going to get ourselves out of this potentially fatal spiral of diet and gain and diet and gain more? As everyone knows, the cause of sickness has to be treated, not the symptoms. And the root cause of all this obesity is, pure and simple …..unhappiness. To explain where I'm coming from on this, I'll tell you my story. Like pretty much everyone, I started off life the right weight…for me. I never worried about what I ate, and I didn't gain an ounce. In fighting form, I topped out at about 145 pounds, and stayed there no matter what. But somewhere in high-school I began to gain weight. I also learned that weight isn't socially acceptable.

That started the diet and gain cycle so many of us are familiar with. A cycle that screws around with our metabolisms and does nothing good for anyone. If you can't identify with this ridiculous and sad problem, you're one of the lucky few that don't spend half their lives gaining and losing weight. Between the ages of 18 and 40, that was me, wandering aimlessly back and forth between 130 and 200 pounds. (Just so you know 200 pounds at five foot seven does not work). Then I woke up and received a big surprise about this obesity puzzle.

And Took It Off

Here's the truth of obesity for you in a nutshell.

Any of God's creatures….people included….going about their lives just being themselves, do not gain weight. Men, women and other animals aren't born to carry around excess fat. Seals, walrus, or peoples in the arctic store up fat, but it's the *right way of being*….for them. That's the key to the obesity puzzle right there. Fear of judgment is keeping us from being ourselves. The resulting soul-destroying unhappiness causes obesity. I know for sure because of what happened to me as I took up my Mission of being myself again. My weight went down and my "natural physical form" emerged once more. Without dieting. This was a truly magical experience and it made me feel the Divine presence of Being Human in my life. I cannot tell you how surprised and delighted I was to discover that my physical person came back with my dreams. For sure I was exercising too….but because I loved it, not to just "lose weight". No question but I'd decline that second bowl of ice-cream as well, but not just to starve myself into smaller jeans. I didn't want it, because the need to comfort myself with food just plain disappeared.

I know this will sound absolutely like a fairy tale to anyone struggling with their weight right now. But it is absolutely true. I believe if you spend ten seconds thinking about it, you'll realize it rings true as well. In short I'm saying here that each of us has a "natural weight" that accompanies "being ourselves". Like deer or mice or elephants do. To find this place in the sun Nature meant for us to be in then, we must learn how to "be ourselves". That is exactly what the Rule of Life can do for you. Being the "right weight" for you, and feeling infinitely worthy at it, is a bonus you get with being yourself.

Sunday, April 6th, 2008, 5:00 A.M.

Today I start training for my motorcycle license. Too bad they didn't have courses like that 40 years ago when I got my first bike. As a matter of fact, they didn't even have motorcycle licenses in those days. Learning how to ride properly might have stopped me from breaking a leg on my Honda on Father's day, June 19th, 1966.

Now The Goofballs Make Sense

Back in the days when I was desperate to figure out what to do with my life, I listened to the conventional wisdom of gurus and tried to find myself in my childhood. I screwed my eyes closed and peered way back into the mists of time, looking for signs of who I might be. I remembered all kinds of things of course, including things I seemed to be interested in. But none of it told me anything important about who I really was. Then, decades later, as my own Vision came back, I turned my Mind's eye to my past and was astonished at what I saw there.

As far back as I could see was an apprentice writing-exploring soul. Days on chair rock at Silver Islet came back to haunt me as I recognized my authentic passionate person writing notes in a funny little diary. Early days pretending to be an engineer, while authoring Big Books of Goofballs became clear as a bell. I was searching for myself in the nature of the world and recording my adventures, much to the dismay of colleagues at the time. As a matter of fact, with newfound insight into who I was, I saw myself writing one sort of Journal time and time again as far back as I could remember.

But why didn't I see those clues about who I am in my life before? Wasn't my natural-born soul always there on display? I wasn't *actually* there…..I was *potentially* there. To make my authentic person real, I had to learn how to "manifest my potential" by dumping fears of judgment. The very same holds true for you. Learn how to be yourself once more and you will see who you are in your past life. On the other hand, if you just can't believe the message in this book, I can give you a guarantee. It won't matter how long and hard you look back at your childhood. You won't *actually* be there.

Just ONE Fear To Worry About

In my travels preaching wholeness I've discovered many people are confused about fear. Everyone knows all kinds of fears are bad for our lives for example. Fear of failing, making mistakes, losing and loving and coming in last to name a few. These fears keep millions of people from getting out and living life. But lots of fears are good too. Fear of fire is a good thing, because it stops us from getting burned. Other fears keep us from leaping off cliffs and flying away…..straight down, or risking our life savings on the flip of a coin. Being able to sort out bad fears from good ones doesn't help much however. There are so many different cures for each life-inhibiting fear, it's all but impossible to make sense of it.

In fact, all these fears that keep people from finding authentic success look suspiciously like symptoms of some illness that doctors can't figure out. If you've ever watched one of those "mystery diagnosis" T.V. programs you'll have some idea what I mean. Some illnesses present all kinds of different symptoms that seem to have no obvious root cause. If you happen to come down with a sickness like this, you can be in big trouble because it may take years before a physician figures you out. Even worse, nobody may discover the single underlying malaise.

Those fears we all know are bad for our lives are just like that. They all come from one single underlying root fear of being judged, and this fear itself comes from our mistaken way of seeing the world. If you learn how to take this fear out of your life, you'll be utterly astonished at what happens. Down will go your fears of failing, making mistakes, speaking in public, being ridiculed, speaking your mind, writing tests, asking girls to dance, changing, etc., etc. etc. Fears of being yourself every which way will disappear. That single root fear has a million branches, but every single one of them will wither up and go away when you see clearly that you and the world are parts of one whole. At bottom then, there is only one fear worth worrying about in the world.

Friday April 11th, 2008, 3:00 P.M.

This morning I picked up my new Hog from the dealer. What a rush this beast is. If you've never ridden a souped-up Harley Davidson motorcycle, it's a bit like throwing your leg over a freight train and riding it down the highway. Half a ton of metal lies between you and the road....and nothing else. It makes you feel like you're driving a cross between a tank and a jet plane too, and can vibrate the fillings out of your teeth. Don't fire one up beside kittens or babies for example, unless they're both deaf. The moral of this story is, stay away from them if you don't like excitement.

Back in '53 Again

Once I had eyes to see once more, I peered back into my own Life and saw myself melting crayons with a magnifier way back in 1953. Like any little kid might, I'd discovered the sun could be focused into a white hot spot with a lens, and it absolutely fascinated me.

But why should that silly little story be stuck in the back of my mind for so many decades? And what important thing could I finally see there when my Vision returned. In a word....*feelings*. To this day I can remember the very special feelings I had on those porch steps. Feelings of discovery. Feelings of mystery. Keep in mind, I had no idea crayons could melt and didn't know magnifiers could melt them either. I felt exactly like Einstein did when he discovered his famous theories. How the heck do I know what Einstein felt? Discovery always feels like that, no matter how big or little or who's the discoverer. It's a combination of surprise, wonder, and even awe, like the impossible happened in front of you. All explorers-at-heart know that magical feeling of enchantment. That's why my crayon days stayed stuck in my mind so long. I'm an exploring fool at-heart. Those crayons were a sign that said ...."you have the soul of a voyager little fellow". One of many such signs along the way, meant to guide me to my destiny. But, sadly, those signs were like black billboards with black writing on a dark night to me until my soul-sight returned. Then I could hardly believe what I saw. Now my road less traveled looks like the Las Vegas strip, with neon signs everywhere telling me who I am and which way to go.

The Old Guy Finally Figures It Out

Back when I was young as grass seed, I used to love padding along the country roads, slowly jogging just for the joy of it. But here's something hard to believe. For decades and decades my inner voice would keep on whispering at me..."you've got the heart of a slow runner my friend, so get out there and enjoy jogging....*your* way". But of course, I Ignored my own heart-song every time, pretending to be something I'm not. Then, in middle age I woke up to "know thyself" and was stunned to realize that message was in my face for years before I saw it.

If that doesn't strike you as unbelievably odd, let's turn to a modern kind of analogy. Imagine you're lost in a foreign land, desperately looking for the way home. Your heart is almost broken because you can't find the Way, but at least you have your MP3 player to console yourself with. So there you are, trying to drown your sorrows in music as you search for the way home. Song after song flows into your head as you go, and you enjoy the melodies while ignoring the words. Unfortunately for you, those lyrics happen to be instructions for finding the way home....set to music. Precisely what you're looking for has been with you all along. Let's say for sake of this story then, that you waste ten years trying to find your way home with the solution in your ears every day. Then by luck or fate you realize what's up. What on earth would you think about that? Ten full years you spent seeking something that was always with you. That is exactly what it felt like to me when I woke up to who I am.....and realized the clues were with me all my life. To say the least, I could hardly believe it. My guess is you'll feel the same way.

Crazy Is Good?

Here's another little story about yours truly being unable to see himself in his own past life for a very long time. Before I was comfortable being myself again, even *I* wondered what my weird sense of humor was about. This strange sense of what's funny goes back as far as I can remember. Back past my youthful days when I'd wow friends and enemies alike with odd twisted jokes. What kind of humor are we talking about here? Why don't I give you a real-life example, I've actually dumped on more than one person over the years. Imagine me coming up to you one day and saying "do you like dogs?". Chances are I can set you up for the fall because most people do. Probably you'll say something like... "as a matter of fact, I love dogs of all kinds", making me rub my hands together in glee as I get ready to deliver the punch line.

"Great!" I reply with what looks suspiciously like tin-plated sincerity. "I have a dead one in my trunk you can have…..let me go get him for you!". Of course you're staring at me in disbelief as I roll around on the floor laughing. What's funny about it you ask? Well, the idea anyone would want a dead dog is obviously absurd, and my brain is tickled pink by absurdities. The question is of course…..why is that? Like I said above, I wondered that myself for many years, because my entire sense of humor appeared to revolve around self-contradictions, absurdities, oxymorons, and other interesting nonsense. Nonsensical enough in fact, I've been called plain crazy more than a few times for it. So what gives here anyway? It was only after I woke up to who I am that the truth of it hit me. It goes like this. In essence, from the time I could speak I've been in touch with the Poem of Life at my center, even as I gave it the wrong meaning that limited my life.

For decades this Poem spoke its message to me, but I was too blind to see what it was saying. My very being communicated wholeness to myself and the world, but it was always mistaken for nonsense by everyone, including me. This amazing Poem is a perfect melding of absolutely incompatible things after all, so it's no wonder I and everyone around me always thought it was nonsense. Only after awakening did I realize my absurd humor wasn't nonsense at all. It's a message about the Joys of wholeness. As it turns out, all humor is one of the real Joys of Being Human that happens when we get past our inhibiting fears of being ourselves. Humor is one characteristically Human thing that flows from the sea of Tao-potential at our core when we are happy. But here's the part I'm getting at. From the age of ten to way into my forties, I cracked nonsense jokes without realizing that they were trying to tell me who I am. And who you are. Who we all are. We're Being Human. It sure took a long time, but now I know this with certainty. I know you too can become Human as well, by learning how to grow yourself your Way.

Sunday April 13th, 4:00 A.M. 2008

Last of three days breaking in my motorcycle today. Maybe I'll cruise out to Grand Bend and back early today. I'd better push it to the edge of town before firing it up though, or wake up the whole neighborhood.

Your Soul Must Understand

There's a gigantic difference between your brain understanding the Tree of Life, and your soul comprehending it. I learned this small fact of life by the time-honored method of trying to get a message to people who weren't ready for it. Soon I discovered the old "horses and water" thing. Sure enough, you can lead a horse right up to the trough, but if he doesn't want to drink, you're out of luck. Chances are you've run into this phenomena yourself. Parents trying to convey life skills to their children find themselves in this predicament all the time for example. Kids understand every word and idea but they seldom benefit from the wisdom. Missionaries looking for converts also find the message falling on deaf ears. Same sort of thing with the Tree of Life. Here's what I mean. If I tell you your life *must be* worth the same as anyone's life, you'll understand what I mean at once, because it's a simple idea. But chances are, this "intellectual understanding" won't help you a bit, and it'll be easy to see you've missed the point. How? You'll still feel bad if you come in last, or if someone says you're not thin enough. You still won't have a clue what to do with your life either. So how do you get your soul to comprehend it's beyond judgment, so you can create your dream life? Gather together as many friends as you can and begin acting like you believed the world around you is who you are. Keep that up until results convince you it is true. How will you know your soul is beginning to get it? You'll begin to see who you really are again.

Nineteen Fifty Seven Memories

Decades ago, in my misspent youth, I'd antagonize librarians near and far by trying to take out bushel baskets of books meant for people ten times my age. Books I could barely read, much less comprehend. It took me many decades to finally understand why I was bound and determined to surf libraries and offend grownups. Here's what I eventually saw. Even by the age of seven or eight I was an exploring soul, turning over rocks in the yard and reading any kind of book you can imagine. Already I was seeking to "know thyself" and knew deep down there were clues everywhere. That's why I wanted to read everything from "A to Z" in the library. My soul knew I could find myself anywhere in the world. But sadly, most librarians couldn't see a little apprentice explorer for who he was. Fifty years later I can tell you this as well. If I hadn't managed to let my inner voice come back into my life, these memories would still be meaningless. But, thankfully, today they tell me who I am. And who you are is always there in your life to be found. All you have to do is learn how to restore your Vision.

Animal People

By the age of five I knew there was something about animals too many people miss. Something profoundly mysterious I couldn't see until Vision returned. Then I saw the full terrible truth, and it made me deeply afraid for Humanity. Now I'm going to spell it out to you whether you want to hear it or not. All creatures great and small are living, feeling *beings*. In essence, they're different *kinds, varieties, or types* of people. Animal people differ dramatically from human people of course but you could morph yourself into any kind of creature at all by changing one aspect of yourself after another. Keep on changing parts of you and you'd eventually look like a dog or cat or horse or whale. But here's the thing. That soul at your center would remain the same.

You'd still be looking out at the world, albeit with very different eyes. So let's imagine you've done precisely that, and changed yourself into a big friendly puppy. Now your own father comes along. Unfortunately this man is not fond of animals. He beats you, deprives you of water and leaves you tied up outside by yourself. You're in great pain and can hardly believe anyone would do this to you…..much less your own father. But you can't speak "human" any more to tell this man what he's doing to you. Even so, the fear and suffering in your eyes is obvious. Sadly for you, your own father doesn't care, because all he sees is "an animal". Unable to communicate in ways your father would recognize, all you can do is cry out in pain and show signs of suffering any human would. But it does no good. Your own father is prepared to let you die.

Does this little story make you uncomfortable? Can you imagine billions of little souls being tortured all over the world right now just like this…..because people can't see they're living, feeling, caring beings? I hope so, because Human people have held dominion over animal beings for a very long time, committing unspeakable crimes against them. That's why creatures have always followed myself and others around. They're crying out for help, because nobody cares how much they suffer. Nobody sees we're torturing our own brothers and sisters. Mark my words. We are not going to like this Karma when it comes back around to haunt us.

Prove You're Blind…To Who You Are

Here's something you can do to start a Rule of Life Journal. Look back over your life, ask yourself some questions, and write the answers down on page one. Here's a few of those questions for you. Do you see what you're here to do anywhere in your own past? Is it obvious what your real passion in life is?

Can you figure out exactly which way to take your life by looking at your interests, skills and native talents? Are there any scraps of true purpose in your youth? Is your Reason for Being written all over your face? Now honestly answer them. I'll bet you don't have much to write home about. Am I correct? That's O.K., just write those little facts of your own life down on the very first page of your Journal. I want you to do that so you're totally stunned later by what happens as fears of being yourself go away. When that happens you'll hardly believe you couldn't find yourself in your own life before. You'll realize you didn't "know thyself" at all. You'll also begin to recognize your authentic self as far back as you can remember in your life….where you saw nothing of interest earlier. But be warned. If you can't see why you're here right now, you're blind to who you are, but won't be able to prove it to yourself yet. The only way to do it is get your Vision back. Believe me, when this special insight into who you are returns, you'll look back at that first page of your Journal in absolute disbelief. It's extremely hard to believe you and I can lose what we need to make our way in the world. But almost everyone does.

Wednesday April 16th, 2008, 5:00 A.M.

Why is it people think everyone on a big motorcycle is a Hell's Angel? There are more doctors, lawyers and housewives out there on bikes than organized criminals.

Integrity is a Sign of the Truth

Gurus tell us integrity is very important, and they're certainly right because people with integrity "do what they say they'll do". But there's another more profound kind of integrity you'll want in your life. I call it "True Integrity" and ordinary "do what you say" integrity is only a pale shadowy sign of this more potent version. Here's how it works.

People with True Integrity are doing what their *hearts* tell them to do. They're not simply speaking words then doing what they say. They're living an authentic life by "doing what their hearts say". Men and women with True Integrity are living a life in sync with their heart-songs. If you know why you're here and what your Life Mission is, you can aspire to a life of True Integrity by making your own dreams real. This kind of Integrity gives you a deep sense of purpose and a Divine sense of being alive. By now you should know there's only one way get this powerful form of Real integrity. You have to learn how to release your inner voice into your life once more. True Integrity is the awe-inspiring Truth beneath the surface of everyday integrity.

Now I Don't Take Things Personally

Once I lost my fears of being judged and stopped taking things personally, I began to see how thin-skinned and hair-trigger defensive so many people are. Soon I realized 90% of the population has to be treated with kid-gloves to avoid hurting their feelings. Everybody is so afraid of being judged and found wanting, they're hyper-vigilant. Tell a joke they don't understand and they'll think you're making fun of them. Mention something they don't happen to know anything about and they'll think you're calling them stupid. Look at them sideways and they'll figure you're putting them down somehow. I'm exaggerating a bit for effect here of course, but not a lot. It's a bit exasperating to feel like you have to walk on egg-shells all the time to avoid bruising egos. It's even more frustrating trying to convince someone to "not take it personally", when they're still terrified of being judged. Just the other day I wasted at least a hundred lungs full of breath trying for instance. It went like this. One opportunity for advancement came up in our company, with two possible candidates. The guy who didn't get it was fit to be tied. He believed absolutely that our company (yours truly that is) was systematically persecuting him.

"You're keeping me down" he said. After about two hours of trying to explain that not everyone can get every opportunity every time, and other simple facts of life, I gave up. He did not understand that each of us is responsible for creating our own dream life, and will get our share of lost opportunities and failed advancements. I just could not convince this man to "not take it personally". He saw the lost promotion as a judgment of his worth and it hurt him right in the pit of his soul. I would have had an easier time convincing a llama to write poetry than make this fellow comfortable with his loss. Unfortunately I now know that "taking things personally" is epidemic in the Western world, because too many don't know their souls can't be worthless.

Being Centered…Where the Truth is

Have you ever wondered exactly what "being centered" means? Back in my own lost years I heard people gushing over how "centered" they were, and tried to figure out what they were doing. I never got it, until I began to wake up to who I am again. Then it became abundantly obvious and clear what being centered is really about. In essence, being centered means there's a central theme to your life. If you're "centered" there's a purpose to everything you do. Here's how I discovered I was getting "centered" by learning how to be myself again. As I began to see what to do with my life, I realized that my dream Life was a multi-faceted thing, with a central theme of happiness. There were Mind, Body, and Spirit components of my Mission, all pointing in the same direction of becoming all I could become. Out on the road jogging for instance, I was "working my dream" of becoming all I could become physically. In my day job I was furthering my aim of getting my message of hope out by stretching my sales and marketing and business skills. All my waking moments were dedicated to growing the different facets of who I am. But they all had that core aim of being myself as best I could.

At the center of it all was that aim of growing human. One day out jogging therefore, I realized that "being centered" was getting in touch with the being at my center. Suddenly I knew I was "centered" because everything I was doing was centered around growing my soul-person the way it was meant to be grown. The very same thing holds for you as well. To "get centered" you need only to take away your fears of judgment to get in touch with the soul at your center. Being centered has nothing to do with a spot in the middle of your body. It has to do with the center of your Life. Now it should be clear why "being centered" has been a mysterious and black art for so long as well. Our misguided worldview has prevented pretty much everyone from being themselves, keeping entire nations from being centered.

Thursday, April 17th, 2008, 4:45 A.M.

I think I'll BBQ salmon tonight. Speaking of BBQ's, our old one goes back five houses now and I bought it when I was in my thirties. Maybe it's time to retire the old soldier.

God. A Four Letter Sign of the Truth

Have you ever noticed how antsy most people get when the word "God" comes up? If you'd like to see someone squirm and dodge and find excuses to disappear, just try to strike up a conversation about God. You'd think God was a four-letter word and any talk about "he, she, or it" was some kind of terrible taboo. This is pretty strange if you stop and think about it. I mean, why should everyone be afraid to talk about good things? God is supposed to be all about love and peace and every good thing known to Man after all. Good things everybody wants and most people have far too little of in their lives. At the very least you'd think folks would speak longingly about God, wishing they had what he represents. But this sure doesn't happen.

Bringing the word "God" up is like throwing a hot potato into a crowd. Everybody tries to get rid of it as fast as they can. But why? The answer is quite simple really. In short, "God" is the wholeness or love we all need to bring authentic happiness into our lives. But wholeness literally defies Reason because it's how absolutely different things are absolutely the same. Therein lies the difficulty. God is unreasonable, and unreasonable people are judged worthless at best. No wonder most people are afraid to embrace God then. Mention the word and you're labeled an irrational flake who can't think right and judged worthless because of it. Who wants to be called names and relegated to the scrap heap? Millions don't, and reject God because of it. I don't know about you, but I find that frightening.

Blind College Memories

Here's what college life was like to me. Four years forcing myself to learn all kinds of amazing things, none of which interested me in the least. But don't get me wrong here. I'm not saying engineering isn't interesting. I'm saying engineering isn't who I am. Anyhow, later in my life as Vision came back, I was taken aback by one huge sign I was going the wrong way, that was there in my college years in spades. A sign the size of Mount Everest that I missed completely. In short, there was no Joy at all in my studies. Here's why that's such a big sign. Anyone living an authentic life will have Joy to look forward to, because Joy is what you get when in sync with your own heart-song. At bottom, Joy is appreciation for life itself, and Life itself is lost when we are. As I resumed growing Human once more however, the sheer absurdity of a Joyless Life presented itself to me. To give you an idea of how crazy living a life without Joy really is, I'll make up a story. Imagine a man with his hand in a pot of boiling water. You can see in his face he's in awe-inspiring pain…..but he's not taking his hand out.

He won't even take it out when you tell him to. What on earth is going on here? Something is obviously wrong somewhere. That pain has a purpose after all. It should be telling him what he's doing isn't right. In the real world, you'd consider a man like that insane. Right? No kidding, but something like this is going on all around you as we speak. In every city there are men and women eking out absolutely Joyless lives because they've taken the wrong Path. Make no mistake as well, the pain of going without Joy is every bit as real as the man with his hand in boiling water. But these people are staying right where they are, just like the crazy guy cooking himself. They're so lost, they think a Joyless life is normal. That's where the real insanity is. And you? If there's very little Joy in your life right now, you're probably in the wrong job, marriage, country, planet……pick one or all. But don't forget. The Rule of Life can help you find your Way.

Saturday, April 19th, 2008, 8:00 A.M.

Pussycats are amazing creatures. Mine will carry on a cat-conversation for minutes at a time. "Murble, squeak, mewl, twitter" he'll say when I speak his name. "Bark, chatter, mip, tweet" says he about birds or squirrels on the lawn as well. I once counted eighteen funny little cat-sounds he can make.

Is It the REAL Tree of Life?

The Tree of Life is an Ages old motif, said to unite all life on earth. Often people say this Tree connects and inter-connects every living thing. As a huge evolutionary Tree, it harks back to the beginning of life, making birds and fish and flowers and Human families all part and parcel of the mystery of living things. Chances are you've heard of it before, but you have to be very careful about this wondrous and ancient symbol.

As it turns out, most men and women aren't talking about the *real* Tree of Life. It's easy to tell if they are too. On the real Tree of Life, every single soul will say….."I am the world", because we're all part of each other and the world. To discover which Tree of Life someone is talking about then, just ask if they think you and they are part of each other. If they look at you like you're crazy, it wasn't the real Tree of Life they were speaking of.

Chapter Twenty-Seven
Autumn Comes to My Life Journal
(You Can Look Forward to a Mission Like Mine)

Monday April 21st, 2008, 5:10 A.M.

Looks like it's time to prune the ornamental grasses again. Trouble is, the darn things are as big as bamboo. Ten feet high and an inch across, they're tougher than nails. Here comes hours on my knees with bolt cutters.

A Gift From John For Your Mission

Anyone on any kind of Mission soon discovers the road is long, tough, and filled with obstacles. Here's something my old friend John G. gave me that helps me every day with my challenges. I hope it helps you. Sadly, John got cancer in his early fifties and died far too long before his time. Several days after his first major surgery I was visiting in the hospital when John suddenly said something that stuck with me forever. "Old buddy" he said…"I'd exchange this cancer for the toughest thing in life you could throw at me and love it". Later it dawned on me what John was saying. He was telling me to love everything in life, no matter how hard, because something like cancer might show up tomorrow. Here's how I apply John's lesson.

When some big painful obstacle gets thrown in my face these days…I pretend I have cancer…. like John did. Then I wish I could exchange the cancer for my trials and tribulations. In my imaginary world I get my wish and I'm happy to take on this difficult task instead of coming to the end of my life. Unfortunately, neither John nor I could make his wish come true, but I've never forgot that lesson, and it makes me love any kind of challenge, because I'm glad to be alive.

Thank-you old friend for that gift of how to appreciate life. I wish you were here to share all my tough, Life-enhancing obstacles with me.

A Universal OFF Switch?

When I was absolutely aimless, I'd party at the drop of a hat and even pop pain killers for fun, because I literally had nothing better to do with my life. But as I began to get my calling back, all the pills and booze switches in my head went OFF... and stayed off. It's very, very easy to see why too. Once you have something to put heart and soul into forever, the very idea of wasting time trying to kill yourself with chemicals is just plain ridiculous. You're far too busy making your dream life and finding Joy in every nook and cranny. You don't have to medicate yourself to try and hide from the pain of being lost. That's really all there is to it.

The cure for all the drug-induced sadness in the world today is showing people how to follow their hearts again. Period. The most important thing in the world to each and every one of us is growing ourselves our way until we blossom. Take that option away and chemical dependencies of every kind take its place. If you don't believe it, it's because you've never experienced the full Joys of Being yourself. You'd have to be brain damaged to choose booze or pills over Being yourself. And here's an even more miraculous thing. Even if you've boozed and binged on pills so long your brain really has been damaged....you can fix it again. Believe it or not, the Rule of Life can heal your brain as well as your Spirit.

How Is That Possible?

How on earth is it possible that the Rule of Life can turn off real live addictions or fix terrible chemical dependencies? Well, the short answer is because Mind and Body are really One.

That's what gets us into trouble in the first place, and it's what can get us back out of it again too. Here's how. When Human Beings are grossly unhappy because they can't figure out how to be themselves, they often try to dull the pain with drugs. Unhappy Minds make people ingest chemicals that literally can change their brains. Their brains become hard-wired to need those chemicals. Now they don't even need an unhappy Mind to get them to the liquor store or street corner for a fix of deadly sins. Damaged brains make them do it. That's what's called being "chemically dependent". But it's possible to turn around and go back down that path as well. It isn't easy of course, but it really is possible. Here's how to do that. As you use the Rule of Life, it will change your Mind about the world and stop the incoming flow of bad ideas about your worth as a Human Being. That will eventually change your brain back to where it came from. That is how Mind changes Body. It will take a while for your brain to heal itself of course, but becoming whole is what heals. Your chemical switches won't turn off overnight, but from personal experience I can tell you they *will* go off. That's exactly what happened to me.

A Mind Blowing Thing

Here's what I mean about turning those chemical switches "off" from personal experience. When I was terrified of being myself, booze had a kind of magnetic pull on me. By that I mean willpower alone could not overcome the attraction. Once and a while I could, by a kind of super-human effort, keep myself from going to the liquor store on a Friday and zoning out with wine that night. But I felt like a guy hanging on to a tree in a hurricane. Every ounce of strength was needed to overcome the pull booze had on me. So much strength I couldn't keep it up. Soon I'd be back at it again.

But as I began to take up my Life Mission once more, and the "switches went off" I was completely flabbergast. The magnet went off and I did not need super-human will to overcome the force of attraction. As a matter of fact, I realized that I'd tapped into a far greater Power of Will and understood what "Thy Will Be Done" means. It means each of us wants above all things to merge with that great source of potential at our center called "Being Human". This Force of greater Will at the core of all of us is infinitely stronger than any individual "will power". It renders any attraction to life-destroying chemicals null and void. That is exactly what I experienced myself. No longer did I need to try avoiding booze by "strength of my own will". There was nothing at all drawing me towards it. In fact, I am now "repelled" by booze or drugs or anything at all that reduces my consciousness of life. So here's something you might want to think about. If you've managed to keep booze or pills at bay with the help of a one of the great multi-step programs out there, ask yourself this.

Does it still feel like a struggle with demons all the time? Do you have to battle against some force trying to pull you back into the pit again every day? Do you have to live your life one day at a time, because you simply don't know when that chemical dependency will pull you back into the abyss once more? If so, I must give you a heart-felt vote of congratulations for your success at staying sober by dint of will power. But you haven't been treating the cause of your disease, and it may come back to bite you some day big-time. If you really want to cut that sickness out of your heart, you have to see what's making you sick and get rid of it. What is making you ill is your fears of being judged. Take that awe-inspiring disease away and you will feel absolutely no attraction for drugs of any kind. None. Zero. I am not kidding either.

A Scary Thought

Once my Vision began to clear up again, I saw something terrifying. Chemical dependencies aren't the only bad sickness our mistaken view of the world is causing. It's *creating* diseases of every kind. Yes I meant to say *creating*. It's easy to see how and why as well. To get an idea where I'm coming from, let's just review what "Reason" is. It's a selfish view of the world that makes us think everything is separate. And here's the thing about "worldviews". They color everything we say or do and make us behave in accordance with beliefs at their core. So what does Reason make us do? It makes us destroy wholeness everywhere by acting selfishly every which way possible. In case you've forgotten, what results from the destruction of wholeness is disease. A few simple examples will suffice.

Men, women, countries and companies see the environment as "separate" from them, and dump poisons into it. Then what? A plague of disease descends upon us. Asthmas, allergies, attention deficit disorders, and cancers to name a few. Industrial farmers trying to corner the market for foods will unleash genetically altered crops on the world as well, not caring if everyone else is made sick by it. Entrepreneurs looking to make a buck for themselves will promote the idea teenage girls are worth nothing if they don't have the right clothing. This causes poor souls desperate for acceptance and love to binge and vomit until they die, sickened by anorexia or other illnesses. And the bottom line, pun intended?

When we treat everything around us as if it can be destroyed for our individual gain, we destroy wholeness on a global scale, inflicting disease upon the planet itself. Symptoms of this sickness are disease, violence, global warming, obesity and extinctions of all kinds. As you might expect, when the entirety of Mother Earth is ill, the signs and symptoms will be many and varied.

But the very worst part of it is that we are creating all the grief ourselves because we cannot see the world is who we are.

Don't Miss Your Chance (to work with others)

Part of the exercise program designed to wake you up is working with others, because it speeds up your progress. You probably won't have too far to go to find others to work with either. Most of us have brothers or sisters and friends nearby for example. As a matter of fact, the old expression "that's what families are for" probably came from parents and kids working together to grow Human. It's supposed to start there after all, but very often it doesn't. Not because parents don't want the best for their children though. It's because parents and children alike are caught up in mistaken beliefs about how the world works. Take my family for example. When I was a kid, I had a little brother around I could have brainstormed with and learned lessons about growing from.

But I was so lost so early in my life, it never occurred to me that Brian was a natural resource, right there in my own backyard. Like a diamond mine out back by the raspberry bushes perhaps. Looking back though, it's clear Brian was actually ahead of me until he too got well and truly lost. No doubt about it, Brian was studying archeology before I could spell the word. Matter of fact, he was going on digs for ancient Indian bones with our local college while I was still chewing on chicken bones. He was pondering classical music when I was pondering the Beatles. Had Brian and I worked together to learn how to be ourselves, we might have overcome the teachings coming at us from every angle, keeping us from finding our Way.

But Brian and I were like completely separate satellites orbiting our family's center. We rarely saw each other, much less came close.

Even by the time I'd got to college, I couldn't see what an amazing personal growth partner Brian would have been. This was a man with a deep intuitive grasp of the world, I could have learned much from. But, sadly, I didn't. A little real-life story will perhaps give you an idea what I mean.

I'm Still Blind

In hindsight I think it's fair to say my departed brother Brian was a truly brilliant person who never managed to let that brilliance out. I have no doubts that Brian's profound curiosity and brainpower could have helped me find my way a lot earlier. But I was so blind I couldn't even see these talents for what they were, despite the obvious evidence in my face all my life. By the time I got to college, Brian had become a plumber like my Dad. The trouble is, I was so brainwashed, I thought a brilliant plumber was an oxymoron. Now I realize the only moron in this picture was yours truly of course, but it's far too late to make amends. At any rate, here's the story that illustrates two simple things. The first is, I didn't recognize Brian for who he was. The second is that I missed a gigantic opportunity to work with him to grow up.

One day myself and a few friends were home from college and gabbing about Albert Einstein's theory of gravity. Little brother Brian happens to be home too and he's sitting in on it all on the side-lines. I'd read somebody's way of explaining Einstein's theory to laymen like my friends and I, so I parroted it out, to make myself look smart. "Here's how to understand Einstein's theory guys" says I... as if I actually did. "Imagine the earth's a big ball sitting on a rubber sheet of space-time"…..I say….pausing for drama. "So what do you think happens to the sheet?". Vacant stares all 'round of course, so I continue. "It sags….I say…trying my best to talk down to the crowd staring back blankly. Then I get ready for the big finale.

With a look of mock intelligence on my face I say…."O.K., so throw a little ball like the moon on the sheet and it'll roll into the hole with the earth". Then the coup de grace. "There you go…..gravity works like that…because space and time sags around the earth!". At this point I'm waiting for the applause…or maybe some kind of prize for my staggering ability to speak stuff I don't understand….when Brian pipes up.

So Blind I Can't See a Star

"That doesn't sound right to me" says Brian. "You just used gravity to explain gravity". Silence from the crowd, yours truly included. He was right. I'd just given a chicken-and-egg sort of explanation, and Brian had seen through it in an instant. He'd just pointed out that none of us had a clue what Einstein was on about, but, truth be told I didn't even notice. My friends and I just fluffed Brian off as a "dumb kid in the presence of wise college men". I didn't even comprehend the kind of brain power behind his response, until some forty years later when I finally woke up. But it was too late. Brian's life had already ended. I missed my chance to work with Brian. It makes me sad just writing about it too. So listen up. Don't miss your chances to work with other folks in your life.

Tuesday, April 22nd, 2008, 6:00 A.M.

Silver Islet and Me

When you're fully alive and awakened with Vision once more, many of your memories will stun you. Here's an example for you. When I finally woke up to who I am again, I realized why memories of our summer cottage at Silver Islet were so special to me.

Silver Islet in my day was a wild place on the North Shore of Lake Superior where the sacred nature of reality stood out on the surface of things for all to see. It was a pristine, quiet place where the Truth at my center could be heard calling out. I felt this Truth bubble up from my heart as a sense of awe and mystery about the world. Always the big lake made me wonder about the beauty of things and its presence in my life. But here's the thing. All these amazing feelings of wonder and amazement were ways my inner voice was speaking to me, imploring me to explore the world and find myself there. Unfortunately, I was so afraid of being judged, all I could do is hear my soul calling from afar. I couldn't heed my heart and venture out, but I knew that heart-song was something special.

Later on in life, as I began growing Human again, the message those feelings contained was clear to me once more. "You're an explorer at heart, whose aim in life is to discover the Truth" they were saying. So here's something to think about. That very same Tao-Force on the shores of Lake Superior will speak to you from your own Life. It's at the core of each of us to tell us who we are. It's there right now and very close by. Just push away your fears of judgment and you'll see what it has to say to you.

Impossible Isn't So Bad

Back when I was lost somewhere on Mars, I thought the impossible was impossible. Now that I'm in the autumn of my Life, I realize that the impossible is what a few awakened souls in every generation keep on doing. The rest of us spend our time making everything impossible. Don't believe it? Just look around you. Most folks throw up impossible roadblocks, to keep from making mistakes and failing and being judged worthless. Not sure what this looks like? I'll give you a real life example of a guy I worked with who was an expert at making things impossible.

You met him before. Barry. Barry is an excellent example because he happens to be very smart. In case you didn't already know, intelligence is a very useful tool for making things impossible. Here's what I mean. Let's say I get a bright idea one day and try it out on Barry. "You know, I think we might be able to make our floor machine work better if we turn it around", I say. "Here's ten reasons that won't work", says Barry so fast it makes my head spin. But I'm not giving up without a fight. "Alright" says I, "but here's how we can get around your first objection." "HA!" says Barry…. "here's ten more reasons it won't work!". Jeepers. I'm flooded with objections….but still game for the chase… so I try again. "I think we can get around your second objection this way" I say. But of course, Barry immediately comes up with ten more reasons it can't work. Holy molasses. Barry can come up with ways to make things impossible faster than I can get around them. Intelligence is really good for that kind of thing. And you? Can you find a million reasons the world can't be whole? Guess what? You're making it impossible to discover who you are.

Waking Up on The Tree of Life

Waking up means you take your rightful place on the Tree of Life and begin to reap the fruits of Spirituality. At bottom, Spirituality is all about growing a deeper and deeper connection with all things great and small. But on the Tree of Life, giving *is* receiving, because giver and receiver are different parts of One whole. This is where the fruit comes in. As you wake up to Being Human again, you discover an astonishing win-win deal like you've never seen before. The more you give to the world, the more you receive. Now you find yourself in the driver's seat. If you want good things to happen to you, give good things to the world.

Wednesday, April 23rd, 7:00 A.M.

Thankfully, it's getting light out early once more these days. I'm not a big fan of darkness.

Who Cares?

If you open your ears a bit, you'll probably hear people shouting "who cares" all over the place. It's a symptom of being lost, and epidemic in the world today. Haven't really noticed all these uncaring people around you? I sure have. I'm very sensitive to this expression nowadays, having had all kinds of bad experience with it myself. When I had no idea what to do with my life, I'd repeat this famous saying at the drop of a hat. Suppose someone accurately suggested I was wasting my life away for instance. In a flash I'd say "who cares?". Same thing if my family doctor reflected on my excess pounds. "That could easily give you a heart attack one day" he'd say. Me to myself? "Who cares?". As a matter of fact, when I was completely lost, I didn't really care about anything. Losing my reason for being cut my depth of caring down to a mere shadow of what it could be. And you? Do you hear yourself saying "who cares!" day after day? Yes? O.K, so here's the deal.

When you get your calling back you'll really and truly care, big-time, about everything. You'll care about doing your best ....because that's how you grow the fastest. You'll care for your body because you'll need it…. to get where you want to go. You'll care about your Life's work because it's making your life. You'll even care about your Life's play, because it'll help you go the distance. In fact, when you get to the autumn of your life, you'll discover that Life is one big Care Package.

"I Don't Care!" A Story

A few weeks ago I came across a real, live, "I don't care" story, so I dropped it in here for you. I was out talking to one of my foremen in our manufacturing plant one morning, when along came a resident bad boy. This unfortunate guy is well-known (to me) for being completely lost. When (hopefully) he's not working he's drinking for example, a really good sign of pure aimlessness. He'll call you names in an instant too, another excellent symptom. As a matter of fact, this sad soul has every sign of losing a calling written all over him. And so, here he comes, wearing a tee-shirt with "I DON'T CARE" plastered across its front. My first thought is that he doesn't really need to spell it out all over his chest. Anyone with eyes to see will know he doesn't care about anything….and why.

But as he got closer, I realized there was a smaller message written on his shirt beneath the big one. I must say, it takes a lot to surprise me these days….but this shirt did. Right there beneath the "I DON'T CARE" message was written……."*And I don't care if I don't care!*". "Wow!" I thought to myself, he's actually *bragging* that he doesn't care? He thinks not caring is a badge of honor? Has the world gone completely bonkers? People are fighting to be best at not caring? Let me out of the lunatic asylum.

In My Autumn I See This

Here's something I'd like you to ponder about the "guru-truths" I've sprinkled liberally throughout this book. Things like Neils Bohr's complementarity and Werner Heisenberg's uncertainty. James Maxwell's demon too and the others. In reality, each of these very different looking discoveries is exactly the same. To get an idea what I mean, we'll use one of those "let's think outside the box" analogies.

It's only an analogy of course, but should do the trick. To get started, imagine our way of seeing the world called "Reason" creates limits to what we can know and understand. It creates the floor, ceiling and walls of our Great House of Knowledge, making it something like a huge box. Inside the box, curious Human Beings explore as much as they can of course, and in every generation, a few passionate souls manage to explore right to the outer limits of this box. They dig down to the deepest parts of the basement and climb to the ceiling and most distant walls. It's when they get to the very limits of our House of Knowledge…the limits of Reason itself….the guru-truths are encountered. Guru-truths are all different forms of the same Dualism Poem of Life.

This great Poem at the furthest reaches of our House of Knowledge is where we can break through the box and get to the "other side", by giving the Poem of Life a new meaning. Instead of seeing everything in the Universe as separate, we can realize everything is a different part of us. But of course, so far we haven't done that. Explorer after explorer has dug down to where the Poem of Life is, but hasn't known what to make of it. So far we haven't been able to get to the "other side". And what exactly is on the "other side"? That peaceful, heavenly world where all men and women are truly created equal. The "other side" is a place where Being Human reigns supreme. Will we ever get there? If this Cry for Help goes unheeded, probably not. We'll destroy ourselves and the world before getting there.

Nothing to Do?

A few pages back, I pointed out that "I don't care" is a symptom of being lost. So too is "I have nothing to do". I'm absolutely certain about that, because it describes me to a tee when I was young and aimless. No doubt about it.

You could have heard me saying...."I've got nothing to do"...ten times before lunch in my wasted years. So was there? Nothing to do I mean. Hardly. There are more things to do in this world than you could shake a zillion sticks at. Just ask anyone on their very own Mission to grow Human. But let's not forget something here. I'm not talking about doing things for the sake of "being busy". I'm talking about creating your dream life. I'm speaking about having a deep sense of knowing what to do to fulfill destiny.....and DOING IT. When you finally see that mountain peak ahead of you with your name on it, you'll do what you have to do to get there. You'll be pushed by passion to get up and at it every day too. Eventually you'll become an *authentically* busy person all those frantic busy bees out there are trying to look like. People without real Vision can't tell the difference between true busyness and the pretend kind of course. But believe me, you'll know. As a matter of fact, you might even become so busy making your own life, you'll have to learn how to manage your time. When that happens you really will have "arrived". "Arrived" means you're busy being yourself. Doing with your life what you're *supposed to*.

Friday April 25th, 2008, 4:00 A.M.

Forty five years ago today, I would have been all excited about Steelhead season in Fort William. For those who don't know, steelheads are big rainbow trout swimming up Lake Superior rivers to spawn each spring. In those days, Ken and I were slapstick crazy over Steelheads. Out to wild places we'd go, to explore the creeks and rivers. We'd cook chili, snap pictures, and hike the wonderful trails. We caught more than our fair share of trout too. That's a lifetime ago now, but I can still see the raging rivers, smell the sweet spring buds, and hear the newly hatched frogs. I'm still inspired by the memories.

Do You Want to Be Your Own Boss?

How many times have you said to yourself…"I want to be my own boss"?...or… "I'd sure like to have my own business some day". Personally I've heard people saying that for as long as I can remember. I've said it myself in fact, and most of my friends have too. But here's a surprise you'll have when you wake up to who you are. When all is said and done, "being your own boss" has nothing to do with running companies. It's all about becoming the "boss" of your very own life. It's about taking charge of the business of building your dream life. No question about it. It's not owning a "business" per se we're after. We're after owning our own lives. We're all here to "take care of business", alright, but it's our very own unique life-business we're supposed to be taking care of. Unfortunately, to do that, you have to know what you're here to do. Here's the best thing about *your* business as well. It won't cost you anything except courage and whatever trials and tribulations you find along the way.

You can begin training to take over the business of your own life wherever you are right now too. Just start growing your native talents in whatever job you're in. Go head. Take some risks and try some new things out. Ask for challenges and don't be afraid to fail. Oh yes. Don't forget to use the Rule of Life to release the courage within you and discover why you're here. There's an infinite ocean of courage at your center and your inner voice will tell you what you need to know. Don't believe a word of what I'm saying? Interview a few folks don't know who they are but actually bought a business. Ask if they greet every day with passion, now that they own their business. If they're honest enough, they'll probably tell you something is still missing in that business of theirs. Can you guess what it is? It's knowing why they're really here. Believe me, these things don't come with the shares of a business.

A Real Want to Run a Business Story

A very old friend of mine has wanted to run his own business for a long time. Here's his story. Back when he and I left college, I was so lost it was pitiful, but my old friend sure didn't look lost. He was eager as a beaver about pretty much everything, and wanted to have his own business as soon as possible. After a few years successfully climbing the corporate ladder, he seemed to be getting closer to his goal too. He'd honed some skills and gained some experience and just needed a few more tools. So off he went and got a Master's degree in business to top it all off. Not long after, he discovered a pub for sale back in our old Home town. Running a pub was always on his list of things to do too, but for reasons unknown, it didn't work out. That's not unusual of course, because opportunities are like clothing. If they don't fit right they don't work, and sometimes you have to try quite a few on. And so, ten years later, my old friend tries again.

This time he actually buys an industrial training franchise designed to help factory personnel do their jobs more effectively. With all his engineering, business, and management skills, it looked like it suited him to a tee. But eventually he gave it up. Today I believe he'd admit it didn't turn him on. I don't think he'd say he had a passion for it. To his credit though, he didn't give up looking for that business to run. Later on he met a fellow at his church who owned and operated a small string of grocery stores in desperate need of business advice. Good Samaritan that he is, my friend provided lots of advice and ideas and worked with the grocer free of charge to improve his profits. Eventually a partnership was offered. But, once again, it didn't happen. My friend had various reservations that stopped him from taking the plunge. It didn't stop him from wanting to run his own business, but we'll have to fast forward another ten years to find his next misadventure.

By now he's been traveling the world for some time, building manufacturing plants from China to Peru, and has just been sent to India to start up another one. There another business opportunity rears its ugly head. This time he has a chance to become the first Canadian franchisee for exotic linens. But after much discussion and investigation..... it falls away. By now you and I and everyone else is probably wondering what's holding him back. Is it just that the right deal hasn't shown up yet? Like in the world of love, it often takes time for "Mr. Right" to come along in business too. But no. That's not it. The trouble is in my old friend's soul. He simply doesn't know what he wants to do with his life, because he's lost his Vision. That's big trouble too, because without Vision, he won't recognize the right deal for his life, even if he ran headlong into it tomorrow. If all this struggle to find the way sounds sad to you though, here's some good news. Very recently my old buddy has been listening to his heart-song once more. He's retired from manufacturing and gone back to graduate school......in Divinity. With a heart as big as all the world, I believe this man has always been destined to go this way. I hope and pray his Spirit guide takes him there.

Feelings Are a Sign of the Truth

I'll bet I've read ten books and watched a hundred T.V. shows that tried like heck to get you and I to "get in touch with our feelings". Gurus, talk show hosts and life coaches keep on hammering this advice into our brains. But for some reason, nine out of ten people steer clear of this touchy feely talk, like it was some kind of plague. If you don't think this is true, just try (honestly) complimenting someone or even thanking them for something. Instead of feeling good about your little acknowledgment, most people will get all embarrassed and tongue-tied over it, as if you'd assaulted them. You might even get a "deer in the headlights" look as the poor victim tries hard to back away a few feet.

Try to make a real and true heartfelt thank-you of it, and your once-was friend might even run in the other direction. Male members of the species especially don't just avoid sharing feelings. They actively suppress them any chance they get. I used to. So what's with all this avoidance of feelings? Step back and look around and you'll see people everywhere all but terrified of "feelings", and the sad, simple truth of it is this. Feelings are ways our inner voices speak to us, trying to show us how to be ourselves. Inner voices don't just communicate in words. The shout out in unspoken intuitions and call to us as desires and loves and likes and awe-inspiring wonders. We're supposed to follow these mysterious feelings to our destiny. But in today's world, being ourselves is scary, because people everywhere will tell us who we are isn't good enough. That's why people don't share feelings.

Who wants to come out of their shell, only to be told they're not wanted? Who wants to put their most precious possession on stage, only to have it booed off? A very sad state of affairs to say the least, but it's not the worst part of all this keeping feelings to ourselves. Some unfortunate souls are so terrified of being themselves, they suppress every scrap of their feelings. That makes for a very frightening man or woman with virtually no feelings at all. These scary people will rape, torture or kill without remorse. Feeling nothing for themselves and others, they simply cannot identify with living things, because most of the life has gone out of them. I don't know about you, but I really don't want to live in this kind of world. But what on earth can we do about it? We can wake up and begin to see that feelings are a sign of a profound Truth in the world. A Truth that can make you and I and all of Humankind feel much better. The Truth is, we're all different parts of each other. Let this Truth grow and thrive and prosper and the world will begin to feel like heaven once more.

Wednesday, May 7th, 2008, 9:00 A.M.

No One Will Do Anything?

One day last month, I was out preaching wholeness when a lady cornered me and asked a good question. I'd been talking about the Tree of Life, and how everyone is profoundly equal on this wondrous Tree when she spoke up. "If everyone is equal" said the woman, "I can't see why anyone would want to do anything anymore". At first I didn't see what she was getting at, so I asked her to explain a bit more. "Who'd bother trying to win or be best or compete if everyone else is already just as good?" she added. Finally it dawned on me where she was coming from. She'd missed the essential teaching of wholeness, but hadn't realized it, so I had to go back and try again.

"The Tree of Life doesn't say people can't win or compete or be best" I said. "Men and women will still work together and play together to each grow their authentic souls as much as possible". "But the prize isn't had by winning or being best or out-competing the other guy". "The prize is the wonderful Journey of personal growth each person will be on". "The trophy is that unique blossom each of us can flower into if we keep on being ourselves". "And the most important thing about the Tree of Life, is that nobody will feel bad or worthless because they didn't win or end up best".

I could see by this time the lady was listening closely, so I carried on. "Think of it this way", I said. "When we finally wake up to the Tree of Life, the world will still be filled with people working and playing and winning and losing". "But everyone will be happy being themselves, whether winners or losers or rich or poor". "People won't have to win or be rich or best to have the sense of purpose and importance they crave.".

"You mean the poorest, weakest, least capable person will feel just as much power and importance as the guy in the castle?" she said. "Exactly", I replied, and her one last word, and how she said it, will probably stick with me for a long time. "Wow" she said, lost in thought about a world a lot different than it is now.

Me and My Shadow

Here's a growing up story, about how the Rule of Life changes things for the better. Just last week I was out on the road, stumbling along, doing my pitifully slow version of jogging. Loving every minute of the beautiful spring morning. Suddenly.... footfalls behind me. Pitta patta pitta patta. Sure enough, here comes a real runner, speeding by so fast she could have been flying. Flowing so smoothly, it was like poetry in motion. Then, as she rounded a corner up ahead, I noticed something. My shadow. What the heck....who's that? It reminded me of my motorcycle. Ka-thunk, ka-thump, ka-shudder. Heaving and thudding and plodding along like something out of a horror movie. But guess what?

As soon as I saw that old duck waddling along the road, a fabulous feeling rose up in me, like seeing an old friend, or putting on a pair of comfy slippers. I was happy to see my authentic self. Then it dawned on me. I remembered another time maybe fifteen years ago. I saw my clunky shadow one snowy day then, but wasn't happy at all. As a matter of fact, I immediately tried to make it look like a real runner, because I was afraid to be myself. There was nobody there but me, and I was still afraid to be myself. Sounds ridiculous? Yes it is, but it's also absolutely true. And me now? Today I greet myself like an old friend, whenever I see him. Believe me, when you do that, you'll know you're on your way. I do and I am.

A Life Mission Story: Learning the Book Biz

Autumn's a time when I also had to wake up to what book writing is all about. Everyone waking up to their own Life Mission will have to learn similar lessons about "How Hard it Is" (to Make a Dream Life). Here's one of mine. Way back in the winter of my life, I had a Princess Picture of authors and books in my brain. I actually believed if you wrote a good book, the world would beat a path to your door. But of course, that doesn't even come close to reality. The best possible book can go nowhere at all if its author doesn't have business skills, because in the real world, book writing is a business. Writing the book is only a small part of the puzzle. You have to sell and market and promote and produce the darn thing too. All of which costs big bucks and requires more than writing skills.

Nothing new there. Everybody knows that. Except overly optimistic, naïve new authors perhaps. Like I was. So what? So this. If you're an aspiring author yourself sitting there right now, eyeballing me like one of those toads less graveled the environmentalists shout about, listen up. That book of yours had better be part and parcel of your very own Life Mission. It'd better be dictated by your inner voice and passionately important to who you are. If you're writing it just because you wannabe important like those book authors you see on T.V., take my advice. Don't. Why? For one thing, you won't be on a Joyful Journey of self-discovery. You won't be living an authentic life either. Chances are the obstacles ahead will make you give up before it hits the shelves too. Oh yes. One more thing. Dr. Steve's lesson. Even if you publish, sell and make lots of money on it….if it isn't coming from your heart, you'll be half-empty at the end of it all.

On the other hand, if that book of yours is truly heart-felt and something "in you" you just have to let out…..for heaven's sake let it out! Even if those agents and publishers won't give you the time of day because you aren't on Oprah twice a week….stick it out. You'll be glad you did…regardless of how it turns out. There you go. Book-Biz-101.

By Autumn Your Journey Will Count

The Autumn of life comes when you're off and running on your own Mission and you've finally mastered the Journey that counts. Age has nothing to do with it. You can be fifteen or fifty when the fall colors come into your life and you're walking your own walk…just for the Joy of it. Here's how to tell if your Journey really does count. We'll make up an example. Say your Mission in life turned out to be building a bridge across a river. So there you are, half-way across the river after many years of hard work. You've learned all kinds of bridge-building skills and pulled all kinds of folks together to help you. You dream of getting across that river every day, and you're well on your way to your own brand of success. Now imagine someone comes along with a crystal ball and gives you a chance to see what your future holds. Peering into the mists of time, you realize that something is going to prevent you from completing your bridge. Now you can tell for sure if your Journey really counts. How? Are you happy knowing you'll only get part-way across the river? Yes? Congratulations, because you really are on a true-blue Life-Mission. You're one of the lucky few who qualify to speak those oft-abused words… "It's the Journey that counts".

Thursday May 8th 2008, 6:00 A.M.

How to Make Luck

Several million pages back I said I'd teach you how to make luck, using the Rule of Life. Remember? Good. Here's exactly what I mean. First let's review what most folks mean by luck. In today's world, luck means winning money….. to get happy. Some folks think they'll be happy instantly by having the world's biggest bank account, because rich people are important and importance is what they crave. Others expect all the things they buy with their winnings will make them happy real soon. Some even think the money will finally let them "do what they want with their lives". But…surprise, surprise….money doesn't buy happiness. Poor people who have no idea what to do with their lives before the big win soon discover they've just turned into rich aimless souls as well. That's ordinary luck for you. It can get you every single thing in the world but your reason for being. On the other hand, the kind of luck you make with the Rule of Life is different. You might even call it "intimate luck" because it takes away everything between you and your dreams, bringing those dreams up close and personal. It gives you something to put heart and soul into for the rest of your life. If you don't believe the Rule of Life is something like a luck machine, just stop and think for a minute. When you see a man or woman making a living following their dreams, what do you say? "What a lucky son of a gun". Right? There you go. Follow the Rule of Life and you'll get luckier and luckier.

Then and Now

Here's a little transformation story for you. As far back as I can remember, I always wanted a big, heavyweight motorcycle, because I thought all the noise and speed made the guys that rode them look powerful. The bad-boy image was attractive too, because I thought tough anti-social folks were forces to be reckoned with.

Unfortunately, by the time I could actually afford one, I'd started growing up again and didn't see the world that way anymore. Now what? Now I wanted one even more, because these machines are just another way to love the gift of life. Like this. Cruising down country roads on a motorcycle, you're no longer kept apart from the world like in a car. Diving down hills you splash into cool air pockets like a crazy dolphin, and swim back out again looking for more. Chugging along farm lanes the earth is so close, you can't help but taste it. Moment by moment you're battered by more fresh air than you can breathe, and showered by sunshine so sweet it's almost musical. Then there's riding with a half dozen biker buddies. Talk about a real rush as you join a herd of wild wildebeest thundering across the plains of Africa, carried back to a place and time from whence we came. And sure. Once and a while you become a wild Angel growling along the tarmac, letting a spark of Bad-Boy peek out from behind your goggles. Just for fun. Never intending to harm a fly. Enjoying the real power of living life.

Another Life Mission Story

By the Fall of my life I was working hard at my Mission. I had a message I was passionate about and was working like crazy to get it out. Finally the book's done and I'm searching for a publisher when something occurs to me. Something that will teach me another life-lesson that all folks on Missions eventually learn one way or the other. It all starts off when I start wondering if I could find a real live guru on a similar adventure to write me a foreword. At this stage of the game I must say I missed the humor of it all, and launched off in my quest with awe-inspiring naiveté. I was convinced there were experts out there who'd help a bird-of-a-feather Missionary. But soon reality kicked in. Soon I learned most gurus aren't interested in helping brand new aspiring start-up gurus at all.

New gurus would be competitors after all, and most businessmen and women don't go out of their way to create more competitors. I guess I'd forgotten that book writing and selling is a business. Even so, I still believed there had to be folks out there with true callings, whose aim in life wasn't just to make money. Men and women who might see other Missionaries as helpful to their cause. And, of course, authentic souls like that are out there, but they get requests from folks whose only goal is to ride their coat-tails to riches every day. By the hundreds. So most successful gurus have no choice to steer clear of requests to read manuscripts, write cover stories, or the like. I discovered this little fact of life myself personally. It went like this. One day a world-class guru happened to be speaking in a city not too far from where I lived at the time. "Here's my chance for a foreword" I said to myself, and forked out big bucks to get V.I.P. tickets to meet the man in person back stage. At the end of his talk, at least five hundred of we V.I.P.'s funneled back stage and lined up to shake the man's hand.

Finally I'm face-to-face with the fellow and get two seconds of fame to blurt out my sales pitch. Right away I know I'm in trouble. I could see it in his eyes as they rolled back to betray his thoughts. "Not another one" I thought I heard him say, as he dismissed me quicker than two bunnies fleeing with five carrots. And what did he see in mine eyes? Hard to say, but I don't think it was a soul on a Mission like himself. Oh well. At least I learned something from it. You'll have to learn this kind of lesson too. Don't give up. Keep trying.

Missionaries Are Nuts

Before you get your very own Life Mission back, you'll probably think Missionaries are….well…..plain nuts. Why is that? It's because Missionary men and women keep on trying to do impossible things.

Things you think are impossible that is. Like building businesses or writing books or climbing mountains for example. Missionaries give up high paying jobs to eke out a meager living doing what they love too. An impossible thing to see if there ever was one….if you're still stuck making big bucks doing something you hate. You'll also see Missionaries swimming upstream against currents, working their butts off for years before anything really happens for them. That'll pretty much prove they're crazy to you if you have no purpose in life, and you'll probably snicker with the best of 'em at these energetic fools. That's the *before* part of the story. Here's what'll happen once you've embarked on your very own passionate aim in life. Now friends, family, and other people will be giving *you* the wink and nod while patting you on the head. "Still figure you'll be a big book author (business gal, farmer, singer…etc.) some day eh?" they'll say….while trying hard not to snicker. "There goes Mr. or Mrs. impossible!" you'll hear echoing from hallways you've just passed through. But by now you'll know something these naysayers don't. The impossible becomes possible every day of the week. Here's a real story about how the impossible became possible one day…..right in my garage.

The Impossible Happens Before My Eyes

One morning last year I was heading off to the office. Out to the garage I went to chuck my briefcase in the car. Suddenly I heard a little "thumpa, thumpa, thumpa, thumpa" sound. Then it stopped. I listened. It started again over in the corner. Curious as heck, I tip-toed closer to where the blue recycling box was, and slowly peeked over the edge. There it was. A little mouse had fallen in and he was desperately jumping….trying to get out. But the box was too high and slippery. It was an impossible obstacle. Until yours truly came along and emptied him out in the garden. There you go. In the Autumn of your life don't forget. The impossible is made possible every day of the week. Sometimes in miraculous ways.

Saturday May 10th, 2008, 10:25 A.M.

Not Much Lost Me Left

Yesterday out jogging I realized how far I'd come working the Rule of Life. There I was clopping along down a country road in May sunshine when a school-bus filled with church kids came by. Kids being kids they were hooting and hollering at me with windows down and heads stuck out. Without a single thought at all, I found myself smiling and waving back…..just like Eddie. Then it hit me. Once again, kids being kids (especially in today's world), they were probably calling me the old slow-poke man every name in the book. But instead of trying to speed up and make myself look like something I'm not….a real runner for instance… like I used to…. I simply beamed back with pride and joy. It was automatic, authentic and real as rain on a cold spring day too. Man. It made me feel like a super-hero. Believe me, it's an absolutely wonderful feeling to be truly happy being yourself. Words can't describe how good it feels. Now you'd be walking down a peaceful path with no worries about those arrows and barbs. Peace of Mind would have broken out in your life.

One Last Goose Bump Story

Here's what I call the "Mother of all goose bump stories". In essence, this book has one simple message in it. It's this. We've given the world the wrong meaning and it keeps us from being happy. It makes us destroy everything around us too. But this mistaken and selfish way of seeing things has done something potentially a lot worse. It's given Mankind an "ego" that makes him reluctant to admit his mistakes. Just like everyday individual people with "big egos" who think they know-it-all and can't be wrong about anything. So?

Think about it. Humankind has made a mistake that's sending everything to hell in a fast car. But Man doesn't want to admit he's wrong. How are we going to get out of the mess? How can we stop, turn around, and go back to where the right Path for Mankind is, if Humanity can't admit it's mistakes? The short answer is…we might not. If that doesn't give you goose bumps I don't know what will. But….where there's Life there's hope. That's why I'm crying out for help. We had better start joining up and crying out together soon too, or time will run out on us. That's what the next chapter is. It's a cry for help to our philosophical brothers and sisters. Like I said before, we will need these passionate exploring souls to help us change our view of reality…and discover who we are.

Chapter Twenty-Eight
A Cry For Help
(We Need You Desperately to Make the World Whole)

"Concern for Man and his fate must always form the chief interest of all technical endeavors. Never forget this in the midst of your diagrams and equations". - Albert Einstein

Why a Cry For Help?

Let's stop for a minute and reflect on what this book is all about. Make no mistake, it's about you. It's about your very soul...your heart-of-hearts...that deepest passion for life buried way down deep in you. The purpose of this book is to help you be yourself. Isn't that the most important thing in the world.....to you? I know for sure it is, because you and I share the same heart, and it's the most important thing ever to me. It's the most important thing ever to millions of people as well. But you and I and all those other people desperate to know who they are have a small problem. Until the way we see the world is changed at its roots, everyone will have an uphill battle understanding that their soul can't be worth less than other souls. Certainly you can retrain your mind and body with the Rule of Life, but it's made needlessly tough with the entire world saying wholeness is crazy. That brings us to the nub of our difficulty.

We'll need our intellectuals to change how we see things. Only they have the authority to give us brand new and completely different beliefs about how the world works. But they don't see it as their job. Philosophical scientists don't yet recognize that the purpose of their work is to help you and I discover who we are. They're interested in big facts of Nature, not our hearts. So how can we get them to listen?

You and I have to cry out for help. The world has to get its priorities straight, and the most important thing possible is freeing the Spirit within each of us. Everything Mankind wants out of Life will follow from setting you and I and our brothers and sisters free. Building bigger factories to make more things isn't important. Putting billions of dollars into yet larger war machines has no real value. Skyscrapers, moon rockets and faster video games are all but irrelevant in the big scheme of things. It's Life itself that we should be concerned about, and we're slowly but surely giving it up. So ask yourself this. Do you want to go to your grave never knowing what Life is really about? Do you want your children and theirs to see less and less of what Life has to offer? If you answered no to those simple questions, you need to begin crying out for help. Luckily for all of us perhaps, there are huge groups of people who will want to join you in asking our philosophers to give us a new view of reality. People on what I call the "six Big Missions" to save us and the earth. Why would they want to cry out with you and I? Because they'll never fulfill their Missions unless our way of seeing the world is changed. It is absolutely impossible for these passionate people to make their dreams of a better planet true as long as we see the world the way we do now. Here's those six Big Missions.

The Cry of Environmentalists

It's fair to say our environment is going to hell in a hand-basket fast. When mercury shows up in polar bears and kids are allergic to peanut butter....something has to be wrong somewhere. When icebergs the size of Rhode Island fall off the polar ice shields and frogs everywhere start going extinct, we should hear the warning bells going off, even in small-town America. But do we? Environmentalists have been trying very hard to make us hear these bells.

They know it's completely possible their grand-children might never know pure white snow or wildflowers. It's obvious to people trying to save the earth that you can't throw poisons everywhere without destroying just about everything. But something really sinister seems to be afoot here, because Mankind knows full well soiling its own nest is really bad….but keeps on doing it anyway. That's a wee bit curious if you think about it. Like somebody eating something clearly marked "poison" for example. He knows it's poison…. but he's eating it anyway? Humanity is pretty much like this right now. It knows for sure that dumping chemicals into the air and water, or destroying the forests is poisonous. You don't have to be an environmental scientist to understand that. So why do we keep on doing it? It's really very simple. Our most sacred beliefs make us think we're separate from each other and the world.

That makes us think like the guy who threw left-over paint into the well he shared with his neighbor. Remember that story? He actually believed there was "his water" and "the neighbor's water" in that well. He figured he could pollute his neighbor's half with impunity. Which is completely insane of course. But, truth be told, our mistaken view of the world makes us think like that. It's why we can't stop polluting. We actually think, way deep down, we can harm the world without harming ourselves. Our profoundly selfish worldview makes us believe we can destroy our neighbor's backyard to enrich ourselves. But that kind of belief system has awe-inspiring consequences. One is this. All the environmentalists in the world will never stop the harm to our environment if our worldview isn't changed. They simply can't stop the extinctions and destruction if we keep on believing in our heart-of-hearts that things are separate. Period. And so, this huge group of impassioned souls has a gigantic interest in helping you and I plead for help from our philosophers. If they want to succeed in their aims, there's no choice.

A Plea For Animal Rights

Elders of our First Nations peoples could teach us a lot about animals...if we'd listen...but we won't. Native Americans knew the creatures around them were different kinds of people and treated them with respect. Coastal tribes knew the salmon people for example and Inuit hunters stalked the walrus tribe for sustenance. Even as these men and women had to kill animals for food, reverence for their lives was the rule. Reverence for their Spirits and the life they made possible was taught in the cradle in these societies. Now compare that to the so-called "modern advanced" peoples of the world. Animals are raised in the most disgusting, inhumane ways imaginable for food, with no regard for their pain and suffering. Creatures great and small are tortured in medical research experiments, in ways that would make most people sick if they actually saw it. People abuse pets daily with impunity. And the vast majority of people don't care.

A smaller minority of "animal rights activists" surely do care however. Down deep in their hearts they realize, at the very least, that these creatures have souls and feel pain as we do. But the full Truth is, it's our souls we're destroying. There's only One Life, we and they share, and we're tearing it to pieces. From personal experience I can say this too. Anybody who sees their very own soul at the heart of all creatures great and small will treat them with compassion. On the other hand, if we continue to wallow in our mistaken view of the world, the hell we're inflicting upon untold creatures will be ours eventually. It cannot be otherwise, because the world really is who we are, even if we can't see it. That's why those so fervently trying to break the Dominion of Man over animals need to join up with you and I to help change how we see the world. If they do, they'll make their dreams of a world that cares for creatures come true. If they don't, it will never happen, because too many are blind to the Truth.

The Great War For Peace

If anything has been around for a while, it'd have to be War. Followed by Peace. Followed by more War. And so on. It's been going on for as long as we have records, and probably long before the first clay tablets recorded it. As a result, most folks believe Mankind is inherently violent and wages war by nature. Maybe we don't much like it, but that's just the way it is. Isn't it? It's certainly the way it has been. But only because Humanity hasn't yet grown up. Violence and war are behaviors of an immature Man. If Mankind were to resume the Path he was meant to be on, and grow fully Human, violence would become only a fact of ancient history. No person committed to Being Human is interested in violating others, because it's violating him or herself. People who aren't violated aren't interested in striking out at the world either. If the way we see the world was changed, that vicious circle of "tit for tat" violence would slowly but surely peter out and die a natural death. Human Beings would be far too busy making a dream world to waste their lives striking out at each other. And so, people interested in abolishing violence really and truly need to help us too. All those wonderfully passionate peace activists can call out to our philosophers to change the meaning of the Poem of Life.

The Song of Freedom For Every Race

In the world today, foolish discrimination probably reaches a zenith in racism. Otherwise sane people will literally hate folks with different colored skin sight-unseen....because they can't see the Truth. The truth is, the world isn't just a brotherhood of different races. It's a multi-colored whole, like a Tiffany lamp or wondrous jig-saw puzzle, with One heart. Every now and then someone like John Howard Griffin comes along and makes this singular soul within us clear as a bell. But are we listening? No we're not.

In case you've never read Griffin's astounding book "Black Like Me" here's the gist of it. Back in the early sixties, John Griffin...a white man...actually turned himself black with drugs and wandered around racially charged states such as Alabama and Mississippi....posing as a black man. In short, Griffin could hardly believe the staggeringly bad treatment he received at the hands of his fellow white men. Knowing he was the same guy he always was...but with different skin color...Griffin was deeply disturbed by his experience.

People treated him as if his soul was worthless....but it was the same soul they treated fairly before. This book should serve as a warning to advocates of racial equality everywhere. If Griffin's profound story cannot make people see how foolish racism really is...something worse than racism itself is going on. Something that literally makes it all but impossible for intelligent human beings to see the truth. What could possibly be worse than savage racism? It's our mistaken way of looking at the world, and unless it's changed, racial equality will never happen. That's why courageous advocates of race-equality need to help persuade the philosophers to change our minds about the world.

The Long Suffering Self-Help Struggle

In the Western world at least, there are hundreds of self-help gurus, life coaches and consultants of all kinds trying to bring authentic happiness to the millions without it. Inspired men and women offer fabulous courses in miracles and explain profound Secrets of true success. Every single one of these writers and speakers has terrific life-wisdoms to share with you and I too, that can really make our stay on earth much better. Even so, there's something these wise people don't really tell us. It's this. If you or I are terrified at heart of being ourselves, the gurus' tools and inspirational offerings simply won't help us get what we want out of life.

Why? Because what each of us wants out of life is to be ourselves, and our worldview won't let us. But let's say the self-help gurus helped you and I convince the philosophers to change that worldview. Then what? Many more people would flock to the gurus ...and every guru's advice would help. Imagine each guru has a different kind of tool-kit for making a dream life for instance. We'd all want as many different tools as we could get, to help us build the life of our dreams. People wouldn't just be going to their one favorite guru like they do now. Everyone would want to sample the tools of many different gurus, to build that wonderful life faster and better and bigger. When all is said and done then, the self-help gurus would profit mightily from crying out for help to change our view of reality.

Science Needs Help To Discover Who We Are

Most of us know science as technology. Computers, cars, and satellites we can see. But beneath technology is science. Most scientists know science as immutable Laws of Nature that can be expressed as formulas. In today's world, these formulas are often massively complex and manipulated by computers to reveal their secrets. But beneath the formulas are deeper, more mysterious and profound questions that far fewer scientists explore. These are sometimes called "epistemological" questions, and they have to do with the limits of what we can know about the world. Often deceptively simple sounding, they're profound questions about nature of light, reality, and life itself. They're the "Big Questions" about who we are, why we're here, and the meaning of your life and mine. Questions that simply can't be answered as long as we see the world the way we do now. Present day explorers will never realize that the famous wave-particle puzzles exhibited by light are artifacts of Reason for instance. Truth is, light isn't a "thing" at all, that goes from A to B like we think it does today.

Light is how Being manifests in the world, and all those pesky particle-wave puzzles are just ways the Poem of Life makes itself known to us. But as long as we stay stuck in our limited way of looking at the world, scientific souls won't be able to explore Being-in-the-world at any depth. They won't be able to see that the world is deeply infused with Being….not filled with many separate things. The modern riddle about "conscious machines" won't be made clear without changing our view of the world either. In actual fact, machines are already conscious….because we and they are different parts of one whole. Every single thing in the Universe is part and parcel of One consciousness. Rocks, plants, animals and oceans for instance. But this simple truth makes no sense according to the way we see things right now. That brings us to all those souls on Mission-6. Scientific souls whose aim is to penetrate the "Big Questions". If they can help you and I get our worldview changed, they'll crack some of the Big Mysteries they so dearly want to understand.

You Too Can Help

You can help the world find its Way again too, by passing a message along two by two until it explodes around the world. The message is…"hear my cry for help to make the world whole". Pass it on to two friends and ask each to do the same. It's kind of like a chain letter, except in this case it's a plea for freedom. Why is this such a powerful way of spreading the Cry for Help? It works like the ancient story of an Emperor and his people that goes like this. Way back in ancient China, an Emperor put a bad tax on his people. To pay for living on his land they had to give him pretty much all their rice, so there was almost nothing to eat. Luckily, a wise man amongst these people knew how to out-fox the Emperor. "All we need is the smallest amount of rice to eat, to keep on paying you taxes sir", said the sage to the Emperor.

"Just give us one grain of rice on the first day of each month, and double the amount every day, starting over again next month" said the wise man. The Emperor wanted to keep taxing folks of course, so he thought hard and long about it. "That's only one grain on day one and two on day two and four on day three and so on" he thought. "I can afford a few grains" he concluded and agreed. Here's where the power of two-by-two comes in. Doubling up on grains every day for a month gives you billions. And billions of grains of rice is more than enough to feed the people. Same thing with spreading the Word two-by-two. If two folks cry out for help to two folks who cry out to two more…..and so on….before you know it …. EVERYBODY is crying for help. Our philosophers will have to listen to EVERYBODY. See what I mean? You too can help.

"We shall require a substantially new manner of thinking if mankind is to survive". – Albert Einstein

Chapter Twenty-Nine
(Not the Final Chapter.... I Hope)

Yesterday morning out jogging, something happened I thought I'd share with you. A fitting end to the book I think. As we speak, it's October 2008 and yesterday around seven thirty A.M. it was cold as ice out. The outdoor thermometer sat just above freezing, but the world was flooded with brilliant sunshine and sure enough, I heard the road less traveled calling. Trouble was, I was running late. I didn't really have the time for my usual 5K jaunt, but stress has been running high of late, so a workout was in order. And off I go to discover traffic is pretty much over this time of day and there's hardly a car on my country road. It's a gorgeous autumn morning out as well. Scents of dark frosty earth and crimson leaves leap at me with every footstep. Brassy bright corn-stubble takes my breath away as I amble along, and it's quiet as can be out, except for the braying Bluejays and neet, neet, neet sounds of nuthatches. Then off in the distance I hear them coming. Geese. Hundreds and hundreds. Soon they're upon me, flying so low I can see little feathers and feet and dark eyes watching. So low I was drawn up into the flock and flew with them, feeling their joyous gabbling song. Then it hit me. It was the Freedom song. The song all wild free creatures sing when they bask in the glorious warmth of sunshine or swim the beautiful oceans. A song of hope and caring and love and joy. A song we can't afford to lose. But we are. I realized that song was being torn from us as those geese went their way without me, because we can't see the Truth. I knew it was the most horrific thing that could befall us. And I cried out loud..."can you hear me ...please ...... *help*....we need the Freedom song".

Short Prayer For Mankind

No doubt about it. If the world really was whole, it'd be obvious every single life is equally important. We'd all have self-esteem the size of the Universe and the world would be a better place. But everyone knows that's impossible. Don't they? Yes they do. So let us pray. "Give Mankind the strength to believe the impossible Truth....that we're all part of each other and the world".

Amen

A CRY FOR HELP

Reading List

The Secret: Rhonda Byrne, Simon & Schuster Nov 2006

Excuse Me! Your Life is Waiting. The Astonishing Power of Feelings, Lynne Grabhorn, Hampton Roads Publishing Company, 2003

Ask and It is Given, Esther and Jerry Hicks, Hay House, 2005

The Law of Attraction, Esther and Jerry Hicks, Hay House 2006

Law of Attraction: The Science of Attracting More of What You Want and Less of What You Don't. Michael J. Losier, Wellness Central 2007

The Attractor Factor. 5 Easy Steps For Attracting Wealth (or anything else) From the Inside Out. Joe Vitale, Wiley 2006

The Science of Success. How to Attract Prosperity and Create Harmonic Wealth Through Proven Principles. James Arthur Ray, Sun Ark Press 1999

Professional Dreamer: 6 Simple Steps That Turn Dreams Into Reality. Ghalil, One Mind Publishing, 2005

A CRY FOR HELP
Reading List

Affirmations – Your Passport to Happiness, Anne Marie Evers, Berkana Books 1999

Affirmations – How to Expand Your Personal Power and Take Back Control of Your Life, Stuart Wilde, Hay House 1995

The Power of Intention, Wayne W. Dyer, Hay House Inc. Dec 2005

Quantum Success, The Astounding Science of Wealth and Happiness, Sandra Anne Taylor, Hay House, 2006

What the Bleep Do We Know? Discovering Endless Possibilities for Altering Your Everyday Reality. Arntz, Chasse, & Vincente, HCI (Mti Edition, 2007)

Manifest Your Destiny: Dr. Wayne Dyer., Element books, 2003

The Power of Positive Thinking, Normal Vincent Peale, Fireside 2003

The Four Agreements: A Practical Guide to Personal Freedom, A Toltec Wisdom Book, Don Miguel Ruiz, Amber-Allen Jan 2001

A CRY FOR HELP
Reading List

The Power of Now, A Guide to Spiritual Enlightenment, Eckhart Tolle, New World Library, 2004

Authentic Happiness: Martin Seligman, Free Press, 2004

The Passion Test: The Effortless Path to Discovering Your Destiny. Janet and Chris Attwood, Hudson Street Press 2007

Mindful Recovery: A Spiritual Path to Healing from Addiction, Thomas and Beverley Bien, Wiley 2002

12 Steps: A Spiritual Journey, Friends in Recovery, RPI Publishing 1994

Addiction: Why Can't They Just Stop? Susan Cheever, Rodale, 2007

In Search of Schrodinger's Cat: John Gribbin, Corgi Adult, 1985,

Suspended in Language: Neils Bohr's Life, Discoveries, and the Century he Shaped, GT Labs, 2004

CRY FOR HELP
Reading List

Uncertainty: The Life and Science of Werner Heisenberg, David C. Cassidy, WH Freeman

Uncertainty: Einstein, Heisenberg, Bohr, and the Struggle For the Soul of Science, David Lindley, Doubleday 2007

The Dancing Wu Li Masters: Gary Zukav, Harper Perennial Modern Classics, 2001

Silent Spring, Rachel Carson, Mariner Books 2002

An Inconvenient Truth, Al Gore, Rodale 2006

Animal Liberation, Peter Singer, Harper Perennial 2001

In Defense of Animals (The Second Wave), Peter Singer, Wiley 2005

Dominion: The Power of Man, The Suffering of Animals, and the Call to Mercy, Matthew Scully, St. Martin's Griffin 2003

About the Author

Born in Fort William, Ontario, Canada in the late forties and educated at Kingston's Queen's University, my qualifications for writing this book are truly impressive and encyclopedic. Namely, being lost for forty years. In case you're not sure what lost means, I'll tell you. Choosing a career your heart isn't in and working your way to the top job will make you well and truly lost. Take yours truly for example. With chemical engineering degree in-hand in the early '70's, I steadily made my way to Chief manufacturing executive, with stints in Montreal, Los Angeles, Calgary, and Toronto. Bystanders would have called out *"success story!"*. Unfortunately, my soul was crying out ….*"you're living a lie"*, because way down deep my mission has always been to write and speak about this great mystery we call "Life". But Fate often has a way of intervening and so it did in my life. Gifted by the kind of insights that strike like lightening, something special was revealed to me. In short, it's this. To find what you're looking for in life, you have to be yourself. A Cry For Help was born to show you how to do exactly that. On a more personal note, I can be counted amongst the long distance runners, Harley Davidson aficionados, wilderness adventurers, and passionate lovers of all creatures great and small.

www.ingramcontent.com/pod-product-compliance
Lightning Source LLC
Chambersburg PA
CBHW031306150426
43191CB00005B/99